Alaska

Other Travellers' Wildlife Guides

Alaska

by Dennis Paulson and Les Beletsky

Illustrated by:
David Dennis (Plate 16),
Linda Feltner (Plates 60–75),
John Myers (Plates A–J),
Colin Newman (Plates 1–15) and
John Sill (Plates 17–59)

Habitat Photographs by:
Dennis Paulson, Richard Droker
and Carol Spaw

Interlink Books

An imprint of Interlink Publishing Group, Inc.
Northampton, Massachusetts

This edition first published 2007 by

INTERLINK BOOKS
An imprint of Interlink Publishing Group, Inc.
46 Crosby Street, Northampton, Massachusetts 01060
www.interlinkbooks.com

Library of Congress Cataloging-in-Publication Data

Paulson, Dennis R.
Alaska : travellers' wildlife guide / Dennis Paulson and Les Beletsky ; illustrated by
David Dennis ... [et al.].
p. cm.—(Travellers' wildlife guides)
Rev. ed. of: Alaska. San Diego : Academic Press, c2001.
Includes bibliographical references and index.
ISBN 1-56656-652-5 (pbk.) ISBN 13: 978-1-56656-652-0
1. Ecotourism—Alaska—Guidebooks. 2. Alaska—Guidebooks. 3. Natural history—Alaska—
Guidebooks. 4. Animals—Alaska—Guidebooks. I. Beletsky, Les, 1956– II. Title. III. Series.
G155.U6P34 2006
591.9798—dc22
2006015058

Cover Image: Gray wolf panting © Tom Brakefield/Photodisc Green, Getty Images

Printed and bound in China

To request our complete 40-page full-color catalog,
please call us toll free at **1-800-238-LINK**, visit our website at
www.interlinkbooks.com, or write to
Interlink Publishing
46 Crosby Street, Northampton, MA 01060
e-mail: info@interlinkbooks.com

CONTENTS

PREFACE

T he books in this series are aimed at environmentally conscious travellers for whom some of the best parts of any trip are glimpses of animals in natural settings. We think this book will be of value to people who, when speaking of a journey, often remember days and locations by the wildlife they encountered: "That was where we saw all the eagles," and "That was the day we saw the sea lion eat the salmon." The purpose of the book is to enhance enjoyment of a trip and enrich wildlife sightings by providing identifying information on several hundred of the most frequently encountered animals of Alaska, along with up-to-date information on their ecology, behavior, and conservation. With color illustrations of 5 species of amphibians, 179 birds, and 64 mammals, this book includes most of the vertebrate animals that visitors are likely to encounter on land or at the water's surface. It also includes 32 of Alaska's most common fishes and 17 marine invertebrates, preparing the visitor for trips to local aquariums, seafood markets, and the beach at low tide. The book features 24 of Alaska's common insects, including highly visible butterflies and dragonflies and the not-so-visible but very persistent flies that will surely make themselves evident at certain times and places. Finally, knowing that most visitors appreciate plants as well as animals, we have illustrated 42 of the most common trees, shrubs, and wild flowers of Alaska.

The idea to write these books grew out of our own travel experiences and frustrations. First and foremost, we found that we could not locate a single book to take along on a trip that would help identify even the larger and more prominent animals – birds and mammals, amphibians and reptiles. Bird field guides are quite adequate for Alaska, as they are for everywhere in North America, but they include every species known from the state, far more than the average visitor will encounter. If we wanted to be able to identify mammals, we needed to carry another book. For "herps" – amphibians and reptiles – we realized that no good, small books existed that might permit us to identify these animals in most parts of the world. Thus, the idea: create a single guide book that travellers could carry to help them identify and learn about the different kinds of animals they were most likely to encounter, not only the big, obvious ones but also some of the common smaller ones that are usually lacking from travel guides and field guides.

Also, we know that ecotour leaders and guides vary tremendously in their knowledge of wildlife. Many, of course, are fantastic sources of information on the ecology and behavior of animals and environments. Some, however, know only about certain kinds of animals – birds, for instance. And some, unfortunately, know precious little about wildlife, and what information they do tell their groups is often incorrect. For example, many guides in Latin America, when asked the identity of any large lizard, respond that it is an "iguana." Well, there certainly are iguanas in the region, but there are also many other types of lizards, and people interested in wildlife need some way to identify the more common ones. The intent of this series of books is to provide that help.

x Preface

Last, like most ecotravellers, we are concerned about the threats to many species as their natural habitats are damaged or destroyed by people; when we travelled, we wanted current information on the conservation status of animals that we encountered. This book provides the traveller with conservation information on Alaska in general, and on many of the animal groups pictured or discussed in the book.

Because this book has an international audience, we present measurements in both metric and English system units. By now, you might think, the scientific classification of common animals would be pretty much established and unchanging; but you would be wrong. These days, what with new molecular methods to compare species, classifications of various animal groups that were first worked out during the 1800s and early 1900s are undergoing sometimes radical changes. Many bird groups, for instance, are being rearranged after comparative studies of their DNA. The research is so new that many biologists still argue about the results. In this book we are using the latest classification that has received general approval by the scientists working on the group.

We must acknowledge the help of a large number of people in producing this book. First, much of the information here comes from published sources, so we owe the authors of those books and scientific papers a great deal of credit. The books from which some of our information was taken are listed in the References section at the end of the text. Perusal of any of them will give you more detailed information about the species or groups of interest to you. We would like to take this opportunity to thank David Pearson, who wrote some of the material on tube-nosed birds and cetaceans; Robert Cannings, for information about flies; Kenelm Philips and David Nunnallee, for information about butterflies; and Joel Elliott, for information about sea anemones.

Our special thanks go to the artists who painted the beautiful plates, David Dennis (amphibians), Linda Feltner (mammals), John Myers (plants), Colin Newman (insects, marine invertebrates, and fishes), Douglas Pratt (Osprey), and John Sill (all other birds). The Slater Museum of the University of Puget Sound was the source of much material for the mammal plates. We also thank the Burke Museum at the University of Washington for kindly allowing access to its facilities, our editors Andrew Richford and Michel Moushabeck, and the editing and production staff at Interlink Books.

Please let us know of any errors you find in this book. We are also interested in hearing your opinions on the book and suggestions for future editions. Write care of the publisher or e-mail: dennispaulson@comcast.net or Ecotravel8@aol.com.

Chapter 1

ECOTOURISM: TRAVEL FOR THE ENVIRONMENTALLY CONCERNED

- *What Ecotourism Is and Why It's Important*
- *The History of Ecotourism*
- *Ecotravel Ethics*

What Ecotourism Is and Why It's Important

Travelling is an essential part of being human. In the distant past, people travelled for the most fundamental reason – to find food. During most of human history, people were nomads or hunter-gatherers, moving almost constantly in search of sufficient nutrition. Then someone made the startling connection between some discarded seeds in the past and the sprouting seedlings of the present; she reported the discovery to her clan, and things have not been the same since. With the development of agriculture, travel, always an inherently risky undertaking, was less needed. Farming peoples could remain close to their familiar villages, tend crops, and supplement their diet with local hunting. In fact, we might imagine that long-distance travel and any venturing into completely unfamiliar territory would have ceased. But it didn't. People still travelled to avoid seasonally harsh conditions, to emigrate to new regions in search of more or better farming or hunting lands, to explore, and even, with the advent of leisure time, just for the fun of it (travel for leisure's sake is the definition of tourism). For most people, still, there's something deeply satisfying about journeying to a new place: the sense of being in completely novel situations and surroundings, seeing things never before encountered, engaging in new and different activities.

During the final quarter of the 20th century arose a new reason to travel, perhaps the first wholly new reason in hundreds of years: with a certain urgency, to see natural habitats and their harbored wildlife before they forever vanish from the surface of the Earth. *Ecotourism* or *ecotravel* is travel to (usually exotic) destinations specifically to admire and enjoy wildlife and undeveloped, relatively undisturbed natural areas, as well as indigenous cultures. The development and increasing popularity of ecotourism is a clear outgrowth of escalating concern for conservation of the world's natural resources and *biodiversity* (the sum total of all the species of animals, plants, and other life forms found within a region). Owing mainly to people's actions, animal species and wild habitats are disappearing or deteriorating at an alarming rate. Because of the increasing emphasis on the importance of the natural environment by schools at all levels and the media's continuing exposure of environmental issues, people have enhanced appreciation of the natural world and increased awareness of environmental problems globally. They also have the very human desire to want to see undisturbe habitats and wild animals before they are gone, and those with the time and resources increasingly are doing so.

But that is not the entire story. The purpose of ecotravel is actually twofold. Yes, people want to undertake exciting, challenging, educational trips to exotic locales – wet tropical forests, wind-blown deserts, high mountain passes, mid-ocean coral reefs – to enjoy the scenery, the animals, the nearby local cultures. But the second major goal of ecotourism is often as important: the travellers want to help conserve the very places that they visit. Fortunately, through a portion of their tour cost and spending into the local economy of destination countries – paying for park admissions, engaging local guides, staying at local hotels, eating at local restaurants, using local transportation services, etc. – ecotourists help to preserve natural areas. Ecotourism helps because local people benefit economically as much or more by preserving habitats and wildlife for continuing use by ecotravellers than they could by "harvesting" the habitats for short-term gain. Put another way, local people can sustain themselves better economically by participating in ecotourism than by, for instance, cutting down rainforests for lumber or hunting animals for meat or the pet trade.

Preservation of some of the Earth's remaining wild areas is important for a number of reasons. Aside from moral arguments – the acknowledgment that we share Earth with millions of other species and have some obligation not to be the continuing agent of their decline and extinction – increasingly we understand that conservation is in our own best interests. The example most often cited is that botanists and pharmaceutical researchers each year discover another wonder drug or two whose base chemicals come from plants that live, for instance, only in tropical rainforest. Fully one-fourth of all drugs sold in the USA come from natural sources – plants and animals. About 50 important drugs now manufactured come from flowering plants found in rainforests, and, based on the number of plants that have yet to be cataloged and screened for their drug potential, it is estimated that at least 300 more major drugs remain to be discovered. The implication is that if the globe's rainforests are soon destroyed, we will never discover these future wonder drugs, and so will never enjoy their benefits. Also, the developing concept of *biophilia*, if true, dictates that, for our own mental health, we had better preserve much of the wildness that remains in the world. Biophilia, the word coined by Harvard biologist E. O. Wilson, suggests that because people evolved amid rich and constant interactions with other species and in natural habitats, we have deeply ingrained, innate tendencies to affiliate with other species and actual physical need to experience, at some level, natural habitats. This instinctive, emotional attachment to wildness means that if we eliminate species and habitats, we will harm ourselves because we will lose things essential to our mental well-being.

If ecotourism contributes in a significant way to conservation, then it is an especially fitting reprieve for rainforests and other natural habitats, because it is the very characteristic of the habitats that conservationists want to save, wildness, that provides the incentive for travellers to visit and for local people to preserve.

The History of Ecotourism

Tourism is arguably now the world's largest industry, and ecotourism among its fastest growing segments. But mass ecotourism is a relatively new phenomenon, the name itself being coined only recently, during the 1980s. In fact, as recently as the 1970s, tourism and the preservation of natural habitats were viewed largely as incompatible pursuits. One of the first and best examples of ecotourism lies in Africa. Some adventurers, of course, have always travelled to wild areas of the Earth, but the contemporary history of popular ecotourism probably traces to the East African nation of Kenya. Ecotourism, by one name or another, has traditionally been a mainstay industry in Kenya, land of African savannah and of charismatic, *flagship*, mammals such as elephants, leopards, and lions – species upon which to base an entire ecotourism industry.

During most of the European colonial period in East Africa, wildlife was plentiful. However, by the end of colonial rule, in the middle part of the 20th century, continued hunting pressures had severely reduced animal populations. Wildlife was killed with abandon for sport, for trade (elephant ivory, rhinoceros horn, etc.), and simply to clear land to pave way for agriculture and development. By the 1970s, it was widely believed in newly independent Kenya that if hunting and poaching were not halted, many species of large mammals would soon be eliminated. The country outlawed hunting and trade in wildlife products, and many people engaged in such pursuits turned, instead, to ecotourism. Today, more than a half million people per year travel to Kenya to view its tremendous wildlife and spectacular scenery. Local people and businesses profit more by charging ecotourists to see live elephants and rhinoceroses in natural settings than they could by killing the animals for the ivory and horns they provide. Estimates were made in the 1970s that, based on the number of tourist arrivals each year in Kenya and the average amount of money they spent, each lion in one of Kenya's national parks was worth $27,000 annually (much more than the amount it would be worth to a poacher who killed it for its skin or organs), and each elephant herd was worth a stunning $610,000 (in today's dollars, they would be worth much more). Also, whereas some of Kenya's other industries, such as coffee production, vary considerably from year to year in their profitability, ecotourism has been a steady and growing source of revenue (and should continue to be so, as long as political stability is maintained). Thus, the local people have strong economic incentive to preserve and protect their natural resources.

Current popular international ecotourist destinations include Kenya, Tanzania, and South Africa in Africa; Nepal, Thailand, and China in Asia; Australia; and, in the Western Hemisphere, Mexico, Puerto Rico, Belize, Guatemala, Costa Rica, Ecuador, and the Amazon Basin. On the North American continent, Alaska is also a favored destination. A great majority of the more than one million visitors to Alaska every year come to the state because of its wilderness and its wildlife.

Ecotravel Ethics

To the traveller, the benefits of ecotourism are substantial (exciting, adventurous trips to stunning wild areas; viewing never-before-seen wildlife); the disadvantages are minor (sometimes, less-than-deluxe transportation and accommodations that, to many ecotravellers, are actually an essential part of the experience). But what are the actual benefits of ecotourism to local economies and to helping preserve habitats and wildlife?

The pluses of ecotourism, in theory, are considerable (some negatives also have been noticed, and they are discussed in Chapter 4):

(1) Ecotourism benefits visited sites in a number of ways. Most importantly from the visitor's point of view, through park admission fees, guide fees, etc., ecotourism generates money locally that can be used directly to manage and protect wild areas. Ecotourism allows local people to earn livings from areas they live in or near that have been set aside for environmental protection. Allowing local participation is important because people will not want to protect the sites, and may even be hostile toward them, if they formerly used the now-protected site (for farming or hunting, for instance) to support themselves but are no longer allowed such use. Finally, most ecotour destinations are in rural areas, regions that ordinarily would not warrant much attention, much less development money, from central governments for services such as road building and maintenance. But all governments realize that a popular tourist site is a valuable commodity, one that it is smart to cater to and protect.

(2) Ecotourism benefits education and research. As people, both local and foreign, visit wild areas, they learn more about the sites – from books, from guides, from exhibits, and from their own observations. They come away with an enhanced appreciation of nature and ecology, an increased understanding of the need for preservation, and perhaps a greater likelihood to support conservation measures. Also, a percentage of ecotourist dollars is usually funneled into research in ecology and conservation, work that will in the future lead to more and better conservation solutions.

(3) Ecotourism can be an attractive development option for developing countries. Investment costs to develop small, relatively rustic ecotourist facilities are minor compared with the costs involved in trying to develop traditional tourist facilities, such as beach resorts. Also, it has been estimated that, in some developing countries with abundant wildlife, ecotourists spend more per person than any other kind of tourists.

A conscientious ecotraveller can take several steps to maximize his or her positive impact on visited areas. First and foremost, if travelling with a tour group, is to select an ecologically committed tour company. Basic guidelines for ecotourism have been established by various international conservation organizations. These are a set of ethics that tour operators should follow if they are truly concerned with conservation. Travellers wishing to adhere to ecotour ethics, before committing to a tour, should ascertain whether tour operators conform to the guidelines (or at least to some of them), and choose a company accordingly. Some tour operators in their brochures and sales pitches conspicuously trumpet their ecotour credentials and commitments. A large, glossy brochure that fails to mention how a company fulfills some of the ecotour ethics may indicate an operator that is not especially environmentally concerned. Resorts, lodges, and travel agencies that specialize in ecotourism likewise can be evaluated for their dedication to eco-ethics.

Basic ecotour guidelines, as put forth by the United Nations Environmental

Programme (UNEP), International Union for Conservation of Nature (IUCN), and the World Resources Institute (WRI), are that tours and tour operators should:

(1) Provide significant benefits for local residents; involve local communities in tour planning and implementation.
(2) Contribute to the sustainable management of natural resources.
(3) Incorporate environmental education for tourists and residents.
(4) Manage tours to minimize negative impacts on the environment and local culture.

For example, tour companies could:

(1) Make contributions to the parks or areas visited; support or sponsor small, local environmental projects.
(2) Provide employment to local residents as tour assistants, local guides, or local naturalists.
(3) Whenever possible, use local products, transportation, and food, and locally owned lodging and other services.
(4) Keep tour groups small to minimize negative impacts on visited sites; educate ecotourists about local cultures as well as habitats and wildlife.
(5) When possible, cooperate with researchers; for instance, researchers in several tropical countries are now making good use of the elevated forest canopy walkways that ecotour facility operators have erected on their properties for the enjoyment and education of their guests.

Committed ecotravellers can also adhere to the ecotourism ethic by disturbing habitats and wildlife as little as possible, by staying on trails, by being informed about the historical and present conservation concerns of destination countries, by respecting local cultures and rules, and even by actions as simple as picking up litter on trails.

Now, with some information on ecotourism in hand, we can move on to discuss Alaska.

Chapter 2

ALASKA: ECOTOURISM, GEOGRAPHY, AND HABITATS

A Brief Eco-history of Alaska

Why should an ecotraveller get on a plane or boat and head for Alaska? First and foremost, because the huge state of Alaska is in many ways an ecological paradise. It is an obvious destination for nature lovers, with more land in preservation than any other of the 50 USA states. By looking at a road map of Alaska, it can be seen that most of the state is roadless wilderness, with humans a dominant presence only in the Anchorage to Fairbanks corridor (Map 3, p. 11) and locally along the coast. The average population density is not quite two persons per square kilometer (per 0.4 sq mile), and many, many of those square kilometers are seldom if ever visited by people. Russians claimed much of Alaska for more than a century, but, overextended so far from their own homeland, they sold the vast piece of land to the USA in 1867 for $7.2 million. Statehood for the Alaska Territory did not come until 1959. Based on its political history, its far northerly latitude, and its physical separation from the remainder of the

USA states (the "Lower 48"), it is not surprising that this wild territory has been so slowly settled.

Fortunately for the ecotraveller, Alaska's wildlife is both varied and well-known. Even though there are huge areas of the state that have been scarcely explored by naturalists, the fauna and flora have been well documented, and the information is available both in technical publications and in field guides. Birds and mammals are diverse and abundant and include not only many interesting species but also spectacular aggregations of some of them. Almost 1600 species of plants grow in the tundra, forest, and wetland habitats of Alaska, the vast majority colorful wildflowers that brighten the landscape. (See, for examples, Plates G to J and Habitat Photos 6 and 8.) The marine environment is just as exciting as the terrestrial one, from tide pools full of fascinating invertebrates to the open sea with its concentrations of seabirds and marine mammals. Importantly also, Alaska has the distinction of having held onto most of its wildlife, while populations of many of the same species have declined or disappeared in the Lower 48 states.

Because of its rich wildlife populations, Alaska has long been a destination for hunters and fishermen. In more recent years, because of its size and spectacular scenery as well as its wildlife, it has become an ecotourism destination as well. Wilderness lodges that sprung up all over the southern part of the state in decades past to accommodate fishing and hunting now also attract birdwatchers and beachcombers. Many people see Alaska only via cruise ships, some of which start at Seattle or Vancouver and cruise up the Inland Passage all the way to Skagway (Map 3, p. 11). Others can be boarded in Juneau or Ketchikan for shorter cruises. Much cheaper than cruise ships, the ferries of the Alaska Marine Highway System run from Bellingham, Washington, north to Skagway. All of these boat trips are superb for scenery – dense forests, narrow fjords, sea-level glaciers, and snow-capped mountains. They are also terrific for wildlife viewing, especially for seabirds and marine mammals. Alaska has a great variety of species in both of these groups, and visitors rarely are disappointed with the show in such rich areas as Glacier Bay, Prince William Sound, and Cook Inlet. For those more interested in terrestrial and freshwater animals and plants, roads through Denali National Park, the Kenai Peninsula, and the Fairbanks area provide unparalleled wildlife viewing. Farther afield, visitors can fly to destinations such as Nome and the Pribilof Islands (Map 4, p. 20) for a taste of tundra and Bering Sea wildlife. The Arctic Circle (Map 1, p. 9) passes south of the Brooks Range and just north of the Seward Peninsula, and a visitor who wants to see the true Arctic, with 24 hours of daylight during midsummer, must visit Kotzebue or Barrow. Beyond even those distant destinations, bush planes can be chartered to deposit the most intrepid travellers in real wilderness almost anywhere in the state.

Alaska has become an increasingly important destination for ecotravellers in recent decades. Over a million visitors come to the state each summer (June to September), and, surprisingly, almost a quarter-million more come in fall and winter. Some, residents and visitors alike, would say this is too many, as the most popular areas now feature crowds in high season, filled-up campgrounds and cruise boats, long lines of cars where a moose or bear is crossing the highway, lodges for which reservations must be made a year in advance, and other problems associated with hot tourist spots.

Other than the crowds in the most popular areas, the problems with visiting Alaska are relatively benign (Grizzly Bears are not a problem only because of the infrequency of interactions with them). Travel can be expensive in the state, but budget-minded travellers don't have to stay at the most expensive lodges. Weather is often less than ideal, especially in the wet coastal areas or arctic regions, but most of us carry adequate clothing, and for most of us there is a toasty-warm lodge, hotel, or ship cabin waiting at the end of the day. Hikers and campers in parts of the state with the potential of particularly foul weather must make sure they are adequately protected from the very environment they are enjoying. Biting insects, although contributing greatly to the biodiversity, are surely the most-cited cause of Alaska being somewhat less than the ecotourism paradise that it might be. Insect repellent, however, goes a long way toward alleviating their presence, and many tourists choose to visit early in the spring or late in the fall, outside "bug season." This is also good from the standpoint of avoiding midsummer crowds, and early- and late-season visits provide some wildlife experiences that are different from those of midsummer.

Geography and Climate

The Bering Strait Connection

Alaska was once politically part of Russia, and from the standpoint of biology, they are inextricably linked. The two countries lie on either side of the Bering Sea (Map 1, p. 9) and share a very large percentage of the marine flora and fauna of that basin. The Aleutian Islands are almost continuous with the Komandorskie Islands of Russia, and the line between the two countries passes between the two small Diomede Islands in the middle of the Bering Strait. The strait itself is so narrow (88 km, 55 miles) that any small land bird can cross it in a few hours, and many of them do so during spring and autumn migration. Some songbirds that breed in Alaska winter in Asia and Africa, while others that breed in Russia winter in South America. The birds passing in opposite directions during migration over the strait are unaware of their significance in joining the hemispheres. Many seabirds that breed on cliffs on either side of the Bering Strait and many fishes and marine mammals that swim in it surely cross between the countries on a daily basis.

But more than the present-day proximity of these two land masses, Asia and North America, is involved with this connection. The two continents are connected by surface ice during winter, so even nonflying animals can cross between them. Although prevailing winds come from the west, plant seeds probably have always blown across the ice in both directions, colonizing one continent from the other. When water levels were lower during glacial periods, there was a very broad land connection between Siberia and Alaska, and large parts of it were ice-free in summer, allowing migration of many plant and animal species in either direction. This so-called *Bering Land Bridge* opened and closed several times during the Ice Ages, and the last connection was broken between 10,000 and 15,000 years ago, when our own species is thought to have invaded North America from Asia.

Thus, although the Old World and New World have almost completely different plants and animals at low latitudes, at the northern end of both of them the fauna and flora are very similar. The species are all adapted to arctic conditions, and many of them occur all across both hemispheres (for example,

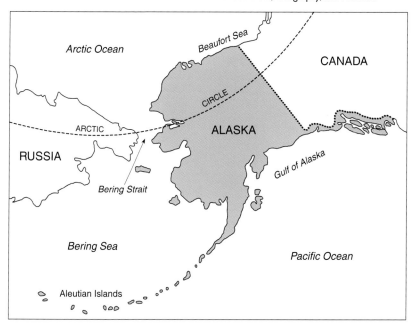

Map 1   The location of Alaska with respect to eastern Russia, the Bering Strait, the Bering Sea, the Arctic Ocean, the Pacific Ocean, and the Aleutian Islands.

Arctic Fox, Snowy Owl, Four-spotted Skimmer) or are represented in each hemisphere by closely related species (Canadian Lynx *vs* Eurasian Lynx, American Wigeon *vs* Eurasian Wigeon). Furthermore, animals and plants that evolved in one hemisphere colonized the other through the same route. Chipmunks, for instance, are restricted to North America, except for the Siberian Chipmunk of Siberia. Wrens are restricted to the New World, but the Winter Wren crossed the Bering Strait and now occurs all the way west to England. Shrikes are an Old World family, but the Northern Shrike crossed the strait in the opposite direction from the wren and now occupies all of northern North America. Farther south, the forest species are more different, because open tundra and muskeg (p. 15) probably always separated the forests of the two continents. For example, the Red Squirrel of Alaska is quite different from the Eurasian Squirrel of Siberia, and the American Robin of Alaska is similarly different from other members of its group in Siberia.

The Structure of Alaska

Alaska is a huge state, one-fifth of the land mass of the USA and extending 2200 km (1400 miles) from north to south and 3800 km (2400 miles) from east to west. Thus, it has plenty of room for both very extensive lowlands and magnificent mountain ranges. On a grand scale, there are three major mountain ranges (Map 2, p. 10): the Brooks Range extending east–west in the north, the Alaska Range extending east–west in the south, and the Wrangell–Chugach–St. Elias Ranges paralleling the coast in Southeastern Alaska. These mountains are impressive; 17 of the 20 highest peaks in North America are in Alaska. Mount McKinley ("Denali"), in Denali National Park, occupies the very top of the North American

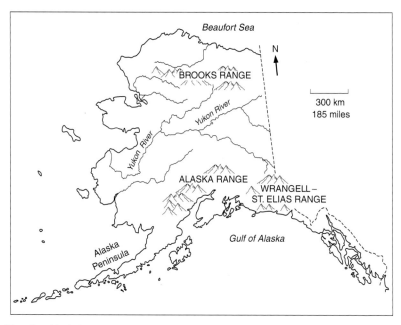

Map 2 Alaska's mountain ranges (the Brooks Range, Alaska Range, Wrangell–St. Elias Range) and the Yukon River.

continent, its summit at 6200 m (20,320 ft) elevation. Some of these ranges are virtually covered by glacial ice, a spectacular sight from land, sea, or air. Because Alaska is so far north, the *tree-line*, where trees and shrubs give way to open tundra, and the line above which there is permanent ice and snow, are at relatively low elevations. This is nowhere more evident than when, by tour-boat, you approach a sea-level glacier at the foot of mountains that rise from the shore, the boat maneuvering among miniature icebergs. The drier mountain ranges in the western part of the state run out to the sea, providing cliffs for nesting seabirds.

Between the Brooks Range and the Alaska Range lies the central plateau of the state, 600 to 900 m (2000 to 3000 ft) in elevation and drained by the lengthy Yukon and Kuskokwim river systems (Map 3, p. 11). Toward their mouths, these rivers flow through a vast lowland of wetlands and tundra. Similar lowland tundra occurs at the base of the Alaska Peninsula, the north side of the Seward Peninsula, and the land between the Brooks Range and the Beaufort Sea. These flat areas are dotted with lakes, probably more than three million of them in the state.

Besides the very large central mass of Alaska, there are two prominent extensions from the state, one to the west and one to the south, that provide it with not only an increase in territory but also an increase in biodiversity. These extensions include many of Alaska's 1800 named islands. The Aleutian Islands form the western extension, along with the Alaska Peninsula (Map 3, p. 11). These islands, many of them with steep coastal cliffs, form the southern border of the Bering Sea and extend almost to Russia; Attu, at their western end, is farther west than the westernmost Hawaiian Islands. In fact, a line directly south from Attu passes through the middle of New Zealand! To the south, Alaska occupies a stretch of the coast that should logically have belonged to Yukon Territory and British

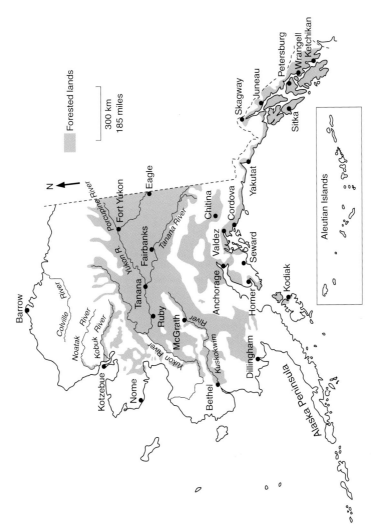

Map 3   Alaska's major towns, major rivers, and forested lands.

Columbia in Canada. This precipitous coastline is occupied largely by the Alexander Archipelago, a collection of large and small islands with deep fjords among them that extends south almost to Prince Rupert, BC. The names of some of the islands – Baranof, Chichagof, Kupreanof – hint of the early Russian colonization of the region, although Spanish (Revillagigedo Island) and British (Admiralty and Prince of Wales Islands) explorers also visited the archipelago.

Climatic Regions

Most people think of Alaska as a cold place, with ice, snow, Snowy Owls, and Polar Bears. Although most of it is indeed cold, it is large enough so that it is influenced by four distinct climatic regimes: maritime, transitional, continental, and arctic. The *maritime* climate is very wet and relatively mild; it influences the southern coast and islands. Southeastern Alaska is wet throughout the year and is just about the wettest part of the North American continent. For example, the average annual precipitation at Ketchikan is 381 cm (150 in), most of which falls as rain; fortunately for the visitor, the driest months are May, June, and July. The temperature differential between summer and winter is least in this climatic zone. Summers are cool and winters cold but not extremely cold; as a consequence, larger freshwater bodies stay ice-free during winter. Daily low and high temperatures at Juneau are about 9° and 18°C (48°F and 64°F), respectively, in midsummer, and −8°C and −2°C (18°F and 29°F) in midwinter. The average precipitation at Juneau is 161 cm (56 in), with March to July the driest months.

The *transitional* climate is considerably drier and quite a bit colder than the maritime zone. It influences much of western Alaska, from the Seward Peninsula to the base of the Alaska Peninsula, with a narrow band extending east between the continental and maritime zones. The Bering Sea's cold water and winter surface ice keep this zone cold for much of the year, and all freshwater bodies freeze during winter. Mean annual precipitation at Bethel, on the Yukon/Kuskokwim delta, is 42 cm (16 in), and daily low and high temperatures there average 9°C and 17°C (48°F and 63°F) in midsummer and −18°C and −11°C (−1°F and 12°F) in midwinter.

The *continental* climate features relatively dry weather, with warm to locally hot summers and very cold winters. It influences the interior of the state between the Alaska and Brooks Ranges, gradually blending with the transitional climate toward the west. Temperature variation is greatest here of anywhere in the state, and the extreme records in Fort Yukon are −61°C (−78°F) in winter and 37°C (100°F) in summer. Temperatures are low enough during winter so that all freshwater bodies freeze. Daily low and high temperatures at Fairbanks are about 11°C and 22.5°C (52°F and 72.5°F), respectively, in midsummer, and −28°C and −19°C (−19°F and −1.5°F) in midwinter. This is the sunniest part of the state, with precipitation much less than near the coast (annual precipitation at Fairbanks is 26 cm, 10 in), and cloud cover here is at its minimal for Alaska. Summer is the rainy season, with over half of the annual precipitation at Fairbanks falling from June to September.

The *arctic* climate is very cold in winter, cool in summer, and very dry. All fresh water freezes during winter, as do the adjacent Beaufort and Chukchi Seas. Daily low and high temperatures at Barrow are about 1°C and 7.5°C (34°F and 45.5°F), respectively, in midsummer, and −29°C and −22°C (−20°F and −8°F) in midwinter. Precipitation is very low (for example, 11 cm, 4.5 in, at Barrow), most

Table 1. Typical weather data in Alaska's four climatic regions.

Region Weather station	Maritime Juneau	Transitional Bethel	Continental Fairbanks	Arctic Barrow
Avg. low temperature, January	−8°C (18°F)	−18°C (−1°F)	−28°C (−19°F)	−29°C (−20°F)
Avg. high temperature, January	−2°C (29°F)	−11°C (12°F)	−19°C (−1.5°F)	−22°C (−8°F)
Avg. low temperature, July	9°C (48°F)	9°C (48°F)	11°C (52°F)	1°C (34°F)
Avg. high temperature, July	18°C (64°F)	17°C (63°F)	22.5°C (72.5°F)	7.5°C (45.5°F)
Avg. annual precipitation	161 cm (56 in)	42 cm (16 in)	26 cm (10 in)	11 cm (4.5 in)

of it falling in late summer (over half from July to October at Barrow). However, with prevailing cool, cloudy weather, evaporation is minimal, and the solidly frozen permafrost near the surface holds water; thus, lowland landscapes are soggy. One of the surprising things about the Arctic is that it can be so wet, with precipitation no more than in some of the driest deserts of the world.

Habitats and Vegetation

Alaska can be conveniently divided into two major regions (Map 3, p. 11), a forested and a non-forested region. The non-forested region consists of open and shrubby tundra, both in the lowlands and the mountains, and areas of permanent snow and ice.

Below we describe Alaska's main habitat types. Many of the common plants you will see in these habitats are illustrated in Plates A to J, following the Habitat Photos.

Tundra

A tundra zone circles the globe at the highest latitudes, where the sun always shines from a low angle and is absent for long periods. In this zone, bare rock and scoured soil are everywhere in areas relatively recently exposed by the withdrawal of glaciers after the last Ice Age, so both harsh climate and lack of nutrients limit plant growth. Tundra is a treeless environment, with thickets of low willows and birches the highest relief. Grasses, sedges, and *forbs* (herbaceous plants other than grasses and sedges) dominate the vegetation, which is surprisingly varied in areas of rich soils. Precipitation is generally low, and the evaporation rate is also low because of the low temperatures. With an underlying layer of *permafrost* (soil at high latitudes that stays permanently frozen), the little water that falls remains on the surface in a maze of ponds and marshes in low-lying areas.

Alaska's western and northern coastal plains are covered by moist and wet tundra, with drier alpine tundra appearing wherever the land is elevated into low mountain ranges. All of the islands in and bordering the Bering Sea and all those in the Gulf of Alaska west of Kodiak Island are tundra-covered. The list of tundra wildflowers (forbs with showy flowers) is a very long one; some of the more common species include poppies, louseworts, saxifrages, fireweeds, mountain avens, many kinds of mustards, forget-me-nots, and heathers.

Coniferous and Mixed Forest

A forest dominated by coniferous trees is characteristic of the *boreal* (a word in-dicating high northern latitudes) forest, or *taiga* (a Russian word, like tundra, that describes this habitat zone), which extends all across North America and Eurasia at high latitudes. With a relatively short growing season, leaves would be difficult to regrow each year, so, instead, conifers keep theirs and fill them with chemicals to deter herbivorous animals. Thus they are evergreens. The ground here is covered with leaf litter and fallen logs and branches, as the low temperatures and acid soils slow down the process of decay. This type of forest covers much of Central Alaska as well as the lowlands of Southcentral and Southeastern Alaska, although the interior forests and the trees in them diminish in size and extent westward toward the Bering Sea coastal plain. Temperatures are lower adjacent to the Bering Sea than in the interior, because of the long-lasting winter ice cover along the shore. The forests that dominate interior Alaska do not extend north of the Brooks Range, nor very far onto the Seward Peninsula, the Yukon/Kuskokwim delta, or the Alaska Peninsula.

Spruces dominate this forest in the interior, producing a great uniformity in appearance, whereas a mixture of conifers in the Southeastern forests produces an environment of more varied aspect. Stands of these trees that have reached maturity, without human disturbance, are called *old growth*. Broad-leaved trees are mixed with the conifers (thus "mixed forest"), especially in areas of *early succession* (where plants recolonize an area after disturbance), and form their own stands in some areas. The forests of Alaska's southern coastal regions are different from those in the interior. Coastal forests are wetter and the trees are larger. There are more species of trees, and many of them are different from those of the interior. Coastal forests are dominated by two huge conifer species – Sitka Spruce and Western Hemlock. Mixed in with them are much smaller numbers of Mountain Hemlock, Western Red Cedar, and Alaska Yellow Cedar; these additional species give these forests a much more varied appearance than the rather monotonous spruce forests of the interior. Numerous species live in the understory and along the edges of these forests, including several species of willows and blueberries as well as Sitka Alder, Salal, Salmonberry, Pacific Red Elder, and Devil's Club.

Interior forests are composed of trees that are considerably smaller than those of coastal forests, and they are dominated by White Spruce. The shrubby understory consists of various species of willows and blueberries, none of them in common with the coastal forests, as well as Crowberry, Prickly Rose, Buffaloberry, and Red-fruit Bearberry. In the interior, there are also extensive low forests with wet, acid soils dominated by Black Spruce mixed with lesser amounts of Tamarack and White Spruce.

Deciduous Forest/Riparian Woodland

Although deciduous broad-leaved trees occur together with coniferous trees all over Alaska, some animals occur in only one or the other of the habitats formed by pure stands of either of these types of trees, so they are listed as a separate habitat. Rather than extensive forests, the forests of deciduous species typically occupy river banks (where they are called *riparian woodlands*) and other disturbed areas, forming light green thickets in the sea of dark green conifers. In the coastal regions, these forests feature Red Alder and Black Cottonwood, while the same habitats in the interior consist primarily of Paper Birch and Balsam Poplar. Many of the same shrubs that occur beneath the conifers also live in the deciduous forests, but in addition, several species of alders are common.

Forest Edge/Shrub Thicket

Because numerous animals inhabit the edges of forest and shrubby thickets in and out of forest, these environments are listed as a separate habitat. The plant species of this habitat type are often those that grow under the tree canopy of the various forests, whether coniferous, deciduous, or mixed, but some shrubs flourish mostly in the open. Also, different shrubs prefer different soil types and soil moistures, so the makeup of shrubs will vary from place to place. The common species of shrubby thickets include numerous kinds of willows and blueberries and several species of alders, willows, currants, and blackberries. Coastal shrub thickets have one set of shrub species, interior floodplain thickets another, and birch–alder–willow thickets near treeline still another.

Open Habitats Other Than Tundra

The tundra is the dominant open habitat in Alaska, but there are open areas scattered all over the state south of the tundra zone. The most extensive is the area of *muskeg*, or treeless bogs, that occurs widely through the forested lowlands. Muskegs are characterized as areas of acid soil too wet for tree growth and instead vegetated with sedges, grasses, and mosses; the most common mosses are sphagnums. Stunted Black Spruce grow in and around these areas, which are often adjacent to black spruce forests. Many shrubs grow on the drier ridges of peat soil that run through the muskegs, for example, Bog Rosemary, Labrador Tea, Crowberry, Mountain Cranberry, and other blueberries. Other open areas south of the tundra include wet meadows, local areas of dry grassland, and the relatively small amount of space devoted to agriculture in the state.

Freshwater

Alaska is a very wet state, with high rainfall in the well-drained southern regions and permafrost that retains water in the drier northern regions. Thus lakes and ponds of all sizes abound, with characteristic aquatic vegetation such as water lilies, horsetails, Mare's Tail, pondweeds, and many sedges. Rivers and streams are also abundant throughout the state, and the very varied topography ensures that most regions have high-velocity mountain streams as well as wide, slow-flowing lowland rivers.

Marine

Marine habitats are nearly as varied as terrestrial ones, although one must look beneath the water's surface to see this variation. These habitats can be viewed as a series of *zones* paralleling the shoreline. Beginning above the high tide line, in the splash zone, the zones are in order supratidal, intertidal, and subtidal. As the names imply, (1) *supratidal* is the zone above average high tides; many land-based species feed there, preying on the few marine species that can exist above high tide; (2) *intertidal* is the zone between average high and average low tides (see Close-up, p. 79); and (3) *subtidal* is the zone below average low tides; in other words, the rest of the ocean. In addition, in open water there are depth zones, from the surface, through the subsurface, to just above the bottom. These zones, together with physical characteristics of the water, the bottom, and the shoreline itself, define the habitats that marine plants, invertebrates, fishes, birds, and mammals use. Alaska's marine habitats can be further divided into *protected* and *unprotected* waters and those with or without strong tidal currents; each type has its own species. The outer coastlines of Southwestern, Southcentral, and Southeastern Alaska face the full force of Pacific winter storms, which affect not only the shoreline but, at their more extreme, well into both subtidal and supratidal realms. Because of this, wind-blown and wave-washed coasts support a collection of species somewhat different from the species that are more common in protected areas. Furthermore, some marine mammals and birds favor either the open ocean or protected bays and inlets, while others are equally at home in both situations.

Tidal currents are strongest at the mouths of harbors and anywhere incoming or outgoing tidal waters are constricted by land. These same currents, characteristic of many of Alaska's islands and inlets, bring nutrients to the surface, increasing productivity and supporting concentrations of fish and invertebrate prey. Thousands of birds gather in season to feed on the fishes that swarm in these situations. Many of the birds float downcurrent, then fly back upcurrent and repeat the foraging run. Seals, sea lions, and cetaceans also travel in these currents, feeding as they go. *Bottom type* is also significant in determining the diversity, abundance, and species representation of the invertebrates that are preyed upon by fishes, birds, and mammals. Bottom types, both subtidal and intertidal, vary from solid rock to cobble to sand to mud, and in each type, there is a different collection of invertebrate and fish species. As with the bottom, the *shoreline* may be composed of rock, cobble, sand, or mud, or mixtures of these elements; each type has its own species of shorebirds. Depending on the intertidal topography, low tides may expose narrow rock ledges or thousands of acres of rich mudflats. In addition, the influence of freshwater and terrestrial habitats is felt everywhere the land meets the sea. For example, areas near river mouths feature a reduced diversity of marine species, because many of them can't thrive where the ocean's salinity is reduced.

Chapter 3

PARKS AND RESERVES: BRIEF DESCRIPTIONS AND GETTING AROUND

- *Getting to Alaska and Getting Around the State*
- *Descriptions of Parks, Reserves, and other Eco-sites*
  Southeastern Alaska
  Southcentral Alaska
  Central Alaska
  Southwestern Alaska
  Western Alaska
  Northern Alaska

Getting to Alaska and Getting Around the State

About half the people who visit Alaska come by air, about half by cruise ship or ferry, and less than one per cent by road, reflecting the great distance of Alaska from everywhere but sparsely populated northwestern Canada. The primary access to Alaska by air is on numerous flights from Seattle to Anchorage. By boat, both cruise ships and ferries provide transportation to many parts of Southeastern Alaska. The Alaska Marine Highway System (**www.akferry.com**) consists of passenger ferries that ply the Inside Passage from Bellingham, Washington, and Prince Rupert, British Columbia, stopping in Alaska at Ketchikan, Wrangell, Petersburg, Sitka, Juneau, Haines, and Skagway. Passengers can arrange to stop over at any of these cities and then reboard.

Finally, although only a small proportion of visitors decide to use the Alcan (or Alaska) Highway between Dawson Creek, British Columbia, and Delta Junction, Alaska, those who do so swear it is the best way to get to Alaska, if there is sufficient time. Bear in mind that about 80% of this highway is in Canada, so it is largely a Canadian experience. After a long history of being a windshield- and tire-destroying gravel road, the entire highway is now paved. Much of its 2430 km (1520 miles) runs through near-wilderness, but gas, food, and lodging are to be found all along its length at frequent intervals, with 160 km (100 miles) the longest stretch between gas stations. Some visitors even get to Alaska by bus, but this is a slow trip that may end up costing more than an airplane fare.

Within Alaska, the road system is limited – that's what makes the state a wilderness – but the main roads are paved and well-constructed, and all of them connect with one another except for the road system around Nome and a few short stretches elsewhere. Essential services (lodging, food, fuel) are not as close together on these roads as they are in the Lower 48 states, but there are usually helpful signs proclaiming the distances between them.

Descriptions of Parks, Reserves, and other Eco-sites

Alaska is full of parks and reserves, from one end of the state to the other, and the remainder of this book could be taken up describing them. But we restrict our list below to a sampler of those we consider of special interest and those that are easily accessible examples of their habitat or wildlife assemblages (Map 4, p. 20). Access is one of the big variables, as many of Alaska's fine wilderness areas are relatively inaccessible; others can be reached easily by highways from the larger cities. For many of the sites described, there are similar sites that are of equal interest, and we advise ecotravellers to purchase a good map of the state (you can't go wrong with the *Alaska Atlas and Gazetteer*, by DeLorme Mapping) and a state travel guide that gives information about not only the highways, lodging, and food stops between the wildlife areas but also about many of the parks and reserves themselves. After all, wilderness and wildlife is what Alaska is all about. We also recommend a few places where animals are kept in captivity, for close-up views of wildlife you will surely see elsewhere at a distance.

The sites are listed under the region of Alaska in which they are found (see Map 6, p. 51, for region locations); we include addresses and telephone numbers for most of the sites discussed. The state has a well-developed tourist infra-structure, and in each of its regions there are many parks and reserves. Further information on parks and reserves is available through publications, local tourism and park offices, and the World Wide Web. The web is a very good source for Alaska information, and some general sites are www.alaskaoutdoors.com, www.alaskashopping.com, www.touralaska.org, www.travelalaska.com, and www2.links2go.com/topic/Alaska.

Southeastern Alaska

Alaska Chilkat Bald Eagle Preserve

This preserve is famous for the large numbers of Bald Eagles that winter there; in fact, it has the world's largest concentration of this species. The eagles come from far and near to feed on the spawned-out carcasses of four species of salmon in late fall and winter; late October to early December is the best time to visit. It is an unmatched spectacle to see dozens of eagles in a single tree, and hundreds scattered in either direction along the river. Total numbers have exceeded 3000 in good years. The best area from which to see the eagles is from miles 18 to 24 on the highway north of Haines. Box 430, Haines, AK 99827;

phone 907-766-2292. (Area: 19,400 hectares, 48,000 acres. Habitats: coniferous and mixed forest, river.)

Chilkat State Park

The park is easily accessible from Haines, situated seven miles south of the town. From it, you can get spectacular views of the Rainbow and Davidson glaciers, as well as Chilkat Inlet. The 10-km (6-mile) Seduction Point Trail follows the coast and alternates between beach and forest. It provides superb scenery and wildlife watching. Harbor Seals, Sea Otters, Dall's Porpoises, and sometimes whales can be seen in the inlet, and Mountain Goats are visible in the hills on the other side. Chinook Salmon spawn in early summer, predictably attracting bears. Both forest birds and seabirds can be seen. This is a family recreational park fairly close to a small city, so it may have more visitors than many of Alaska's wilder parks. There are camping and picnic sites and a boat launch; telescopes are available at the visitor center. There is an entry fee. Mud Bay Road, Haines, AK 99801; phone 907-465-4563. (Area: 2450 hectares, 6045 acres. Habitats: coastal coniferous forest, saltwater.)

Gastineau Salmon Hatchery

This modern $7 million hatchery, located three miles north of Juneau, is a great place to observe how salmon populations are augmented by hatchery stock. The hatchery incubates about 163 million eggs each year of Chum, Pink, Coho, and Chinook Salmon. Fish are kept in large pools and tanks, carefully managed to grow rapidly and be released into nature. Aquaculture methods are shown and explained with underwater viewing, and there is also a saltwater aquarium, where local sea life is on display. There is an admission fee, and tours are offered.

Glacier Bay National Park

Tens of thousands of visitors visit Glacier Bay by cruise ship, and no one goes away dissatisfied. The scenery is spectacular, with sea-level glaciers on all sides, and the wildlife is awesome. Huge Humpback Whales are among the primary attractions, but many other marine mammals compete for attention, including Sea Otters, Harbor Seals, Steller's Sea Lions, Killer Whales, and porpoises. Seabird colonies abound, and visitors from the south are enthralled by Horned and Tufted Puffins and large numbers of Black-legged Kittiwakes. Access is only by boat or plane, but the abundance of cruise ships – varying in length of cruise, luxuriousness of boat, and cost – makes the area very accessible. Those who wish to be land-based can fly into Gustavus and arrange to stay at the Glacier Bay Lodge at Bartlett Cove. Glacier Bay National Park, PO Box 140, Gustavus, AK 99826; phone 907-697-2230. (Area: 1.3 million hectares, 3.3 million acres. Habitats: coastal coniferous forest, glaciers, saltwater fjords.)

Mendenhall Wetlands State Game Refuge

This popular destination is located in the center of Juneau, and it attracts thousands of water birds, from herons and geese to shorebirds and gulls. Large numbers of Dusky Canada Geese, a subspecies with a restricted breeding range, are an attraction, as are Bald Eagles. Birders have recorded 140 species here, including Peregrine Falcons. There is an interpretive center at Lemon Creek, but the refuge is otherwise undeveloped. There are trails for hiking, jogging, and cross-country skiing, and at some times the refuge is much used, but birds are always common somewhere in the refuge, in particular during spring, fall, and

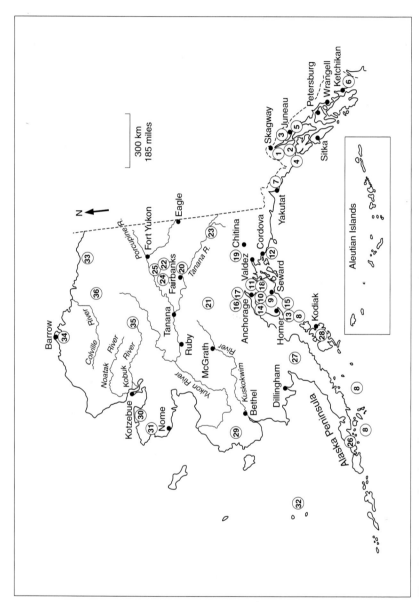

Map 4 Locations of parks and reserves mentioned in the text (key on p. 21).

Key for Map 4

Southeastern Alaska

1. Alaska Chilkat Bald Eagle Preserve
2. Chilkat State Park
3. Gastineau Salmon Hatchery
4. Glacier Bay National Park
5. Mendenhall Wetlands State Game Refuge
6. Misty Fiords National Monument
7. Situk River

Southcentral Alaska

8. Alaska Marine Highway
9. Alaska SeaLife Center
10. Anchorage Coastal Wildlife Refuge
11. Chugach State Park
12. Copper River Delta
13. Kachemak Bay
14. Kenai National Wildlife Refuge
15. Kenai Fjords National Park
16. Nancy Lake State Recreation Area
17. Palmer Hay Flats State Game Refuge
18. Potter Marsh State Game Refuge
19. Wrangell–St. Elias National Park

Central Alaska

20. Creamer's Field Migratory Waterfowl Refuge
21. Denali National Park
22. Steese Highway
23. Tetlin National Wildlife Refuge
24. White Mountains National Recreation Area
25. Yukon Flats National Wildlife Refuge

Southwestern Alaska

26. Izembek National Wildlife Refuge
27. Katmai National Park
28. Kodiak National Wildlife Refuge
29. Yukon Delta National Wildlife Refuge

Western Alaska

30. Bering Land Bridge National Preserve
31. Nome road system
32. Pribilof Islands

Northern Alaska

33. Arctic National Wildlife Refuge
34. Barrow
35. Gates of the Arctic National Park
36. James Dalton Highway

winter. Relatively few water birds but many songbirds breed in the refuge. While you're in Juneau, check out the nearby Mendenhall Glacier, no less magnificent because of its proximity to an urban center. (Area: 1500 hectares, 3800 acres. Habitats: tidal estuary with mudflats, grassy meadows, willow thickets.)

Misty Fiords National Monument

This is one of the many huge wilderness areas of Alaska that reward the intrepid ecotraveller. National Monument status protects ecological, cultural, geological, historical, prehistorical, scientific, and wilderness values. The lowlands here are heavily forested, and the greatly eroded peaks extend up into tundra, ice, and snow. Several major rivers and hundreds of streams are fed by misty rain and snow each year, as well as by meltwater from glaciers that begin near the Canadian border. Mineral springs and volcanic lava flows are among the area's diverse geological features. Marine life, from seals and seabirds to shellfish, is abundant in the fjords, and the lowland forests and muskegs support a wide variety of wildlife species. There are no roads into the monument, which can be reached only by boat or plane, but the very long Portland and Behm canals that border it allow access over a very large part of its perimeter. The monument maintains and operates a system of recreation cabins located in a variety of forest settings, from open ocean beaches to high alpine lakes. Recreation cabins are available to the public on a reservation basis for a fee. Reservations may be made up to 6 months in advance, and are booked on a first-come, first-served basis at the monument headquarters in Ketchikan. 3031 Tongass Ave., Ketchikan, AK 99901; phone 907-225-2148. (Area: 930,000 hectares, 2.3 million acres. Habitats: coastal coniferous forest, muskeg, freshwater wetlands, rocky fjords.)

Situk River

Near Yakutat, the Situk River is famous for its salmonid runs. All five Pacific salmon spawn there, and steelhead (sea-run form of Rainbow Trout) and Dolly Varden are common as well. The steelhead fishing is considered among the best anywhere. Because of the fish abundance, both Black and Brown Bears and Bald Eagles congregate during spawning seasons. Water-loving mammals such as Moose, Mink, and River Otters are often seen. Nine Mile Bridge is considered the best place to watch salmon. Lodging is available in Yakutat. (Area: 4 hectares, 10 acres. Habitats: coastal coniferous forest, riparian, river.)

Southcentral Alaska

Alaska Marine Highway

The Alaska ferry system runs all along the coast in this region, connecting many of the coastal port cities, from Cordova and Valdez in the east all the way to Dutch Harbor, on Unalaska Island in the eastern Aleutians. Passengers on all of these voyages can expect to see beautiful scenery and much marine wildlife. The routes from Homer to Kodiak and then on to Dutch Harbor travel far enough from shore that pelagic birds such as albatrosses, shearwaters, and storm-petrels can be seen, and there is a possibility of sighting some of the larger whales not usually seen from land. The Homer to Kodiak round-trip takes only 27 hours, but the trip to Dutch Harbor and back (six times each summer) takes six days and is only for the intrepid, as it can be a rough voyage. For such a lengthy trip, you should reserve a cabin or plan to sleep in a sleeping bag in the solarium. There are free showers, and you can bring your own snacks or eat the expensive food available in the dining room. For reservations, call 1-800-642-0066.

Alaska SeaLife Center

This center for the study of marine life opened in 1998 and is now a major visitor attraction in Seward. Funded largely with funds from the *Exxon Valdez* oil spill settlement, it devotes considerable efforts to rehabilitation of marine animals and research on them and their habitats. It features naturalistic exhibits of local marine birds and mammals, as well as fishes and invertebrates, and is the perfect place to visit before taking one of the boat tours from Seward. The center also includes exhibits of the oil spill and its effects. There is an admission fee.

Anchorage Coastal Wildlife Refuge

This refuge protects extensive mudflats and salt marsh on Turnagain Arm, just south of Anchorage. It supports over 130 species of birds and is an important area for waterfowl and shorebirds. There are boardwalks with interpretive signs, and naturalists are often present to answer questions. Look for Belugas all along Turnagain Arm, especially at high tides, when they come nearer to shore. (Area: about 12,000 hectares, 30,000 acres. Habitats: salt marsh, tidal flats.)

Chugach State Park

This park, which has been listed as one of the USA's "top 10" state parks, occupies much of the area immediately east of Anchorage. It extends from sea level at Turnagain Arm through lowland lakes and rivers up to alpine tundra above 760 m (2500 ft). It is well known for its views of the Chugach Mountains, with their glaciers, rugged peaks, and wild valleys. Wolf packs, Grizzly Bears, and Lynx, symbols of wilderness, are all in this park, so close to Alaska's largest city. Dall

Sheep, Mountain Goats, Collared Pikas, and Golden Eagles inhabit the high, rocky slopes. The park's campgrounds, picnic areas, and trails, and the Eagle River Visitor Center receive nearly one million visits each year, but the park also offers wilderness solitude and mountaineering. The headquarters are at Potter Section House, a state historic site 19 km (12 miles) south of Anchorage. HC 52, Box 8999, Indian, AK 99540; phone 907-345-5014. (Area: 198,000 hectares, 490,000 acres. Habitats: coniferous forest, deciduous forest, alpine tundra, freshwater wetlands, coast and mudflats.)

Copper River Delta

This very large estuary supports the largest concentrations of shorebirds anywhere in the world. Millions of sandpipers and plovers stop in the delta on their way to breeding grounds farther north, feed voraciously, and build up fat deposits to allow them to make the last flight in their long migration. Western Sandpipers, Dunlins, and Short-billed Dowitchers are particularly abundant, but large numbers of a dozen other species can also be seen. Waterfowl are also abundant. Spring is the best time to visit, and this migration magic is celebrated each year with the Copper River Delta Shorebird Festival in early May. Most of the area is inaccessible, but tour boats cruise along channels bordering the mudflats. (Habitats: estuarine mudflats, coastal coniferous forest, riparian woodland, willow thickets.)

Kachemak Bay

Kachemak Bay is famous for its large numbers of waterfowl and shorebirds during migration. Every year in early May, the Kachemak Bay Shorebird Festival is held at Homer, with guided birding trips and guest speakers. Alaska specialties such as Aleutian Terns and Kittlitz's Murrelets may be seen from the tip of Homer Spit, which is a prime location for migratory birds of all kinds. Sea Otters rest at the surface in virtual rafts, twined in the offshore kelp beds. Lodging, food, and gas are available in Homer. Boat tours are available from Homer Spit to Gull Island, where thousands of seabirds nest. The most common species are Black-legged Kittiwakes, Common Murres, Glaucous-winged Gulls, and Pelagic Cormorants, but there are also a few pairs of less common species, such as Red-faced Cormorants and Tufted Puffins. You can also charter a boat or float plane to Kachemak Bay State Park (Mile 168.5, Sterling Hwy, Homer, AK 99603; phone 907-235-7024), across the bay, where campsites are provided. (Area: 160,000 hectares, 400,000 acres. Habitats: coastal coniferous forest, estuarine mudflats, gravel spit.)

Kenai National Wildlife Refuge

This area, on the relatively flat northwestern part of the mountainous Kenai Peninsula, is easily accessible from Anchorage, on a good highway to Soldotna. Many side roads lead into the refuge, and there are numerous campgrounds, good freshwater fishing, and some river float trips. The Kenai River has the most large Chinook Salmon spawning in it of anywhere in the state, and Humpback Salmon are very abundant. With its profusion of lakes and marshy wetlands, the area is paradise for wildlife, and Moose and other freshwater mammals such as Muskrats, Beavers, and River Otters are especially common. Marsh-dwelling birds such as shorebirds (snipe, yellowlegs, dowitchers) and waterfowl are also abundant. Common Loons and Trumpeter Swans nest on some of the larger lakes, and the smaller ones have a rich assortment of waterfowl, as well as Sandhill Cranes.

Songbirds and small mammals such as Red Squirrels abound in the scenic boggy countryside. Box 2139, Soldotna, AK 99669; phone 907-262-7021. (Area: 800,000 hectares, 2,000,000 acres. Habitats: coastal coniferous forest, deciduous forest, freshwater wetlands of all sorts, saltwater and shoreline.)

Kenai Fjords National Park

Most people who visit this park do so by taking boat tours, which, from mid-May to mid-September, are booked at a visitor center in Seward. The town can be crowded with tourists, and reservations for boats should be made the evening before. Midsummer provides the greatest likelihood of good weather, but it can be rainy and windy any day of the year. The boats carry ecotravellers to islands with breeding seabirds such as Tufted and Horned Puffins, Black-legged Kittiwakes, Pelagic Cormorants, and Glaucous-winged Gulls. A shorter trip to Cape Resurrection is excellent, but even more wildlife will be seen on the longer trip to the Chiswell Islands (in the Alaska Maritime National Wildlife Refuge) and Holgate Glacier. Many marine mammals are seen on these trips, including Steller's Sea Lions, Sea Otters, Killer Whales, Dall's Porpoises, and Humpback Whales. PO Box 1727, Seward, AK 99664; phone 907-224-3175. (Area: 260,000 hectares, 650,000 acres. Habitats: coastal coniferous forest, saltwater fjords, rocky islands.)

Nancy Lake State Recreation Area

This popular recreation area is located near mile 67 on the Parks Highway, north of Anchorage. The Parks Highway runs up the flat Susitna River valley, with mountain ranges on both sides. The marshy lowlands around Nancy Lake are among the few extensive areas of wetlands available for recreation in settled regions of southern Alaska, most of which is mountainous. Beaver lodges are everywhere, Moose can be seen feeding near the road, and Common, Pacific, and Red-throated Loons, as well as ducks and geese, can be found nesting at the numerous lakes. There are good canoe trails offering superb wildlife viewing, and many visitors come to fish for trout and pike. There are cabins for rent (reservations are needed) and campgrounds. (Area: 9200 hectares, 22,685 acres. Habitats: spruce and deciduous forests, riparian woodland, shrub thickets, muskeg, lakes, streams.)

Palmer Hay Flats State Game Refuge

This refuge is located north of Anchorage, at the upper end of Knik Arm. It is a stopover site for tens of thousands of waterfowl, including both Trumpeter and Tundra Swans, three species of geese, and ten or more species of ducks. Sandhill Cranes also use the area in migration. Migrant birds are most abundant during the spring, but many are there in fall as well. The freshwater marshes have Beavers, Muskrats, and Moose, and the upland areas are full of songbirds during the breeding season. Small mammals such as Red Squirrels and Snowshoe Hares inhabit the scattered spruce islands. Coho Salmon spawn in Cottonwood and Wasilla creeks, draining into the refuge. A number of side roads allow access to the north edge of the refuge for good viewing. (Area: 11,650 hectares, 28,800 acres. Habitats: spruce forest, shrub thicket, wet meadow, freshwater marshes, lakes, streams, and tidal flats.)

Potter Marsh State Game Refuge

Next to Anchorage, this easily accessible refuge is great for a morning visit to observe its waterfowl and other water birds. Female ducks of several species with their young can be seen during midsummer, and large numbers of salmon and trout crowd into the small stream that drains the wetland during spawning season. Moose and many smaller mammals occur at the edge of the marsh and in the surrounding woodland. (Area: 220 hectares, 540 acres. Habitats: spruce forest, shrub thicket, freshwater marsh, stream.)

Wrangell–St. Elias National Park

This is the largest USA national park, the size of six Yellowstones, and the premier mountain wilderness in North America. The northern part of the park lies in the continental climate zone and is much drier than the coastal part, in the maritime climate zone. Four major mountain ranges meet here, and the park includes 9 of the 16 highest peaks in the USA. The Bagley Icefield is the largest subpolar icefield in North America. On a clear day, you can see the steam plume rising from the active volcanic crater of Mt. Wrangell. The sparkling-clear lakes and creeks teem with waterfowl and fish. The park is accessible by aircraft and from the Alaska Highway system on two rather poor gravel roads that penetrate it. The Nabesna Road, off the Tok Cutoff, offers access to lowland forest and meadows, home to Moose, Caribou, wolves and bears. The picturesque highlands of the Mentasta and Wrangell Mountains, at close hand on either side, offer opportunities to spot Dall Sheep and Mountain Goats. The McCarthy Road, coming in from Chitina in the west, passes through forested lowlands and ends at the foot of a glacier at McCarthy. There are lodges on both roads, as well as campgrounds or at least good camping sites. The park headquarters visitor center is at mile 105 on the Richardson Highway, and the Slana Ranger Station is at the beginning of the Nabesna Road. There are no maintained trails in the park, but several hiking routes and abandoned roads lead deep into the park. PO Box 439, Copper Center, AK 99573; phone 907-822-5234. (Area: 5.3 million hectares, 13.2 million acres. Habitats: coastal and interior coniferous forests, shrub thickets, alpine tundra, freshwater wetlands, saltwater.)

Central Alaska

Creamer's Field Migratory Waterfowl Refuge

This refuge, on the north side of Fairbanks, was originally a dairy farm. Begun in 1903, it had several owners until the mid-1960s, when it was converted into a refuge and environmental education center. Creamer's Field is very popular with Fairbanks birders: it is close at hand, about 150 species of birds have been seen there, and something of interest always turns up on the refuge during migration. There is a 3-km (2-mile) self-guided nature trail and a visitor center. (Area: 730 hectares, 1800 acres. Habitats: spruce forest, fields, wetlands.)

Denali National Park

Close to a million visitors per year enjoy this park, which most people consider Alaska's prime eco-attraction. The view of Mount McKinley (also known as "Denali") alone makes the visit worthwhile, on the relatively rare days when the clouds lift; and almost all visitors, no matter what their interests, are impressed by the wildlife. The experience starts with the cute squirrels that beg for handouts at campgrounds and visitor centers. Most visitors take the shuttle bus to Camp Denali, a 147-km (92-mile) ride through pristine forest, tundra, and river valleys. Moose, Caribou, and Dall Sheep are likely to be seen, but the biggest excitement comes from the occasional sighting of Gray Wolves or Grizzly Bears, and the bus driver is sure to stop for a good look. There are numerous points along the way to stop at a visitor center or campground, to spend some time wandering about the roadside, or to take a short day hike, to be picked up by a later bus ("shuttle bus surfing"). There are few trails, as most of the park is open terrain. There are both campgrounds and wilderness lodges at the end of the road, but reservations should be made at least six months in advance for one of the lodges. To prevent "loving the park to death," restrictions have been placed on visitors. In fact, you should get to the Visitor Access Center at the entrance as soon as it opens, at 7 a.m., because you'll have to get permits there for some of your activities. No private vehicles are allowed on the park's single main road, 40% of campsites and bus seats are reserved (the others are first come, first served), and you may be faced with crowds trying to get into the peaceful wilderness. But any inconvenience is worth it, as soon as you get away from the crowds, around a bend in the trail in your own little part of the park, with majestic Mt. McKinley filling the sky in front of you. PO Box 9, Denali National Park, AK 99755; phone 907-683-2294. (Area: 2.4 million hectares, 6 million acres. Habitats: shrubby river valleys, alpine tundra, freshwater lake, spruce forest.)

Steese Highway

This highway runs northeast from Fairbanks to Circle, passing through all the major interior Alaska habitats and – of special note – furnishing access to alpine tundra at Twelvemile Summit and the even higher Eagle Summit. Although wildlife is scarce in the open, rocky, alpine habitat, some special birds, such as Surfbirds and Northern Wheatears, can be found nowhere else without long hikes. There are also Rock Ptarmigan, American Golden-Plovers, Long-tailed Jaegers, and other tundra birds. At lower elevations, typical wildlife of central Alaska can be found in spruce and aspen forests and freshwater wetlands; the latter are common in the flatter terrain between Central and Circle. The area is easily reached on day trips from Fairbanks. (Length: 259 km, 162 miles. Habitats: spruce and deciduous forests, shrub thickets, alpine tundra, muskeg, freshwater lakes and ponds.)

Tetlin National Wildlife Refuge

This large and diverse refuge features all of the habitats of the area around Fairbanks, as it contains both river valleys and foothills. A total of 114 species of birds have been found nesting on the refuge, and 68 additional species visit it during spring and fall. The many lakes and marshes provide habitat for waterfowl, of which there is a dense nesting population, and Sandhill Cranes and swans move through in large numbers during migration. Extensive forests of spruce, birch, aspen, and willow hold large populations of woodland songbirds. Moose are distributed throughout the wetlands of the refuge, and Caribou can be seen from the highway during winter. Brown and Black Bears are also common, along with a host of smaller carnivores such as Gray Wolves, Coyotes, and Red Foxes. Fishing is a popular pastime at the many lakes and rivers, and common fish include Grayling, Northern Pike, and Burbot. Access is easy, because the Alaska Highway borders the refuge for 112 km (70 miles), and there are interpretive stations along the road as well as nature trails and campgrounds. PO Box 779, Tok, AK 99780; phone 907-883-5312. (Area: 295,000 hectares, 730,000 acres. Habitats: spruce and deciduous forests, muskeg, riparian, freshwater wetlands.)

White Mountains National Recreation Area

This is the largest National Recreation Area in the USA (but you've already learned that everything in Alaska is superlative). The low spruce forests of the river valleys quickly give way to alpine tundra on the hillsides in this popular recreation area. Miners and trappers live here, practicing subsistence life styles, but wildlife is abundant, too. The birds and mammals are those of the northern edge of the boreal forest and include many interesting species. Although the shyer mammals always prove a challenge to see, a quiet hike along one of the many trails would be pregnant with possibilities. Views of a Spruce Grouse, Great Gray Owl, or Northern Hawk Owl might reward the persistent watcher. The refuge can be reached by car on US Creek Road into the Nome Creek valley, accessible from the Steese Highway. There is a campground at either end of the Nome Creek Road. The refuge also lies adjacent to the Elliott Highway on the west. This refuge is especially popular for winter cross-country travel; fortunately, some of the trails are closed to snowmobiles. Phone 907-474-2200. (Area: 445,000 hectares, 1.1 million acres. Habitats: spruce forest, shrub thickets, alpine tundra, lakes and rivers.)

Yukon Flats National Wildlife Refuge

Yukon Flats is about 160 km (100 miles) north of Fairbanks. Here the Yukon River breaks free from canyon walls and runs in braided channels for 320 km (200 miles) through a vast flood plain. In the spring millions of migrating water birds arrive on the flats before ice moves from the river. The refuge has one of the highest nesting densities of waterfowl in North America, with over 40,000 lakes and ponds for nesting pairs. The Yukon Flats contributes more than two million ducks and geese to the migration flyways of North America. The area is similarly notable for its fish populations. Salmon from the Bering Sea ascend the Yukon River to spawn in the freshwater streams of their birth, some of them moving nearly 3200 km (2000 miles) from the sea. Runs of Chinook, Coho, and Chum Salmon pass through and spawn in the flats each summer – the longest salmon run in the USA. Mammals on the refuge include Moose, Caribou, Gray Wolves, Black and Grizzly Bears, and a host of smaller species. Both the Dalton and Steese highways pass within sight of the refuge, but the only access is by plane or boat. The area's waterways are much used for canoe, kayak, and raft float trips. 101 12th Ave., Room 264, Fairbanks, AK 99701; phone 907-456-0440. (Area: 4.5 million hectares, 11.1 million acres. Habitats: spruce forest, muskeg, shrub thickets, freshwater wetlands.)

Southwestern Alaska

Izembek National Wildlife Refuge

This refuge, near the end of the Alaska Peninsula, is famous because of the large numbers of waterfowl and shorebirds that visit the lagoon during migration. Eelgrass is abundant, so most of the Brant that breed in Alaska stop here for "refueling." Two waterfowl virtually restricted to the Bering Sea and environs – Emperor Goose and Steller's Eider – visit this area in large numbers. The mudflats provide high densities of invertebrates for migrant shorebirds such as Ruddy Turnstones, Western and Rock Sandpipers, and Dunlins; up to 40,000 shorebirds have been seen at once in fall. Streams in the area are full of spawning salmon of four species in summer, and Brown Bears are common. The tundra supports large numbers of voles and Arctic Ground Squirrels. The refuge is accessible from Cold Bay, which itself can be reached on the Alaska Marine Highway or by commercial airline service. A 64-km (40-mile) gravel road system leads from town to the refuge on Izembek Lagoon. Cold Bay itself has interesting birds such as Gyrfalcons, Rock Sandpipers, and Gray-crowned Rosy-Finches, as well as Sea Otters and Harbor Seals. Visits to the refuge should be arranged in advance by writing to the refuge office. Box 127, Cold Bay, AK 99571; phone 907-532-2445. (Area: 1.2 million hectares, 2.9 million acres. Habitats: moist and wet tundra, salt marsh, muddy/sandy lagoon, rocky shore and bay.)

Katmai National Park

The main visitor center for this park is in King Salmon, which is accessible by plane from elsewhere in southern Alaska. From King Salmon, visitors can take boat trips on Naknek Lake, rich in waterfowl and other water birds during nesting season and migration. Brooks Camp is the center of visitor activities for the park. The Katmai Wilderness Lodge, on Kukak Bay, is a luxurious but very expensive way to see the coast of the park, with great seabird and bear watching and outstanding fresh- and saltwater fishing opportunities. Brown Bears can be seen all along the shore, feeding on the tideline; as the lodge advertises, "The guests of Katmai Wilderness Lodge do not have to stand in line, stand on a platform, or look out a bus window to view these magnificent carnivores." PO Box 7, #1 King Salmon Mall, King Salmon, AK 99613; phone 907-246-3305. (Area: 1.7 million hectares, 4.1 million acres. Habitats: coastal coniferous forest, shrub thickets, muskeg, freshwater wetlands, wet tundra, marine shoreline and waters.)

Kodiak National Wildlife Refuge

Kodiak Island is one of Alaska's major islands, and it is famous for its "Kodiak" Brown Bears, the largest land carnivores in the world. With its varied habitats, the island supports large populations of wildlife, including Black-tailed Deer, Sea Otters, and many seabird colonies with puffins, cormorants, and gulls. The main town, Kodiak, is reached by air or the Alaska ferry system. From there, you can charter a small boat or plane into the refuge. There are public-use cabins, available by reservation and lottery, and guided wildlife tours. Many people visit the island to see the bears, and the easiest way to do so is by charter flight into bear-viewing country. The airplanes can set down near enough to feeding bears for excellent viewing and photography. Bears are often accompanied by scavengers such as Red Foxes, Bald Eagles, ravens, and gulls. 1390 Buskin River Road, Kodiak, AK 99615; phone 907-487-2600. (Area: 607,000 hectares, 1.5 million acres. Habitats: Sitka spruce forest, shrub thicket, alpine tundra, muskeg, freshwater wetlands, shoreline, saltwater.)

Yukon Delta National Wildlife Refuge

This refuge is very special because it protects one of the most important bird breeding areas in North America. The Yukon and Kuskokwim rivers have long flowed to the sea on this part of the Alaska coast, depositing material from the interior and building up a huge delta area just above sea level. With virtually as much water as land surface, its productive freshwater and saltwater wetlands serve as nesting habitat for many thousands of waterfowl and shorebirds. Substantial parts of the world's populations of Black Turnstones, Emperor Geese, Spectacled Eiders, Greater White-fronted Geese, Black Brants, and Cackling Canada Geese breed on the flats, and the very locally distributed Bristle-thighed

Curlews nest in the surrounding hills. Over 170 species of birds and 45 species of mammals are known from the refuge. To reach the refuge, most people fly to Bethel, where the refuge headquarters is located, and from there catch a commuter flight to a nearby Yupik community, from which boats can be chartered to see wildlife. Nunivak Island, just off the delta and also in the refuge, has large herds of Muskoxen and Reindeer, and there are guides based in Mekoryuk. PO Box 346, Bethel, AK 99559; phone 907-543-3151. (Area: 7.9 million hectares, 19.6 million acres. Habitats: spruce forest, wet tundra, cliffs, coastal mudflats, freshwater wetlands.)

Western Alaska
Bering Land Bridge National Preserve
This preserve offers the ultimate in wilderness, as it is far off the tourist routes, and so very few people visit it. Yet it is of great historic importance as the pathway between two hemispheres, and it holds spectacular wildlife, from Caribou and Belugas to Muskoxen and Gray Wolves. The tundra is alive with bird life during summer, especially shorebirds and waterfowl but including Gyrfalcons and Snow Buntings. Located on the north side of the Seward Peninsula, this refuge is reachable by bush plane from both Kotzebue and Nome. Serpentine Hot Springs is one of the primary attractions, with granite towers providing a scenic backdrop for the springs; cabins are available here by reservation. As in so much of the Far North, it is easier to get around during winter – on trails used by dog sleds and snowmobiles. At that time, most of the animals in the area will be species that are white, such as Snowy Owls and Polar Bears, or turn white in winter, such as ptarmigans, Arctic Foxes, Arctic Hares, and Collared Lemmings. They are difficult to see but wonderful to look at when you do see them. PO Box 220, Nome, AK 99762; phone 907-443-2522. (Area: 1.1 million hectares, 2.7 million acres. Habitats: wet tundra, sandy shore, ocean.)

Nome Road System
The small, isolated town of Nome is a popular destination for tourists because it allows easy access to tundra habitats. Although a thriving town, it is adjacent to the huge wilderness area furnished by the Seward Peninsula, and its roads give access to strikingly beautiful habitats with abundant wildlife. The wildflower show in July is alone worth the visit. Nome is set in the midst of tundra, but there are also willow and alder thickets along the rivers and even spruce forest on one road. There is no better place in the state to see a large number of tundra breeding birds from the comfort of your car, with relatively easy hikes onto the tundra anywhere that looks interesting. Three road systems leave Nome, the Teller Road to the northwest, the Kougarok (Taylor) Road to the north, and the Council Road to the northeast. All of them pass through varied habitat, including alpine as well as lowland tundra. The Teller Road goes all the way to Teller, a smaller village on the Bering Sea. The Kougarok Road, where it crosses the Kougarok River, is the only place in North America where the rare Bristle-thighed Curlew breeds near a road, although the hilly tundra there is very difficult walking. The Council Road passes the Nome River mouth and Safety Lagoon, premier birding sites, where bird tours often encounter rare visitors from Siberia during spring migration (which can last into June). The Council Road also passes through stands of spruce, with forest birds such as Spruce Grouse and Bohemian Waxwings. (Length:

365 km, 228 miles. Habitats: wet lowland to dry alpine tundra, willow/alder riparian thickets, freshwater, sandy shore, ocean.)

Pribilof Islands

Far enough out in the Bering Sea to seem a long way from anywhere, the Pribilof Islands are nevertheless easily reached by regular flights from Nome (although bad weather can delay flights at either end). The trouble in getting there is well worth the trip, as St. Paul Island, which most ecotravellers visit, is a paradise of wildlife. In midsummer, it is also dotted with patches of multicolored wildflowers, some of them found nowhere else but around the Bering Sea. The two common mammals are Northern Fur Seals, gathered in a large colony with good watching from a blind (hide), and Arctic Foxes, everywhere on the island but most readily seen on the bird cliffs. The foxes are often as curious about you as you are about them! The bird cliffs are spectacular, and there are numerous points of access to them; here puffins, murres, cormorants, kittiwakes, and auklets perch on rock ledges as nature photographers' dreams come true. Like Nome, this is a place where any Siberian bird might occur, and birders flock to the islands for not only the breeding seabirds but also the great variety of migrant shorebirds and songbirds that stop briefly on the island during their spring and fall passage. Among these migrants there are always a few off-course Siberian species, adding to the exotic flavor of these windswept islands. (Area: 21,000 hectares, 51,000 acres. Habitats: tundra, sea cliffs, freshwater, ocean.)

Northern Alaska

Arctic National Wildlife Refuge

Undisturbed wilderness awaits the ecotraveller who is able to visit this vast area of lowland and alpine tundra, dotted with lakes and rivers and rich in wildlife. All the typical arctic mammals are present, including the huge Porcupine Caribou herd, the females of which have their calves in the refuge in early summer. Bird life is abundant and diverse; the sky rings with shorebird songs and loon cries through the 24-hour summer daylight. All four eider species breed here, and – in a good lemming year – there are Snowy Owls and jaegers everywhere. Like other premier wilderness areas of Alaska, this one is accessible only by airplane, but the most adventurous and hardy wilderness travellers fly in to lakes and rivers throughout the area each summer. Bush planes can be chartered from either Kaktovik or Arctic Village, the two points of access. There are many lakes, rivers, and gravel bars on which planes can land, so the choice of where to set up a camp is up to you. You will very likely not see any other people from the time you are dropped off until the time you are picked up. This kind of camping trip is only for the hardiest and most experienced ecotraveller, as it is true wilderness. Planes can be delayed by bad weather, so extra food and supplies are a must. It is hard to know if there is more biomass of Grizzly Bears or mosquitoes in this area, but between the two of them, you will know you've had an adventure. 101 12th Ave., Room 236, Fairbanks, AK 99701; phone 907-456-0250. (Area: 7.8 million hectares, 19.3 million acres. Habitats: wet lowland tundra, freshwater, sandy shore and ocean.)

Barrow

Barrow is an obvious destination for travellers who wish to visit the High Arctic (it is well north of the Arctic Circle) and Beaufort Sea coast. It is easily reached by commercial flights, there is food and lodging (albeit very expensive), and rental vehicles are available. It is possible to see a wide variety of birds on foot, but a vehicle allows greater mobility, as there is a road system to take you out of town. The tundra and ponds have many breeding shorebirds and waterfowl, Snowy Owls can almost always be seen, and tremendous numbers of migrant birds pass along the Beaufort Sea coast both spring and fall. Black Guillemots, a species of the Arctic and Atlantic oceans, nest under debris on the shore on the spit that ends at Point Barrow. Mammals are scarce around the village but become more common farther away. After the ice goes out, Arctic cetaceans and pinnipeds can be seen from shore. The Beaufort Sea coast of Alaska (including the Barrow area) is icebound until midsummer. (Area: 7800 hectares, 19,200 acres. Habitats: wet lowland tundra, freshwater, sandy shore and open ocean.)

Gates of the Arctic National Park

Another of Alaska's great wilderness parks, Gates of the Arctic protects large swathes of the Brooks Range. The headwaters of the Noatak River Valley, a World Biosphere Reserve, also lie in the park. This and other rivers in the park are much used for float trips, and moving through the landscape in a rubber raft is an incomparable way to see wildlife. Large mammals such as Caribou, Moose, Dall Sheep, Grizzly Bear, and Gray Wolf are all likely sightings along the way, and this is the stronghold of the Alaska Marmot. Inconnu and other arctic fish are caught for supper at sand-bar camps along the way. Thirty-six mammal species and 133 bird species have been observed in the park. The park is accessible by air, usually from Coldfoot or Anaktuvuk Pass, or by a lengthy hike in from the Dalton Highway, which passes near its eastern boundary between mileposts 190 and 276. 201 First Ave. (Doyon Building), Fairbanks, AK 99701; phone 907-456-0281. (Area: 3.4 million hectares, 8.4 million acres. Habitats: northern coniferous forest at its northern edge, shrub thicket, wet lowland to dry alpine tundra, freshwater.)

James Dalton Highway

The Dalton Highway, constructed for the Alaska Pipeline, is now open to the public, and intrepid travellers traverse it every summer. It begins at Livengood, in the boreal forest, moves up into and across the Brooks Range at Atigun Pass, then down onto the Arctic Coastal Plain along the Sagavanirktok River to Prudhoe Bay. It offers a chance to see arctic and subarctic wildlife of many kinds, although encounters, as is usual with wildlife, are entirely fortuitous. Nevertheless, a drive of this length through country that is largely wilderness provides many opportunities for interesting sightings. Most of Alaska's large mammals are possible along this road, and the small mammals are there too, if you look for them. Breeding birds include many of those that attract visitors to the Arctic, from Snowy Owls and Bluethroats to three species of jaegers and four species of eiders. You have a very good chance to see nesting birds of many species, as they are very conspicuous on the open tundra. Wildflowers abound, and the rivers are full of catchable fish, including Grayling, Dolly Varden, Arctic Char, and Burbot. You will need to carry two spare tires, emergency repair supplies, and camping equipment; food, fuel, and lodging are available only at Yukon River Crossing (mile 56), Coldfoot (mile 175), and Deadhorse (mile 414, just before Prudhoe Bay). The Bureau of Land Management manages most of the land surrounding the Dalton Highway from the Yukon River (mile 56) to Slope Mountain (mile 300). Recreational camping, with a 14-day camping limit, is permitted on most of these lands. (Length: 662 km, 414 miles. Habitats: northern coniferous forest, shrub thicket, wet lowland to dry alpine tundra, freshwater, saltwater.)

Chapter 4

ENVIRONMENTAL THREATS AND CONSERVATION IN ALASKA

- *Changing Viewpoints about Animals*
- *Wildlife Management*
- *Overfishing*
- *Oil Exploration, Pipelines, and Oil Spills*
- *Logging*
- *Problems to Come*
- *The Great Value of National Lands*
- *Ecotourism and Conservation*

Changing Viewpoints about Animals

Environmentalism in Alaska can be shown readily by a chronology of events over the last century that both reflected and shaped changing American viewpoints about wildlife and the environment. In 1911, the Treaty for Preservation and Protection of Fur Seals was passed; it banned commercial seal hunting at sea. In 1913, the Migratory Bird Act was passed, setting uniform federal limits on bird hunting. In 1915, the Bureau of Biological Survey began a campaign to eliminate bears, wolves, and other predators. In 1924, the first federal waterfowl refuge was established. In 1934, Roger Tory Peterson's *A Field Guide to the Birds* was published; the first printing sold out in days, even though the USA was in the midst of the Great Depression. Alaska paid a bounty on Bald Eagles until its statehood in 1959, even though the species had been protected in the USA since 1940. In 1962, Rachel Carson's *Silent Spring* was published; the book pointed out the largely unnoticed devastation in America's environments and wildlife. In 1967, the Bald Eagle was listed as Endangered in the Lower 48, as its populations had declined sharply because of the effects of DDT. In 1969, the National Environmental Protection Act was passed. In 1972, the Marine Mammal Protection Act was passed; it placed total protection on all North American marine mammals. In 1973, the Endangered Species Act was passed, for the first time giving the federal government the power to halt development because of the presence of a single threatened species of plant or animal. In 1986, a total ban on whaling was declared by the International Whaling Commission. In 1994, the eastern North Pacific population of Gray Whales was removed from the Endangered Species List; this was the first marine mammal to have recovered by a concerted effort to protect it. In 1999, removal of the Bald Eagle from the Endangered Species List was proposed; the USA's national symbol was considered restored to robust health.

Wildlife Management

Wildlife species interact both with each other and with human populations, and these interactions are often the subject of intense interest and debate among biologists, the general public, and those who are given the responsibility of managing the species. Although *wildlife management* is a relatively recent term, we have been controlling populations of wildlife species for a long time. For the last several centuries in North America, large predatory mammals were routinely eliminated from areas of heavy human settlement. This treatment was because they were considered a threat to livestock such as horses and cattle and – in the case of wolves, bears, and large cats – even to humans. By early in the 20th century, the hunting of these and other animals by private individuals was largely regulated, and government agencies took over *predator-control programs*. More recently, the same sort of control programs were initiated against smaller predatory animals, such as Coyotes, foxes, and hawks, that fed on smaller livestock such as chickens and sheep. Seals, sea lions, and Bald Eagles were also subject to persecution because they preyed on fish that fishermen were unwilling to share. Throughout human history, our predators and competitors have been so treated.

The first programs to *increase* populations of wildlife species in North America were also initiated early in the 20th century, primarily as a response to the wishes of hunters. Since then, much effort has been made to increase populations of hunted species such as large hoofed animals and waterfowl. The *national wildlife refuge system* was initiated to furnish habitat for waterfowl, and it has succeeded very well. More recently, there have been concerted efforts to reverse population declines in many wildlife species, both large and small. But efforts to save two species sometimes brings agencies and managers into conflict, when one of the animal species eats the other; hard decisions have to be made.

Just this sort of conflict is ongoing in Alaska. The state has the healthiest populations of Gray Wolves and Brown Bears of anywhere on the continent, but these predators, where protected from hunting, increase to levels that have a negative effect on their prey populations. But when attempts have been made to limit wolf numbers, only lengthy and large-scale reductions of their populations have had any effects on populations of their primary prey species, Caribou and Moose. These wolf-control programs in turn cause great concern among environmentalists and animal lovers. The most recent management program was begun in 1993 on the Tanana Flats, south of Fairbanks, prompted by a continued decline in Caribou numbers and the accompanying concern of sport hunters. Wolves were hunted and trapped very effectively, but video footage of a game agent killing a trapped wolf sparked such outrage among the general public that tourists began to boycott the state; the program was quickly halted. One of its consequences, however, was the initiation of a Committee on Management of Wolf and Bear Populations in Alaska by the National Research Council. The results of the committee's deliberations were published in 1997. Among their conclusions: wolves and bears do limit prey populations but are not the only factors involved; conflicts over wildlife management policies may continue indefinitely; economic costs and benefits must be assessed; and more research and interagency cooperation is needed.

Overfishing

It is amazing to think that nets and other fishing methods can wipe out virtually entire populations of fish and shellfish from the immense oceans, but it has happened all around the world, including around Alaska. In part because of the usual "bottom line" of making a profit at the expense of natural resources, and in part because commercial fishing on the high seas has been difficult to regulate, overfishing is commonplace. Typically techniques are developed to harvest a *fishery* (one or more species of commercially important fishes or invertebrates), and if fishing is profitable, more and more boats set out to profit from it. Harvesting techniques may become sufficiently efficient that large proportions of the species are removed from its preferred habitat. The harvest may take primarily breeding adults, in which case reproduction is insufficient to continue the stock; or it may take primarily young fish, in which case recruitment into adulthood diminishes, and – again – there are not enough breeders. Or, very commonly, all age stages are harvested, and the population crashes even more quickly. One of the major consequences of some fisheries is the *bycatch*, the capture of great quantities of other species taken along with the target species. Perhaps a fourth of the fish captured around the world are tossed overboard as bycatch, dead or dying, or, if undamaged, far from their home territory and almost assured of death. For example, in 1997, fishermen capturing Sablefish were ordered to reduce their bycatch of Shortraker Rockfish and Rougheye Rockfish, or fisheries officials would be forced to close the season before quotas of Sablefish were reached. As you might imagine, catching one species of fish in huge nets, while deliberately not catching other species, can be a difficult, if not sometimes impossible, task.

Both the Bering Sea and North Pacific are extraordinarily rich ecosystems, and Alaska's marine resources are tremendous; for example, more than half of the United States' seafood production comes from the Bering Sea. Not only do residents of Alaska fish in the Bering Sea and North Pacific Ocean, but boats from the Lower 48 arrive in summer to take their portion. In addition, fishermen from several Asian countries fish in these waters, further harvesting marine biological resources that must be shared among different nations.

Interestingly, a September 1997 Report on the Status of Fisheries of the United States by the National Marine Fisheries Service identified no Alaska fish or shellfish stocks that were considered overfished or in imminent danger. This was in stark contrast to many fisheries farther south in the Pacific, as well as throughout the western Atlantic and Caribbean, that were considered overfished. However, the status of 42 of the 105 fisheries stocks assessed for the Gulf of Alaska and Bering Sea was listed as "unknown." That report notwithstanding, depletion of stocks of common Alaska species such as Red King Crab, Walleye Pollock, and Pacific Halibut is well documented. During recent years, Steller's Sea Lion populations have decreased by 80%, Northern Fur Seals by 50%, and Sea Otters by 40%. These three marine mammals feed on fish or shellfish, but it has been difficult to pin down whether declines in their prey are responsible for these alarming declines. Murres and kittiwakes, both fish-eating birds, have also declined greatly during the same period. Overfishing, prolonged El Niño events, and oil spills have all been suggested as being responsible for reduced numbers of some of these species, and any or all of them might be to blame. The Bering Sea is a huge and complex ecosystem, and most biologists are forced to concede the great distance yet to travel to reach a sufficient understanding of it to ensure its long-term health.

A new kind of fishing net has been developed that allows immature pollock and other small fish to swim through "escape hatches" in the top of the net. The first trials indicated a high survival rate among escapees, with bycatch of juveniles reduced by up to 75%. After witnessing the results of these trials, some fishermen have begun to use this net. With such developments, there is hope that intelligent management of marine resources is possible.

Oil Exploration, Pipelines, and Oil Spills

Alaska has rich oil resources under its territory, and there are strong feelings, both positive and negative, about that oil; it has given the state both extravagant riches and devastated beaches. The oil pumped from beneath the ground at Prudhoe Bay is of great importance to the economy of the USA, but the fact that it is adjacent to the Arctic National Wildlife Refuge has caused considerable concern among environmentalists. The oil is transported to the south coast of Alaska at Valdez through the 1280-km (800-mile) Trans Alaska Pipeline, which cost $8 billion and employed about 70,000 people during its three years of construction. It was designed to be heavily safeguarded against not only leaks but also earthquake damage. A major leak in this pipeline would do irreparable damage to tundra, forest, and/or wetland environments, depending on where it happened. A leak near or over a river would be particularly harmful. Another problem could have been the melting of permafrost that would occur around the pipeline, because oil rushing at high speed through a pipe warms it up. The pipeline is supported above the tundra in areas of unstable permafrost to avoid this problem.

Being the terminus for the pipeline has made Valdez one of the richest towns in Alaska; up to 30% of the people living there now work on pipeline-related jobs. Because the oil pipeline from Prudhoe Bay to Valdez was such a potential threat to the environment, it caused substantial controversy during its planning, but broad-based opposition didn't stop it. Nevertheless, the Alyeska Pipeline Service Company has had to make great efforts to mitigate the environmental problems the pipeline might cause. In those sections where the pipeline is elevated, 579 crossings were provided for wildlife, mostly by elevating it to 3 m (10 ft) above the ground but in a few cases by burying 60 m (200 ft) stretches of it. This was considered necessary especially because of the fear that it would interrupt the migration of thousands of Caribou.

Once the oil reaches Valdez and is pumped onboard a tanker, the environmental risk jumps an order of magnitude. A marine oil spill has the potential to affect a huge area, depending on the amount of oil spilled, the type of oil, the currents, and the winds. All marine animals are affected by oil spills, and such spills are among Alaska's worst potential environmental disasters. That potential was realized in 1989 when the tanker *Exxon Valdez* ran aground and spilled 11 million gallons of crude oil into Prince William Sound. Over 30,000 birds of 90 species were picked up dead on beaches in the three months after the spill, but the actual mortality has been estimated in the range of a quarter of a million birds or more. Large numbers of marine mammals were also found dead, including more than a thousand Sea Otters; it was estimated that only one-fifth of the otters that died were actually seen and recorded.

Sea Otters are especially vulnerable to oil spills, because oil mats their fur coat in a way to make it lose its value as a necessary insulation against the cold ocean. This loss of insulation is surely the cause of death among many seabirds as well. Marine birds and mammals come ashore to avoid heat loss, and die of starvation. On top of that, as they groom their feathers and fur to try to rid it of oil, they ingest the oil, usually causing death. Some birds survive while sparsely oiled, but, if they are incubating, their reproduction is at risk, because oil on the surface of eggs has been shown to cause the death of embryos within them. Finally, populations of many species of marine fishes and invertebrates are reduced by the spill, and many birds and mammals surely die because of the lack of their usual prey.

Seabirds are differentially vulnerable to oil spills by way of their foraging habits. Those that remain on the water, feeding either on the surface (many waterfowl) or by diving beneath it (loons, grebes, cormorants, diving ducks), are more vulnerable than those that remain out of the water most of the time, feeding from the water surface in flight (gulls) or on the shore (shorebirds). It is noteworthy that diving birds such as loons, grebes, and alcids have always suffered the most substantial mortality from spills.

Some residual oil remained on the bottom, on the shore, and even in the water column of Prince William Sound, years after the 1989 spill, and even very small concentrations can continue to affect wildlife. In experiments, Pink Salmon embryos were killed by extremely low doses (1 part per billion) of highly weathered Prince William Sound oil. By 1996, Bald Eagle populations had reached previous levels in the region, but Harlequin Ducks had not. Nevertheless, superficially at least, Prince William Sound has recovered. The best place to observe this recovery is at Seward, where the $56 million dollar Alaska SeaLife Center opened in 1998. Funded by money paid by Exxon after a historic court settlement, the center offers exhibits about both the oil spill and the formerly and again abundant Prince William Sound wildlife. Many of the same wildlife species can be seen near the center in the sound itself.

As part of its environmental responsibility, Alyeska has prepared very detailed contingency plans in the event of leaks in the pipeline, at its marine terminal, or in the waters surrounding it. In addition, a few months after the *Exxon Valdez* disaster, a Ship Escort Response Vessel System was established for oil spill prevention and response in Prince William Sound that could serve as a model for any other region.

Logging

Logging has been a potential environmental problem only in Southeast Alaska, where most of the state's big trees grow. The Tongass National Forest is the scene of most of the controversy surrounding the logging industry in Alaska. It is not only the USA's largest national forest, at 7 million hectares (17 million acres), but is one of the most important, as the largest stand of temperate coastal rainforest remaining in the world. At this time, it contains about 29% of all the temperate rainforest remaining unlogged. Timber companies would like to be able to log those parts of the Tongass that contain prime stands of old-growth, and a concerted effort is being made to prevent that from happening. Previous to 1990, logging had been the primary goal of the forest, but in that year, Congress passed the landmark Tongass Timber Reform Act to reform the Forest Service's management of the Tongass. More than 400,000 hectares (one million acres) of important fish and wildlife habitat were protected by the act, about the same amount of land that had been clear-cut since 1954, when serious logging began. There is still an on-going battle between those who favor clear-cutting the forest and those who want to preserve it intact.

Problems to Come

Besides the usual ways in which humans are detrimental to plant and animal populations (for example, overhunting, overfishing, pollution, and habitat destruction), we are actually changing the entire Earth in ways that could prove to be more serious yet. Two of these ways that have received much attention in recent years are *ozone depletion* and *global warming*.

Alaska, because it is situated in high latitudes, is vulnerable to the excess of *ultraviolet rays* (UV) that accompany the thinning of the ozone layer over the planet. In 1974, ozone was found to be affected by chlorofluorocarbons (CFCs), chemicals found in aerosol cans and refrigerators. Fearing the effect of these chemicals on a vital protective layer, the USA banned the use of CFCs in aerosol cans in 1978. In 1985, the first hole in the Antarctic ozone layer was reported, with an associated increase in UV radiation. The hole has become bigger since then, and a similar, but smaller, hole has been reported in the Arctic. UV radiation has increased in many areas, and its toxic effects cannot be overstated. UV-B causes sunburns in humans and is particularly harmful to life; most plants and animals have adaptations to keep its rays from reaching vulnerable tissues. In fact, the black pigment on frog eggs, the black lining of the body cavity in many desert lizards, the light-colored reflective surfaces on many dragonflies, and the carotenoid pigments in plants may all represent such adaptations.

Global warming is caused by excess amounts of carbon dioxide being produced by the burning of fossil fuels, and the "greenhouse effect" produced by the increase of that gas. Average temperatures have risen slightly in recent years in most parts of the Earth, and some effects of this on living organisms are already being seen. In the British Isles, for example, flowers are blooming earlier and birds breeding earlier than ever before, apparently a response to earlier springs because of the higher average temperatures. This seems little cause for concern, but there are other, potentially more ominous consequences of global warming. One of the most likely consequences is a latitudinal shift in the distribution of plants and animals, exactly as happened during the Ice Ages. At the time when the Ice Ages' glaciers reached their southernmost extent, much of Alaska was buried under ice, and the spruce forests that characterize the state at present occurred in a belt from Nebraska to New Jersey. As the glaciers receded, the spruce forest migrated north after them and returned to its northern range. Such migrations of whole ecosystems will occur during global warming, but what is happening now is changing temperatures much more rapidly than occurred during the northward retreat of the glaciers. During their migration, some of these ecosystems will run into impediments to an orderly northward progression: rivers, the Great Lakes, areas especially dry or especially wet, and soils unsuitable for certain plants. Species could easily be lost because of these barriers, unable to shift their distribution while other species of their ecosystem did so.

The overall effects of global warming on Alaska may not be very severe. They could involve, as well as extended breeding seasons, an invasion of southerly distributed plants and animals into the state, a retreat of many of its glaciers, and a melting of the southern edge of the permafrost. However, as the ice fields and glaciers of the world continued to melt, sea levels would rise, inundating the low-lying lands along Alaska's coast, with effects on shoreline environments and wildlife.

The Great Value of National Lands

As they do in most states, lands under federal jurisdiction play a very large part in conservation. In 1916, the National Park Service was created; the next year, Mount McKinley and its surroundings became a national park. The National Wilderness Preservation Act was passed in 1964 and has been responsible for protecting 42 million hectares (104 million acres) of federal land in the USA as wilderness areas. The fundamental premise of that act was that the process of building roads is a death sentence for an ecosystem. Numerous studies have shown that the fragmentation of habitats often leads to their disintegration, and roads are especially responsible for that fragmentation, as they allow incursion by more and more people, with all the disturbance and habitat modification that entails. Grizzly Bears are good examples of animals that are pushed farther and farther back into wilderness as roads invade their range. Thus, wilderness areas are defined to be roadless.

The year 1980 was the really significant milestone for the Alaska environment. The Alaska National Interest Lands Conservation Act of that year set aside more than 60 million hectares (150 million acres) of federal land as parks, wildlife refuges, wilderness, and national forests, totaling 40% of the state's land area! Of this total, 23 million hectares (56 million acres) were designated as wilderness. About 55% of all lands set aside as wilderness in the USA are in Alaska. There are 48 such areas, the largest of which is more than 3.6 million hectares (9 million acres) inside Wrangell–St. Elias National Park and Preserve, the largest designated wilderness in the USA. Beneath the coastal plain of the Arctic National Wildlife Refuge is one of the large oil reserves for the nation, and the need for that fossil fuel exerts strong pressure to drill for it there. However, environmental groups such as The Wilderness Society are lobbying to have that area designated as wilderness to protect the biological treasures there, including the 155,000 Caribou of the Porcupine Herd.

Although not all are wilderness areas, federal lands in Alaska protect vast wildlife populations. Of all the land designated as national wildlife refuge land in the USA, 84% is in Alaska. The Arctic National Wildlife Refuge is the largest of the entire 37 million-hectare (92.5 million-acre) system. The Alaska Maritime Wildlife Refuge supports populations of 40 million seabirds, including some of the largest seabird colonies in the world. The 14 other refuges in the state protect other important wildlife concentrations and ecosystems.

Two-thirds of all the land in the national park system is in Alaska, which is home to 16 national parks, totaling 22 million hectares (54 million acres). Among them are the world-famous Denali National Park, home of the highest peak in North America, and Wrangell–St.Elias National Park and Preserve, at 5 million hectares (12.3 million acres) the largest park in the USA, six times the size of Yellowstone.

But even with this much protection, it was shown by a recent study that 15 of Alaska's 28 *ecoregions* (divisions of the state characterized by distinct environments) still lack sufficient protection to ensure the conservation of their unique floras and faunas. The ecoregions at risk include the Arctic Coastal Plain, Copper River Basin, Upper Yukon Highlands, and Cook Inlet Lowlands, each of which is an important environment for wildlife.

Ecotourism and Conservation

Ecotourism can contribute to environmental preservation. In Chapter 1, we discussed ecotourism's economic and ecological advantages to its destinations. But does ecotourism always help local economies and significantly preserve visited habitats and wildlife? This question is important because increasingly, the fostering of ecotourism is suggested by indigenous people in developing nations, by the nations themselves, and by international conservation organizations, as one of the best methods to preserve natural resources and biodiversity almost anywhere that they are threatened. Certainly it works to a degree – witness success stories in countries such as Kenya and Costa Rica and, in Alaska, cities such as Nome, Juneau, and Seward, and St. Paul Island in the Bering Sea. However, as with any popular program that undergoes rapid growth, there are problems. Many people who monitor tourism – researchers and government officials – believe that in the rush to make money from ecotourism, benefits are often overstated and problems ignored.

Some private companies purporting to be "ecotour" operators are "eco-" in name only; they are interested solely in profits, and are not concerned about local economies or the wild areas into which they take tourists. There is increasing concern about monetary "leakage": despite attempts to keep most of the ecotourist revenues in local destination economies, many of those dollars, more than 50% by recent estimates, leak back to higher levels of government or are siphoned off as profit in the private sector; relatively little actually is spent on conservation. Also, popularity as an ecotourism site has the potential to lead to its failing. As ecotourism expands dramatically, sites that are over-used and under-managed will be damaged. Trails in forests and especially tundra gradually enlarge and deepen, and erosion occurs; cruise ships and wildlife-viewing boats leak oil and may make waves that damage fragile shorelines; "wilderness" lodges are built that immediately end the wilderness; and crowds of people are incompatible with natural animal behavior. Also, ecotourism's success harms itself in another way: when any area becomes too popular, many travellers wanting to experience truly wild areas and quiet solitude no longer want to go there. That is, with increasing popularity, there is an inexorable deterioration of the experience. In Alaska, this is particularly true of helicopter and airplane tours of the wilderness, which – although they allow spectacular views for a few – thoroughly compromise the experiences of others.

Thus, ecotourism is not a miracle cure-all for conservation; these days it is understood to be a double-edged sword. Clearly, large numbers of people visiting sites cannot help but have adverse impacts on those sites. But as long as operators of the facilities are aware of negative impacts, careful management practices can reduce damage. Leakage of ecotourist revenue away from the habitats the money was meant to conserve is difficult to control, but some proportion of the money does go for what it is intended and, with increased awareness of the problem, perhaps that proportion can be made to grow. Finally, environmentally sensitive travellers can take steps to ensure that their trips help rather than hurt visited sites (see p. 3).

Chapter 5

HOW TO USE THIS BOOK: NATURAL HISTORY AND ECOLOGY

- *What is Natural History?*
- *What is Ecology?*
- *How to Use This Book*
  Information in the Family Profiles
  Information in the Color Plate Section

What is Natural History?

The purpose of this book is to provide ecotravellers with sufficient information to identify many common animal species and to learn about them and the groups of animals to which they belong. *Natural history* includes the study of animals' natural habits, especially their distribution, classification, ecology, and behavior. This kind of information is important for a variety of reasons. Animal researchers need to know natural history as background on the species they study, and wildlife managers and conservationists need natural history information because their decisions about managing animal populations must be partially based on it. More relevant for the ecotraveller, natural history is simply interesting. People who appreciate animals typically like to watch them, touch when appropriate, and know as much about them as they can.

What is Ecology?

Ecology is the branch of the biological sciences that deals with the interactions between living things and their physical environment and with each other. Animal ecology is the study of the interactions of animals with each other, with plants, and with the physical environment. Broadly interpreted, these interactions take into account most everything we find fascinating about animals – what they eat, how they forage, how and when they breed, how they survive the rigors of extreme climates, why they are large or small, or dully or brightly colored, and many other facets of their lives.

An animal's life, in some ways, is the sum of its interactions with other organisms – members of its own species and others – and with its physical environment. Of particular interest are the numerous and diverse ecological interactions that occur between different species. Most can be placed into one of several general categories, based on how two species affect each other when they interact; they can have positive, negative, or neutral (that is, no) effects on each other. The relationship terms below are used in the book to describe the natural history of various animals.

Competition is an ecological relationship in which neither of the interacting species benefit. Competition occurs when individuals of two species use the same resource – a certain type of food, nesting holes in trees, etc. – and that resource is in insufficient supply to meet all their needs. As a result, both species are less successful than they could be in the absence of the interaction (that is, if the other species was not present).

Predation is an ecological interaction in which one species, the *predator*, benefits, and the other species, the *prey*, is harmed. Most people think that a good example of a predator eating prey is a cougar eating a deer, and they are correct; but predation also includes interactions in which the predator eats only part of its prey and the prey individual often survives. Thus, deer eat tree leaves and branches, and so, in a way, they can be considered predators on plant prey. Furthermore, some plant parts are especially valuable to the plant: a mouse eating all the seeds produced by a dandelion is having the same effect as a weasel eating a nestful of baby mice.

Parasitism, like predation, is a relationship between two species in which one benefits and one is harmed. The difference is that in a predatory relationship, one animal kills and eats the other, but in a parasitic one, the parasite feeds slowly on the *host* species and usually does not kill it. There are internal parasites, like many kinds of worms, and external parasites, such as leeches, ticks, and mites. Vampire bats and lampreys are examples of vertebrate parasites.

Some ecological interactions involve what we call *symbiosis*, which means living together. Usually this term suggests that the two interacting species do not harm one another; two kinds of symbiotic interactions – mutualisms and commensalisms – are discussed here.

Mutualisms are among the most compelling of ecological relationships – they are interactions in which both participants benefit. Plants and their pollinators engage in mutualistic interactions. In arctic Alaska, crane flies often sit in cup-shaped flowers. They benefit because the flower acts as a parabolic reflector, and the fly warms itself in the sun's rays. These flies transmit pollen between flowers, benefiting the plants by aiding them in their reproduction – just as bees do when they visit flowers for their nectar. Sometimes the species have interacted so long that they now cannot live without each other; theirs is an *obligate* mutualism. For instance, termites cannot by themselves digest wood. Rather, it is the single-celled animals, protozoans, that live in their gut that produce the digestive enzymes that digest wood. At this point in their evolutionary histories, neither the termites nor their internal helpers can live alone.

Commensalism is a relationship in which one species benefits but the other is not affected in any way. A classic example of a commensal animal is the Remora, a fish that attaches itself with a suction cup on its head to a shark, then feeds on scraps of food the shark leaves behind. Remoras are *commensals*, not parasites – they neither harm nor help sharks, but they benefit greatly by associating with sharks. In Alaska, a commensal relationship occurs between grebes and scoters. Horned Grebes often associate with feeding flocks of scoters, large ducks that prey on mussels and other bivalves. When the scoters root around in a mussel bed, they scare up small fish and shrimp that the grebes can then capture.

How to Use This Book

The information here on animals is divided into two sections: the *plates*, which include artists' color renderings of various species together with brief identifying and location information; and the *family profiles*, with natural history information on the families or larger taxonomic groups to which the pictured animals belong. The best way to identify and learn about Alaskan animals may be to scan the illustrations before a trip to become familiar with the kinds of animals you are likely to encounter. Then when you spot an animal, you may recognize its general type, and can find the appropriate pictures and profiles quickly. In other words, it is more efficient, upon spotting a bird, to be thinking, "Gee, that looks like a sandpiper," and be able to turn to that part of the book, than to be thinking, "That bird is mostly brown" and then, to identify it, flipping through all the bird pictures, searching for brown ones.

Information in the Family Profiles

Classification, Distribution, Morphology

The first paragraphs of each profile generally provide information on the classification (or *taxonomy*), geographic distribution, and *morphology* (shape, size, and coloring) of the group. The "family profiles" in the book cover different levels of classification, from phyla in the invertebrate chapter and orders in the insect chapter to families in the bird and mammal chapters. Classification information is provided because it is how scientists separate animals into related groups, and often it enhances our appreciation of animals to know these relationships. You may have been exposed to classification levels sometime during your education, but if you are a bit rusty, a quick review may help. *Kingdom*: all the species profiled in the book (except the plants in Plates A to J, of course) are members of the animal kingdom, Animalia, which is divided into phyla. *Phylum*: the species in the book are included in several phyla, from the jellyfish of the phylum Cnidaria to the mammals of the phylum Chordata; these are divided into classes. Most of the phyla include only *invertebrates*, animals without backbones, but most of the species discussed in the book are *vertebrates*, animals like ourselves with backbones. *Class*: the book covers several vertebrate classes: Petromyzontoidea (lampreys), Osteichthyes (bony fishes), Amphibia (amphibians), Aves (birds), and Mammalia (mammals), as well as numerous classes of five invertebrate phyla. *Order*: each class is divided into several orders, the animals in each order sharing many characteristics. For example, one of the mammal orders is Carnivora, the carnivores, which includes mammals with teeth specialized for meat-eating – dogs, cats, bears, raccoons, and weasels. *Family*: families of animals (all of which end in *-idae*) are subdivisions of each order that contain closely related species that are very similar in form, ecology, and behavior. The family Cervidae, for instance, contains all the deer, which, in Alaska, includes Moose and Caribou. *Genus*: within each genus are grouped species that are very closely related – they are all considered to have evolved from a common ancestor. All Pacific salmon and Rainbow and Cutthroat Trout are in a single genus. *Species*: the lowest classification level; all members of a species are similar enough to be able to breed and produce living fertile offspring.

Example: Classification of the Gray Wolf (Plate 66)

Kingdom: Animalia, with more than a million species
Phylum: Chordata, Subphylum Vertebrata, with about 40,000 species
Class: Mammalia (mammals), with about 4600 species
Order: Carnivora, with about 240 species; includes bears, weasels, cats, dogs, civets, hyenas, seals, and others
Family: Canidae, with 34 species; dogs, wolves, foxes, and jackals
Genus: *Canis*, with 7 species; the most diverse and most "doglike" of dogs; includes Gray Wolf, Coyote, Africa's Black-backed Jackal, and others
Species: *Canis lupus*, the Gray Wolf

The distributions of species vary tremendously. Some species are found only in very limited areas, whereas others range over several continents. Distributions can be described in a number of ways. An animal can be said to be *Old World* or *New World*; the former refers to the regions of the globe that Europeans knew of before Columbus – Europe, Asia, Africa; and the latter refers to the Western Hemisphere – North, Central, and South America. When species or groups are said in the book to occur on every continent, we are excluding Antarctica, where all the vertebrate animals are of marine origin and visit that continent only to breed. Alaska falls within the part of the world called the *Nearctic Region* by biogeographers – scientists who study the geographic distributions of living things. A Nearctic species is one that occurs within North America, excluding Mexico except for its high central plateau. The terms *tropical*, *temperate*, and *arctic* refer to climate regions of the Earth; the boundaries of these zones are determined by lines of latitude (and ultimately, by the position of the sun with respect to the Earth's surface). The tropics, always warm, are the regions of the world that fall within the belt from 23.5° north latitude (the Tropic of Cancer, where the sun is directly overhead on the Summer Solstice) to 23.5° south latitude (the Tropic of Capricorn, where the sun is directly overhead on the Winter Solstice). The world's temperate zones, with more seasonal climates, extend from the Tropics to 66.5° north and south (the Arctic and Antarctic Circles, at those latitudes, are the farthest from the poles that daylight lasts at least 24 hours at midsummer). Arctic regions, more or less always cold, extend from 66.5° north and south to the poles. The position of Alaska with respect to these zones is shown in Map 5, p. 46.

High latitude, in the case of Alaska, refers to the state's northerly location; the higher the latitude, the farther north is the location (the Equator is at zero degrees latitude; the North Pole is at 90 degrees north latitude). *Boreal* means "northern," and refers to high northern latitudes (and *austral* means "southern").

Several terms help define a species' distribution and describe how it attained its distribution.

Range. The particular geographic area occupied by a species.

Native or *Indigenous*. Occurring naturally in a particular place.

Introduced. Occurring in a particular place owing to people's intentional or unintentional assistance with transportation, usually from one continent to another; the opposite of native. For instance, pheasants were initially brought to North America from Europe/Asia for hunting, Europeans brought rabbits and

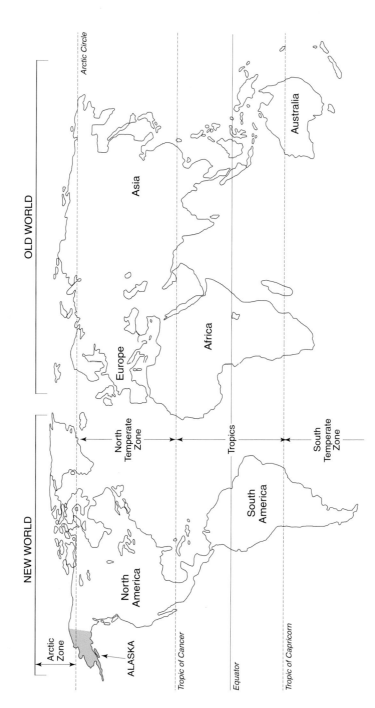

Map 5 Map of the Earth showing the position of Alaska; Old World and New World zones; and tropical, temperate, and arctic regions.

foxes to Australia for sport, and the British brought European Starlings and House Sparrows to North America.

Endemic. A species, a genus, an entire family, etc., that is found in a particular place and nowhere else. Galápagos finches are endemic to the Galápagos Islands; nearly all the bird and mammal species of Madagascar are endemics; all species are endemic to Earth (as far as we know).

Cosmopolitan. A species that is widely distributed throughout the world.

Ecology and Behavior

In these sections, we describe some of what is known about the basic activities pursued by each group. Much of the information relates to when and where animals are usually active, what they eat, and how they forage.

Activity Location – *Terrestrial* animals pursue life and food on the ground. *Arboreal* animals pursue life and food in trees or shrubs. *Cursorial* refers to animals that are adapted for running along the ground. *Fossorial* means living and moving underground.

Activity Time – *Nocturnal* means active at night. *Diurnal* means active during the day. *Crepuscular* refers to animals that are active at dusk and/or dawn.

Food Preferences – Although animal species can usually be assigned to one of the feeding categories below, most eat more than one type of food. Most frugivorous birds, for instance, also nibble on the occasional insect, and carnivorous mammals occasionally eat plant materials.

Herbivores are predators that prey on plants.
Carnivores are predators that prey on animals.
Insectivores eat insects.
Granivores eat seeds.
Frugivores eat fruit.
Nectarivores eat nectar.
Piscivores eat fish.
Omnivores eat a variety of things.
Carrionivores, such as vultures, eat dead animals.

Breeding

In these sections, we present basics on each group's breeding particulars, including type of mating system, special breeding behaviors, durations of egg incubation or *gestation* (pregnancy), as well as information on nests, eggs, and young.

Mating Systems – A *monogamous* mating system is one in which one male and one female establish a pair bond and contribute fairly evenly to each breeding effort. In *polygamous* systems, individuals of one of the sexes have more than one mate (that is, they have harems): in *polygynous* systems, one male mates with several females, and in *polyandrous* systems, one female mates with several males. All of these systems imply some sort of parental care; but in the great majority of animals, mating is *promiscuous*, with no pair bonds and, for the most part, no parental care.

Condition of offspring at birth – *Altricial* young are born in a relatively undeveloped state, usually naked of fur or feathers, eyes closed, and unable to feed themselves, walk, or run from predators. *Precocial* young are born in a more developed state, with eyes open, and soon are able to walk and/or swim and perhaps feed themselves.

Ecological Interactions

These sections describe what we think are intriguing ecological relationships.

Groups that are often the subject of ecological research are the ones for which such relationships are more likely to be known.

Lore and Notes

These sections provide brief accounts of folklore associated with the profiled groups, and any other interesting bits and pieces of information about the profiled animals that do not fit elsewhere in the account.

Status

These sections comment on the conservation status of each group, including information on relative rarity or abundance, factors contributing to population declines, and special conservation measures that have been implemented. Because this book concentrates on animals that ecotravellers are most likely to see – that is, on more common ones – few of the profiled species are immediately threatened with extinction. The definitions of the terms that we use to describe degrees of threat to various species are these: *Extirpated* is used to refer to species or populations that have become extinct entirely or in a particular area. *Endangered* species are known to be in imminent danger of extinction throughout their range, and are highly unlikely to survive unless strong conservation measures are taken; populations of endangered species generally are very small, so they are rarely seen. *Threatened* species are known to be undergoing rapid declines in the sizes of their populations; unless conservation measures are enacted, and the causes of the population declines identified and halted, these species are likely to move to endangered status in the near future. *Vulnerable* to threat are species that, owing to their habitat requirements or limited distributions, and based on known patterns of habitat destruction, are highly likely to be threatened in the near future. For instance, a fairly common bird species restricted to old-growth forest might be considered vulnerable to threat if it is known that these forests are being logged at a high rate. Several different organizations publish lists of threatened and endangered species, but agreement among the lists is not absolute.

Where appropriate, we also include threat classifications from the Convention on International Trade in Endangered Species (CITES) and the United States Endangered Species Act (ESA) classifications. CITES is a global cooperative agreement to protect threatened species on a worldwide scale by regulating international trade in wild animals and plants among the 130 or so participating countries. Regulated species are listed in CITES Appendices, with trade in those species being strictly regulated by required licenses and documents. CITES Appendix I lists endangered species; all trade in them is prohibited. Appendix II lists threatened/vulnerable species, those that are not yet endangered but may soon be; trade in them is strictly regulated. Appendix III lists species that are protected by laws of individual countries that have signed the CITES agreements. The USA's Endangered Species Act works in a similar way – by listing endangered and threatened species, and, among other provisions, strictly regulating trade in those animals.

Information in the Color Plate Section

Paintings

Among most invertebrates, amphibians, reptiles, and mammals, males and females of a species usually look alike, although often there are size differences, and in a few cases (for example, dragonflies), the sexes may be quite different-looking. For many species of birds, however, the sexes differ in color pattern and even anatomical features. If only one individual is pictured, you may assume that male and female of that species look much alike; when there are major sex differences, both male and female are depicted. The animals shown on an individual plate have been drawn to the correct scale relative to each other, although in a few cases a horizontal line across the plate separates species illustrated at different scales.

Name

We provide the common English name and the scientific (Greek or Latin) name for each profiled species. Many species have alternate English names, but we include the one used in recently published authoritative checklists.

ID

Here we provide brief descriptive information that, together with the paintings, will enable you to identify most of the animals you see. The lengths of amphibians given in this book are their *snout–vent lengths* (SVLs) unless we mention that the tail is included. The *vent* is the opening on their bellies that lies approximately where the rear limbs join the body, where mating occurs and wastes exit. Therefore, long tails of salamanders, for instance, are not included in the reported length measurements, and frogs' long legs are not included in theirs. Similarly for mammals, size measures given are generally the lengths of the head and body, but do not include tails except where indicated. Birds are measured from tip of bill to end of tail. For birds commonly seen flying, such as seabirds and hawks, we provide wingspan (wingtip to wingtip) measurements. We describe relative size in terms of the group to which the animal belongs, for example, a *large shrew*, a *small bear*, a *mid-sized songbird*. Total lengths can be misleading, as a very long-tailed bird has a larger measurement given than a much heavier, short-tailed bird. Our size designations thus relate to relative bulk (weight) of birds; a magpie with a length of 48 cm (19 in) is only a bit bulkier than a Steller's Jay at 28 cm (11 in), and both are considered mid-sized.

Habitat

In this section we list the habitat types in which each species occurs, along with symbols for these habitats to give an instant overview. For birds that are migratory, habitats used for breeding and wintering are listed separately unless they are the same; in some cases, habitats used in migration are also different.

Explanation of habitat symbols:

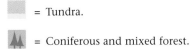

= Tundra.

= Coniferous and mixed forest.

= Deciduous forest.

= Forest edge/shrub thicket.

= Meadows and grassland other than tundra.

= Freshwater. For species typically found in or near lakes, streams, rivers, marshes, swamps.

= Saltwater/marine. For species usually found in or near the ocean.

Regions

In this section we list the regions of Alaska in which the species is likely to be found (see Map 6, p. 51). *Southeastern* (SE) Alaska is the southern peninsular part of the state, south of Yakutat and Skagway; *Southcentral* (SC) includes the coastal lowlands from Yakutat west to Homer, including Anchorage and the Seward Peninsula; *Southwestern* (SW) includes the Alaska Peninsula, Kodiak Island, and the Aleutian Islands; *Western* (W) includes the Yukon Delta, Seward Peninsula, and generally the western edge of the state, as well as the Bering Sea islands; *Northern* (N) includes the coastal plain from the Brooks Range north; and *Central* (C) includes the remainder of the state, the huge area centering around Fairbanks and including the Alaska and Brooks ranges and everything between them.

Example

Plate 42d

Tufted Puffin

Fratercula cirrhata

ID: Large black alcid with big, colorful bill; breeding adult has white head with yellow tufts, huge yellow and orange bill; winter adult with dark head, loses yellow at bill base; juvenile all dark, much smaller dull yellow bill; often flies around boats; 38 cm (15 in).

HABITAT: Breeding in burrows and rock crevices on coastal cliffs and islands, foraging offshore; wintering offshore.

REGIONS: SE, SC, SW, W (winter SW)

Map 6   Alaska divided into the six regions used to describe animal ranges in the species profiles.

Chapter 6

INSECTS

General Characteristics and Natural History

Insects are the most diverse living organisms, with over a million described species and perhaps tens of millions of undescribed ones; as in most groups, diversity is highest in the tropics. No one has estimated the number of species of insects in Alaska, but it is probably relatively low. Like amphibians and reptiles, the body temperature of insects is that of the surrounding air or water, so none of these groups flourishes in the cold environments of high latitudes. However, the abundance in Alaska of some individual species of insects, such as mosquitos, is legendary.

Insects are classified in the phylum Arthropoda and class Insecta. See p. 74 for a discussion of arthropods. Insects are the only group of arthropods with exactly six legs. Almost all insects are terrestrial, like spiders but unlike the mostly marine crustaceans (two other arthropod groups). Insects have three body parts, a *head*, *thorax*, and *abdomen*. The antennae, eyes, and mouthparts are on the head, the three pairs of legs and usually two pairs of wings are on the thorax, and the reproductive structures are on the abdomen. Insects vary among themselves tremendously: in where they live, what they eat and how they eat it, how they escape their predators, how they reproduce, and how their immature stages develop. They also vary greatly in how they affect humans, from the predatory wasps that eat caterpillars that are crop pests, through the beautiful butterflies that please our aesthetic senses, to fleas and flies that carry human diseases.

Because of their great diversity, it is not surprising that insects eat just about everything. What is especially interesting is that they do it in so many ways. Insect groups vary in their basic feeding anatomy, or mouthpart structure. Many insects, for example, dragonflies and beetles, have *biting* mouthparts, consisting of a pair of strong mandibles with which they chew up plant or animal prey. Others, such as butterflies and moths, have *sucking* mouthparts, the same structures modified into a long, coiled tube through which they suck nectar produced by flowers. Still others, especially many types of flies, have *piercing* mouthparts, which they insert into plant or animal tissues to deliver venom and suck blood and tissues.

The reproductive biology of insects varies especially in how they develop to adulthood. Primitive insects such as silverfish exhibit direct *metamorphosis*, the immature form going through a series of *molts*, shedding its outer covering each time and growing while it is soft. These immature stages change gradually into the reproductively mature adult. More advanced insects such as grasshoppers, cockroaches, and bugs have an immature stage called a *nymph*, which becomes increasingly adultlike as it goes through a series of molts. The final molt turns the immature-looking nymph into a mature adult, usually with wings and a quite different appearance. The most extreme change is undergone by advanced insects such as beetles, butterflies, flies, and wasps, in which there is a *larval*, a *pupal*, and an *adult* stage, all very different from one another (see the Environmental Close-up, p. 63). Almost all insects lay eggs, but some aphids and others give birth to live young. Most aphid births are *parthenogenetic*, females giving birth to other females without the benefit of fertilization.

Seeing Insects in Alaska

You needn't worry about looking for insects in Alaska – they'll come to you. But the ones that find you may not be the ones you were seeking! They will most likely be one of Alaska's Big Four – the mosquitos, black flies, no-see-ums, and horse flies that plague the northern traveller. However, with a modicum of protection, you can get along just fine in the midst of these pesky flies while spending your time looking for the showier insects, the butterflies and dragonflies.

Butterflies and dragonflies are sun lovers, so don't look for them during bad weather. But when the summer sun warms the northern landscape, they will appear in the right places as if by magic. Dragonflies can be found wherever there are lakes, ponds, marshes, and bogs. Ponds heat up during the summer, but Alaska's running waters are too cold for dragonflies; however, there is one stream species, the PACIFIC SPIKETAIL, at the far southern tip of the state. Butterflies are not particularly associated with water, but they are attracted to plants, some for their nectar and others for their leaves, which furnish food for butterfly larvae. If it's a windy day, look for both of these insect groups in the shelter of trees or other situations out of the wind. On cooler days, they are likely to be most active at midday or just afterwards, at the warmest time. Just as is the case in birds and mammals, different habitats support different species of dragonflies and butterflies, so look in all sorts of places to see the greatest variety.

Insects are small animals, and one way you can add to your enjoyment of them is to make them larger. You can do this by looking at them through a 10× hand lens, available in nature stores and many book stores. Ten times magnification is much better than the 3× to 5× magnifiers sold "to reveal the secrets of nature."

Some naturalists carry their lens on a string around their neck, for immediate use, but a pocket will suffice. If you're a birder, already carrying binoculars, you can reverse them to produce an excellent pair of magnifying glasses. When that next mosquito lands on your arm, don't swat it – study it!

Family Profiles

1. Dragonflies

Dragonflies are members of the order Odonata (they are often called *odonates*). The group is characterized by having four large wings that are abundantly provided with supporting veins and that have characteristic structures called the *triangle*, the *nodus*, and the *pterostigma*, which are lacking in all other insects. The wings do not fold flat over the abdomen, as in more recently evolved insects, but instead project out to the side or are closed vertically over the abdomen. On their head they have tiny antennae that may function as air-speed indicators; large compound eyes that give them excellent vision; three simple eyes, or *ocelli*, between the compound eyes that may function as flight-attitude indicators; and biting mouthparts. The first pair of legs are on the rather small, necklike prothorax, while the two rear segments of the thorax are fused into a large synthorax containing the flight muscles and supporting the two pairs of wings. Finally, they have a long, 10-segmented abdomen bearing the genitalia and terminal appendages. Alaska dragonflies vary in length from the SEDGE SPRITE at 2.5 cm (1 in) to the PACIFIC SPIKETAIL at 7.5 cm (3 in), and this encompasses a large part of the variation in odonate size.

There are about 5400 species of dragonflies worldwide, and 26 of them occur in Alaska. Dragonflies have been poorly sampled in the state, and there may be additional species along the southern and eastern borders. Six of the species are damselflies in the suborder Zygoptera. Damselflies are relatively small and slender, with smallish eyes at either end of the rather wide head. Their forewings and hindwings look alike and are held over the abdomen in *pond damsels* of the family Coenagrionidae (including the BOREAL BLUET, Plate 1) but half open in *spreadwings* of the family Lestidae (including the COMMON SPREADWING, Plate 1). *True dragonflies*, in the suborder Anisoptera, are larger, with much larger eyes that touch one another and hindwings – broader at their base than their forewings – held outspread from the body. The large blue dragonflies that are common in Alaska are *darners*, family Aeshnidae (including the SEDGE DARNER, Plate 1), while the smaller brown, red, and black species are *skimmers*, family Libellulidae (including the FOUR-SPOTTED SKIMMER, Plate 1). A dark dragonfly with emerald-green eyes is one of the *emeralds*, family Corduliidae.

Natural History
Ecology and Behavior
Almost all dragonflies have an aquatic larval stage, so wherever they are, they must return to the water to breed. The larvae have their own habitat preferences, and the females presumably can recognize favorable larval habitats from above water, perhaps because of the types of aquatic plants growing there; the females will lay their eggs in these habitats. Furthermore, males also should be able to recognize these habitats, as that's where they can find females! Knowledgeable

students of dragonfly biology, at least as smart as the dragonflies, know just where to look for each species.

Males of some species, for example, the FOUR-SPOTTED SKIMMER, set up territories at waterside and defend small areas from other males of the same species. They are often aggressive to males of other species as well, especially those of similar size and color – perhaps a case of mistaken identity. Males of other species, including many kinds of darners, cruise along lake shores or over sedge marshes, chasing and being chased by other males of their species when they come in contact; however, they don't defend a fixed territory. Although damselflies don't usually defend territories, they tend to localize over a much more restricted area because of their small size.

Breeding

The point of males being at the water, whether defending a territory or not, is to encounter females of their species. When they do, there is no time spent on delicate courtship, at least not in Alaska. The male lands on the female, grabs her head (dragonflies) or thorax (damselflies) with the clasping appendages at the end of his abdomen, and the *tandem* (connected) pair either remains in flight or lands on a nearby perch. The tandem position, with the pair connected head to tail, is unique to dragonflies; other insects mate tail to tail. Just after grabbing her, the male bends his abdomen forward and transfers sperm from the tip of his abdomen (where it ought to be) to the underside of the second segment, where a copulatory organ is located. If the female is receptive (and it's always her decision), she will swing her abdomen up and hook up with that segment. This *wheel* position, with male and female connected at two places, is also unique to dragonflies. Both the tandem and wheel positions appear to be adaptations to allow the pair to fly rapidly, both of them facing the same direction. A mating pair can elude a predator (or collector) about as easily as a single dragonfly.

At lower latitudes, especially in the tropics, many damselflies have evolved complex courtship behavior that may involve the male's hanging in the air directly in front of the female, fluttering his brightly marked – often iridescent – wings or, in some species, holding the hind wings almost stationary to best display their colors. Others add to this white or red much-widened legs that they dangle and display prominently to the female. In these species, after a bout of courtship, the male finally lands on the female, and she accepts his attentions.

After mating has taken place, in many species the pair remains in tandem and flies to just the right spot for *oviposition* (egg-laying). Damselflies and darners oviposit *endophytically* (*endo* = within, *phyto* = plant), pushing eggs into substrates such as plant stems with the sharpened tips of their ovipositor valves. The other dragonflies oviposit *exophytically* (*exo* = without), dropping their eggs directly into the water. Watch mated pairs, and you should soon see egg-laying.

Each egg (they may number in the low thousands) hatches quickly into a tiny *prolarva*, the function of which is to flip around until it lands in the water. This stage molts quickly into the true *larva*, which remains in the water for a few months to a few years, depending on the species. The larva grows by molting into a succession of about a dozen *instars*, each one larger than the one before; growth occurs right after the molt, while the larva is still soft. During the last few instars, wing pads form from the thorax, and during the last instar, metamorphosis begins to take place, the adult body forming within the larva. Finally, the larva stops feeding and heads for shore. It will typically climb up a plant stem, anchor itself firmly, the larval cuticle will split, and the adult will emerge in a seemingly miraculous transformation. Its wings expand, then its abdomen, and soon it will open its wings and fly away as a *teneral* (the soft, pale-colored adult right after emergence).

The immature adult stays away from the water for a few days (damselflies) to a few weeks (darners), during which time it develops mature coloration and sexual maturity. It then returns to the water to breed, and the cycle begins again.

Ecological Interactions

Dragonflies are all predators; none of them show the least interest in flowers, fruits, or any other plant parts, although plants do make excellent perches. The adults eat a wide variety of insects, mostly quite small, although the larger darners may take butterflies and other dragonflies half their size. They are such committed predators that they could well be called "bugs of prey" as a take-off on "birds of prey," the feathered raptors.

Dragonfly larvae lead a more interesting life *vis-à-vis* predation. One of their mouthparts, the *labium*, is extended and jointed and can be quickly shot out by hydraulic pressure to grasp a smaller animal in a pair of hook-tipped labial palpi at the end. This "killer lip," as it has been called, allows them to catch both stationary and swimming critters, up to the size of small fish and tadpoles. Larger dragonflies are the dominant predators in ponds that lack fish.

Lore and Notes

For some reason, dragonflies have always had bad press. Known as Devil's darning needles, they have been said to sew up people's eyes, ears, or mouths. Perhaps children were threatened with this by ignorant parents, the children themselves growing up to pass on the myth. In the southern USA, dragonflies are called "mosquito hawks," a more appropriate name, as they eat many mosquitos and other small flies – unfortunately, however, they don't make a dent in Alaska mosquito populations. In some countries, they are associated with darker images, for example, in Mexico dragonflies are called *caballito del Diablo* (little horse of the Devil).

Although among the earliest evolved of living insects, dragonflies excel in numerous ways in addition to their unique way of mating. They are arguably the best fliers among the insects, or at least the most versatile, with wings that beat independently of one another (the forewings and hindwings of most insects are linked together during flight) and allow them a continuous range of speeds from slow forward to fast forward, hover, and reverse. Even more impressive, they can turn amazingly fast and somersault like any Olympic athlete. They have without a doubt the best vision among the insects, each compound eye of the darners that are such a prominent feature of Alaska wetlands having up to 12,000 *ommatidia* (simple eyes). No wonder they can spot another dragonfly flying above them too high for us to see.

Status

No Alaska dragonfly is thought to warrant special concern, although a few of the species that occur in the state just barely occur in Alaska and, as such, should have their wetland habitat protected. Many species are at great risk in the tropical parts of the world. In these areas, a river system may have its own unique set of forest-dwelling odonate species. Some of them occur nowhere else, and most of them disappear when the forests flanking the rivers are cut down.

Profiles

Boreal Bluet, *Enallagma boreale*, Plate 1a
Common Spreadwing, *Lestes disjunctus*, Plate 1b
Sedge Darner, *Aeshna juncea*, Plate 1c
Four-spotted Skimmer, *Libellula quadrimaculata*, Plate 1d

2. Flies

No account of Alaska natural history would be complete without mention of flies. Relatively free of the pesky house flies and blow flies that support the window-screen industry across the Lower 48, instead Alaska has its own wilderness flies that occupy the attention of the ecotraveller. Flies are members of the insect order Diptera (*di* = two, *ptera* = wing), the only flying insects in which the hindwing is not used for flight. Instead, this pair of wings has been reduced to nubs, which are called *halteres*, apparently organs of balance. Don't think for a second, however, that a fly can't function just as well with one pair of wings as other insects do with two. Flies are superlative fliers, reaching high speeds and turning or stopping incredibly fast. Most of them hover very well and can reverse direction instantaneously while doing so. Watch a mosquito hovering over your arm and realize that this is one of the poorest-flying flies; try to swat it and you'll be even more impressed.

There are two large groups of flies, a more primitive group (suborder Nematocera) that has thread-like antennae and that includes *crane flies, mosquitos*, and their relatives; and a more advanced group (suborder Brachycera), with more highly modified antennae, that includes *hover flies, horse flies* and *deer flies, house flies*, and their relatives. Of the former group, we profile CRANE FLIES (Plate 2), Tipulidae; MIDGES (Plate 2), Chironomidae; MOSQUITOS (Plate 2), Culicidae; NO-SEE-UMS (Plate 2), Ceratopogonidae; and BLACK FLIES (Plate 2), Simuliidae. Of the advanced group, we profile HORSE FLIES (Plate 2), Tabanidae.

There are more than 120,000 species of flies in the world, of which perhaps 25,000 occur in North America. An estimate of the number of species that occur in Alaska remains to be done, but flies represent an increasingly large proportion of insect life as the traveller moves to higher latitudes and, in fact, are the dominant insects in the Arctic and Subarctic. Alaska flies vary in size from tiny no-see-ums with wings 1 mm (1/25 inch) long to big crane flies with wings 2.5 cm (1 inch) long. Elsewhere in the world, fly size varies much more, the largest being 125,000 times the smallest in bulk!

Natural History

Ecology and Behavior

Flies are everywhere. The numerous families in this order occur, among them, in all terrestrial habitats. Many have larvae in fresh water, and Alaska, with its abundant wetlands, is especially well provided with members of the aquatic groups. Flies have sucking and lapping rather than biting mouthparts, but the basic mouthparts are modified in so many ways that flies as a group eat just about all the food items provided by this planet. ROBBER FLIES are among the fiercest predators in the insect world, readily capturing and instantly killing dragonflies larger than themselves; HOVER FLIES and BEE FLIES take nectar from flowers, and are pollinators as important as bees and butterflies; and still others feed on organic detritus of all sorts. Some adult flies don't feed; their only functions are to disperse between larval habitats and to breed.

Breeding

The different groups of flies in Alaska have somewhat different life cycles, but there are some basics in common. All flies undergo complete metamorphosis, just like butterflies, with larva, pupa, and adult; there are of course actually four stages, if we include the egg. In the flies profiled here, eggs are laid in or near the water. BLACK FLIES, HORSE FLIES and DEER FLIES lay their eggs on floating vegetation or leaves hanging into the water. Most Alaska MOSQUITOS deposit theirs on plants or on the bottom, but some species lay them on the water surface, singly or in floating rafts of eggs. Hundreds of eggs are laid by the aquatic breeders, and egg mortality is very high. The larval life may be very short in mosquitos or last up to a year in horse flies. One of the most noteworthy aspects of reproduction in some of these flies is the swarming of male MIDGES. These relatively insignificant insects (it has been estimated that it would take about a half million to weigh an ounce) form swarms of hundreds to thousands of males on warm summer evenings, dancing up and down rhythmically to attract females (exactly the reason, for example, that groups of male prairie-chickens get together).

The larvae in the five fly families discussed herein are all quite different from one another. Mosquito larvae swim actively in ponds, especially those without fish, and eat algae and detritus. They hang at the water surface, taking in air through a breathing tube, but dive for the depths when disturbed. One Alaska species breathes by tapping into the underwater stems and roots of cattails and other water plants, which have air in their tissues. Deer fly and horse fly larvae live at the bottom of stagnant ponds or in wet soil, also feeding on vegetation and detritus. CRANE FLY larvae are called *leatherjackets* because of their thick cuticle, a trait shared with the horse flies; this thick "skin" presumably protects them from environmental extremes, even pollution. Crane fly larvae live in most aquatic and terrestrial habitats, and the water-dwelling ones can be either herbivorous or carnivorous. Black fly larvae attach to rocks in streams by means of a sucker at their rear end and hang out into the current, filtering tiny organic particles with a set of elaborate mouth-brushes. NO-SEE-UM larvae are aquatic or semiaquatic and probably feed on organic detritus.

The pupal stage is a resting stage, so it is surprising that the pupae of mosquitos are quite mobile, able to swim jerkily away from potential predators. This is a great adaptation for a "dormant" animal that is quite visible at the water surface.

Ecological Interactions

When you have dark thoughts about the flies in Alaska, remember that it's not their fault. They have evolved to take advantage of large populations of birds and mammals, the blood of which is rich in nourishing compounds. In some groups of flies, including many of those that, in Alaska, visitors and residents alike learn to hate, females must have a blood meal to grow eggs within their body. No blood, no babies. Note that only the female of the species is the biter; male MOSQUITOS, HORSE FLIES, etc., are harmless to people and in fact in many cases are nectar feeders. Because of this, fly biologists speculate that the ancestors of these blood-sucking flies were nectar feeders, the "butterflies" of their order. Over evolutionary time, the mouthparts became more and more elongated to reach the nectar at the base of a long flower tube, and some relatives of nectar-feeding crane flies may have become mosquitos! Many blood-sucking flies have varied diets, but all apparently must have a blood meal to mature their eggs. Adult CRANE FLIES, unlike the other profiled groups, are nectar feeders, and adult MIDGES live such a short life that they don't feed at all. Travel and sex, nothing more.

The populations of these little animals are prodigious. Horse flies are relatively large, and a warm-blooded vertebrate may have to contend with only a few at a time, but their bites are fierce enough that they irritate all out of proportion to their numbers. The other biting flies irritate similarly but all out of proportion to their size. Everyone can recognize a mosquito, but watch for their smaller cousins, the BLACK FLIES and NO-SEE-UMS, the bites of which can draw blood and can itch for days from your immune responses to the flies' saliva. Bites from very large numbers of black flies have been known to cause death in livestock and humans. In contrast, crane flies and midges are abundant but harmless, their numbers furnishing fodder for thousands of migratory songbirds and shorebirds that migrate to high latitudes in summer to take advantage of this flush of flies.

Status

Flies as a group are a perfect example of how little we know about insects. North American flies are typically not on lists of threatened or endangered species, perhaps because the only flies that are well known are the common ones. Many species, even in North America, are known from only a few specimens from one locality, and we lack even such basic information as where they live and what they do; such information needs to be collected before we can consider any of the flies in peril. Many an Alaska visitor doubtless wishes for quick extirpation of the entire dipteran fauna!

Nevertheless, there is an endangered fly in North America, the DELHI SANDS GIANT FLOWER-LOVING FLY, which occurs only on remnant dune fragments in a small area in southern California. It has been the subject of some political controversy because of development in its habitat. As its name indicates, it is a large fly, so its population decline has been noticeable.

Profiles

horse fly, Tabanidae, Plate 2a
black fly, Simuliidae, Plate 2b
crane fly, Tipulidae, Plate 2c
midge, Chironomidae, Plate 2d
mosquito, Culicidae, Plate 2e
no-see-um (sand fly), Ceratopogonidae, Plate 2f

3. Butterflies

Butterflies are perhaps the first insects one notices as a child, and they are often the most obvious insects to ecotourists. They are big, active, brightly colored, and day-active, much like birds, and have often been called "birdwatchers' insects." They are characterized by their large wings, covered with colored scales, and their sucking mouthparts. The tiny scales that cover their wings and give them their characteristic patterns make them unique in the insect world; their wings beneath the scales are transparent, like those of a wasp. Butterflies, together with moths, make up the insect order Lepidoptera (*lepido* = scale, *ptera* = wing). They can be distinguished from the *moths*, their very diverse nocturnal cousins, by the little bulbs at the ends of their antennae. Their larvae are the familiar *caterpillars*, less conspicuous than the adults but no less interesting. Alaska butterflies vary in wing spread from the 2.5 cm (1 in) of several species of blues to the 7.5 cm (3 in) of the CANADIAN TIGER SWALLOWTAIL (Plate 3), but there are butterflies considerably smaller and much larger in other parts of the World.

There may be as many as 20,000 species of butterflies in the world, of which 79 are known to occur in Alaska. They include 5 swallowtails (Papilionidae), 16 whites, marbles, and sulfurs (Pieridae), 12 blues, elfins, and coppers (Lycaenidae), 42 brush-footed butterflies (Nymphalidae), and 4 skippers (Hesperiidae). Extremely abundant and diverse in the tropics (Costa Rica has more than 10 times as many species as an area the same size at the latitude of New York), their numbers decrease with latitude until they are merely moderately common in the far North. In Alaska, they are least common near the coast and high in the Arctic and most common in the warm interior valleys, even well up in the mountain ranges, and they can be common indeed in favored localities on sunny summer days.

Natural History

Ecology and Behavior

Butterflies are most active on warm, sunny days. Usually first seen in flight, they move about the landscape looking for flowers for a nectar meal, for host plants on which to lay their eggs (if a female), and for females with which to mate (if a male). Their flight is deceptively lazy, as they can accelerate and zigzag to avoid a predator. Adult butterflies in Alaska have few predators, because specialized butterfly predators have evolved mainly in the tropics, where butterflies are much more diverse and abundant. Instead, physical conditions – temperature and cloud cover – control butterfly populations at high latitudes. The summer season is short, both for larvae and adults, and so a persistently bad summer (cool and cloudy) can affect local populations severely. Fortunately, butterflies have a high reproductive rate, and during a good summer, their populations rebound readily.

Caterpillars lead a more mundane existence, perhaps spending their entire life in one clump of plants. Wormlike, they are yet distinct from all other insect larvae in having four sets of prolegs, extensions of the body on abdominal segments three to six, that give them a bit more versatility in locomotion. Moths are more diverse than butterflies, so some of the Lepidoptera larvae you see will surely be moths.

Breeding

Butterflies, like beetles, flies, and wasps, have a complex life cycle with four distinct stages: egg, larva, pupa, and adult. Starting with the adult, males and females have to meet to reproduce, and females are extremely valuable resources. This was never more elegantly described than by E. B. Ford (1957): "No attraction ... is as potent as that which the female butterfly exercises for the male; to the Purple Emperor it even surpasses the appeal of a decomposing rat." Males of some species stake out favored perches and fly out after any passing butterfly, including other species and males of their own, but they are really searching for receptive females. Males of other species patrol large areas actively looking for females. Often females hang around larval food plants, where they will lay their eggs, and males are programmed to look for the same plants to find the females. Some tropical butterflies exhibit elaborate courtship behavior, in which males flutter in front of females, wafting *pheromones* (chemical substances produced by specialized structures on the wings) toward them to convince the females that they are males of the correct species and in mating condition.

Butterflies are not seen mating nearly so often as dragonflies, perhaps because the latter fly well united, so they can afford to be conspicuous. Butterflies mate tail to tail, the female hanging below the male in flight, and they are relatively clumsy in flight because of this, so during mating they tend to stay at rest and so be inconspicuous.

The eggs are laid on appropriate host plants. If you see butterflies laying, take out your pocket hand lens and look at the eggs. Butterfly eggs are beautiful works of natural art, varying from perfect spheres to elongate spindles, each with a distinctive sculpturing. Look quickly, as the eggs will hatch in less than a week. Females lay their hundreds of eggs singly or in clumps, directly on the plants that will host the *larvae*. The larvae (better known as caterpillars) that hatch from these eggs go through five larval *instars*, molting their outer skin and growing substantially at each molt. They eat voraciously and grow rapidly during the long Alaska days, typically for only a few weeks. They then stop feeding and search for a sheltered spot in which to become a butterfly. They enter the third stage of their life, the *pupa*, by producing a structure called a *chrysalis* around them; the chrysalis may hang from a branch or be on the ground. Chrysalids (plural of chrysalis) are also beautiful and varied, distinctive for each butterfly group, and, as you would expect, quite well camouflaged. At this time the butterfly seems to be dormant, but in fact a wonderful change is taking place. Larval tissues are broken down and rearranged into adult tissues with amazing rapidity. After a period of another week or two, this *metamorphosis* is complete and the butterfly emerges from the chrysalis, spreads its wings, dries off, and flies away, to live its brief week-long adult life and complete the cycle. In Alaska, all butterflies fly during June and July, in the fairly brief warm season.

There are many variations on this theme; for example, each stage of the life cycle can be greatly prolonged to place the next stage at a season favorable for it. Different stages may overwinter, typically the pupa but sometimes the egg or even the hibernating adult. MOURNING CLOAK (Plate 4) adults hibernate (in hollow trees or under loose bark), are usually the first butterflies to be seen in spring, and may live nearly a year!

This system of *complete* metamorphosis, with larva, pupa, and adult, is very different from the dragonfly system of changing directly from a larva to an adult without going through a dormant pupal stage.

Ecological Interactions

All Alaska butterflies are nectar-feeders, so don't expect to find many of them where there are no flowers. Alaska has a great diversity of wildflowers, and many of them are pollinated by butterflies of one sort or another. The butterflies depend on the flowers for their nectar diet, and the flowers depend on the butterflies for *pollination* – the transfer of pollen among them; this aids fertilization and is therefore essential to successful reproduction. This dependence of one on the other is a *symbiotic* relationship, specifically one called *mutualism*, in which both members of the pair benefit from the interaction. The butterfly tongue (also called a *proboscis*) is long and held in a tight curl in flight. When a butterfly lands on a flower, it uncurls its tongue, probes deep into the flower, and sucks from the nectaries at the base of the corolla. Nectar contains not only sugars but also essential amino acids, so the butterflies are getting more than a straight carbohydrate diet. Butterflies in other parts of the world have a more varied diet, different types eating tree sap, pollen, rotting fruit, and even animal carcasses and feces. Many species visit wet soil to lick essential minerals, especially salts, from its surface.

An interaction equally important is the relationship between the butterfly larva and its host plant(s). Some butterflies will lay their eggs only on a single species of plant, others may use all the members of a genus or family, while the larvae of some species will eat the leaves of, say, most of the deciduous tree species where they occur. The *coevolution* of butterflies and their host plants in very tight, specialized relationships is without question one of the reasons that there are so many species of both groups in the tropics, where the butterflies are particularly specialized. What seems to have happened is that over evolutionary time the butterfly has overcome the *antiherbivore* defenses of a species or group of plants, both chemical and physical, by its own very specific adaptations, and these adaptations fit it for living only on those kind of plants. Other butterflies have done the same thing for other types of plants.

Butterflies escape their predators by their camouflage at rest (many hold their wings closed, and the underside is usually dull) and their rapid and erratic flight. Many tropical species are toxic if eaten and are brightly (*aposematically*) colored to warn predators to leave them alone; birds typically learn this by a taste test. Few Alaska butterflies use this defense mechanism, but the PHOEBUS PARNASSIAN (Plate 3) has a strong odor and is distasteful to birds and humans (chipmunks apparently eat them, however). Its showy coloration may advertise its taste. In addition, the larvae of this species apparently mimic distasteful millipedes!

Lore and Notes

Butterflies have always been favored insects, without any of the negative publicity that most of the other insects ("creepy crawlies") suffer. Of course, this meant ignoring the fact that their larvae were as creepy and crawly as any other insects! Some of the more famous butterflies include the highly migratory MONARCH of points south of Alaska, the brilliant blue MORPHO butterflies of the New World tropics, and pest species such as the CABBAGE WHITE, the caterpillar of which feeds on many economically important members of the mustard family. If Alaska's butterflies were to be famous for something, perhaps it would be for how surprising it is that there are so many of them!

Status

It's nice to be able to say that Alaska has no threatened butterflies. Some of the rarest butterflies in the state are those that are among the most common elsewhere in North America but just barely make it into the southern panhandle. We probably shouldn't be overly concerned that CABBAGE WHITES, for example, hugely abundant over much of North America, are rare in Alaska. Many butterflies at lower latitudes are threatened, and a few have become extinct, for example, the XERCES BLUE, a subspecies restricted to San Francisco sand dunes. Prime real estate for this butterfly was unfortunately prime real estate for humans.

Profiles

Phoebus Parnassian, *Parnassius phoebus*, Plate 3a
Old World Swallowtail, *Papilio machaon*, Plate 3b
Canadian Tiger Swallowtail, *Papilio canadensis*, Plate 3c
Arctic White, *Pieris angelika*, Plate 3d
Hecla Sulfur, *Colias hecla*, Plate 3e
Dorcas Copper, *Lycaena dorcas*, Plate 4a
Northern Blue, *Lycaeides idas*, Plate 4b
Mourning Cloak, *Nymphalis antiopa*, Plate 4c

White Admiral, *Limenitis arthemis*, Plate 4d
Painted Lady, *Vanessa cardui*, Plate 4e
Green Comma, *Polygonia faunus*, Plate 5a
Silver-bordered Fritillary, *Boloria selene*, Plate 5b
Common Alpine, *Erebia epipsodea*, Plate 5c
Melissa Arctic, *Oeneis melissa*, Plate 5d

Environmental Close-up 1:
Why Are There Both Caterpillars and Butterflies?

Many of us know the story of the Ugly Duckling that grew up to be a beautiful swan. If you watched that duckling day after day, you could see the change taking place, and in hindsight it would not be so surprising. But how about the change from a caterpillar to a butterfly? This change is so drastic that the caterpillar (*larva*) has to pass through a resting stage (*pupa*) during which its larval tissues are replaced by those of the butterfly (*adult*). All advanced insects (including beetles, butterflies and moths, bees and their relatives, and flies) pass through these three stages. During the pupal stage, *metamorphosis* occurs, the dramatic change from larva to adult.

You are familiar with other animals that undergo metamorphosis, for example, tadpoles turning into frogs, but did you know that most of the marine invertebrates discussed in this book also have larval stages very different from the mature animals? You would never recognize a halibut or herring as such, much less a crab, sea urchin, or jellyfish, if you saw its tiny larva.

You may think that a larval insect turning into an adult insect is comparable to a robin's egg turning into a robin, but it's not. The egg is just a place to keep an embryo protected as it develops outside its mother's body, and the bird growing within it develops gradually until it hatches at a stage at which the parent can take care of it. The larva and adult phenomenon described here for insects and other animals involves a complete reorganization from one stage to the next. The time spent in different stages can be very unequal, too. Some Alaska dragonflies are in the larval stage for three or four years, the adult stage for only a month. The well-known "seventeen-year locusts" (cicadas) in eastern North America spend 17 years underground in the immature stage, then emerge from the ground, transform into an adult, breed, and die in a few days!

What possible advantage is there in such a dramatic change? The answer is simple: the larva and the adult serve different functions during the animal's life. In marine animals, the larva is often the *dispersal stage*, the period during which it may float around in ocean currents, finally to settle on some distant or not so distant shore. It then changes dramatically to another form (see the accounts of marine invertebrates and fishes for further details) and continues its growth as a miniature of the adult, finally growing to reproductive size and age. In insects, the larval stage is typically when feeding and growth occurs, and the adult is the dispersal and reproductive stage. In fact, some adult insects are so specialized for dispersal and reproduction that they do not feed – ever! These stages serve such different functions that natural selection has acted upon them independently, causing them to diverge more and more over evolutionary time until they are highly specialized for their larval or adult roles. The wonderful phenomenon of metamorphosis ties them back together.

We should add a few words about dispersal, a phenomenon found in all living organisms. Dispersal occurs when a young bird leaves its nest and settles a few miles from its parents. It occurs when the winged seeds of a pine are blown a few hundred yards downwind from the parent tree. It occurs when the larvae of a crab drift downcurrent for hundreds of miles from where the eggs were laid. These are cases of both active and passive dispersal; the former occurs in most *motile* (travelling under their own power) animals, the latter in most *sessile* (attached to the substrate) animals and plants. Dispersal has at least three benefits. First, it moves offspring away from parents, so they don't compete with parents for food or space, for example. Second, it lowers the probability of harmful inbreeding, a consequence of the mating of close relatives. Third, by the spread of individuals of particular genetic types into new areas, it increases genetic variation in both populations and individuals, making it more likely that some of them will survive environmental hardships. This genetic variation, in fact, is a basic and necessary feature of organic evolution.

Chapter 7

MARINE INVERTEBRATES

General Characteristics and Natural History

Invertebrates are animals without backbones. The only animals with backbones (vertebral columns made of bone or cartilage) are the *vertebrates*, with which we are all familiar: mammals, birds, reptiles, amphibians, and fishes. Each of these groups represents a class of vertebrates, except the fishes, which include four classes (see p. 82). Vertebrates are included with two other groups of small animals, the *tunicates* (sea squirts, commonly seen marine invertebrates) and *lancelets* (burrowing fish-like animals), to make up the phylum Chordata. All other animals are invertebrates, and they are so diverse that they have been separated into numerous *phyla* (singular *phylum*). In fact, there are at least 33 phyla of living animals recognized at this time, several of them discovered as distinct phyla only within the past few decades. For example, peculiar animals were recently collected that matched nothing else known; they were described as the new phylum Loricifera in 1983, and there are now about 25 known species. It is easy to imagine why this discovery wasn't made any sooner, as these tiny (less than 1 mm, 1/25 in) animals live among the sand grains on the ocean bottom. The total number of known invertebrate species is vast, and there are very likely millions more undescribed species, particularly in those groups that have many small species. This includes not only familiar animals such as freshwater and land snails and insects but also roundworms (nematodes), which occur in vast numbers in the soil, in fresh water, and as parasites of a wide variety of animals and plants. Biologists interested in the Earth's biodiversity have theorized that there is probably at least one distinct species of parasitic roundworm specialized to live within every animal species!

The various phyla of animals are distinguished from one another by very basic differences. Some of these differences include whether the body is *bilaterally symmetrical* (like an earthworm or squid) or *radially symmetrical* (like a sea star or sea anemone); whether the digestive tract has one opening (like a jellyfish or flatworm) or two openings, a mouth and anus (like most animals); and whether the *blastopore* (the opening into the first hollow ball of cells that appears early in embryonic development) eventually becomes the mouth (as in insects and snails) or the anus (as in sea urchins and vertebrates). It may be hard to believe that we are more closely related to sea urchins than we are to lobsters, but, based on these kinds of classifying characteristics, it is true.

Marine invertebrates vary greatly in their lifestyles. For example, they can be attached to the bottom or free-swimming. Many marine animals are *sessile*, being attached to rocks and gravel on the bottom. Numerous groups include sessile animals, for example, sponges, sea anemones, tubeworms, mussels, and barnacles. All other marine animals are *motile*, not attached to the bottom and able to move. Another basic ecological division concerns whether animals live on the bottom or in the open water above it. Animals that spend their adult life on the bottom are called *benthic*, and those that spend their life above the bottom are called *pelagic*. Of pelagic animals, many are *planktonic*; they drift with currents and don't have much ability to move out of harm's way or toward any goal. Most planktonic animals are very small, including the larvae of many benthic species. The abundance of plankton in the sea is what allows so many animals to be sessile; they can remain in one spot and have their food come to them, drifting on currents and tides. By contrast, animals that swim actively are called *nektonic*. Fishes are good examples of nektonic animals, but many invertebrates also swim actively, and squids swim as well as fish. Crabs, of course, swim sideways. Knowledge of these terms can aid in understanding the lives of marine animals.

The majority of animal phyla occur in the sea, and the marine environment has been very important in the evolution of life on Earth. Of the many invertebrate phyla, only five are profiled here; however, they include a large proportion of the marine invertebrates a visitor to Alaska is likely to see. Sponges (phylum Porifera) comprise the only phylum that is common and readily visible in the Alaska marine environment but is not profiled in this book. No more will be said about the distribution of marine phyla, as virtually all of them occur worldwide in the sea, from tropical to Arctic and Antarctic waters.

Seeing Marine Invertebrates in Alaska

Intertidal marine invertebrates live in the zone between average high tide and average low tide, and such animals can be seen most vividly at rocky shores anywhere in southern Alaska (see Environmental Close-up 2, p. 79). From mid-Bering Sea north, invertebrates are scarce near shore because of the scouring by the heavy shore ice that forms each winter, but south of that, a large array of species may be visible at low tides. Most of them will be dormant, their bodies closed up while waiting for the water to return, but you can see the shells of bivalves and barnacles, the bodies of anemones, and, especially in tide pools, sea urchins and sea stars. Tide pools are always the best places to look, especially at extreme low tides, as they contain a rich assemblage of the local marine creatures, and, by retaining water, they allow the animals to remain active. Watch your footing, as the algae that grow on the rocks can be extremely slippery. You may wish to turn over a few small rocks, and you will find many animals sheltering beneath them. Be sure to replace the rocks carefully. At high tide, everything will be hidden but the few hardiest snails and barnacles that live at that level. In southern Alaska, lie down on a dock near the water and look over the edge. Sometimes the pilings are covered with invertebrates, and on docks that lie right at the water surface, whole communities of animals may be very close at hand. You may have difficulty telling the plants (marine algae) from the animals, as many marine animals are sessile (fixed in place) and don't look that different from plants. The algae are usually shades of green, red, purple, or brown, and they look leafier than the animals.

The very determined ecotraveller might be able to arrange a ride on a fishing boat, where the diversity of the sea is evident in every haul of a net or bottom dredge, or visit a marine aquarium (for example, Alaska SeaLife Center, p. 22, or the Gastineau Hatchery, p. 19) or marine laboratory, where some species will be visible in aquaria – probably with better viewing than would be possible in nature. Just as with fish, the edible marine invertebrates of Alaska can be seen at seafood markets, sometimes even alive in holding tanks.

Family Profiles

1. Cnidarians – Jellyfish and Anemones

The *cnidarians* (pronounced "nye-DARE-ians") of the phylum Cnidaria could be called "water animals," as they are made up largely of water (95% in the case of jellyfish). The great majority of them live in the oceans, although a few species occur in fresh water. They are simple, with no well-developed body systems, but they exist quite well either floating with currents or attached to the sea floor. The defining characteristic of the phylum is that all have *tentacles* that capture prey by means of *nematocysts*, tiny structures that contain a coiled tube with a harpoonlike barbed point at one end. When stimulated by touch, a nematocyst bursts open and harpoons whatever touched it. The "harpoon" is small but contains toxic chemicals that can paralyze a smaller animal instantly; and, because there are thousands of nematocysts on each tentacle, the "sting" of some kinds of cnidarians is powerful enough to be felt by human skin. Not all nematocysts penetrate; some are adhesive, either because they produce a sticky substance or because their slender tip wraps around part of the prey.

There are over 9000 species of Cnidaria. *Jellyfish*, in the class Scyphozoa (*scypho* = cup, *zoa* = animal), are free-floating cnidarians. A jellyfish consists of a *bell*, the main part of the body, and a variety of organs that hang down from the bell, including tentacles around the edge and a feeding organ, the *manubrium*, in the center. A few species are large enough to dwarf a Scuba diver, the LION'S MANE (Plate 7) with a bell 2 m (6.6 ft) across. All jellyfish, beautiful and symmetrical as they slowly pulse through the water by rhythmic contractions of their bell, turn into blobs when they wash up on the beach. They would surely have been called "jellofish" had that gelatinous dessert been around when they were first named.

Anemones, in the class Anthozoa (*antho* = flower), attach themselves to the sea floor, usually rocky areas, by means of their sticky *pedal disk*, the flat part on the bottom. The *oral disk* at the other end bears the mouth (which also serves as the anus) and ring of tentacles. Anemones are supported by a *hydrostatic skeleton*, an interesting feat of biological engineering. They imbibe water and close their mouth, then move the water in their body around to move and to change shape. Anemones are almost unrecognizable when they are exposed to air, as their tentacles are withdrawn, and they shrink to a fraction of their full size. A search for anemones at low tide is a search for symmetrical rounded bumps. As soon as water covers them, they expand into the beautiful animals they are.

The class Anthozoa also includes corals, both the familiar *hard corals* with calcareous (calcium carbonate) skeletons, which look like rocks with beautiful patterns on them, and the *soft corals* such as sea fans and sea whips. The third class, Hydrozoa, includes not only the freshwater hydras and their marine relatives but also many kinds of jellyfishes, including the PORTUGUESE MAN-OF-WAR.

Natural History
Ecology and Behavior
Amazingly, sea anemones are not really sessile; they can move about, if only very slowly. PLUMOSE ANEMONES (Plate 6) can move over rocks at about 8 cm (3 in) per week, but one traveled 5.8 cm (2.25 in) in an hour on the smooth surface of an aquarium. This ability allows them to seek out more favorable situations, if they have sufficient time to do so. They don't, however, go after their food but must wait until it comes to them, either stumbling into the anemone's tentacles or being swept in with a wave.

The anemones profiled here are all distinct from one another in their use of the environment. The Plumose Anemone is characteristic of the low intertidal and subtidal levels, so it is not a species you normally see in tide pools. Instead, at extreme low tides, look for it on pilings and rock walls in protected bays, where it forms clusters of small, rather slender, whitish, tan, or orange anemones with frilly tentacles. The tentacles are finely divided and capture only very small planktonic prey. The GIANT GREEN ANEMONE (Plate 6) grows through the whole range of the intertidal zone, so this species is easy to see on beach walks in rocky areas, especially on the open coast. Although it is solitary, many individuals occur together in favorable locations, characterized by clear water and an abundance of marine life. Anything small enough to be subdued by the tentacles is fair game, including sea urchins, mussels, crabs, and small fish. This anemone, especially its tentacles, also furnishes food for certain sea slugs (technically called *nudibranchs*, these snails without shells are usually recognized by their colorful bodies) and sea stars. The AGGREGATING ANEMONE (Plate 6) is a fascinating creature because it forms large *clones* (groups of genetically identical individuals) by asexual reproduction, and the groups can get very large (some clones occupy 100 sq m, 1100 sq ft). When two of these expanding colonies meet, they recognize genetically different individuals, and there is war between them, a tension zone where individual anemones battle it out tentacle to tentacle. The outermost tentacles of each anemone possess very powerful nematocysts that can injure or even kill another anemone. The boundary between two colonies is often evident as a distinct gap.

Jellyfish drift about on ocean currents. They feed on whatever smaller organisms their tentacles can snag, which, in the case of the LION'S MANE, can be fairly large, as its tentacles extend 2 m (6.6 ft) or more; fish and swimming crustaceans are common prey. The sting of this species is painful to humans, and the effects of it can last four or five hours. Lion's Manes become very common in late summer, when – presumably because of tidal currents that concentrate them – their density in some bays can become spectacularly high, just about one per cubic meter of seawater near the surface.

Breeding

You might be hard-pressed to consider jellyfishes and sea anemones closely related, but in fact they represent the two stages in the life cycle that characterize most cnidarians, the wandering *medusa* and the stationary *polyp*. Cnidarians are quite unusual in their *alternation of generations*, with a sexually reproducing generation (the medusa) alternating with an asexually reproducing generation (the polyp). Jellyfish emphasize the medusa stage, while sea anemones have lost that stage and instead emphasize the polyp. This reproductive system, interestingly, is much like that of many primitive plants, which also alternate sexual and asexual reproduction.

Jellyfish shed eggs and sperm into the water, and the fertilized eggs develop into tiny larvae that are carried in currents until they touch something solid on the bottom such as a rock. They then quickly transform into a polyp and attach to the rock. The polyp grows, and eventually other polyps bud off from it and grow until they are big enough to be self-contained. After some time of this asexual reproduction, the polyp begins to bud off tiny medusae, which drift off in the current and grow up to full-sized jellyfish, which begin the reproductive cycle again.

Sea anemones are surprisingly varied in their reproduction, considering that all of them lack the medusa stage. The GIANT GREEN ANEMONE reproduces sexually, individual anemones being either male or female and shedding their eggs and sperm into the water; the embryo develops into a larval stage much like that of the jellyfishes. The larvae swim around as part of the plankton before settling on the bottom and transforming into tiny anemones. AGGREGATING ANEMONES also practice sexual reproduction, but in addition they reproduce asexually, dividing by longitudinal fission, each anemone splitting in two; this is how their colonies form. The PLUMOSE ANEMONE reproduces sexually and asexually, much like the Aggregating Anemone, but it forms smaller clones, and in addition its pedal disk can shed fragments that grow into new anemones!

Ecological Interactions

The most prominent interaction between some anemones and other organisms is their symbiotic relationship with algae of two types, with the wonderful names *zooxanthellae* (zo-o-zan-THELL-ee) and *zoochlorellae*. The algae live just under the outer surface of the anemone and apparently receive both a living place and light, water, and carbon dioxide, essential for the photosynthesis that provides them with their nutrition. The anemone, in turn, presumably benefits from both the oxygen and some of the organic byproducts produced by the algae during photosynthesis. These algae are what give GIANT GREEN ANEMONES and AGGREGATING ANEMONES their green color. As might be expected, when these green species of anemones grow in caves, where insufficient light penetrates for photosynthesis, they lack the algae and are whitish to dull brown in color.

They survive perfectly well in the cave, but if brought into sunlight, they do not grow as well as anemones with algae.

Many large anemones eat small fishes, but one of them in turn furnishes shelter for fish. Young Painted Greenlings shelter from their predators next to the columns of SPOTTED RED ANEMONES, the tentacles of which droop over and form a hiding place for these small fish. The greenlings are the only fish in their habitat that do not stimulate a feeding response in the anemone; they are protected from the tentacles by a substance in their skin. The unrelated anemonefishes of the South Pacific, which live associated with large sea anemones, are similarly protected. These relationships are also symbiotic, as the fish get shelter and protection from predators. The benefits to the anemones have been harder to determine, but the Painted Greenling eats small crustaceans that parasitize the Red Anemone, and the fecal material of the anemonefishes adds nutrients essential to the symbiotic algae that live in the anemones. These simple animals are at the center of a complicated set of relationships! In addition, many tropical jellyfish have small fish that stay with them as they ride the ocean currents, the fish gaining protection from larger predatory fish that are repelled by the cnidarian tentacles with their potent nematocysts.

Lore and Notes

Larger jellyfish, for example, the PORTUGUESE MAN-OF-WAR of tropical waters, can cause quite a bit of discomfort even to humans, and the sting of the Australian BOX JELLY has caused human fatalities. No Alaska jellyfish could be called really dangerous, but if their tentacles are touched, the larger ones can cause painful reactions, especially on mucous membranes such as those that cover your eyes or tongue. It is best to avoid jellyfish tentacles anywhere in the world. Some Alaska anemones have powerful defensive nematocysts that can irritate mucous membranes, but you will feel nothing more than an adhesive effect if you stick your finger gently onto the ring of tentacles.

"Anemone" is one of the most commonly mispronounced words, whether by plant or animal lovers. The correct pronunciation is a-NEM-o-nee, with the accent on the second syllable. Many people corrupt it to "anenome," with the 'm' in the wrong place. We feel rewarded that by pointing this out to the readers of this book, we can, in our own small way, uplift literacy standards.

Status

As long as the oceans of the world remain largely unpolluted, sea life such as cnidarians that are of no economic importance (that is, no one is fishing for them) should remain abundant. However, the vigorous aquarium trade in BLACK CORALS has had a deleterious effect on the populations of these striking animals. Furthermore, some cnidarians – watery, stinging animals such as they are – are dried and eaten in parts of Asia.

Profiles

Plumose Anemone, *Metridium senile*, Plate 6a
Giant Green Anemone, *Anthopleura xanthogrammica*, Plate 6b
Aggregating Anemone, *Anthopleura elegantissima*, Plate 6d
Lion's Mane, *Cyanea capillata*, Plate 7b

2. Worms

Many invertebrates are called *worms*, but technically, worms include members of at least 15 different phyla. All of these phyla have marine representatives, and most of the phyla are restricted to the sea. The worms treated here are segmented worms, or *annelids*, in the phylum Annelida (a-NEL-ida). This phylum includes the *oligochaetes* (OLLY-go-keets) (class Oligochaeta, about 6000 species), which burrow in soil (where they are known as *earthworms*) or live in fresh water; the *leeches* (class Hirudinea, about 500 species), which are blood-sucking parasites on larger animals (a few are predators); and the *polychaetes* (POLLY-keets) (class Polychaeta, about 9000 species), the major group of marine annelids. Annelids are recognized as such because their entire body is divided into many segments, easily seen on the outside. Most people can recognize an earthworm or a leech, because the members of each of those groups are all rather similar to one another. Most of us have seen earthworms on our lawns, and those of us who wade in freshwater lakes have probably seen leeches on our ankles. Oligochaetes and leeches lack any sort of obvious appendages, while most polychaetes have prominent appendages projecting from each segment (one name for the entire group is "paddle-footed worms"). The largest annelids are the huge earthworms of Australia, reaching 3 m (10 ft) in length.

Natural History

Ecology and Behavior

Worms, as one might guess, are animals adapted to tight spaces. Many worms burrow in sand or mud substrates. Others thread their slender bodies through the tiny spaces in rock piles and gravel. A small number of worms swim in open water, where their relatively slow mode of locomotion would seem to make them subject to easy capture by faster-swimming predators. More than most other worms, polychaetes vary tremendously in shape and lifestyle. Typical polychaetes include long worms with prominently segmented bodies, a pair of appendages on each segment for locomotion, and large biting jaws. Some of them are fierce-looking predators on smaller invertebrates, and a few even have poison fangs. Other worms are short and thick and creep around on rocks or in mussel beds. Many polychaetes, some of them extremely elongate (and called "thin worms") burrow in sand or mud. Still others create tubes in the bottom in which they live, filtering out organic detritus that drifts past them. Finally, some worms have taken filter-feeding to its logical end by becoming sessile, constructing tubes that they attach to rocks. The worm lives in the tube, from which it projects a crown of filtering appendages (often beautifully colored) to strain tiny plankton and organic materials from the water. The CALCAREOUS TUBEWORM (Plate 6) profiled here is a member of this last group.

Breeding

Annelid worms breed in a great variety of ways. Leeches and earthworms are hermaphroditic; each copulates with another individual to transfer sperm, and both individuals then produce eggs that hatch and develop in a cocoonlike structure and emerge as miniature adults. Polychaetes have separate male and female sexes, and most kinds shed great numbers of eggs and sperm into the water, where fertilization takes place. The CALCAREOUS TUBEWORM falls in this group. In some sedentary species, parts of the abdomen break off and swim to the surface, where they spawn in great numbers. These worms and a variety of other polychaetes swarm by the millions when tidal conditions, moon phase, or temperature stimulates them all to breed synchronously. The fertilized eggs grow into plankton-feeding larvae that swim around for a while and then undergo metamorphosis into adult worms.

Lore and Notes

Leeches have been known for their medicinal value for many centuries. They produce an anticoagulant and an anesthetic saliva to facilitate their attaching onto other animals and sucking their blood, and this adaptation fits them for bloodletting from human patients. A MEDICINAL LEECH can be placed anywhere that tissue is swollen with damaged blood cells, and it will pierce the skin and begin to feed. It clears out the damaged blood with the help of a symbiotic bacterium that digests blood; in addition, the bacterium produces an antibiotic that kills other bacteria.

The budded-off segments of a South Pacific polychaete, called the PALOLO WORM, are eaten by many people during the spectacular spawning aggregations of the worms at the sea surface during certain lunar cycles.

Status

Like other invertebrates with little or no direct economic importance, annelids will persist as long as their habitats remain available. Most of them are poorly known, in any case, so a decline in their numbers would not necessarily be noted. The GIANT AUSTRALIAN EARTHWORM is a well-known species that has indeed declined, and it is considered endangered in its small range in southeastern Australia. Worms are used as fish bait the world over, but the effects of this have been little documented. One study found that shorebirds had poorer feeding success in areas where BLOODWORMS (a primary component of the birds' diets) were harvested by people in the Bay of Fundy.

Profiles

Calcareous Tubeworm, *Serpula vermicularis*, Plate 6c

3. Mollusks

Mollusks (phylum Mollusca) are soft-bodied animals, most of which enclose their body in a hard shell or shells. The shells are calcareous, that is, made of calcium carbonate, which is an abundant material in the sea. There are well over 65,000 species of mollusks, and they are very diverse in both fresh and salt water as well as on land. Although the various classes of mollusks look very different from one another, they share common molluskan structures. The *mantle* is an important organ, as it secretes the shell, covers much of the body, and produces the siphons that move water in and out of the shell and over the gills. The *foot* is a muscular structure variously modified for locomotion. The *radula* is a specialized organ for feeding, consisting usually of a cartilaginous base bearing a ribbon of chitinous teeth (*chitin* is the hard substance that makes up the outer coating of insects) that are pulled back and forth over the base to rasp prey.

The major groups of mollusks include *chitons* (KYE-tons) (class Polyplacophora), with a series of eight joined plates down the length of their body, a broad foot, and a radula; *gastropods*, including snails, slugs, and sea slugs (class Gastropoda), which also have a radula and crawl on a broad foot (*gastro* = stomach, *poda* = foot) but are typically protected by a spiral shell (the shell is not spiral in some snails and is internal in some slugs and sea slugs; and most slugs and sea slugs lack a shell); *bivalves*, including clams, mussels, and their relatives (class Bivalvia), with paired shells completely enclosing the body and a muscular foot that is used in some species for digging; and *cephalopods*, including squids and octopuses (class Cephalopoda), with no shell or an internal shell, and the foot modified into 8 or

10 arms or tentacles that surround a horny beaked mouth. As we move away from terrestrial vertebrates, most of which are basically like ourselves in anatomy, our naming of anatomical structures becomes less precise; thus the squid's "arms" have evolved from the basic mollusk "foot."

The largest shelled mollusks are several species of GIANT CLAMS, reaching 1.3 m (4 ft) in width; the largest living mollusks are GIANT SQUIDS, with at least a 4 m (13 ft) long body and 16 m (52.5 ft) long tentacles.

Natural History
Ecology and Behavior

Feeding behavior varies greatly in mollusks. Chitons and herbivorous snails use their radula to scrape algae off rocks (this method of feeding is easily seen on the glass of an aquarium). Other snails are predatory, and their radula is modified into a drilling organ that can penetrate the shells of other mollusks. Still others, for example the CONE SHELLS of tropical waters, have a radula modified into a venomous dart that they shoot into large prey such as fishes; humans have been fatally poisoned from picking up one of these beautiful but deadly snails. Bivalves by and large are plankton- and detritus-feeders; they sit in one spot, open their shells slightly, and bring water over their gills by means of the mantle siphons. While all marine mollusks use gills for respiration, the bivalves use them as their feeding system. The gills strain out small particles from the water and carry them to the mouth. At intervals, the clam expels larger particles that won't fit into its mouth. You can appreciate the force of the clam's pumping system when you see one squirt water into the air at low tide. Some bivalves burrow in sand or mud and extend just their siphons up into the water. Others, such as the PACIFIC BLUE MUSSEL (Plate 8), secrete *byssal threads* with their foot that serve to attach them to rocks; they are effectively sessile. The GIANT PACIFIC OCTOPUS (Plate 7) and other octopuses and squids are predators. Octopuses crawl in and out of rock piles and capture crabs and other large invertebrates, which they bite with their strong, horny beak (the hardest part of a cephalopod). Squids are fast swimmers, using their large siphons for jet propulsion; most of them are predators on small fish. Cephalopods squirt opaque "ink" into the water to hide their escape from their own predators.

Breeding

Mollusk breeding systems are as varied as their feeding techniques. Land snails, some sea slugs, and some bivalves are hermaphrodites – each is a male and female, capable of fertilizing and being fertilized; and fertilization is internal. However, most marine mollusks practice external fertilization, shedding their eggs and sperm into the water. Most mollusks have separate sexes; some change sex as they age, and oysters reverse their sex repeatedly during their lives. Egg laying is very variable, with eggs being deposited in gelatinous clumps, horny capsules, bubble rafts, or collars made of sand. Female octopuses stay with their eggs to keep them clean, sweep water over them to aerate them, and defend them against predators. The eggs of most kinds of marine mollusks hatch into larvae that become part of the plankton, moving with ocean currents. Larvae of gastropods and bivalves transform into a second type of larva that swims more actively than the first type, then that larva settles on the bottom and transforms into a miniature adult.

Ecological Interactions

The EMARGINATE DOGWINKLE (Plate 8) is one of the major predators on the PACIFIC BLUE MUSSEL and other mollusks of similar size. The dogwinkle drills through the shell with its very hard radula and inserts its very long proboscis into the shell to feed on the prey's body. Some mollusks can escape this by climbing up on the shell of the predator, but mussels have a special trick. The byssal threads by which they attach to rocks can be produced rapidly, and a mussel quick enough can glue some threads to the predator and their other ends to a rock or other mussel shell, then close its valves and wait for the hog-tied dogwinkle to die of starvation.

Lore and Notes

Mollusks are among the best-represented invertebrates in the fossil record because of their hard shells. Fossil cephalopods are especially abundant, as many ancient cephalopods had shells. Ancient fossil beds are full of the mineralized shells of relatives of the present-day CHAMBERED NAUTILUS, and the coiled shells of the largest types had a diameter of about 3 m (10 ft). Other nautiluses had similar shells, but they were straightened out in long, narrow cones, some as long as 5 m (16 ft) in length.

Although *paralytic shellfish poisoning* has been infrequently reported in Alaska, the frequency has increased in recent years, and you should be cautious about eating mussels, clams, or snails from unmonitored beaches. Restaurant owners are careful about the sources of their delicacies, however. The Alaska Division of Environmental Health will have the latest information about which beaches are safe.

Status

Most benthic marine organisms in Alaska are endangered only by truly wide-ranging disturbances such as oil spills, which quickly clog the feeding apparatus of filter feeders, grazers, and predators alike. Intertidal and beach areas that have been hit by oil spills may take many years to recover from the local extinction of large sections of the marine invertebrate community. Because so many of the species have larvae that disperse by currents, they will eventually repopulate the area. Of course, any species of economic importance, for example some of the clams and mussels that are eaten by humans, is at risk of overharvesting. But so far, nothing of that sort has happened with any Alaska mollusks.

Profiles

Giant Pacific Octopus, *Octopus dofleini*, Plate 7a
Emarginate Dogwinkle, *Nucella emarginata*, Plate 8a
Sitka Periwinkle, *Littorina sitkana*, Plate 8b
Lined Chiton, *Tonicella lineata*, Plate 8c
Shield Limpet, *Lottia pelta*, Plate 8d
Pacific Blue Mussel, *Mytilus trossulus*, Plate 8f

4. Crustaceans

Crustaceans are members of the phylum Arthropoda and class Crustacea. Arthropods are all those animals that have a hard exoskeleton (*exo* = outside) and jointed appendages, including crustaceans (crabs, shrimps, lobsters, barnacles), arachnids (spiders, scorpions, and their relatives), millipedes, centipedes, and insects. Arthropods have a basic body plan of *bilateral symmetry*, and they are divided into three parts – head, thorax, and abdomen (the head and thorax are fused in arachnids). Crustaceans are characterized by having multiple sets of appendages, including five sets of appendages (antennae and mouthparts) on the head and one pair on each segment of the thorax and abdomen. Leglike appendages in the different groups of crustaceans are modified for either walking or swimming locomotion. Crustaceans are a very diverse group, with over 26,000 species described from marine, freshwater, and terrestrial environments. Land crustaceans include relatively few groups, but some of them, such as *isopods* (pillbugs), are common throughout the world. Very few of the animals we normally think of as crustaceans occur on land, but there are a few species of *land crabs*; they have to return to the water to breed. Many marine crustacean groups have freshwater representatives, including crabs and shrimps, but especially the many tiny forms that make up the plankton of fresh water. These phenomenally abundant *copepods, cladocerans* (water fleas), *ostracods*, and other creatures less than 3 mm (1/8 in) in length make looking at water samples through a low-powered microscope an adventure comparable to an African safari but on a very tiny scale.

Crustaceans are so diverse that the discussion here will focus on the species profiled, the RED KING CRAB (Plate 7) and the ACORN BARNACLE (Plate 8). Although they do not look much like them, King Crabs belong to the same group of crustaceans that include the *hermit crabs*. Hermit crabs have a curled and twisted abdomen to allow them to fit in snail shells, while King Crabs are quite symmetrical. King Crabs are much like other crabs in having four pairs of legs, the first pair furnished with a pinching claw and the other three used for walking. The claw is used for both feeding and defense.

Barnacles, on the other hand, don't look much like anything else. They have been defined fancifully as animals that stand on their head and kick food into their mouth with their legs, and that just about describes them. The Acorn Barnacle is typical of the group; it consists of six plates in a circle with a basal plate cemented to a rock or mussel shell, with the animal inside. Groups of barnacles may cover vast expanses of the intertidal zone with their shells.

Natural History
Ecology and Behavior
Adult RED KING CRABS live on most types of bottom from near shore (the young crabs) to depths of 366 m (1200 ft). They forage for just about any animal they can capture – worms, snails, clams, other crabs, even sand dollars and sea urchins. When they molt their exoskeleton, they lose a great amount of calcium carbonate, and it is thought that the barnacles and echinoderms that they prefer at certain times of year may be the source of replenishment of that vital material.

An ACORN BARNACLE is unlikely to come into contact with a King Crab, as the barnacles live in the high and middle intertidal zones, where they are exposed by most low tides. They are well adapted to this level, as they can obtain oxygen from both air and water. A barnacle's plates can be held open or closed at the top. They are open for feeding when it is covered by water, and it is easy to see the barnacle feeding technique in a tidepool. When feeding, a barnacle opens its plates and extends six pairs of slender, feathery "legs," actually appendages called *cirri* (singular *cirrus*). These appendages beat constantly, straining small particles of food from the current and carrying it to the barnacle's mouth. The plates close when the barnacle is uncovered by a falling tide but also when it is disturbed, and this can be seen by causing your shadow to fall on a barnacle with its shell open.

Breeding

RED KING CRABS may live 15 to 20 years. They mature reproductively at five to six years of age, and the adults move inshore during winter to breed. Males seek out females and grasp them at the base of their front legs. The pair stays like this for a few days or even as long as two weeks, until the female molts. The male then deposits sperm on her body near her genital openings; as the eggs are extruded from these openings, they are fertilized. The female lays the eggs on her own abdomen and broods them for up to a year; large females may carry almost a half-million eggs. The young go through several larval stages after hatching and spend much of their two- to three-month larval stage in the water column, migrating nearer the surface during the day and deeper during the night. At two to three months of age, they sink to the bottom and metamorphose into tiny crabs. The young crabs spend their first few years in relatively shallow water, where they form dense aggregations that may offer them protection from some predators. They then move out into deeper water.

Most sessile marine invertebrates mate by broadcasting their eggs and sperm into the water, but ACORN BARNACLES – in fact all barnacles – are quite different. Each barnacle has the organs of both sexes; it is *hermaphroditic*. The male's copulatory organ may be up to five times the length of the barnacle itself, allowing it to extend into the opening of a nearby barnacle, where it deposits sperm. That barnacle produces eggs that are then fertilized and retained within the shell until they reach an early larval stage, at which time they are released into the water. These larvae join the plankton and can be very abundant locally (densities of up to 4500 per cubic m, 125 per cubic ft). After six molts, they transform into a very different sort of larva that looks like a little bivalve with appendages. It does not feed but instead heads for the shore and settles on a rock, usually among others of its own species (which indicate a good settling site). The larva attaches to the rock by cement glands on its first antennae and transforms into a juvenile barnacle, surrounded by delicate transparent plates. It is then ready to begin its decade-long life, assuming it avoids predation and being crushed by wave-washed logs.

Ecological Interactions

ACORN BARNACLES are not quite as resistant to desiccation (drying out) as their smaller relative, the LITTLE BROWN BARNACLE, so they do not colonize the upper levels of the upper intertidal zone. However, the Little Brown Barnacle cannot colonize areas inhabited by the Acorn Barnacle, as the latter is a superior competitor and crushes or undercuts the Little Browns. The lower level in the intertidal zone that can be inhabited successfully by the Acorn Barnacle is set to some extent by its predators, an array of species including sea stars, limpets, dogwinkles, and sea slugs.

Lore and Notes

Some barnacles grow on long stalks and look rather different from the ACORN BARNACLE and its near relatives. These stalked barnacles are called *goose barnacles* because people in Europe long ago believed that Barnacle Geese hatched from them. Perhaps the long "neck" of the barnacle suggested the long neck of the goose to these people, who clearly did not have quite enough curiosity to check the truth of the statement for themselves.

Status

Crustaceans are of great economic importance in many parts of the world, and the RED KING CRAB is one of the most important. This species and a deep-water relative have supported a large fishery and been the source of most of the canned crab meat eaten in the USA. Because the crabs are fairly easy to capture, their populations have diminished in many parts of their range, to the point at which it is not economically profitable to fish for them in these areas. When formerly abundant, people collected King Crabs around Juneau by wading at very low tides; alas, this activity is no more.

Profiles

Red King Crab, *Paralithodes camtschaticus*, Plate 7c
Acorn Barnacle, *Balanus glandula*, Plate 8e

5. Echinoderms

Echinoderms (ee-KINE-o-derms) are among the most characteristic of marine organisms, as they are diverse and common in salt water but are completely absent from fresh water. The group seems primitive, because the species are *radially symmetrical*, but in fact echinoderms are fairly advanced invertebrates, on the same evolutionary line as vertebrates. What radial symmetry does for an animal that moves is to give it the opportunity to go just as easily in any direction, and these slow-moving animals seem not to need anything more. Echinoderm symmetry is not radial in the same way as that of a jellyfish; instead, it is a five-parted symmetry, derived from ancestors that were bilaterally symmetrical like most invertebrates. Echinoderms (*echino* = spine, *derm* = skin) have a hard calcareous skeleton that seems to cover them, but in fact it is an internal skeleton, because there is a skin layer over it. Echinoderms are the only animals that have a water-vascular system, a closed system of canals that moves water through the animals and is important in locomotion. Water is squeezed into the extensible *tube feet* (picture a flexible cylinder with a bulb at one end and a shallow cup at the other), and each tube foot alternately sticks to the surface, pulls the animal along, and lets go; with hundreds of tube feet, these awkward-looking animals can move faster than you might think. You can see how this works by looking at a sea urchin or sea star in motion.

There are over 7000 species of echinoderms, organized into five classes. The class Crinoidea includes primitive echinoderms called *sea lilies* and *feather stars*. Sea lilies, which occur mostly in deep water, are sessile and attached to the bottom by stalks. Feather stars, which live on tropical coral reefs, break loose from their stalk as they grow and can change positions, although they tend to move very little. Members of this class are *suspension feeders*; mucous on their arms traps minute particles in the water, and these bits of food are carried down the arms and into the mouth. The common echinoderm groups in Alaska waters include sea cucumbers (class Holothuroidea), sea urchins (class Echinoidea), sea stars (class Asteroidea), and brittle stars (class Ophiuroidea), all of which are motile. *Sea cucumbers* are smooth echinoderms shaped as their name implies, as if a sea urchin were grabbed at the top and pulled upwards, then stripped of its spines. They rest in one spot, sometimes in large numbers, and extend highly branched tentacles (actually modified tube feet) into the water or onto the bottom to snag microscopic prey. They have been called "vacuums of the sea."

One species of sea cucumber, at 2 m (6.6 ft) in length, is the largest echinoderm. *Sea urchins* are spiny, pincushion-shaped echinoderms that move slowly along the bottom, either on tube feet or by moving their spines, and graze on plants. This group includes the *sand dollars*, which are very much flattened and lie on sandy substrates feeding on organic matter. *Sea stars* have five or more distinct arms that radiate out from the central disk; most are predators that crawl on tube feet. Finally, *brittle stars* have a distinct central disk and five very long, slender arms that are moved sinuously for locomotion; they are nocturnal detritus feeders, sheltering under rocks by day. This group includes the *basket stars*, large deep-water forms with many-branched arms.

Natural History
Ecology and Behavior
The two groups of echinoderms profiled here have had a long and independent evolutionary history, the sea stars becoming specialized as predators and the urchins as herbivores. Both are extremely good at what they do. Large sea stars are among the most effective predators on shellfish, making up in persistence what they lack in stealth and speed. A sea star is unlikely to be a very good predator on fast-moving fishes and shrimps, but some of the organisms with which it shares the bottom are similarly slow-moving, for example snails, bivalves, and other echinoderms. It's not easy to envision how a sea star could eat anything, and its way of predation is indeed unusual. A sea star crawls right over a potential prey animal and everts its stomach through its mouth, enveloping the prey in the stomach. The digestive juices can penetrate the most tightly closed mollusk shell and kill and digest the prey at the same time, the nutrients being absorbed into the sea star's stomach as it feeds. SUNFLOWER STARS (Plate 9) are particularly voracious predators, moving over the sea floor at high speed (for a sea star) and attacking many other species in their environment. Putting a few drops of Sunflower Star extract into a marine aquarium full of its prey species provides a lesson in varied escape responses; in fact, it creates what seems to be a panic. Scallops close their shells and shoot around the aquarium, sea urchins and other sea stars increase their speed dramatically, abalones twist their shells rapidly, and periwinkles may leave the water entirely.

Echinoderms have many adaptations to protect them from predators. The spines of sea urchins present an effective defense, except to certain predators that are able to turn the urchins over and eat out their unprotected underside. Also, Sea Otters smash them against each other or on a rock held on the otter's chest, sea stars digest them from the outside, and gulls and crows pick them up and drop them on rocks. Many sea stars can easily lose an arm and regenerate it; amazingly, in one type of sea star, the arm itself can regenerate an entire animal. Some sea cucumbers, when harassed by a predator, eviscerate themselves (shed the contents of the body cavity) and then regrow their digestive and respiratory organs and gonads in as little time as a month or two.

Breeding
The sexes are separate in most echinoderms. Many species shed eggs and sperm into the water, and the fertilized eggs develop into planktonic larvae. However, there is a surprising amount of parental care in this phylum, with females of some small species of sea cucumbers, sea stars, and brittle stars retaining eggs either inside or outside their bodies and releasing small young into the water.

Ecological Interactions

The OCHRE STAR (Plate 9) is a dominant predator of the low intertidal and subtidal zones. A common species, it eats just about everything in its habitat, and it is especially attracted to sessile animals such as barnacles and mussels. The presence of large numbers of Ochre Stars in the subtidal zone restricts the lower limit to which mussels and barnacles normally grow. Because of its importance over a long stretch of Pacific Ocean coast, the Ochre Star has been called a *keystone species*, defined as having an influence on its ecological community far out of proportion to its abundance.

GREEN SEA URCHINS (Plate 9) are also highly significant in marine communities. When abundant, they wipe out plant growth to the degree that some large areas of rock are transformed into "urchin barrens." The Sea Otter (p. 208) is one of the few animals that eats enough sea urchins to keep their populations from exploding, and it too has been called a keystone species.

Lore and Notes

Echinoderms don't seem like human fare, but in fact, the eggs of sea urchins are eaten all over the world, usually uncooked, and dried sea cucumbers are considered a delicacy in Asia.

Status

Alaska echinoderms are not threatened, but both sea cucumbers and sea urchins are heavily fished in some regions, and they may become locally extirpated. Perhaps the most pressing environmental problem in the Galápagos Islands is the sea cucumber fishery that has brought too many fishing boats and thus too many people to these fragile islands. The cucumbers are shipped to distant Asian markets, one among many examples showing that a resource in demand is not safe anywhere in the modern world.

Profiles

Ochre Star, *Pisaster ochraceus*, Plate 9a
Green Sea Urchin, *Strongylocentrotus droebachiensis*, Plate 9b
Red Sea Urchin, *Strongylocentrotus franciscanus*, Plate 9c
Sunflower Star, *Pycnopodia helianthoides*, Plate 9d

Environmental Close-up 2:
Life in the Intertidal Zone

The inshore marine environment is at the mercy of Earth's tidal cycles. At every place along the ocean's shore, the sea level rises and falls each day. At some times and places, there is only one tidal cycle per day, but in most parts of the world the tide comes in and goes out twice each day. The amplitude of the tidal cycle (the difference in elevation between high tide and low tide) varies tremendously, from less than 1 m (3.3 ft) at many oceanic islands (this is the actual bulging of the water from the moon's and sun's gravitational pulls) to much higher in estuaries, where the rising and falling sea is pushed rapidly through narrow channels. The largest variation at extreme tides is about 17 m (56 ft) at the Bay of Fundy, on the Atlantic coast of Canada, but southern Alaska also experiences dramatic tidal ranges, for example, an average range of 8.2 m (27 ft) at Auke Bay, near Juneau.

The *intertidal zone* is the habitat between average high tides and average low tides. Because of the long existence and wide distribution of this special habitat, there are many species of plants and animals adapted to live in it. In fact, in Southeast Alaska, it is one of the most productive environments for animal life. Acorn Barnacles reach densities of 70,000 per sq m (6500 per sq ft) in this zone, and a visitor to the shore can stand in one spot and see barnacles and Pacific Blue Mussels completely covering the intertidal rocks in both directions. Both of these abundant species are filter feeders, filtering small organisms and organic particles from the water during high tide and closing up their shells during low tide. Sea anemones growing in the same area extend their tentacles to capture similar small prey when covered by water, then shrink to unrecognizable blobs when uncovered. Other very common animals include limpets, snails, chitons, and sea urchins that graze on the algal coating of the rocks; other snails that drill holes in these shelled invertebrates; and sea stars that prey on most of the other species. Even fishes can be found in the intertidal zone, as long as there are small *tide pools* that retain water as the ocean recedes.

Rocky shores furnish much habitat for animals, both on solid rock and among boulders and cobbles. However, as water drains off rocks quickly, they also dry out faster at low tide. Sand and mud furnish a less diverse habitat that stays moister as the tide goes out, so intertidal zonation is not so dramatic there, and many of the animals merely burrow more deeply as the surface dries out.

Numerous physical factors determine which species are most successful on rocky shores. The very water itself can be inimical to survival, especially on outer coasts where huge waves crash onto the shore. The waves can wash away many invertebrates not fixed in place, and – even more severe – they can carry sand, pebbles, logs, and chunks of ice that can severely damage whole invertebrate communities. Sun, high temperature, and wind add the serious problem of desiccation (drying out). And, of course, low temperature will have its own effect, an extreme cold snap freezing many of the exposed animals. Large numbers of Pacific Blue Mussels are killed when low tides occur during very cold weather. Light is also an important physical factor, as marine algae – the food for many animals – need adequate light levels for growth and photosynthesis.

Biological factors also determine intertidal distribution. Many species are predators, and some of them may control the distribution of their prey, for example the Ochre Star that, when common, sets the lower level for mussel beds (that is, mussel beds exist where Ochre Stars don't). Competition is also an important factor, in particular competition for space among all of these sessile animals. Mussels and some barnacles are successful competitors, while other barnacles are forced out of communities by competition for space. Competition also occurs between motile animals, especially when they compete for the same prey. Ochre Stars and Six-armed Sea Stars eat the same prey, and the Ochre drives the Six-armed away wherever their paths cross.

The intertidal zone varies greatly from top to bottom. The *upper intertidal* is exposed to the air for a longer time, and relatively few species exist there. These are mostly shelled animals – barnacles and mollusks such as periwinkles and limpets that can close up tightly enough at each exposure to the air (and sometimes sun) to keep from drying out. One can easily see how high the tide reaches, on the average, by looking for the upper edge of the colonies of barnacle species that are the most resistant to desiccation. Above them is a splash zone with scattered barnacles and limpets and, often, a coating of black lichens.

The *middle intertidal* supports a great diversity of invertebrates that are not quite as resistant as those of the upper intertidal, but they nevertheless are able to close up and protect themselves from drying out during the briefer period of exposure. These animals include other barnacles, many snails and chitons, beds of mussels, sea anemones, and numerous echinoderms. There are often tide pools in this zone that shelter a whole array of animals that cannot withstand drying. Tide pools also shelter actively feeding and thus fully open individuals of many of the species that are dormant out of water. Beds of barnacles and especially mussels furnish very significant habitat, and a great variety of small invertebrates live in them, sheltering among the larger sessile animals. One can well imagine what a good habitat a mat of mussels would be for the polychaete worms that can slither among them.

Finally, animals of the *lower intertidal* are much less often exposed, so more delicate species abound there. A visit to the shore, whether rocky or sandy, is most interesting at extreme low tides, when many species of animals and plants are exposed that could otherwise be seen only by taking a dip in the chilly ocean.

Chapter 8

FISHES

General Characteristics and Natural History

Fishes are aquatic vertebrates that are supported by an internal skeleton, respire by gills, and swim with a set of fins. Generally thought of as a single group, in fact they comprise four different classes of animals: Myxinoidea (hagfishes), Petromyzontoidea (lampreys), Chondrichthyes (cartilaginous fishes – sharks and rays), and Osteichthyes (bony fishes). There are about 40 species each of Myxinoidea and Petromyzontoidea, 800 of Chondrichthyes, and over 20,000 of Osteichthyes. The bony fishes have long been the most diverse – and easily the most abundant – group of vertebrate animals, and they occur everywhere in the world in fresh and salt waters. The cartilaginous fishes, although much less diverse, remain the dominant predators in the marine environment; the huge, carnivorous WHITE SHARK and the even larger, plankton-feeding, WHALE SHARK are much larger than any living bony fishes. Unlike birds and mammals, fishes are independent from a very young age, and many of them have larvae very different from the adults. During growth, many fishes change shape and habits dramatically.

To know fishes, you should know their fins (Figure 1, p. 83). They have paired *pectoral* and *pelvic* fins, the precursors of the limbs that all land vertebrates use for locomotion, and, in addition, a series of unpaired vertical fins – one or more *dorsal* fins on the back, an *anal* fin on the underside behind the *vent* (opening of the digestive and urogenital tracts), and a *caudal* fin at the rear. These fins work together to stabilize the fish in its watery world as well as to provide propulsion and steering, but they have been much modified to function in different ways for fishes with many different life styles.

A fish extracts oxygen from the water through its gills. Either by swimming forward or by taking in water and then closing its mouth, or both, a fish forces water through its gills. The gills are basically a mass of tiny blood vessels, supported by bony or cartilaginous *gill arches*, that extract oxygen from the water and excrete carbon dioxide back into it. A series of *gill rakers* on the front of each gill arch strains particles from the water to prevent damage to the delicate gills, and these gill rakers perform double duty by capturing food particles that can then be swallowed. They are especially fine in plankton-feeding fishes; if you get the chance, compare the gill rakers of a plankton-feeding SOCKEYE SALMON (Plate 12) with those of a fish-feeding CHINOOK SALMON (Plate 12).

Salmonids (trout and salmon) are very important fish in Alaska, and they are treated separately below. The other two groups that are profiled include fresh-water and anadromous fishes other than salmonids, and marine fishes.

Seeing Fishes in Alaska

Fishes, being underwater creatures, are not much seen by ecotravellers, except those who spend time snorkeling or scuba diving, and Alaska is not exactly a popular destination for such activities. Underwater researchers and serious sport divers dive in Alaska, but it takes heavy-duty equipment and adequate diving experience to stay warm and safe in these frigid waters.

The rest of us can nevertheless see fish in Alaska. Some ecotravellers enjoy fishing, and the fish species profiled here are among those most frequently sought by anglers. Furthermore, about half of them regularly appear on the menus of Alaska seafood restaurants.

But the most likely species to be seen are the salmonids: the salmon, trout, and graylings that inhabit Alaska's streams and rivers during the spawning season, if not year-round. Fish-watching, even including identification of species, is surprisingly easy with a pair of binoculars. At close range, polarized sunglasses are also helpful. Stand quite still on a bridge over any clear, fairly shallow river or

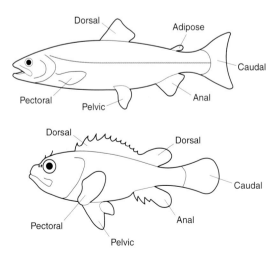

Figure I   Two typical fish forms, showing positions of fins.

stream and watch for fish. During the nonbreeding season there are always a few to see, especially in quiet pools, where the stillness of the water allows relatively undistorted viewing. These should include adults of freshwater species and young of those anadromous species, such as COHO SALMON (Plate 12) and DOLLY VARDEN (Plate 11), that stay in fresh water for a year or more. But during spawning season the pools and riffles may be alive with salmonids, usually one or more of the group called "Pacific salmon" (Plate 12). They are in full breeding colors, the males with grotesquely hooked jaws, and they furnish one of nature's most impressive spectacles (see Close-up, p. 93).

Quiet marine waters sometimes furnish reasonably good fish-watching. Lie on a dock and peer beneath it, where reflections are absent; you may see sculpins (Plate 13) resting in clumps of seaweeds or schools of herrings moving to and fro, or with luck, a larger predatory fish such as a greenling or rockfish. If you can see the bottom, watch for flatfishes moving; don't expect to see them if they aren't! On a protected sandy beach, with luck you might see a PACIFIC SAND LANCE (Plate 15) burying itself in the sand as a wave recedes. Sit quietly at the edge of a tide pool and watch for the shapes of sculpins darting about. Finally, try carefully lifting up small rocks (and just as carefully replacing them) at low tide; you may be startled by the wiggling of an eel-shaped prickleback or gunnel, some of them very colorful.

Family Profiles

1. Salmon and Trout

Salmon and trout are members of the family Salmonidae, and they are collectively called *salmonids*. They include not only the familiar trout and salmon but also the less familiar but closely related ARCTIC GRAYLING (Plate 11) and the somewhat different whitefishes. The family is characterized by having soft-rayed fins (that is, none of the fin rays are spiny, as in more advanced fishes) and an extra, fleshy, *adipose fin* on the back just in front of the tail. There are 68 species worldwide and 21 in Alaska, including 10 whitefishes (one of which, the INCONNU [Plate 11], is profiled in the next section), the Grayling, 4 "chars" of the genus *Salvelinus*, and 7 salmons of the genus *Oncorhynchus* (which also includes the RAINBOW [Plate 11] and CUTTHROAT TROUTS). Most salmonids are medium to large fish, with CHINOOK SALMON reaching 147 cm (58 in), while whitefishes are relatively small, the PYGMY WHITEFISH only 28 cm (11 in) in length.

Natural History
Ecology and Behavior

Most salmonids are *anadromous*, the term used for fishes that spend much of their adult life in the ocean but ascend freshwater rivers and streams to breed. They are supremely adapted to this life, with pointed heads and bodies oval in cross section to slide smoothly through the water, strong swimming muscles, and large, forked caudal fins to provide powerful thrust for both ocean swimming and the more difficult task of fighting the strong currents and even ascending waterfalls in their spawning rivers. To see a large salmon leap three or four of its body lengths up into a waterfall, and then continue to drive itself up the torrential flow with powerful strokes of its tail, is to see one of the wonders of nature.

Even though the five species of "Pacific salmon" are thought of collectively and have many traits in common, each species is quite distinct, with its own preferred feeding habits, spawning areas, and life histories. All of them make prodigious ocean journeys, but the PINK SALMON (Plate 12) spawn at the mouths of big rivers, while others move farther upriver, some of them flexing their powerful muscles for many days more and travelling hundreds and even thousands of miles farther upstream. The CHINOOK SALMON is legendary for its long spawning runs, at their farthest to the upper reaches of the Yukon River system in interior Alaska, over 1600 km (1000 miles) from the river mouth.

The salmonids that are not anadromous are mostly smaller species, in Alaska including the whitefishes and ARCTIC GRAYLING. However, the LAKE TROUT is a large char restricted to inland lakes, and many ARCTIC CHAR (Plate 11) remain in fresh water all their life. Interestingly, a near relative of these two chars, the DOLLY VARDEN, is anadromous.

Salmonids are generalized carnivores, eating insects and other invertebrates when young but switching quickly to a diet of small fishes as they enter the ocean. Young SOCKEYE SALMON are plankton feeders, however, and most of them spend a year in a freshwater lake, where plankton is more abundant and easily harvested than in their birth stream. The adults continue to feed on plankton after reaching the ocean, although they eat small fishes as well.

Breeding

The life histories of fishes of this family are very well known, thanks to the great economic importance of its members. Females of the anadromous species make nests, called *redds*, by scraping a depression a few inches deep in the gravel bottom of their breeding stream. Males compete for the opportunity to mate, and eventually a single male will associate with the breeding female, fertilize her 2000 to 5000 eggs when she lays them (by releasing sperm into the water around the eggs), and defend the nest against other males and other fish that might threaten the eggs. Some male ARCTIC CHAR remain in fresh water all their lives and do not grow as large as their anadromous relatives; they nevertheless breed with sea-run females, often sneaking in to fertilize eggs just laid in the redd of a mating pair. The relatively large eggs of salmon take about 50 days to hatch. Each larva is well endowed with a large *yolk sac* to provide it with nutrients for the several weeks until it leaves the gravelly nest and begins to feed successfully.

The larval salmon are called *alevins*, and they don't begin to look like real salmon and trout until a few more weeks of growth, when they develop dark vertical bars on the sides. At this stage they are called *parrs*, and the markings are parr marks. When they move out to sea, they lose these marks and become silvery; they are then called *smolts*.

The breeding of some other salmonids diverges from this typical Pacific salmon mode. LAKE TROUT, for example, merely broadcast their eggs among the rocks on the bottom of their breeding lakes with no nest construction. Males rub the rocks before spawning occurs, possibly depositing scent marks to guide or stimulate the female or perhaps just cleaning algae and detritus away. ARCTIC GRAYLING show a more complex interaction between the sexes. Males court females by erecting their very large dorsal fin; then, when a female shows that she is receptive, the male presses her down into the bottom gravel with his dorsal and caudal fins, and she lays her eggs there.

Most of the anadromous species spawn in the fall, when river levels are lowest and ascent is therefore easiest. Some species, for example ARCTIC GRAYLING and freshwater populations of CUTTHROAT and RAINBOW TROUT, breed in spring. By breeding in spring and having rapid egg and larval development, graylings can move into small arctic streams, and their young can move back downstream with the adults before the streams freeze in winter. DOLLY VARDEN are good examples of *partially anadromous* fish: some populations move into the sea, while others remain in fresh water and overwinter in lakes, where not only are there fewer predators than in the ocean, but also temperatures are lower than in the ocean, so the fish are less active and require less food.

Ecological Interactions
These fish are among the most numerous in Alaska's streams and rivers, and – especially when spawning in great numbers – represent a fabulous source of food for predators of all kinds. Although the most impressive of these predators, the Brown Bear, is single-pawedly responsible for attracting great numbers of ecotravellers to Alaska every year, the salmon themselves remain the state's biggest attraction, as trophies for anglers, menu items everywhere, and an accessible and spectacular concentration of wildlife.

Lore and Notes
The first human inhabitants of Alaska came across the Bering Strait from Siberia more than 10,000 years ago. Hunters of birds and mammals, they did not discover the rich marine resources of Alaska until they settled farther south along the coast. There they encountered rivers so full of salmon it seemed that one could walk across on their backs. They quickly adapted to this new and seemingly inexhaustible source of protein by developing sophisticated fishing methods and became experts in salmon harvest. Dried salmon could last until next year's runs and could be supplemented by the abundant shellfish and other marine life of coastal areas. Because of the salmon, the marine life, the varied woods for constructing boats and lodges, and the relatively benign climate, the Native people of the Pacific Northwest, including southern Alaska, reached the highest population density and in many ways became the "richest" of North America's indigenous people. Here was the home of the potlatch, a ceremonial feast at which gifts were exchanged in a rivalry to display wealth!

Some Northwest Indians believed that the five species of Pacific salmon were actually five tribes of salmon people living under the sea; and that the tribes sent their young men and women every year to feed the Indian people as a voluntary gesture of good will. The first salmon to be sighted each year were greeted formally in First Salmon ceremonies, and the salmon were asked respectfully to send all their family members to be honored by being eaten.

Status
For decades it had been known that Pacific salmon runs were declining along the coast from British Columbia to California, but only in 1999 were many of them finally declared Endangered or Threatened. By that time, 75% of the runs in that region were extinct or severely diminished. So many factors have contributed to the declines that it's hard to pick out any one as paramount, but they include overfishing by both sport and commercial fisheries, with obvious effects; dams on major rivers that not only prevent adults from moving farther upstream but also kill many of the young salmon produced by the spawning that does take place

above them; the need for water both to generate electricity and to irrigate agricultural fields that keeps the dams in place; logging that clears the forests that protect the stream environments; and, until recently, inertia on the part of policymakers.

Fortunately, Alaska has been relatively free of many of these problems, and its salmon runs are still prodigious. Furthermore, resident salmonids such as RAINBOW TROUT have not been genetically tainted by hatchery stock, as is the case farther south. As the state's natural resources become the focus of more and more special interests, fisheries managers are taking note of the problems to the south of them and trying to steer a safe course. The collapse of some of Alaska's marine fisheries (p. 92) also provides a stark lesson!

Profiles

Arctic Grayling, *Thymallus signifer*, Plate 11b
Arctic Char, *Salvelinus alpinus*, Plate 11c
Dolly Varden, *Salvelinus malma*, Plate 11d
Rainbow Trout, *Oncorhynchus mykiss*, Plate 11e
Sockeye Salmon, *Oncorhynchus nerka*, Plate 12a
Chum Salmon, *Oncorhynchus keta*, Plate 12b
Chinook Salmon, *Oncorhynchus tshawytscha*, Plate 12c
Coho Salmon, *Oncorhynchus kisutch*, Plate 12d
Pink Salmon, *Oncorhynchus gorbuscha*, Plate 12e

2. Other Freshwater and Anadromous Fishes

There are a total of 42 species of freshwater fishes in Alaska, of which 9 are fully anadromous. Many of these anadromous species are salmonids, but those in other families are included here. Interestingly, there are also 14 *partially anadromous* species, in which some populations are anadromous and others live permanently in fresh water. This leaves only 19 species that are restricted to fresh water, a very small list for a large state such as Alaska, but, like many other *ectotherms* (animals whose body temperature is regulated by environmental temperatures), fishes are much less diverse at high latitudes. One way to think of the reasons why there might not be many species of freshwater fish in Alaska: imagine the life of a fish in a shallow arctic pond that is frozen to the bottom three-fourths of the year!

The fishes in this group are varied, almost every species in a different family, and range from an eel-like lamprey and a freshwater cod (BURBOT, Plate 10) through slender, silvery, fast-swimming smelt (EULACHON, Plate 10) and whitefish (INCONNU; Plate 11) to the rather more chunky, mottled ALASKA BLACKFISH (Plate 10), a member of the mudminnow family, and two tiny, spiny sticklebacks. The sticklebacks are only 9 to 10 cm (3.5 to 4 in) long, while the INCONNU reaches 125 cm (49 in).

The most unusual species in this group is the PACIFIC LAMPREY (Plate 10), first because it is not really a fish but instead a primitive fish ancestor with a round sucking mouth instead of jaws, and second because of what it does with that mouth. Rather than feeding on smaller organisms, lampreys are parasitic on fishes. They approach a fish, often one considerably larger (salmonids get much attention from them), and suck onto its side much like the rubber cup of a toy arrow sticks to a wall. The tongue has rasping teeth on it, and the lamprey scrapes a hole in the fish's side and sucks its blood and lymph. After a while it drops off and seeks another host. Many fishes damaged by lampreys survive, but some of them don't. The amount of damage done by lampreys to fish populations is difficult to estimate, as scarred fish can be counted but dead ones can't.

Natural History

Ecology and Behavior

Although not especially diverse, freshwater fishes are abundant in Alaska and occupy all of its freshwater habitats – marshes, ponds, lakes, streams, and rivers. Fresh water is spectacularly abundant in Alaska, not only because massive glaciers cut grooves in the landscape everywhere but also because permafrost is close to the surface in northern areas, trapping a layer of water above it even in areas of relatively dry climate. Many isolated ponds, however, lack fish entirely.

Of the species profiled here, the PACIFIC LAMPREY is anadromous, as are some populations of the INCONNU and both species of sticklebacks. BURBOTS and ALASKA BLACKFISHES are resident in still waters, the former mostly in deep lakes and the latter in shallow ponds and lakes, the Inconnu occurs in rivers, and the sticklebacks live in most vegetated shallow freshwater bodies.

Fish diets are usually fairly generalized, the smaller species feeding on whatever invertebrates are common in their habitat, the larger ones typically on other fishes. Some of the salmonids are famous for preferring the eggs and young of other salmonids. DOLLY VARDENS, for example, eat tremendous numbers of the eggs that their anadromous relatives deposit, but they may not be as significant predators as they seem, as most of the eggs they eat are those that have been dislodged from their gravel nests.

Breeding

There are as many kinds of spawning as there are fish families. PACIFIC LAMPREYS ascend gravelly streams and spawn in nests scraped in the bottom, much as salmon do. Both sexes construct the nest by carrying rocks in their sucking mouths and digging with their tails. The females lay between 10,000 and 100,000 eggs, which hatch in a few weeks. The larvae drift downstream and burrow into the mud of pools, where they spend up to five years before transforming to the parasitic adults.

Even more parental care is shown by the THREESPINE STICKLEBACK (Plate 10), in which males build a hollow nest of plant materials among aquatic vegetation, then court females and convince them to lay in their nests. The male guards the eggs and young when they emerge from the nest.

Most other Alaska fishes abandon their eggs when they are laid. Some species come together in mass spawnings near the surface or in midwater. EULACHON come in from the sea to the lower reaches of rivers and lay their eggs into the water, where they sink to the bottom and adhere to sand and gravel. BURBOTS live in the open water of deep lakes and rivers but move to the surface to spawn, usually under the ice; their eggs also drift to the bottom. Other species spawn in smaller groups or pairs. Female INCONNU skitter along the surface while spawning, followed by one or more males that fertilize their eggs. ALASKA BLACKFISH lay their eggs on vegetation.

Ecological Interactions

Fish play a major role as predators in freshwater ecosystems, and this is easy to see by comparing fish-inhabited ponds and lakes with fishless ones. Planktonic crustaceans and insects that live in the open are particularly prone to fish predation, and members of some of these groups are found only in fishless lakes. Some crustaceans develop long spines, surely adaptations to avoid predation, when in fishy lakes but lack them in fishless lakes. Even the fish themselves are affected by this; THREESPINE STICKLEBACKS tend to develop their sharp spines in lakes with the larger fish, such as trout, that prey on them, but have smaller spines when those fish are absent.

Lore and Notes

ALASKA BLACKFISH are real survivors, very well adapted to arctic conditions. First, they can breathe air by gulping it at the surface, so they can withstand the greatly lowered oxygen content of shallow, warm tundra pools. Also, they can exist with a minimum of water, so they can inhabit ponds that dry out, leaving only wet mud or moss until the next rain or snow refills them. Native Alaskans capture Blackfish and throw them in the snow, which their bodies melt to produce just enough water to keep them alive, and the fish can be harvested for meals for several days. Finally, these fish can cope with their aquatic habitat freezing to the bottom. Contrary to prevailing wisdom, Blackfish cannot survive freezing, but their cells contain glycerol, which acts as an antifreeze, keeping the cells from freezing even though the fish is enclosed in ice.

THREESPINE STICKLEBACKS are of special interest because they occur in marine anadromous and freshwater populations, and the two types look different, the marine forms having a large number of conspicuous bony plates along the sides and the freshwater ones having few or no plates. The two kinds have been thought to represent different species, but they do interbreed where they meet, albeit over a rather narrow zone.

In French, *poisson inconnu* means "unknown fish," and the name stuck to the large whitefish we now call the INCONNU. It is also called Sheefish by many Alaskans, and it is part of the staple diet of Native Alaskans of the Far North.

An even more important staple to Native inhabitants of Alaska is the EULACHON, which spawns in vast numbers in river mouths, where writhing masses of them can be dipped from the water. This fish is so oily that not only can it be rendered easily into cooking oil, but whole dried fish can have a wick inserted and be burned like a candle. The name, in fact, derives from the Chinook word for "candlefish."

Status

The freshwater fishes of Alaska's mostly pristine lakes and streams are flourishing, but the same cannot be said for these animals in other parts of North America. Numerous fishes of rivers and springs in arid western USA are listed as Endangered because the limited water in their habitat is used by humans for consumption, irrigation, and/or recreation. The names of some of these species (each from a different fish family) tell of the wetlands so affected: GILA TROUT, COLORADO SQUAWFISH, MODOC SUCKER, DEVIL'S HOLE PUPFISH, PAHRUMP KILLIFISH, and CLEAR CREEK GAMBUSIA.

Profiles

Alaska Blackfish, *Dallia pectoralis*, Plate 10a
Pacific Lamprey, *Entosphenus tridentatus*, Plate 10b
Eulachon, *Thaleichthys pacificus*, Plate 10c
Burbot, *Lota lota*, Plate 10d
Ninespine Stickleback, *Pungitius pungitius*, Plate 10e

Threespine Stickleback, *Gasterosteus aculeatus*, Plate 10f
Inconnu, *Stenodus leucichthys*, Plate 11a

3. Marine Fishes

There are many more marine than freshwater species of fish in Alaska, but we profile only a small percentage of them, as the ecotraveller is unlikely to encounter most of them. Most of the profiled species are relatively large and are included here because they are more likely to be seen in a commercial aquarium or fish market or on the dinner table, but remember that there are actually many more small than large species, as is typical of most animal groups. We also include two small species, the PACIFIC HERRING (Plate 15) and PACIFIC SAND LANCE (Plate 15), of great importance in the diet of a wide variety of marine fishes, birds, and mammals. Alaska's largest fish, the BASKING SHARK, reaches a length of 12 m (40 ft), while the smallest species are many sculpins in the range of 5 to 7.5 cm (2 to 3 in). Peruse the plates to see the great range of shapes and colors in this group.

Natural History
Ecology and Behavior
The fish profiled in this section run the gamut of fish natural history. Just by looking at a fish, it is possible to conclude much about its life-style. For example, about half the fish species profiled here have relatively large mouths and thus would appear to be predators, in most cases on other fishes. The LINGCOD (Plate 14) and GREAT SCULPIN (Plate 13) are good examples. Small-mouthed species such as the STARRY FLOUNDER (Plate 14) feed on smaller prey, primarily invertebrates.

Dark-colored mottled fish such as sculpins and greenlings would be well camouflaged against bottom rocks and algae, and indeed that is where they hang out. The *flatfishes* (flounder, halibut, and sole) go even further in being confirmed bottom-dwellers, always resting on one side, which has become depigmented. As they swim, this whitish side always faces the bottom. Furthermore, during early growth, the eye on that side migrates over to the side that is exposed, so both eyes end up on the same side of these quite asymmetrical fishes. Other fishes, such as rays and skates, also live on the bottom but are flattened (*depressed*) rather than narrowed from side to side (*compressed*). Fishes that swim in open water are better camouflaged by being plain-colored and *countershaded* – dark above and light below – so the light shining on them from above lightens their dark upperside, and their own shadow darkens their light underside. Thus from the side they blend amazingly well with the water. Both predators, such as the SABLEFISH (Plate 15), and prey, such as the herring and sand lance, show this type of coloration.

Fish fins also vary substantially. The WOLF-EEL (Plate 13) has long dorsal and anal fins that are continuous with the caudal fin, enhancing its locomotion, which consists of the body moving in *sine waves*. These are waves of muscle contraction that travel backward along the body to move the fish forward, or with equal facility, forward to move it backward! This *undulatory* locomotion is characteristic of all very long-bodied fishes. Most fishes move by using *oscillatory* locomotion, the body flexing back and forth and propulsion furnished primarily by the large caudal fin. In this type of locomotion, steering and braking are accomplished by the paired pectoral and pelvic fins. The large group tank in a marine aquarium is a great place to observe different locomotory styles.

Breeding

Most marine fishes lay their eggs on the bottom (*demersal* eggs). In some of the species profiled here, males choose nest sites and defend them against other males. Females visit the males, spawn with them, and leave their eggs behind to be guarded by the male. This is true in the greenlings (including the LINGCOD), sculpins, and WOLF-EEL, although the latter takes parental care one step further because both sexes guard the eggs, a rather unusual breeding strategy in fishes. Parental care serves two functions, protection of the eggs against the many smaller fish that would make a meal of them, and maintaining a steady supply of oxygenated water over the eggs by fanning with their fins. Amazingly, the "reward" for many males that guard eggs is to eat a small percentage of them during the guarding period. As the males are often too busy to forage, and as they may attract a number of females to lay in their nests, they are probably cropping a surplus from a nest in which not all the eggs would hatch anyway (if, say, they were laid too densely or became conspicuous enough to attract predators that might overcome the males' defenses). As a further complication, the eggs of some sculpins are poisonous and brightly colored, perhaps the same sort of warning coloration that protects unpalatable tropical butterflies.

None of the fishes that guard eggs extends parental care to its young, which are on their own after hatching, either to spread out gradually through their habitat or, in some fish families, move up into the water column and disperse in prevailing currents.

PACIFIC HERRING participate in mass spawnings, with millions of fish aggregating near the shore in shallow bays to lay their eggs on all available substrates, including kelp. Each female lays tens of thousands of eggs, and there is so much *milt* (the sperm-containing fluid) that the water looks milky white from a distance. These spawning frenzies attract thousands of seabirds and dozens of pinnipeds that gorge themselves on fresh herring; some of the same predators and many invertebrates feast on the eggs. PACIFIC SAND LANCE spawn in much smaller groups but are unusual in laying eggs on the open sand, even riding in on waves to lay them on wet sand above the tide line. The larvae that hatch from the eggs are washed off the beach by later high tides.

Other species spawn in open water, the eggs floating free in the current (*pelagic* eggs). This group includes the cods, SABLEFISH, and, surprisingly, the flatfishes. These eggs typically develop into pelagic larvae, which continue to drift in the current and either mature as midwater fishes or, in the case of the flatfishes, settle to the bottom and undergo metamorphosis into an immature fish much like the adult; growth to sexual maturity follows. In both of these spawning types, the young are consumed by larger predators as they grow, and very few reach maturity.

Ecological Interactions

The way that biologists view how animals distribute themselves within an area has been partially worked out by thinking about how fish might arrange themselves in a lake or in the ocean. Predation is a major worry for many animals, including fish, and it doubtless influences many aspects of their lives. Often, there is safety in numbers, the rationale being that, although a group is larger than a single animal and therefore more easily located by a predator, the chance of any one animal in the group being taken is low, and so associating with the group, instead of striking out on one's own, is advantageous to an individual. But within the group, where should an individual herring, say one named Harry, position himself to minimize his chances of being eaten?

If the predator is a large fish such as a salmon that for lunch will take one smaller fish, the best place for Harry is between two other herrings, so that his left and right are "protected," the neighbor fish there to be eaten first. To gain such advantageous positioning, clearly Harry's best move would be to find two fish near each other and move into the gap between them. If such a strategy exists, then the neighboring fish should move in turn, also trying to fit into small gaps. Eventually, all the herrings in the area, if playing this game, should end up in a school, the best protected fish at its center. The formation of a fish school needs no other explanation than a bunch of fish heading for the center of their group! This *selfish herd* explanation for the formation of fish and other animal aggregations was first proposed about 30 years ago.

Not all fishes can benefit by getting together in schools. Herrings eat *plankton*, minute crustaceans that can be very abundant in the productive Alaska waters, so large numbers of the fish can travel together and still find enough to eat. Larger fish can't aggregate in such large groups, as they couldn't find enough to eat and would get in each others' way when chasing prey.

Lore and Notes

What is really impressive about fish schools is their cohesion, which of course you would expect, if they were all trying to stay very close together. If you watch a school of herrings, especially as they are being attacked, you can see how they almost seem to move as one, a remarkable feat when you consider that they have no known means to communicate with one another. In flying bird flocks, it appears that an individual on one edge of the flock begins to turn, and the action spreads almost immediately through the entire flock. They seem to be synchronous, but in fact there is an almost imperceptible delay from bird to bird. For more about this, see under Shorebirds (p. 132).

Status

Fishes are among the creatures most at risk on our planet, in particular those that are used as food by humans. A number of the most common Alaska fishes, for example, PACIFIC COD, WALLEYE POLLOCK, and PACIFIC HAKE (all Plate 15), have had abundant fisheries in the Bering Sea decline precipitously ("collapse" is a word that has been used to describe the situation) after a few decades of heavy fishing pressure. It may also be that some of the population declines are to be attributed to severe El Niño situations (periodic shifting of some Pacific Ocean currents and associated warming of oceanic regions) that have reached so far north that they affected food chains far from their tropical origins.

The Walleye Pollock is perhaps the best example of overfishing disasters. Probably more of these fish are caught by commercial fishermen each year than any other fish species in the world. The Bering Sea is dotted with boats every summer, both the fishing boats themselves and huge "factory" ships that process the fish as they are brought in by their fleet. The methods by which the pollock are caught are sufficiently efficient to decimate local populations and to have a major effect on the entire Bering Sea stock. It may not be a coincidence that Steller's Sea Lions, Common Murres, and Black-legged Kittiwakes have all decreased in Alaska – Walleye Pollock are mainstays in their diets. It would seem a shame to lose these species to the world's desire for surimi and sushi. Fortunately, a new net has recently been designed that greatly reduces the capture of juvenile pollocks and other "bycatch" (the unwanted sea life brought up in fishing nets that are not commercially useful but nevertheless perish during the process).

Profiles

Pacific Staghorn Sculpin, *Leptocottus armatus*, Plate 13a
Pacific Ocean Perch, *Sebastes alutus*, Plate 13b
Yelloweye Rockfish, *Sebastes ruberrimus*, Plate 13c
Great Sculpin, *Myoxocephalus polyacanthocephalus*, Plate 13d
Wolf-eel, *Anarrhichthys ocellatus*, Plate 13e

Petrale Sole, *Eopsetta jordani*, Plate 14a
Kelp Greenling, *Hexagrammos decagrammus*, Plate 14b
Starry Flounder, *Platichthys stellatus*, Plate 14c
Lingcod, *Ophiodon elongatus*, Plate 14d
Pacific Halibut, *Hippoglossus stenolepis*, Plate 14e

Pacific Herring, *Clupea pallasii*, Plate 15a
Pacific Sand Lance, *Ammodytes hexapterus*, Plate 15b
Pacific Cod, *Gadus macrocephalus*, Plate 15c
Walleye Pollock, *Theragra chalcogramma*, Plate 15d
Pacific Hake, *Merluccius productus*, Plate 15e
Sablefish, *Anoplopoma fimbria*, Plate 15f

Environmental Close-up 3:
The Miracle of the Salmon

One of the features that makes the life of an individual salmon so fantastic is the distance it may travel in that life. When one comes upon a salmon river in autumn, the bank littered by dying, dead, and decomposing fish (with their hooked jaws, sharp teeth, and tattered flesh, they look like monsters), one has to ask "why did they die?" Salmon are considered *semelparous*, a technical term meaning "breeding only once," that is usually reserved for small animals and plants that live only a year. Most large animals are *iteroparous*, breeding more than once. But one spawning is all a big Chinook or any other Pacific salmon gets, after a fairly long and very full life of finding food, escaping predators, and always travelling, travelling, travelling. The distance a salmon travels during its lifetime is awesome; a single Chinook may hatch 1600 km (1000 miles) up the Yukon River system in interior Alaska, make the perilous journey downriver to the sea, then move out into the Bering Sea or North Pacific Ocean, travelling in currents and perhaps moving as far seaward as 4000 km (2500 miles) from the river mouth. But that's only half the journey; the same fish must make it all the way back whence it came, to that same tributary of the Yukon River! Journeys of this distance seem to make sense for birds, but salmon have to propel themselves through a dense medium, water, and they must swim upcurrent for a substantial part of their journey.

The first question to ask is "why anadromy?" That is, why do many marine fishes spend much of their life in salt water but move into freshwater rivers to spawn? The answer to this is straightforward, especially in this part of the world. Marine habitats of Alaska are very productive, and a fish such as a salmon can grow much more rapidly in salt water than in fresh. Thus a salmon in salt water can grow to be a large salmon, and a large salmon has a greater reproductive potential than a small one. Why go back to fresh water, then? This probably has to do with predation. Predators are abundant in salt water, and salmon eggs laid on the bottom would be subject to intense predation, as would the newly hatched young. The adults could not guard the eggs, as many bottom-dwelling marine fishes do, as they are not bottom fish; they travel and feed in midwater. Well up freshwater rivers, predators on both eggs and young are few. So this round trip is an evolutionary answer to the ecological conditions prevailing throughout the range of the Pacific salmons.

Recent research has attempted to answer the question of why these fishes get only one chance at reproduction. In a way, it's not surprising. The salmon stop feeding when they get to their appropriate river mouth, then have to undergo physiological changes to suit them for the freshwater environment. As they move upstream, never feeding again, their bodies begin to self-digest, their muscles fueled by the breakdown of other tissues, for example in the digestive system.

But why has this peculiar pattern evolved? It turns out that the streams in which salmon spawn are, for the most part, not very productive. The water is cold, sunlight doesn't penetrate the forest canopy in many of them (so there is almost no plant growth), and populations of aquatic insects are generally sparse. Much of the productivity in the stream, interestingly enough, comes from its surroundings, plant matter and soil that wash into the stream and give it some organic nutrients, which in turn support freshwater invertebrates that in turn feed the young salmon.

Well, guess what all those dead adult salmon provide for these nutrient-poor streams. You're right, nutrients! The decaying salmon add quite measurably to the nutrient level in the streams, and although many drift downstream well below where their own eggs will hatch, the overall productivity of the system is much enhanced, and all young salmon in the stream surely benefit as this nutrient pulse goes up the food chain. In addition, it has been discovered that not only do the salmon feed quite a variety of predators and scavengers, but also their carcasses increase the productivity of the nearby uplands; and those are the source of still more nutrients.

Finally, to answer the question that's been on your mind since you started reading this section: how does a fish, which, let's admit, is probably not the brightest animal in the world, find its birth stream after years in the ocean? Well, first of all, they probably navigate through the ocean by a variety of means, including the position of the sun, the direction of currents, and the Earth's magnetic field. Salmonids have been shown to be receptive to magnetic fields, and the receptors are almost surely tiny bits of *magnetite* (an iron-containing compound) in cells associated with the nostrils. As they approach the coast, another mechanism takes over, their sense of smell. Apparently each river system has a unique mixture of chemicals, and anadromous fishes can find their way to the mouth of their own river, then ascend that and pick out their own home stream in the same way. These fish essentially follow their noses!

Chapter 9

AMPHIBIANS

- *General Characteristics and Natural History*
- *Seeing Amphibians in Alaska*
- *Family Profiles*
  1. *Salamanders*
  2. *Toads*
  3. *True Frogs*

General Characteristics and Natural History

Amphibians first arose during the mid part of the Paleozoic Era, 400 million years ago, developing from fish ancestors that had lungs and thus could breathe air. The word "amphibian" refers to an organism that can live in two worlds, and that is as good a definition of the amphibians as any. Most stay in or near the water, but many spend at least portions of their lives on land. In addition to lungs, amphibians generally have wet, thin skins that aid in gas exchange (breathing). Amphibians were also the first animals to develop legs for walking on land, the basic design of which has remained remarkably constant for all other land vertebrates. Many have webbed feet that aid locomotion in the water.

Approximately 4800 species of living amphibians have been described. Almost all reptiles, birds, and mammals living on Earth have been identified, but most experts agree that many more amphibians, with their small size and secretive ways, remain to be discovered. They are separated into three groups. There are about 400 species of *salamanders*, of the order Caudata (*cauda* = tail); most have four limbs and look like lizards with smooth skin. The *caecilians* (sih-SEA-lians), of the order Gymnophiona (*gymno* = naked, *ophio* = snake), with 165 species in the tropics, look for all the world like giant earthworms with big mouths and beady eyes. The *frogs* and *toads*, of the order Anura (*an* = without, *ura* = tail), make up the bulk of the group, with about 4200 species. Tailless and with extra-long hind legs, they are easily recognizable. The great diversity of frogs is in the tropics, where new species are discovered every year, but some groups are common in the temperate zones.

Most amphibians live in the water during part of their lives. Typically the larval stage is spent in the water and the adult stage on land. Because amphibians need to keep their skin wet, even when on land they are mostly found in moist habitats – in marshes and swamps, around the periphery of bodies of water, and in wet forests. Adults of most species return to the water to lay eggs, which must stay moist to develop. Some amphibians – a few hundred species of frogs, salamanders, and caecilians – are entirely terrestrial, laying eggs on land in moist places.

Salamanders are an almost exclusively north temperate-zone group. In the tropics they usually inhabit moist, cool areas, such as middle and higher elevation cloud forests. About 175 species are completely terrestrial. Females of these species lay eggs in moist places, and most stay with the eggs, sometimes coiling themselves around them and protecting them until hatching. *Newts* are a group of aquatic salamanders, often with rough-textured skin. Many lay their eggs singly on pond bottoms or on vegetation, but other aquatic salamanders lay their eggs in large, jelly-covered clusters, which they attach to sticks or plants in the water. The aquatic salamanders do not protect their eggs.

Most species of frogs and toads live in tropical or semi-tropical areas but some groups are abundant in temperate latitudes. Frogs can be either mostly aquatic or mostly terrestrial; some of the terrestrial species spend most of their life in trees. A few species of frogs live in deserts by staying underground, remaining moist enough to survive. At the arrival of periodic rains, they dig to the surface and breed in temporary ponds before heading back underground. The eggs hatch, and the froglets burrow underground before the ponds dry. Toads constitute a group of frogs that have relatively thick, dry skin that reduces water loss, permitting them to live on land. Most frogs and toads leave their eggs to develop on their own, but a few guard nests or egg masses, and some species actually carry their eggs on their backs or in skin pouches. Two species swallow their eggs, and they develop in the vocal sacs of a South American species and the stomach of an Australian species, the live young later emerging through the mouth.

Frogs and toads are known for the vocal communication of males, which during breeding periods call loudly from land or water, attempting to attract females. Each species has a different call. Some species breed *explosively* in synchronous groups; on a single night thousands gather at ponds, where males call and compete for females, and females choose from among available suitors. Many frogs, such as BULLFROGS, fight fiercely for the best calling spots and over mates. Because frogs have no weapons such as teeth or sharp claws with which to fight, size usually determines the winners. Some species of frogs and toads have developed *satellite* strategies to obtain matings. Instead of staking out a calling spot and vocalizing themselves (which is energy-draining and risky because calling attracts predators), satellite males remain silent but stay furtively near calling males, and attempt to intercept and mate with approaching females. Smaller males are more likely to employ such "sneaky" tactics.

All amphibians as adults are predatory carnivores – as far as it is known, there is not a vegetarian among them. Larval salamanders are also carnivores, but most larval frogs (*tadpoles*) graze on algae and other aquatic plants. Many animals eat amphibians, although it is not as easy as you might think. At first glance amphibians appear to be among the most defenseless of animals. Most are small, many are relatively slow, and their teeth and claws are not the types appropriate for aggressive defense. But a closer look reveals an array of ingenious defenses. Most, perhaps all, amphibians produce skin toxins, many of which are harmless to humans and so not very noticeable, but a few of which are very poisonous, even lethal. These toxins deter predators.

Most amphibians are *cryptically colored*, often amazingly difficult for people, and presumably predators, to detect in their natural settings. The jumping locomotion of frogs probably evolved as an anti-predator strategy; it is an effective way of escaping quickly through leaves, dense grass, thickets, or shrubby areas and, especially, straight into the water. When captured, some frogs give loud, startling screams, creating opportunities for escape.

In general, amphibians are under less direct threat from people than are other vertebrate groups, there being little commercial exploitation of the group (aside from certain people's taste for frogs' legs). However, amphibians are very sensitive to pollution, both because their moist skin absorbs chemicals from both air and water and because their aquatic eggs and larvae are very susceptible to toxic substances. Many amphibian populations have been declining noticeably in recent years, although the reasons are not entirely clear. Much research attention is currently focused on determining which of these reported population changes are real and significant and their causes. Not all ecologists agree on what is going on, but possible causes include the increase of ultraviolet radiation reaching the earth because of a thinning ozone layer caused by air pollution; acid rain from polluting industries changing the chemical balance of breeding ponds; the introduction of non-native predatory fishes, crayfishes, and bullfrogs into many wetlands; and, most recently and perhaps most devastatingly, a deadly virus that has been killing frogs in regions as far apart as Australia and Central America.

Seeing Amphibians in Alaska

Amphibians, although tolerant of cold, don't thrive at high latitudes with hard-frozen winters, so the first step in seeing amphibians in Alaska is to get as far south as you can in the state! In most of the state, if you see a frog, you can be assured it is a WOOD FROG (Plate 16), but in the far south, you might see another frog, a toad, and three salamanders. All of Alaska's amphibians have aquatic larvae, so look for adults in moist areas near water and larvae in lakes and ponds. Only the NORTHWESTERN SALAMANDER is truly difficult to see; you have every chance of encountering the other five amphibian species that occur in Alaska.

Amphibians will most likely be found in moist habitats – wet forests, near bodies of water, in small pools and puddles, and along streams. One of the best ways to find secretive salamanders is to turn over rocks and logs in these habitats, or look through and under leaf litter. But make sure you replace your divots! Most adult salamanders are nocturnal, so a night walk with flashlight or headlamp is often a good way to see them. The best time is during a rainy night (although not during torrential downpours) in spring, when most species breed. They are often found crossing roads on these wet nights, sometimes even during daylight hours. ROUGH-SKINNED NEWTS (Plate 16) are often seen near shore in their breeding ponds, where they swim slowly, crawl along the bottom, or cling to aquatic vegetation. In many parts of the world, the breeding calls of male frogs are the best clues of their presence, but Alaska frogs by and large are relatively quiet, the loudest species, the WOOD and COLUMBIA SPOTTED FROGS (Plate 16), uttering short croaks that can be heard only at the breeding pond.

Family Profiles

1. Salamanders

Salamanders are long, generally slender amphibians with four limbs. They loosely resemble lizards in body plan, but their skin is smooth and moist – both from the aquatic or moist locales that they inhabit and the skin secretions that keep their skin wet for breathing. Salamanders are secretive and usually nocturnal in their activities, much less frequently encountered than frogs. Three species occur in Alaska.

Natural History

Ecology and Behavior

In contrast to frogs, with their vegetarian tadpole phase, all salamanders, both juveniles and adults, are carnivores. They feed opportunistically, essentially snapping at and trying to ingest whatever squirms and will fit into their mouths. This includes insects and spiders on land, but also small frogs and other salamanders. Because studying salamanders in the wild is difficult, relatively little is known about what eats them, but the list includes snakes, other salamanders, frogs, fish, and a few birds and mammals. Both of the salamanders we profile are terrestrial as adults but must return to the water to breed.

Breeding

Breeding occurs in spring, typically as soon as the pond surface becomes ice-free. Salamanders are known for their complex mating behavior. Unlike frogs, salamander males do not call to advertise territories or attract mates, but males do fight each other for females. Losers employ various strategies to try to interfere with the winners' mating – either physically inserting themselves between a female and a courting male, or approaching the mating pair, which distracts the male, causing him to pause or stop.

How sperm gain access to eggs in salamanders is different from the way one might expect. Following a surprisingly complex courtship ritual, the male deposits a tiny, cone-shaped packet, called a *spermatophore*, on the substrate, either on land or in the water. The spermatophore contains the male's complement of sperm for that breeding episode. The female maneuvers until she can pick it up with her *vent* (the opening on her underside to reproductive, excretory, and digestive systems), which permits the sperm to gain access to her reproductive tract. She can then store the sperm for many months, having it always available to fertilize her eggs.

In the two profiled salamanders, females lay a clutch of eggs associated with an aquatic plant. The LONG-TOED SALAMANDER (Plate 16) lays its 6 to 60 eggs in a jellylike mass about the size of a walnut, typically surrounding a plant stem, while the ROUGH-SKINNED NEWT (Plate 16) lays its eggs singly, often in the axils of leaves, where they are well hidden. Egg masses of NORTHWESTERN SALAMANDERS, also found in southern Alaska, are very conspicuous in the spring, often green from symbiotic algae that grow within the masses. There is no parental care. Eggs hatch in 2 to 9 weeks, the shorter times at higher water temperatures. The larvae that emerge from the eggs are quite different from the adults that laid them. Larval aquatic salamanders have conspicuous external gills for extracting oxygen from the water and high tail fins to swim rapidly away from potential predators. The larvae undergo *metamorphosis* (change from larval to adult stages) at about six months to a year of age and mature sexually in another 2 to 5 years.

Ecological Interactions

Salamanders are usually inconspicuous and hidden to casual observers. Actually, however, they are integral parts of the forest animal community, often being very abundant in good habitat. Therefore, they are one of the predominant predators on insects, acting to keep many bug populations in check. The species discussed here spend much time in fresh water, where they take many kinds of small crustaceans, insects, clams, snails, and the eggs and larvae of other amphibians.

In addition to hiding, escaping down a hole, and, in some species, biting, to prevent themselves from becoming another animal's meal, salamanders employ an arsenal of chemical weapons. All of them apparently have skin secretions that are sufficiently toxic or distasteful to render them unpalatable to most potential predators, and some of the secretions contain potent poisons. Numerous vertebrates (including a Pied-billed Grebe, a Mallard, a Bullfrog, and a catfish) have been found dead after eating a ROUGH-SKINNED NEWT (however, a trout that had eaten one appeared healthy), and it has been estimated that the toxin from a single individual of this species, when diluted, could kill 25,000 laboratory mice! The NORTHWESTERN SALAMANDER is considerably less toxic but, if you capture one, you will see, oozing from large glands on its head and along its tail, a white liquid that presumably protects it from some predators. Amazingly, Common Garter Snakes have evolved immunity from salamander toxins and eat them freely, even the very poisonous newts. Garter snakes from outside the range of the Rough-skinned Newt do not possess this immunity.

Lore and Notes

Many salamanders apparently lead long lives, as do several other groups of cold-blooded animals. They have low metabolisms and they grow slowly in cool habitats, at times eating infrequently and going through long periods of in-activity. In captivity, some salamanders – for instance, one species from Japan – have lived more than 50 years, but the Alaska species probably live no longer than about 10 years.

Status

None of the Alaska salamanders is thought to be rare or threatened, although many salamander species in other parts of the world have declined as part of a seemingly general decline of amphibians (see p. 97).

Profiles

Rough-skinned Newt, *Taricha granulosa*, Plate 16a
Long-toed Salamander, *Ambystoma macrodactylum*, Plate 16b

2. Toads

Scientists sometimes have trouble formally differentiating *toads* from frogs, but not so nonscientists, who usually know their toads: they are the "uglies" of the frog world that one finds on land, not built for speed and with a rough, lumpy, warty appearance. Actually, toads are a kind of frog, both of them included in the amphibian order Anura. They have some special anatomical and reproductive traits that are used to set them apart (for instance, frogs lay eggs in jellied clusters, toads in jellied strings), but for our purposes, toads are squat, terrestrial frogs with short limbs, thick, relatively dry skin, and glands that resemble warts spread over their bodies. A few families of frogs are called toads, but the predominant group, hugely successful, is the *true toads*, family Bufonidae (*bufo* is the word for toad in Latin), which spread naturally to all continents except Australia (and has been introduced to that continent); all the toads occurring in the USA are in this family. *Bufonids* usually have two prominent *parotoid glands*, which look like really big warts, on each side of the neck area. Shades of olive or brown with black markings, toads vary in size from 2.5 to 20 cm (1 to 8 in) long and weigh up to 1200 g (2.5 lb) – the largest would be a dinner-plate-sized toad! Worldwide there are about 350 bufonid species; one occurs in Alaska, the WESTERN TOAD (Plate 16).

Natural History
Ecology and Behavior
Although their relatively heavy, dry skin (compared with that of other frogs) permits adult toads a permanently terrestrial existence, they experience some water loss through their skin, so unless they stay near water or buried in moist soil, they dry out and die in just a few days. Although freed from an aquatic life, their existence is still governed by water. Toads are primarily nocturnal, avoiding the sun and its drying heat by sheltering during the day under leaf litter, logs, or rocks, and coming out to forage after sundown. Toad tadpoles are vegetarians, feeding on green algae and bacteria in their aquatic habitats, but adult toads are all carnivorous, foraging for arthropods, mostly insects, amid the leaf litter. As one natural historian defines the toad diet, "if it's bite-sized and animate it is food, no matter how noxious, toxic, or biting/stinging." Beetles and ants are frequent prey, as are small vertebrates such as small frogs and salamanders.

With their short legs, toads are capable of covering only very short distances per hop, but they have two methods to escape being eaten. They can be extremely hard to detect, concealing themselves with their *cryptic coloration* and habit of slipping into crevices or under leaves or actually burying themselves in the earth. Also, apparently quite effectively, they exude noxious fluids from their skin glands – those funny-looking warts are an effective defense mechanism. When a toad is grabbed, a viscous, white fluid oozes from the warts. The fluid is very irritating to mucous membranes, such as those found in a predator's mouth and nose. At least some toads also have muscle control over the poison glands, and one large species was seen to spray the poison more than 25 cm (10 in). Most predators that pick up a toad probably do not do it twice; pets such as cats and dogs that put toads into their mouths have been killed by the poisons.

Breeding
Toads in Alaska breed in early summer. To breed, males migrate to ponds, where they swim actively in search of females. This is very competitive, as there may be 20 males per female. Males stay at the water and breed as much as they can, females visit just long enough to lay their eggs. After appropriate mating maneuvers of both sexes, sperm are released by a male in a cloud into the water, followed by a female releasing her eggs into the cloud. Thus fertilization is external; it happens outside of the animal. The eggs are laid within jellied strings, the jelly protecting the eggs physically and also, because it contains toxins, discouraging consumption by potential predators. Depending on species and size, a female may lay from 100 to 25,000 eggs at a time. The two long strings laid by a female WESTERN TOAD may extend 9 m (30 ft). Eggs hatch in only a few days,

releasing young in the larval feeding stage known familiarly as tadpoles (it's tempting to call them "toadpoles"). They feed, grow, and develop, transforming themselves into *toadlets* after a few weeks, which then swarm up the banks and disappear into their terrestrial existences. Toads generally reach sexual maturity in a year or two, although the period before breeding is longer in some species.

Ecological Interactions
A few predators, such as raccoons and opossums, having learned their way around toad anatomy, avoid the poison glands on the back and legs by eating only the inside of the toad, entering through the mostly wart-free belly. Skins of WESTERN TOADS that are found turned inside-out were probably left that way by raccoons; the rest of the toad is inside the raccoon. The tadpoles are as well protected by toxins as the other life-history stages. They swarm in tight aggregations of hundreds to thousands of individuals, and their shiny black coloration makes these swarms very conspicuous. Some swarms extend into a line, resembling a huge, coal-black snake slowly moving through the shallows. A predator that samples one of these bitter tadpoles will never bother such a swarm again.

Lore and Notes
The claim that a person will contract warts by handling toads is not true. Human warts are caused by viruses, not amphibians. The glands on toads' skin that resemble warts release noxious fluids to discourage predators. Various poisons have been identified in these fluids that, among other effects, cause increased blood pressure, blood vessel constriction, increased power of heartbeat, heart muscle tissue destruction, and hallucinations. Because these fluids minimally are irritants, a smart precaution is to avoid handling toads or, after such handling, make sure to wash your hands. Caustic irritation will result if the fluids are transferred from hands to eyes, nose or mouth. Some reports have it that voodoo practitioners in Haiti use the skin secretions of toads in their zombie-making concoctions.

Status
The WESTERN TOAD has decreased substantially farther south in its range, in Washington and Oregon, and Alaska populations need to be closely monitored. Some toads in other regions, for example, the GOLDEN TOAD of Costa Rica, have become extinct with the recent worldwide declines of amphibian populations. The cause of these declines is still poorly known, but one or more viruses have been implicated in Central America and Australia.

Profiles
Western Toad, *Bufo boreas*, Plate 16c

3. True Frogs

Frogs of the family Ranidae are known as *true frogs* not because they are less likely than other frogs to tell a lie but because they are the most common frogs of Europe, where the early classification of animals took place. With over 650 species, the true frogs, or *ranids*, now have a worldwide distribution, excepting most of Australia; most are in Africa. True frogs include many of what most people regard as typical frogs – green ones that spend most of their lives in water. Among frogs familiar to many North Americans, BULLFROGS and LEOPARD FROGS are members of the Ranidae. Typically ranids are streamlined, slim-waisted frogs with long legs, webbed hind feet, and thin, smooth skin. They are usually shades of green. Size varies greatly, up to the 30-cm (12-in) GOLIATH FROG of West Africa.

Natural History

Ecology and Behavior

These are aquatic frogs that are good swimmers and jumpers. With their webbed toes and long, muscular hind legs, they are built for speed on land or in water. This is fortunate for these frogs, because most lack the poison glands in their skins that many other types of frogs use to deter predation. They have thin skin through which water evaporates rapidly, and thus they tend to remain in or near water, often spending much of their time around the margins of ponds or floating in shallow water. Except during breeding seasons, they are active only during the day. True frogs feed mainly on insects, but also on fish and smaller frogs. In turn, they are common food items for an array of beasts such as wading birds, fish, turtles, and small mammals. Because they are such tasty morsels to so many predators, these frogs are very alert to their surroundings, attempting escape at the slightest movement or noise; the splashing heard as you walk along a pond or lakeshore is usually made by frogs on the shore leaping into the water. This is often accompanied by a loud vocalization, somewhere between a squeak and a shriek, perhaps given as a way to startle a potential predator.

Breeding

These frogs reproduce under what most would consider the standard amphibian plan. Eggs are released by the female into the water, where they are fertilized by sperm released by the male. In both the WOOD FROG (Plate 16) and COLUMBIA SPOTTED FROG (Plate 16), the eggs are laid in a jellied plum- to orange-sized mass containing hundreds of eggs, often those of several females sticking together. They are either laid at the surface or soon float up there. The eggs, black above and white below, hatch in a few weeks, and the tadpoles develop during the summer or into the following summer, metamorphosing into little 2-cm (3/4-inch) *froglets*. Sexual maturity occurs in from 1 to 4 years.

Ecological Interactions

Frogs are voracious predators on anything smaller than themselves. As they are mostly aquatic, they feed while in the water, but most of their food is at and above the surface. Swimming insects, other frogs, salamanders, and even small fish at the surface are fair game. Above the surface, a host of flying insects are taken. A dragonfly, for instance, slowly patrolling over the pond is out of luck if it passes over a large frog, which will leap up to 0.5 m (1.5 ft) into the air after it. The dragonfly disappears down the frog's gullet, the pond surface calms, and the frog awaits another such meal.

Lore and Notes

The true frogs have always provided a minor source of protein to people throughout the world – there's no accounting for national and ethnic taste. These frogs are non-toxic, abundant, and large enough to make harvesting and preparation economically profitable. American BULLFROGS are not only hunted from boats with gigs (multipronged spears such as Neptune, God of the Sea, carries) but also raised in captivity for this purpose. In much of Europe and pockets of the USA, the muscles of the long bones of the hind legs, often dusted with flour and fried in butter, are eaten. Although perhaps an acquired taste, they are unquestionably tasty.

Status

Alaska has not obviously suffered declining amphibian populations, but farther south the OREGON SPOTTED FROG, a very close relative of Alaska's COLUMBIA SPOTTED FROG, has disappeared from much of its former range in western Washington and Oregon.

Profiles

Columbia Spotted Frog, *Rana luteiventris*, Plate 16d
Wood Frog, *Rana sylvatica*, Plate 16e

Chapter 10

BIRDS

- *Birds: Animals to Watch*
- *General Characteristics and Natural History*
- *Seeing Birds in Alaska*
- *Alaska's Seabirds*
- *Family Profiles*
    1. *Loons and Grebes*
    2. *Tube-nosed Birds*
    3. *Cormorants*
    4. *Waterfowl*
    5. *Raptors*
    6. *Chickenlike Birds*
    7. *Cranes*
    8. *Shorebirds*
    9. *Jaegers, Gulls, and Terns*
    10. *Puffins and Their Relatives*
    11. *Owls*
    12. *Hummingbirds*
    13. *Kingfishers*
    14. *Woodpeckers*
    15. *Flycatchers*
    16. *Larks and Pipits*
    17. *Swallows*
    18. *Crows and Jays*
    19. *Chickadees, Nuthatches, and Creepers*
    20. *Wrens and Dippers*

Birds: Animals to Watch

Most of the vertebrate animals one sees on a visit to just about anywhere at or above the water's surface are birds, and Alaska is no exception. Regardless of how the rest of a trip's wildlife-viewing progresses – how fortunate one is to observe land or marine mammals, or amphibians – birds will be seen frequently and in large numbers. The reasons for this pattern are that birds, as opposed to all other vertebrates but fish, are most often active during the day and are visually conspicuous. In addition, they are often quite vocal as they pursue their daily activities. But why are birds so much more conspicuous than other vertebrates? The reason goes to the essential nature of birds: they fly. The ability to fly is, so far, nature's premier anti-predator escape mechanism. Animals that can fly well are relatively less prone to predation than those that cannot, and so they can be reasonably certain of daily survival even while being somewhat conspicuous in their behavior. Birds can fly quickly from dangerous situations, and, if you will, remain above the fray. Flightless land vertebrates, tied to moving in or over the ground or on plants, are easy prey unless they are quiet, concealed (including being nocturnal), and careful; very large or fierce; or equipped with special defense mechanisms such as poisons or venoms.

A fringe benefit of birds being the most frequently encountered kind of vertebrate is that birds are, to the ecotraveller, entirely innocuous. Typically the worst that can happen from an encounter is a soiled shirt. Contrast that with close encounters with certain insects (any one of Alaska's biters), amphibians (salamanders with toxic skin secretions), and mammals (bears). Better yet, birds do not always depart with all due haste after being spotted, as do most other types of vertebrates. Again, their ability to fly and thus easily evade our grasp permits many birds, when confronted with people, to go about their business (keeping one eye at all times on the strange-looking bipeds), allowing us extensive time to watch them. Not only are birds among the safest animals to observe and the most easily discovered and watched, but they are among the most beautiful.

Experiences with Alaska's birds will almost certainly provide some of any trip's finest, most memorable moments. A human visitor at a seabird colony, for instance, with a half-dozen or more species and many thousands of individual birds in view, has all senses stimulated to the maximum, far past the familiar and bordering on the overwhelming. That soiled shirt is surely worth it.

General Characteristics and Natural History

Birds are vertebrates that can fly. They began evolving from reptiles during the Jurassic Period of the Mesozoic Era, perhaps 150 million years ago, and saw explosive development of new species occur during the last 50 million years or so. Debate about their exact ancestors (were they in the same group as the *Velociraptor* made famous by the movie *Jurassic Park*?) at this time is intense. As diverse as birds are now, it is thought that there were even more species prior to the Ice Ages. The development of flight is the key factor behind birds' evolution, their historical spread throughout the globe, and their current ecological success and arguably dominant position among the world's land animals. Flight, as mentioned above, is a fantastic predator-evasion technique, but it also permits birds to move over long distances in search of particular foods or habitats, and its development opened up for vertebrate exploration and exploitation an entirely new and vast theater of operations – the open air.

At first glance, birds appear to be highly variable animals, ranging in size and form from 135-kg (300-lb) ostriches to 4-kg (10-lb) eagles to 3-g (a tenth of an ounce) hummingbirds. (Some extinct birds were about twice the size of living ostriches!) Actually, however, when compared with other types of vertebrates, birds are remarkably standardized physically. The reason is that, whereas mammals or reptiles can be quite diverse in form and still function as mammals or reptiles (think how different in form are lizards, snakes, and turtles), if birds are going to fly, they more or less must look like birds, and have the anatomy and physiology of birds. The most important traits for flying are:

(1) feathers, which are unique to birds;
(2) powerful wings, which are modified forelimbs;
(3) hollow bones;
(4) warm-bloodedness; and
(5) efficient respiratory and circulatory systems.

These characteristics combine to produce animals with two overarching traits – high power and low weight, which are the twin dictates that make for successful flying machines. Bats, the only flying mammals, have followed a similar evolutionary pathway.

Currently about 9700 species of birds are recognized. Bird classification is in a state of flux at this time, with several competing systems. Depending on which system is followed, birds are divided into 23 to 30 orders, 145 to 170 families, and more than 2000 genera. For our purposes, we can divide birds into *passerines* and *nonpasserines*. Passerine birds (order Passeriformes) are the perching birds, with feet specialized to perch on tree branches. They are mostly the small land birds with which we are most familiar – swallows, robins, wrens, finches, sparrows, etc – and the group includes more than 50% of all bird species. The remainder of the birds – seabirds and shorebirds, ducks and geese, hawks and owls, kingfishers and woodpeckers, and a host of others – are divided among the other orders. Of the passerines, about three-quarters are *songbirds*, those with a more complex syrinx (the *syrinx* is the sound-producing organ, located where the trachea branches into two bronchi leading to the lungs, that produces the beautiful songs we associate with birds). The other fourth of the passerines consists of the flycatchers and their relatives, which are mostly confined to the New World Tropics and do not produce true songs (although they are quite able to communicate vocally).

Seeing Birds in Alaska

All of Alaska's common birds and many of its uncommon ones are illustrated in this book. Large birds (most of them aquatic in Alaska) are often out in the open, active at all times of day, and relatively easy to find. Small birds take a little more effort. The best way to spot them is to follow three easy steps:

(1) Look for them at the correct time. They are often most active, and vocalize most frequently, during early morning and late afternoon, and so can be best detected and seen during these times.
(2) Be quiet as you walk along trails or roads, and stop periodically to look around carefully. Not all birds are noisy, and some, even brightly colored ones, can be quite inconspicuous when they are in dense vegetation. Some species are so well camouflaged that hearing them is almost always the best way to find them.
(3) *Bring binoculars* on your trip. You would be surprised at the number of people who travel with the purpose of viewing wildlife and don't bother to bring binoculars. They need not be an expensive pair, but binoculars are essential for birdwatching. They also work for viewing dragonflies, mammals, fish, and any other wildlife that might not be at close range when encountered.

It would be a shame to leave Alaska without seeing at least some of its spectacular birds, such as loons, swans, cranes, oystercatchers, eagles, ptarmigans, and puffins. If you have trouble locating such birds, ask people – tour guides, resort employees, park personnel – about good places to see them. Fortunately, the period when most tourists visit Alaska – the summer – is the breeding season for most bird species, and birds are often most conspicuous when breeding. Song and courtship behavior are common in May and June, nesting is underway in June, and young birds abound in July; a few species have earlier or later seasons. Many people visit Alaska in late August and September because of fall colors and the absence of biting flies, but this is not a particularly good time for birdwatching because so many of Alaska's birds are migratory, leaving the state by late summer. Of course, some species are always present, and marine species will be common in late summer anywhere along the southern coast. There are lots of interesting seabirds in southern Alaska throughout the winter, but if you visit then, you had better be prepared psychologically and physically for cold, windy, rainy weather.

Alaska's Seabirds

Because of the irregular shoreline, varying climates, juxtaposition of deep and shallow waters, and currents and bottom topography that promote upwellings, Alaska's marine waters are extremely productive. Prodigious amounts of phytoplankton, zooplankton, pelagic and benthic invertebrates, and fishes are produced at increasingly higher levels of the food chains that characterize coastal and offshore environments. At the top of these rich marine food chains are seabirds and marine mammals, which are as abundant in the waters of Alaska as anywhere in the world.

Birds that use coastal waters are of two types: (1) *obligate marine species*, in which all populations use salt water; and (2) *facultative marine species*, in which only some populations use salt water, the others occurring in fresh water. The obligate species include most of the loons, all the tubenoses, Pelagic and Red-faced Cormorants, sea ducks, many shorebirds, and all alcids (puffins and relatives). Facultative species include Common Loon, Great Blue Heron, Double-crested Cormorant, and many waterfowl. In both of these groups, there are *resident marine species*, those that are present in Alaska throughout the year, and *seasonal marine species*, those in which breeding occurs in freshwater or upland environments, and marine environments are used only during the nonbreeding season. There are no marine-breeding bird species that move to freshwater or upland habitats after the breeding season, although individuals of some species do so.

Seasonality is the rule in natural systems. Few of the marine birds of Alaska are equally common in every month. Even those that are resident – present all year – vary in numbers seasonally because of the influx of additional birds from the south in summer, from the north in winter, or passing in either direction during the spring and fall migration periods. A relative minority of species, including the familiar Bald Eagle and Glaucous-winged Gull, are present in equal numbers throughout the year. On the other hand, many species are present primarily or only in summer. Many seabird species winter to the south but move north into Alaska to breed, including all those species that breed on shorelines adjacent to parts of the ocean that freeze during the winter – the Beaufort Sea and much of the Bering Sea. Some species that are pelagic in the nonbreeding season move inshore to coastal islands to nest while continuing to feed at sea, for example, Fork-tailed Storm-Petrel, Cassin's Auklet, and Tufted Puffin. Pelagic species from other parts of the Pacific also move into Alaska's productive waters during summer. They include Black-footed and Laysan Albatrosses from Hawaii, Sooty Shearwaters from New Zealand, and Short-tailed Shearwaters from Australia. That individuals of some of these species fly over 11,000 km (7000 miles) to reach the Bering Sea is testimony to the productivity of this rich water body.

No seabirds are present in the state only during winter, but hundreds of thousands of birds that breed in freshwater and tundra habitats in the interior and northern parts of Alaska retreat to the southern coast (and farther south) and become seabirds during the winter. These birds include loons, grebes, waterfowl, shorebirds, and gulls. Other species, especially shorebirds, migrate through southern Alaska in great numbers, present only in spring or fall or, more commonly, both. Some shorebirds move through Alaska from Siberia on their way to tropical or even southern hemisphere wintering grounds on either side of the Pacific.

The magnitude of seabird migrations must be seen to be believed. At times, especially during April and May and again from July through October, migration can be observed directly and migrants can be censused accurately, as single birds and flocks of dozens to hundreds move past observers stationed on projecting points and jetties on the outer coast. Movements in excess of 100,000 birds per day have been recorded. Shorebird migration is similarly spectacular. The Copper River Delta in particular provides food for hundreds of thousands of individuals of sandpipers and plovers each spring, a spectacle that has generated sufficient public interest to warrant a Shorebird Festival at Cordoba during that period.

Three major diet categories support Alaska's seabird populations: plants, invertebrates, and fishes. Only a few species of waterfowl are obligate plant feeders, but they include locally abundant species such as Tundra Swan, Snow Goose, Brant, and American Wigeon. Invertebrates form the primary food for many species of waterfowl and most shorebirds. Fishes predominate in the diet of diving birds such as loons, grebes, cormorants, and alcids, and birds that fish from the air such as gulls and terns. Some species combine two of these three groups in their diets.

Clearly, a persistent base of food resources is essential to maintaining populations of marine bird species. A collapse in numbers of any organism at any level of the food web represents a potential threat to the concentrations that characterize seabirds at nesting colonies and favored feeding areas. They may withstand local resource collapse but, especially when tied to breeding areas, may not be able to travel sufficiently far to find food; complete breeding failure over fairly large areas may ensue. Fortunately, seabirds are long-lived and are thus not severely affected by single breeding failures, but multiple breeding failures, as from long-term perturbation by human activities, have more serious consequences.

Family Profiles

1. Loons and Grebes

Loons and *grebes* are diving birds, not closely related to one another but similarly modified for a life spent foraging for fish underwater. Their similarities include compact bodies, sharply pointed bills, relatively small wings, short (loons) or virtually absent (grebes) tails, short legs, and feet modified for underwater propulsion. Their differences are apparent as soon as one looks at their feet, which in loons have the front three toes connected by webs, as in most swimming birds; grebe feet, however, are not webbed, but their toes have lobes extending out from them. The result is the same: birds of both groups are amazingly fast swimmers underwater, where they pursue and capture fast-moving fishes. Being such effective divers handicaps them greatly for the terrestrial world, however; because of the structure of their legs and feet, neither of them can move about on land. When a grebe or loon washes up on the beach, the best it can do is propel itself back into the water with a series of grasshopperlike hops and flops.

Worldwide, there are five species of loons, family Gaviidae, and 22 species of grebes, family Podicipedidae. Alaska is the only place in the world where all five loon species breed, and most visitors have a chance to see four of them. Grebes are a more southerly group, and only three of them breed in the state, with another a rare visitor. Loons and grebes are *countershaded* – dark above and light below – like many birds that swim underwater. With light coming from above, the back of a countershaded bird (or fish or dolphin) is illuminated, and the underside is shadowed, and this causes them to blend amazingly with the water. All loons and the grebes profiled here have bright, contrasty breeding plumages and dull, brown to black nonbreeding plumages. All of Alaska's loons and the Horned Grebe have bright red eyes, which are obvious if you are close enough. Loons are easily distinguished from grebes by their much larger size and relatively shorter necks; they are also much more often seen in flight.

Natural History

Ecology and Behavior

Loons and grebes breed on fresh water but spend much of their year on salt water, where feeding conditions are better and the surface remains unfrozen in winter. They are among the most accomplished diving birds, disappearing below the surface with a thrust of their powerful feet and reappearing many meters away, perhaps with a fish held crosswise in their bill. When in deeper water, they typically jump into the air at the beginning of a dive, presumably to give them added momentum. Loons are very mobile, and some of them fly strongly among feeding grounds in response to the movements of schooling fishes, such as herrings and sand lances, that are carried by tidal currents. Others remain in shallow bays and capture bottom fishes such as sculpins and soles. Grebes are more sedentary but at times, like the loons, can be seen pursuing a special feeding strategy of repeatedly floating downcurrent, diving as they do so, and then flying upcurrent for another pass through rich feeding waters. Grebes have another special adaptation to deal with a fish diet; they swallow their own feathers, which apparently protect their stomach lining from sharp fish bones until the bones are sufficiently digested to pass down the rest of their gut.

Grebes often have a commensal relationship with other diving birds. HORNED GREBES (Plate 18) hang around flocks of feeding Surf Scoters; when the scoters dive, the grebes follow them. The scoters pop back up to the surface and quickly coalesce into a flock; the grebes surface randomly but immediately seek out the scoter flock. We don't know what is going on underwater, but it seems almost certain that the grebes follow the scoters and benefit whenever the mussel-eating scoter flushes a small fish or shrimp from the mussel bed.

Breeding

Both loons and grebes form *monogamous* pairs, the male and female forming a *pair bond* and sharing in all parental care, including nest-building, incubation of the eggs, and brooding and feeding of the young. They typically unite with their mate of the previous year, if both are still alive, when they encounter one another at the breeding lake. If one of the mates doesn't show up, the other has no hesitation in mating with another bird. Both loons and grebes have striking courtship displays, the loons displaying in flight and moving in unison on or under the water, and the grebes standing up breast to breast and shaking their heads simultaneously or taking brief runs across the water's surface; all this activity is accompanied by loud vocalizations. The nesting habits of both groups are somewhat similar, but the differences tell a nice ecological story. Their nests are big piles of aquatic vegetation at or on the water, as neither kind of bird can move about on land. Loon nests are built right at the shore, where the adults can slide on and off them; grebes, even less agile at maneuvering on a solid substrate, build floating nests. In both cases, vegetation is added to the nest continually, as it decays (and sinks, in the case of grebe nests). Loons typically lay 2 eggs and presumably can not rear more than 2 young in the large lakes where they breed. Some lakes at which loons nest contain no fish at all, and the adults, which are strong flyers, must travel to nearby, larger lakes to find food. Grebes, weaker flyers, must find productive waters on which to nest, and they can thus feed more young, so their clutches range from 4 to 6 eggs. Both sexes incubate the eggs alternately for 23 to 31 days in loons, 20 to 25 days in grebes. Young loons are plain-colored but still stand out in the open waters of large lakes; young grebes have strikingly striped heads, presumably to facilitate the adults' finding them among marsh vegetation. In both families, the adults feed the young until they are able to fly, 7 to 11 weeks after hatching. Because loons migrate during the day, the birds can keep together visually, so the young may remain with their parents in migration. Young and adult grebes part soon after the young can feed themselves.

Ecological Interactions
Loons are typically seen in small numbers and so you wouldn't think they would have much impact on fish populations. However, PACIFIC LOONS (Plate 17) sometimes collect into very large flocks, up to thousands of individuals, in which they feed on schooling fishes in deep passages. These spectacular aggregations, combined with similar numbers of cormorants, mergansers, gulls, and other fish-eating birds, are impressive in their visual impact and, presumably, in their ecological impact.

Lore and Notes
"Crazy as a loon" refers not to the dramatic aerial and aquatic courtship chases of a pair of loons on the breeding grounds, but instead to the weird but beautiful calls they give at that time. Loons often call at night, and their loud tremolos coming off a quiet northern lake are enough to produce chill bumps. All loons have memorable voices, although the typical flight call of the RED-THROATED LOON (Plate 17) sounds more like the croaking of a giant frog than the musical notes coming from the throats of its near relatives.

With their strong flight, loons migrate both day and night, but grebes do so only at night, probably because they are smaller and poorer fliers and during daylight would be at the mercy of hunting falcons and eagles.

Status
The COMMON LOON (Plate 17), although much reduced in numbers as a breeding species in the Lower 48 because of increased human disturbance to its breeding lakes, is still abundant in Canada and Alaska, in areas where wilderness prevails. The YELLOW-BILLED LOON (Plate 17) has a restricted wintering range, and large numbers of that species were killed during the *Exxon Valdez* oil spill of 1989; overall populations are not threatened, however.

Profiles
Red-throated Loon, *Gavia stellata*, Plate 17a
Pacific Loon, *Gavia pacifica*, Plate 17b
Yellow-billed Loon, *Gavia adamsii*, Plate 17c
Common Loon, *Gavia immer*, Plate 17d
Red-necked Grebe, *Podiceps grisegena*, Plate 18a
Horned Grebe, *Podiceps auritus*, Plate 18b

2. Tube-nosed Birds

The seabird order Procellariiformes includes the *albatrosses, shearwaters, petrels,* and *storm-petrels.* All are found only in marine (sea water) habitats, and they spend their entire lives at sea (a *pelagic* existence) except for relatively brief periods of nesting on islands. They have peculiar tube-shaped nostrils and distinctly hooked bills. Like other seabirds, they have a large gland above each eye that permits them to drink seawater; it filters salt from the water and concentrates it. This highly concentrated salt solution is excreted in drops from the base of the bill; the nostril tubes then direct the salt drops to the end of the bill, and the drops are then discharged by a toss of the head. Some of these tube-nosed seabirds, or *tubenoses,* will be seen by travellers to Alaska who take cruises; one of them, the NORTHERN FULMAR (Plate 19), breeds on many Alaska sea cliffs. The tubenoses include the largest and smallest seabirds, the largest of all being the WANDERING ALBATROSS, with a wingspan to 3.5 m (11.5 ft)! Alaska's tubenoses range from the very rare SHORT-TAILED ALBATROSS, at 91 cm (3 ft) long, to the small LEACH'S STORM-PETREL (Plate 18), at 20 cm (8 in). Albatrosses are large, heavy birds with very long wings and long, heavy, hooked bills. Shearwaters are small to mid-sized seabirds with slender, hooked bills. Storm-petrels are very small seabirds with longish wings and medium-length, slender, black bills. Most tubenoses, like many seabirds, are either all dark or dark above and lighter below.

The family Diomedeidae contains 14 albatross species, which are distributed over the world's southern oceans and the northern Pacific; 3 occur in Alaska waters. The family Procellariidae, with an essentially worldwide oceanic distribution, has 75 species of fulmars, petrels, and shearwaters; 4 species are seen regularly around Alaska. The family Hydrobatidae, also worldwide when at sea, includes 21 species of storm-petrels; 2 are found in Alaska.

Natural History
Ecology and Behavior

Albatrosses feed, either solitarily or in small groups, on fish and on squid and other invertebrates (crab larvae, krill) near the surface at night (and sometimes during the day). Larger species sit on the water and seize prey in their bills; smaller, more agile species can also seize prey from the surface while flying. Also, albatrosses are not above eating garbage thrown overboard from ships, as well as floating carrion such as dead whales and seals. They may go to sea for as long as a month to bring food back to nestlings. Albatrosses use a type of non-flapping flight, known as *dynamic soaring,* that takes advantage of strong winds blowing across the ocean's surface. Their efficient but peculiar soaring flight takes them in huge loops from high above the ocean surface, where the wind is fastest, down and across the wind at increasing speed toward the surface, where friction slows the wind. The birds then turn up into the higher wind speed again to give them lift for the next loop – a kind of roller coaster flight that requires virtually no flapping. Albatross wings are so long and narrow that these birds must have wind to help them fly, and on absolutely calm days (which, luckily for them, are rare on the open ocean), they must wait out the windless hours sitting on the sea's surface. In very windy conditions, whether they are on land or on the water, albatrosses need only spread their wings, and the wind moving past the wings provides sufficient lift to get them airborne. In low winds, they face into the wind (like an airplane taking off) and make a takeoff run; at island breeding colonies, often there are actual "runways," long, clear paths on the island's windward side, usually on slopes, along which the large birds make their downhill takeoff runs.

Petrels and shearwaters are also excellent flyers, some using dynamic soaring like albatrosses, some alternating flapping flight with gliding. They feed at sea by day or by night, often in groups, on squid, fish, and crustaceans, and some species dive underwater to feed. Storm-petrels pluck prey from the surface of the sea, using their wings to flutter and hover just above the water. The North Pacific and Bering Sea are so productive of sea life that flocks of tens of thousands of fulmars and shearwaters sometimes gather where their prey is especially abundant.

Tubenoses have perhaps the best developed sense of smell of any birds, and they use this ability not only to locate odoriferous food at the surface but also to locate their nest sites when returning from extended foraging trips. Tubenoses produce a vile-smelling stomach oil that they regurgitate to feed to nestlings and to squirt at enemies. The oil reputedly makes an excellent suntan lotion, but its smell would surely wreak havoc on your social life.

Breeding

Tubenoses breed usually in large, dense colonies, often but not always on small oceanic islands. Albatrosses are monogamous, and most breed with the same mate for life. On their remote breeding islands they engage in elaborate courtship dances in which male and female face each other, flick their wings, bounce their heads up and down, and clack their bills together. This behavior probably strengthens the pair bond and also coordinates hormone release and synchronizes mating readiness. Nests vary from a scrape on the bare ground to scrapes that are lined by vegetation, soil, and pebbles. The female lays one large egg. Male and female alternately incubate and brood the young, in shifts lasting several days to weeks. The other adult flies out to sea and searches for food. When it returns, it feeds the chick regurgitated fish and squid and stomach oil and takes over its turn at brooding again. When the chick's demand for food becomes overwhelming, both adults leave it alone for long periods as they search great distances over the ocean for enough food. An albatross you see in the Aleutian Islands may have flown there on a single lengthy foraging trip from Hawaii! Tubenose young store great amounts of fat when they are getting a lot of food, to tide them over leaner times, and at some point in its nestling period, a young albatross can actually weigh more than either of its parents. After about 7 months, the chick is large enough to fledge and leave the colony. Albatrosses take 5 to 7 years to mature, staying at sea during this period before finally returning to their birthplace to breed. Although they may return to their nesting island at 5 years of age, most individuals do not breed until they are 7 to 9 years old; some albatrosses in the wild live 40+ years.

The breeding of fulmars, shearwaters, and storm-petrels is basically similar to that of albatrosses. Some nest in the open, with nests simply small depressions in the ground, and fulmars nest on cliff ledges, but most are burrow or cavity nesters, nesting in a burrow they dig themselves or take over. The burrow or cavity is re-used each year by the same pair. In both fulmars and storm-petrels, one large egg is incubated for 6 to 10 weeks, both parents incubating the egg and feeding and brooding the chick, which remains in the nest for another 6 to 10 weeks. Both the incubation period and fledging period are exceptionally long in storm-petrels for the size of the birds; because these oceanic feeders must fly so far to find food, they are forced to neglect both eggs and young for longer periods than most birds.

Ecological Interactions

Although land-based naturalists may not see many of them, tubenoses are some of the most abundant birds in the world. Vast flocks of petrels, shearwaters, and storm-petrels are seen in different parts of the oceans, typically where marine productivity is very high and some fish, squid, or crustacean species is sufficiently abundant to support such bird numbers. The SOOTY SHEARWATER (Plate 19) has been nominated as the world's most abundant bird, but such an honor may be difficult to assign, as the more common a bird is, the more difficult it is to determine its actual population size. Nevertheless, anyone who sees streams of shearwaters migrating offshore, when good estimates tally hundreds of thousands of birds in a day, has to be impressed. Flocks of many thousands of Sooty Shearwaters can be seen in the Gulf of Alaska, and huge flocks of both SHORT-TAILED SHEARWATERS (Plate 19) and NORTHERN FULMARS are often spotted in the Bering Sea, one of the world's most productive marine ecosystems.

Lore and Notes

Petrels get their name from the Greek word "petros," which refers to the biblical disciple Peter, who tried to walk on water, just as *storm-petrels* appear to be doing (some species, although not those in Alaska, drag their long, dangling legs in the water as sea anchors to hold their position as they feed).

Sailors have long believed albatrosses contained the souls of lost comrades, so it was considered bad luck for one's ship and shipmates to kill one. Albatrosses are highly respected birds in many cultures, perhaps owing to the respect accorded the birds for their amazing flight capabilities, and killing them is frowned upon. Samuel Taylor Coleridge's 1798 *Rime of the Ancient Mariner* brings the matter into sharp focus ("Ah wretch! said they, the bird to slay, That made the breeze to blow!"). On a lighter note, albatrosses are sometimes called "gooney birds" because of their awkwardness on land and the untidiness of their takeoffs and landings; crashing into beach shrubbery is a common occurrence.

Status

Because of their often highly restricted nesting sites on small islands and vulnerability during the nesting period, many species of tubenoses are at risk. Albatrosses cannot become airborne readily from land and are easy victims for humans and introduced predators. Cats and rats, if carelessly released by people, can wreak havoc on an entire island's population of petrels. Albatrosses during the 1800s and early 1900s were widely killed for their feathers, entire breeding colonies destroyed. For example, from the reports of a few early ornithologists, the SHORT-TAILED ALBATROSS was common in Alaska's waters a century and a half ago. Late in the 19th century, this species was so common on the coast of Alaska that Natives sometimes speared them from their kayaks (their bones are abundant in middens). But the population had dropped to no more than a few birds by the 1940s, decimated not only by feather hunters but also by several volcanic eruptions on their tiny breeding island of Torishima. Fortunately, albatrosses take so long to mature that there were always young birds out to sea when disaster struck the island; with strict protection after World War II, the population has been slowly increasing (nearing a thousand individuals) and is on the way to becoming secure (volcanoes willing).

Humans are the greatest enemies of most wildlife, but we also have the potential to alleviate our effects. For example, airplanes landing and taking off at Midway Island, part of a national wildlife refuge in the Northwestern Hawaiian chain, frequently hit low-flying albatrosses, causing some damage to the planes and much damage to the albatrosses. The simple solution that allowed both flying objects to use the island safely was to restrict airplane takeoffs and landings to night-time, when the birds are inactive.

Profiles

Leach's Storm-Petrel, *Oceanodroma leucorhoa*, Plate 18c
Fork-tailed Storm-Petrel, *Oceanodroma furcata*, Plate 18d
Black-footed Albatross, *Phoebastria nigripes*, Plate 19a
Northern Fulmar, *Fulmarus glacialis*, Plate 19b
Sooty Shearwater, *Puffinus griseus*, Plate 19c
Short-tailed Shearwater, *Puffinus tenuirostris*, Plate 19d

3. Cormorants

There are 37 species of *cormorants*, family Phalacrocoracidae, distributed throughout the world except on oceanic islands. Four occur in Alaska, the three species profiled here and BRANDT'S CORMORANT, a rare breeder in the southern part of the state. Cormorants are large birds, the Alaska species in the 60 to 70 cm (24 to 28 in) range. They are fairly heavy-bodied and rest low in the water when swimming, typically with their bill pointing upward. They are unusual among seabirds in that, after foraging, they leave the water to roost on dry land. Cormorants have long, snaky necks, strongly hooked bills, and large webbed feet, all of which are very useful adaptations for fish-catching birds. Not only are the front three toes connected by webs, as in many swimming and diving birds, but the hind toe is quite large, directed to the side, and connected to the other toes by the same webbing. With these expanded swimming paddles, cormorants can easily swim rapidly enough to capture their fishy prey. Their relatives, pelicans and boobies, have similarly *totipalmate* feet. Cormorants also have relatively long tails, unlike other diving birds such as loons and grebes. Their long tail provides them with agility in flight, which allows them to land on perches such as rocks, cliff ledges, pilings, and even trees. Loons, grebes and diving ducks just splash into the water when they land.

Adult cormorants are typically all black or black above and white below, with some variations on these themes. Immatures are usually duller, often brownish. At close range, cormorants are actually quite beautiful, as most of them have bright emerald green or blue-green eyes and bright colors on their naked facial and throat skin. The RED-FACED CORMORANT (Plate 20) is particularly striking among Alaska's species. The PELAGIC CORMORANT (Plate 20) is just as impressive, with its spectacularly iridescent plumage best seen in bright sunlight.

Natural History
Ecology and Behavior

Cormorants are the ultimate fishing machines, and it is sad that we can't observe them and other diving birds under water very easily (they flee from Scuba divers). Scientists who could watch these birds below the surface without disturbing them would surely add greatly to our understanding of seabird foraging. Cormorants forage primarily on bottom fishes such as sculpins, gunnels, and soles. Some species, for example the BRANDT'S CORMORANT of the American Pacific coast and the GUANAY CORMORANT of South America, feed in groups on surface and midwater schooling fishes such as herrings, anchovies, and sand lance. Cormorants can swallow fishes of greater diameter than their heads, as their throat and neck skin is quite elastic. If you watch a feeding cormorant long enough, you are sure to see it bring up a fish and manipulate it at the surface for a while to assure that it is dead. A live fish going down a bird's gullet might erect spiny fins and get stuck, killing the bird; this has happened often enough that there are notes about it in ornithological journals.

Some species, including the DOUBLE-CRESTED CORMORANT (Plate 20), characteristically hold their wings open for several minutes after arriving at their roost, apparently to get rid of excess water that both weighs them down in flight and perhaps makes it more difficult to stay warm. It is an amusing sight to see a long line of cormorants standing with spread wings, some of them waving their wings back and forth, presumably to dry them that much faster. One gets a very prehistoric, almost reptilian, impression from cormorants, as they wave their snaky heads about. This effect is heightened on their breeding grounds, where they vocalize with grunts and hisses.

Breeding
Cormorants are monogamous, the members of the pair meeting back at their nesting colony shortly before breeding is to take place. A few species, including the DOUBLE-CRESTED, nest in trees, but the majority nest on the ground on islands or on narrow cliff ledges inaccessible to predators. Cormorant nests are big, bulky structures of branches and twigs in tree colonies and typically piles of seaweeds in island colonies. Cormorants are among the very few birds that forage for nesting material below the water's surface. Three to five chalky bluish-white eggs are laid, and incubation is by both sexes for 28 to 34 days. Nestlings are black and featherless at birth and very reptilelike in appearance. They grow relatively slowly, as a clutch of 3 to 5 is large for a fish-eating bird, and the parents must work hard to feed that many young. The young fledge after about 5 to 8 weeks.

Ecological Interactions
Many ecological interactions are complex, involving a chain of events in which three or more species interact. The relatively inconsequential interaction of one species with another may represent an excellent opportunity for a third. For example, although cormorants nest in relatively inaccessible places, they are nevertheless subject to nest predation during disturbances. Crows living near a cormorant colony, for instance, know exactly when the approach of Bald Eagles or humans causes the nesting cormorants to take flight, and they arrive promptly to pillage temporarily unprotected eggs.

Lore and Notes
GREAT CORMORANTS are used in Asia as fishing birds. Each fisherman has his own small group of perhaps a half-dozen birds, which he releases into the water from bamboo cages. Each bird is attached to the boat by a line that goes to a ring around its neck. The line allows the fisherman to pull in the bird after it has caught a fish, and the ring keeps it from swallowing its prey. Of course, not all birds are released at once; the tangle of lines would be hopeless. Anyone who knows cormorants wouldn't think they are trainable, but the fishermen actually communicate with their birds by a series of whistles and grunts. The birds get fed

regularly as they fish, and they are apparently unharmed by the fishing process. These fishermen depend on their cormorants more than most of us do on our pets, so it is not surprising that they take good care of their birds.

Status

Alaska cormorants are not threatened, at least as long as good populations of bottom fish remain all along the coast. However, the BRANDT'S CORMORANT of Alaska's far South is a rare breeder anywhere north of Oregon, so it deserves special concern in the state. Cormorants elsewhere in the world have not always fared well. The SPECTACLED CORMORANT of the western Bering Sea became extinct by the middle of the 19th century, a victim of sailors who found themselves with inadequate rations in that harsh region.

Profiles

Double-crested Cormorant, *Phalacrocorax auritus*, Plate 20a
Pelagic Cormorant, *Phalacrocorax pelagicus*, Plate 20b
Red-faced Cormorant, *Phalacrocorax urile*, Plate 20c

4. Waterfowl

Members of the Family Anatidae are universally recognized as *waterfowl*. They are aquatic birds distributed throughout the world in habitats ranging from open seas to high mountain lakes. The family includes 158 species of *ducks*, *geese*, and *swans*. An especially abundant and diverse group throughout temperate regions of the globe, waterfowl are well represented in Alaska, where 50 species, a third of the world fauna, occur. The 27 profiled here represent all of the common species, the other 23 being American species that, in Alaska, are at the northwest edge of their distribution, or Asian migrants that end up in the wrong hemisphere (a few of the Asian species, such as the EURASIAN WIGEON, come across the Bering Sea in large numbers). All of Alaska's waterfowl are migratory, and because it is such a large state, some species may breed in the north, migrate through the interior, and winter in the south.

Waterfowl vary greatly in size and coloring, but all share the same major traits: characteristic duck bills on big heads on rather long necks, pointed wings for strong flight, short tails, and relatively short legs with webbed toes. Plumage color and patterning vary, but the group divides up neatly into swans and geese on one hand, in which the sexes look alike and plumages tend toward white, gray, or brown, and ducks on the other hand, in which males are much brighter than females and are among the gaudiest of our birds. A special feature of many ducks is the *speculum*, a rectangular patch of contrasty, often iridescent, color on the rear edge of the wing near the body; it is prominent in flight and usually partially visible on the resting bird. Male ducks are unusual in bearing a bright, species-specific plumage throughout the winter (normally thought of as the nonbreeding season) and holding that plumage through spring, until the females are nesting. The males then molt into a dull plumage in which they look very much like the mostly brown, camouflaged females. This dull nonbreeding plumage, which occurs during the summer, is called *eclipse* plumage. Waterfowl are also unusual in having a *simultaneous flight-feather molt* during the late summer, in which all of the wing feathers are dropped at once, and the birds become flightless. They usually do this out on deep water, where they are safe from terrestrial predators. This molting strategy allows them to replace their wing feathers more rapidly than can be done by birds that molt these feathers sequentially over a period of months.

Natural History
Ecology and Behavior

Waterfowl, as their name implies, are birds of wetlands, spending most of their time in or near the water. Geese are the most terrestrial waterfowl, most species spending a large amount of time grazing on terrestrial vegetation such as grasses and sedges. Both the BRANT (Plate 22) and EMPEROR GOOSE (Plate 22) are exceptions to this generalization, because of their strong association with the marine environment. The Brant feeds largely on eelgrass (a higher plant) and sea lettuce (an alga) and the Emperor Goose on marine algae but also clams and mussels during migration and winter. The ducks are divided into *diving ducks* and *dabbling ducks*. Divers, such as scaups and scoters, plunge underwater for their food; dabblers, such as mallards, wigeons, and teals, take food from the surface of the water or submerge their heads to reach food at shallow depths. When they reach underwater, their rear ends tip up into the air, and a flock of duck behinds all tipped up at once is one of nature's more ludicrous sights. Ducks vary from virtually pure *herbivores* (wigeon spend much time grazing like geese, teal eat seeds of aquatic plants) to pure *carnivores* (mergansers eat fish, goldeneyes eat snails and shrimps, eiders and scoters eat bivalves), but many species eat both plant and animal matter. It is easy to watch ducks such as SURF SCOTERS (Plate 26)
and BARROW'S GOLDENEYES (Plate 27) feeding, as they dive and then surface, clutching mussels up to several centimeters long. The ducks prefer those at their upper limit of swallowing, because with large mussels, they get more energy intake relative to their energy output in each dive; this is as efficient a cost/benefit estimate as made by any accountant. The mussel is ground up in the duck's muscular *gizzard* (the main part of a two-part stomach), with the help of small pieces of gravel, and the shell fragments are regurgitated.

In the nonbreeding season, almost all waterfowl gather together in flocks, usually of their own species but sometimes mixed. Small ducks fly in clumps, larger ones such as scoters and eiders fly in lines, and geese and swans are well known for their V-formations. Lines and V-formations are thought to allow a modicum of energy saving in these birds because the turbulence produced by the wingtips of the bird in front of them furnishes some lift for the bird behind. This still has not been shown for sure; a good alternative explanation is that the formations allow the birds to organize their flying together with a minimum of accidents!

Breeding

Ducks place their nests on the ground (dabblers, eiders) or water surface (scoters, scaups) in dense vegetation or in tree holes or rock crevices (goldeneyes, mergansers). Typically nests are lined with down feathers that the female plucks from her own breast; in those species that nest in the open, the down is brown and pulled over the whitish eggs to hide them whenever the female leaves the nest to forage. In Alaska ducks, females perform all of the breeding duties, including incubation of the 4 to 12 eggs (eiders have the smallest clutches) and shepherding and protecting the ducklings. Geese and swans, on the other hand, have lifelong pair bonds, during which male and female share more equally in breeding duties; the female incubates the 3 to 7 eggs, but the male stays nearby and helps raise the young. In these larger species, the presence of the male is a significant asset in protecting the young, so there has been strong evolutionary pressure for monogamy. Ducks have a quite different mating system, however. Males begin their courtship early in winter, each species with a different courtship behavior that shows off its distinctive color patches. This of course is why their bright breeding plumage is held through the winter, when males and females are together and interacting, and lost in midsummer, when females have already mated and are on their nests. Males fight among themselves for the privilege of courting an individual female, and unmated females are badly harassed, sometimes by a whole flock of unmated males. Because copulation involves getting on the female's back and often submerging her, females are sometimes killed in these situations. As soon as female ducks are on their nest with a full clutch of eggs, the males desert them and begin their molt into eclipse plumage.

Young waterfowl are *precocial*, able to run, swim, and feed themselves soon after they hatch. They remain with the adult female or pair until full-sized and able to fly well, at one or two months of age in the smaller ducks, ranging up to four months in the TRUMPETER SWAN (Plate 21). Young geese and eiders from several broods are often seen in a *crèche* (a group of young from several families that cluster together), which may be better protected from predators by the presence of additional care-givers. Young geese and swans remain with their parents and migrate south in family groups, in some species the groups staying together through the next spring migration. In ducks, on the other hand, the female deserts the young at about the time they fledge, and they move south separately. Most ducks mature in their first year, but the larger swans may not breed until they are four or more years of age.

Lore and Notes

Ducks, geese, and swans have been objects of people's attention since ancient times, chiefly as a food source. These birds typically have tasty flesh, are fairly large and thus economical to hunt, and are usually easier and less dangerous to catch than many other animals, for example, large mammals. Because they were much used as food, a few species of waterfowl were first domesticated thousands of years ago. The MALLARD (Plate 23) is familiar in its many domestic forms, ranging from iridescent black (Cayuga duck) to pure white (Peking duck). The MUSCOVY DUCK, native to Latin America, is another common farmyard inhabitant in many parts of the world, and it is one of only two New World birds that have been domesticated for food (can you think of the other?). Wild ducks also adjust well to the proximity of people, to the point of taking food from them – a practice that surviving artworks show has been occurring for at least 2000 years. Hunting ducks and geese for sport is also a long-practiced tradition. As a consequence of these long interactions between ducks and people, and the research on these animals stimulated by their use in agriculture and sport, a large amount of scientific information has been collected on the group; many of the ducks and geese are among the most well-known of birds. In fact, many North American duck species have hunters to thank not only for research studies but even for their very existence. The system of national wildlife refuges that superbly protects waterfowl in North America was created primarily to keep duck populations large for hunting, and much of the cost of the refuges is covered by fees paid annually by hunters for federal and state duck stamps (beautiful paintings of waterfowl on stamps that must be attached to hunting licenses).

One of the most used waterfowl "products" is goose and duck down, the down feathers that waterfowl use to line their nests. Eider down is unexcelled as an insulating material and is much in demand for filling jackets and sleeping bags. In regions where the birds are common, people encourage eiders to nest at high densities by protecting their loose colonies from predators. The down is collected from each nest at the beginning of incubation, and the female replaces it readily; the second batch is taken after the ducklings leave the nest. Interestingly, eiders defecate on their eggs, perhaps to protect them from predators that are very sensitive to smell; the stink of an eider nest can be detected a few meters (yards) away. The eider-down industry has presumably developed a way to deodorize the down.

Status

Waterfowl are much affected by human actions, in particular the draining of wetlands. Even in the USA, which has a stated federal policy of "No net loss of wetlands," wetlands are continually being destroyed. Alaska, with its millions of acres of wetlands, still supports substantial breeding populations of ducks, geese, and swans. But they are all affected by habitat destruction and water pollution that takes place on their wintering grounds and along their migration routes (Canada, the Lower 48 states, and Mexico). The status of the TRUMPETER SWAN provides an example of another activity that has affected waterfowl: although much of the breeding range of that species was on inaccessible lakes in southern Alaska and northern British Columbia, it was nevertheless reduced to a tiny remnant of its former numbers by the 1930s, mostly as a result of hunting on its winter range. However, with full protection, it has flourished and continues to increase.

Only one Alaska waterfowl has been listed as Endangered, the Aleutian subspecies of the CANADA GOOSE (Plate 22); it was, in fact, one of the first species listed after the passing of the Endangered Species Protection Act in 1966 (changed to the Endangered Species Act in 1973). Confined to the Aleutian Islands, this small goose was nearly extirpated by populations of Arctic and Red Foxes that were introduced for fur farming. Breeding programs and the removal of foxes from many of the islands have brought this subspecies back to acceptable population levels, and in 1990 its status was changed to Threatened, not at such high risk. Finally, in 1999 the US Fish & Wildlife Service proposed to delist the subspecies, its present population of 30,000 birds assuring its survival; it is one of the notable successes of the Endangered Species program.

Presently declining in Alaska are two species of ducks that leave the continent after breeding and spend their winters at sea. These are the SPECTACLED and STELLER'S EIDERS (Plate 25), both of which are restricted as nesting birds to Alaska and far eastern Siberia. The Spectacled in particular was being considered for Threatened status when very large wintering flocks were discovered in 1998 in unfrozen openings (*polynia*) in the ice-covered Bering Sea.

Profiles

Tundra Swan, *Cygnus columbianus*, Plate 21a
Trumpeter Swan, *Cygnus buccinator*, Plate 21b
Snow Goose, *Chen caerulescens*, Plate 21c
Greater White-fronted Goose, *Anser albifrons*, Plate 22a
Emperor Goose, *Chen canagicus*, Plate 22b
Canada Goose, *Branta canadensis*, Plate 22c
Brant, *Branta bernicla*, Plate 22d

Green-winged Teal, *Anas crecca*, Plate 23a
Mallard, *Anas platyrhynchos*, Plate 23b
Northern Pintail, *Anas acuta*, Plate 23c
Northern Shoveler, *Anas clypeata*, Plate 23d
American Wigeon, *Anas americana*, Plate 24a
Greater Scaup, *Aythya marila*, Plate 24b
Bufflehead, *Bucephala albeola*, Plate 24c
Harlequin Duck, *Histrionicus histrionicus*, Plate 24d

Common Eider, *Somateria mollissima*, Plate 25a
King Eider, *Somateria spectabilis*, Plate 25b
Spectacled Eider, *Somateria fischeri*, Plate 25c
Steller's Eider, *Polysticta stelleri*, Plate 25d
Long-tailed Duck, *Clangula hyemalis*, Plate 26a
Black Scoter, *Melanitta nigra*, Plate 26b
Surf Scoter, *Melanitta perspicillata*, Plate 26c
White-winged Scoter, *Melanitta fusca*, Plate 26d
Common Goldeneye, *Bucephala clangula*, Plate 27a
Barrow's Goldeneye, *Bucephala islandica*, Plate 27b
Common Merganser, *Mergus merganser*, Plate 27c
Red-breasted Merganser, *Mergus serrator*, Plate 27d

5. Raptors

Raptor is another name for *bird of prey*, birds that make their living hunting, killing, and eating other animals, usually other vertebrates. When one hears the term raptor, one usually thinks of soaring hawks that swoop to catch rodents, and of speedy, streamlined falcons that snatch small birds out of the air. Although these are familiar forms of raptors, the families of these birds are large, the members' behavior diverse. The two main raptor families are the Accipitridae, containing the *hawks* and *eagles*, and the Falconidae, including the *falcons* and their tropical relatives. The reasons for classifying the two raptor groups separately have to do with differences in skeletal anatomy and hence, presumed differences in evolutionary history. They differ substantially in nesting behavior as well. Owls (p. 140), which are nocturnal birds of prey, can also be considered raptors. Raptors are common and conspicuous animals in many parts of Alaska. Many are birds of open areas, above which they soar during the day, using *thermals*, currents of heated air, that rise from the sun-warmed ground to support and propel them as they search for meals. But raptors are found in all types of habitats, including wetlands and the sea coast as well as forests and woodlands.

The accipitrid hawks are a worldwide group of 238 species. Alaska is home to nine regularly occurring species – the OSPREY (Plate 28), six hawks, and two eagles – and two eagles from Siberia that do not occur annually. Falcons likewise are worldwide in their distribution. There are 63 species, of which four are regular in Alaska and two additional Siberian species occur rarely. Some falcons have very broad distributions, with the PEREGRINE FALCON (Plate 30) found almost everywhere. Peregrines may have the most extensive natural distribution of any bird.

Raptors vary considerably in size and in patterns of their generally subdued color schemes, but all are similar in overall form – we know them when we see them. They are fierce-looking birds with strong feet, hooked, sharp claws, or *talons*, and strong, hooked and pointed bills. Accipitrids vary in size in Alaska from the 27-cm (10.5-in) long male SHARP-SHINNED HAWK (Plate 29) to 86-cm (34-in) long eagles. Females are usually larger than males, in some species noticeably so. Most raptors are variations of gray, brown, black, and white, usually with brown or black spots, streaks, or bars on various parts of their bodies. The plumages of these birds are actually quite beautiful when viewed close-up, which, unfortunately, is difficult to do. Males and females are usually alike in color pattern, the NORTHERN HARRIER (Plate 28) and AMERICAN KESTREL (Plate 30) being conspicuous exceptions. Juvenile raptors often spend several years in *subadult* plumages that differ in pattern from those of adults. In Alaska, falcons can be distinguished from hawks by their long, pointed wings, which allow the rapid, acrobatic flight for which these birds are justifiably famous.

Natural History
Ecology and Behavior

Raptors are meat-eaters; most hunt and eat live prey. BALD EAGLES (Plate 28) have a reputation as carrion eaters, but they will also take live and healthy prey of many kinds. Raptors usually hunt alone, although, when mated, the mate is often close by. Hawks, eagles, and falcons take mainly vertebrates, including items up to the size of Chinook Salmon, Canada Geese, and young Mountain Goats. Fish are the sole food of OSPREYS and very important in the diet of Bald Eagles. When a hawk makes a capture, the prey is snatched with the sharply pointed and curved talons and usually killed by the puncturing of internal organs by those same talons. Falcons kill by a swift bite to the base of the skull with their specially toothed and notched bill. In both groups, the very sharp-edged bill is then used to dissect the prey into bite-sized morsels.

Alaska's raptors can be divided into groups based on how they pursue and capture prey. *Falcons* are long-winged, high-speed bird chasers, from the ptarmigan-eating GYRFALCON (Plate 30) to the sparrow-eating AMERICAN KESTREL (Plate 30). Most people are familiar with stories of PEREGRINE FALCONS *stooping* (diving vertically from height to gain speed and force) at speeds of 160 kph (100 mph) or more to stun, grab, or knock from the sky an unsuspecting bird.

The fish-eating Osprey, in a classification group of its own, dives to the water surface from flight. *Harriers*, including the NORTHERN HARRIER, look for small birds and mammals while drifting low over the ground, their wings held up in characteristic fashion and – just as in the unrelated owls – their large ears tuned to the sound of potential prey. *Accipiters*, including the SHARP-SHINNED HAWK and NORTHERN GOSHAWK (Plate 29), are forest-based bird chasers with long legs that can reach into dense shrubbery after their prey; the largest species also takes small mammals. *Buteos*, including the ROUGH-LEGGED and RED-TAILED HAWKS (Plate 29), hunt from the air, either soaring or hovering, and take primarily rodents and other small mammals. The GOLDEN EAGLE (Plate 28) is basically a big buteo that takes good-sized mammals spotted from high in the air. The stoop of this species may start so high in the air that, to an observer on the ground, the eagle isn't even a speck. It folds its wings and drops like a stone, its speed increasing throughout the descent; the prey is captured as the eagle levels out just above the ground, its legs shooting forward at the last moment. Bald Eagles may hunt in the same fashion but usually do it over water, plucking from the surface fish, young Sea Otters, and water birds. Many Bald Eagles make a living by searching the seashore for dead seals and the rivers for spawned-out dead salmon.

Many raptors are territorial, a solitary individual or a breeding pair defending an area for feeding and, during the breeding season, for reproduction. Displays that advertise a territory and may be used in courtship consist of spectacular aerial twists, loops, and other acrobatic maneuvers. Although many raptors are common birds, typically they exist at relatively low densities, as is the case for all *top predators* (a predator at the pinnacle of the food chain, preyed upon by no other animal). That is, there usually is enough food to support only one or a pair of a species in a given area. For example, a typical density for a small raptor species, perhaps one that feeds on mice, is one individual per square kilometer (0.4 square miles). A large eagle that feeds on marmots may be spaced so that a usual density is one individual per thousand square kilometers (386 square miles).

Breeding
Hawk and eagle nests are constructed of sticks that both sexes place in a tree or on a rock ledge (on the ground in harriers). Nests are often lined with freshly collected leaves, which are thought to produce chemicals that deter nest parasites that could harm the young birds. The female (sometimes assisted by the male in the OSPREY) incubates the 1 to 6 eggs (only 2 or 3 in the larger species) for 28 to 45 days and gives food to the nestlings. In all raptors, the male hunts for and feeds the female during the egg-laying, incubation, and early nestling periods. Both sexes feed the young when they get a bit older. Youngsters can fly at 4 to 12 weeks of age, depending on species size. After fledging, the young remain with the parents for several more weeks or months until they can hunt on their own. Falcon breeding is similar but differs in a few particulars. Falcons lay their 3 to 6 eggs in a tree or rock cavity or on a ledge but do not construct a nest; in this they are quite different from hawks. Some of them, in fact, lay their eggs in abandoned nests of other birds, for example MERLINS (Plate 30) using crow and magpie nests. Incubation is from 28 to 35 days, performed only by the female. The young fledge after 4 to 7 weeks in the nest.

Ecological Interactions
Surely the most conspicuous raptor in much of Alaska is the BALD EAGLE. Not only are these birds familiar sights around towns and villages throughout the southern coastal parts of the state, but they are also common over the biggest city, Anchorage. The concentrations of these huge birds that gather to feed on dead Chum Salmon in late fall on southern Alaska rivers must be seen to be believed. In fact, they may be the largest concentrations of raptors anywhere outside of the truly awesome flocks of hawks that can be seen in more southerly areas during migration. Bald Eagles are large birds, and to see 500 or 1000 from one spot on the Chilkat River – already as scenic a spot as one would wish to see – is one of nature's most magnificent spectacles. Glaucous-winged Gulls, Common Ravens, and other predators up to the size of Brown Bears also share the salmon feast; the eagles, however, dominate all of them but the bears, which are sufficiently scarce to present little in the way of real competition for this resource.

Very different in flying from the big, almost lumbering, eagles, are the rapid, acrobatic falcons. Falcons hit birds in flight with their talons or closed foot, stunning the prey and sometimes killing it outright. Fast as falcons are, an individual prey bird, even one caught unaware in the open, has a fairly good chance of escaping these avian killing machines. Most bird-eating hawks, falcons included, have a success rate of only about 10 per cent. Smaller birds that are chased may not be as fast as falcons, but they can turn on a smaller circle, and often they can continue to evade their pursuer until the falcon gives up or the potential prey finds cover. Birds in groups have two additional defenses. First, each individual in a group benefits because the group, with so many eyes and ears, is more likely to spot a falcon at a distance than is a lone individual, thus providing all in the group opportunities to watch the predator as it approaches and so evade it. This sort of anti-predation advantage may be why many animals stay in groups. Second, some flocks of small birds, such as sandpipers, which usually fly in loose formations, immediately tighten their formation upon detecting a flying falcon. The effect is to decrease the distance between each bird, so much so that a falcon flying into the group at high speed and trying to take an individual risks injuring itself – the sandpipers form an almost solid wall of birds. Starling flocks take this one step further and sometimes dive as a group on a hawk, trying to injure or at least intimidate it.

Lore and Notes

Large, predatory raptors have doubtless always attracted people's attention, respect, and awe. Wherever eagles occur, they are chronicled in the history of civilizations. Early Anglo-Saxons were known to hang an eagle on the gate of any city they conquered. Some North American Indian tribes and also Australian Aboriginal peoples deified large hawks or eagles. Several countries have used likenesses of eagles as national symbols, among them Turkey, Austria, Germany, Poland, Russia, and Mexico. Eagles are popular symbols on regal coats of arms, and one of their kind, a fish-eater, was chosen as the emblem of the USA (although, as most schoolchildren know, Benjamin Franklin would have preferred that symbol to be the Wild Turkey). People have had a close relationship with falcons for thousands of years. Falconry, in which captive falcons are trained to hunt and kill game at a person's command, is a very old sport, with evidence of it being practiced in China 4000 years ago and in Iran 3700 years ago. One of the oldest known books on a sport is *The Art of Falconry*, written by the King of Sicily in 1248. Falconry reached its pinnacle during medieval times in Europe, when a nobleman's falcons were apparently considered among his most valued possessions.

Status

The USA's national symbol, the BALD EAGLE, has been closely associated with the rise of environmentalism in North America. In the early part of the 20th century, Alaska fishermen declared war on this fish-eating species; 100,000 eagles were killed. Bald Eagles declined dramatically during the period of DDT use (the middle part of the 20th century), with populations reaching a low of about 400 pairs in the Lower 48. Fortunately, Alaska's eagles, most of which were well away from agriculture, were not affected by this environmental pollutant. DDT becomes more concentrated as it passes up the food web (*bioconcentration*), so eagles that ate seabirds that ate fish that ate invertebrates that had DDT in their tissues were greatly at risk. Listed as Endangered in most of the Lower 48 in 1967, the species has recovered very well with the banning of DDT in its range in 1970. It was "downlisted" to Threatened status in all of the Lower 48 in 1995, and in 1999, a proposal was made to remove it completely from the Endangered Species list. It remains very well protected by the Bald Eagle Protection Act of 1940, which makes it a serious crime to kill or disturb an eagle. GOLDEN EAGLES are vulnerable because of powerline collisions and occasional shooting by farmers who consider them a threat to stock; they are also protected by this act, which was renamed the Eagle Protection Act and amended to include Golden Eagles in 1962.

Similarly, the PEREGRINE FALCON was drastically affected by DDT, the effects of which are to cause problems in calcium metabolism such that eggs receive less calcium in their shells; these eggs are thinner than normal and actually crack under the weight of the incubating bird. Populations of the most widespread breeding American subspecies of this falcon were listed as Endangered in the USA in 1970 and Canada in 1978. With DDT no longer used in the USA and Canada, falcon populations began to increase slowly. They were aided by an extensive program of releasing captive-bred young in nest boxes to which some of them would return to breed; several thousand birds were released in this way. This program, called *hacking*, has been used for raptors worldwide with some success. Peregrines were "downlisted" from Endangered Species status in 1999.

Profiles
Bald Eagle, *Haliaeetus leucocephalus*, Plate 28a
Golden Eagle, *Aquila chrysaetos*, Plate 28b
Osprey, *Pandion haliaetus*, Plate 28c
Northern Harrier, *Circus cyaneus*, Plate 28d
Northern Goshawk, *Accipiter gentilis*, Plate 29a
Sharp-shinned Hawk, *Accipiter striatus*, Plate 29b
Red-tailed Hawk, *Buteo jamaicensis*, Plate 29c
Rough-legged Hawk, *Buteo lagopus*, Plate 29d
American Kestrel, *Falco sparverius*, Plate 30a
Gyrfalcon, *Falco rusticolus*, Plate 30b
Merlin, *Falco columbarius*, Plate 30c
Peregrine Falcon, *Falco peregrinus*, Plate 30d

6. Chickenlike Birds

There are 17 species of *grouse* in the world; seven occur in Alaska. Grouse are part of a large family, the Phasianidae, which, with 176 species, includes most of the chickenlike, or *gallinaceous*, birds in the world. Grouse are much like chickens – plump, short-winged, and strong-legged, and only rarely taking to the air. Grouse spend much of their time on the ground and are resident all year in Alaska, so, more than most birds, they walk around in snow. Accordingly, in winter they grow extra scales along their toes that make the toes broader, a *snowshoe* effect. Some grouse, known as *ptarmigans*, grow a complete set of feathers on the toes as well, effectively insulating surfaces that would lose valuable body heat (the Snowy Owl is another bird with entirely feathered feet for the same reason). Ground birds that they are, it is not surprising that grouse are among the best camouflaged of birds, with mostly brown or gray-brown plumages. Although the woodland species remain brown all year, ptarmigans, which live out in the open, are well-known for their molt into pure white plumage in winter. Their tail, which molts only once each year, is black, but it is well hidden by the long, white rump feathers that cover it, and visible only in flight. A ptarmigan's beady black eyes and black bill actually look like dark dots in a motionless bird and deflect attention away from the white body against white snow. Male and female grouse either look alike or the males are a bit more brightly marked, especially around the head. Males are often larger, in some species considerably larger.

Natural History
Ecology and Behavior
Grouse are leaf-eaters, among the few groups of birds that get most of their nourishment from the leaves of plants. Leaves are difficult to digest because of their thick cellulose coat, and, even with specialized intestinal bacteria to aid the process, they are digested slowly. Thus leaf-eaters usually have longer intestines than other animals, and the leaves pass through them slowly (the longer material to be digested is in the intestine, the longer the animal has for nutrients to be absorbed into its body). Because of this rather inefficient system, they must eat a lot of leaves to survive. Many mammals are leaf-eaters, as they can afford to increase their weight considerably during a meal; this is not a good strategy for birds, however, which may have to jump into flight at any moment. Probably because grouse spend so much of their time on the ground and are well-camouflaged from predators, and so do not have to fly very often, they can afford to be leaf-eaters. Some of them are even rather specialized in their diets, as one might infer from their names – SPRUCE GROUSE (Plate 31), SAGE GROUSE, HAZEL GROUSE, WILLOW PTARMIGAN (Plate 31). You can go only so far with names, however; ROCK PTARMIGAN (Plate 31) don't eat rocks. You can easily detect the presence of Spruce Grouse, as their cylindrical fecal pellets are usually full of spruce needles (next time you prick your finger on a spruce needle, think about that!). Grouse also eat many berries and flowers in season. The chicks feed heavily on insects at first, which makes sense, because a growing bird needs more protein than can be furnished by a strictly herbivore diet.

Breeding
Grouse are popular among ornithologists who study bird mating systems because so many of the species are *promiscuous* (p. 47), with no pair bond between males and females. Some of the promiscuous species form *leks*, communal displays that may include several dozen males spread out over a traditional "dancing ground." Of Alaska's grouse, only the SHARP-TAILED GROUSE is a lekking species, but its displays are memorable. Males run around like little wind-up airplanes taxiing in circles, with wings outspread and tail up, all the time stamping their feet, rattling their tail feathers, and inflating their pink neck sacs, which make a hollow cooing sound as they deflate. At intervals the birds jump into the air and flutter to the ground. Dominant males keep subordinate ones away from favored parts of the lek, which are usually toward the center of the group (battles among males have led to natural selection for large size, and some male grouse of other species, in other parts of the world, are almost twice the size of females). Females enter the lek from time to time, wandering through the males and raising their display fervor to a frenzy; the females may then wander out the other side of the lek or may approach a particular male and indicate readiness to mate. Mating occurs quickly. Then the female goes away to her own territory and lines a shallow depression on the ground with grasses and other plant material for a nest. Male SPRUCE GROUSE display singly rather than at leks but still furnish no parental care. Male ptarmigans typically mate with one female and often stay with their mates until they begin incubating the clutch of eggs, when there is no chance of another male fertilizing those eggs. WILLOW PTARMIGAN go one step further in

parental care, typically remaining near the female and often defending the nest and brood against predators.

Females incubate the 5 to 12 eggs for 20 to 25 days. Grouse young are amazingly *precocial*, able to run after their mother and begin pecking at small prey just hours after hatching. Precocial young, tiny and conspicuous because of their movements, are greatly at risk from predators. Ducklings at least live in the water, so they are safe from most land-based predators. Grouse, on the other hand, are tasty tidbits for just about any carnivorous bird or mammal, and their way of coping with this is to grow miniature but functional wings very rapidly. Young grouse can fly at 6 to 12 days of age, at least giving them an even chance of survival. It's a startling sight to see a brood of diminutive grouse burst into the air as they are approached. The young birds nevertheless stay with their mother, who knows the territory and can lead them to productive feeding areas, for another 10 to 15 weeks.

Female RUFFED GROUSE (Plate 31) give spectacular distraction displays, jumping up at an approaching predator with strongly beating wings and a rather ferocious growling sound. One of the authors of this book discovered this firsthand when his wife screamed so loudly nearby that he expected a bear and found, instead, an effectively protective Ruffed Grouse and her brood.

Ecological Interactions

Grouse are actually surprisingly common for their size, and this indicates an important ecological principle. Animals higher up on the food web must sustain themselves on the next level below them, and that level therefore has to be much more common. Conversely, as we move up the food web, from plants to plant-eaters to animal-eaters, the species at each level become much less common. That is, for example, each hawk must eat many mice each day to survive, so in places where we see a few hawks, we expect there to be many mice. Paul Colinvaux used this principle to title his 1990 ecology textbook *Why Big Fierce Animals are Rare*. A grouse is about the same weight as a large hawk, but it can be much more common, because it is feeding very low down on the food web, on plants, while the hawk is feeding at a higher level, on the grouse and other plant-eaters and on smaller animal-eaters.

Lore and Notes

Grouse are so easily approached that they are sometimes considered stupid. But the reason they are apparently so tame is that they are wonderfully camouflaged; they depend heavily on this *cryptic coloration* to protect them from predators. In the grouse's universe, it probably "thinks" that if it sits very still, you won't see it. Spruce Grouse are especially known for being "fool hens," being the easiest grouse to approach closely. This may be because they roost in trees, which makes them even harder to detect than ptarmigans and other grouse that spend more of their time on the ground in the open.

Grouse have more than one line of defense. They have short, stiff wings and specially adapted flight muscles that allow for amazingly quick take-offs and rapid acceleration. When approached closely, they take off like a rocket, and this, combined with the loud whirring sound of their wings, produces a *startle effect* that surely must save many from predators. Many a hunter, birder, or woodsperson who has spent much time in the northern forests can attest to how well it works.

Status

Alaska grouse are all common, even the SHARP-TAILED GROUSE, which is found only in certain areas in the interior. That species, however, has disappeared from large parts of its former range in the Lower 48, largely because its grassland habitat has been replaced by farmland. Grassland animals are among the most threatened in the world, because their habitat is sublimely suited to the growth of grains such as wheat, corn, barley, rye, sorghum, and others in the grass family.

Profiles

Ruffed Grouse, *Bonasa umbellus*, Plate 31a
Spruce Grouse, *Falcipennis canadensis*, Plate 31b
Rock Ptarmigan, *Lagopus mutus*, Plate 31c
Willow Ptarmigan, *Lagopus lagopus*, Plate 31d

7. Cranes

There are 15 species of *cranes*, family Gruidae; members of the family occur on all continents but South America. Two species of cranes occur in North America, and one, the SANDHILL CRANE (Plate 21), is a regular visitor to Alaska. These are large, long-necked and long-legged wading birds that stride across prairies and wetlands. The tallest of them stand as high as a person. Cranes are sometimes confused with herons, which are also tall wading birds, but the two are very different. Both groups have long, pointed bills, but the crane bill is less compressed than the heron bill, and the nostrils are *perforate* (see-through). Most cranes have a patch of red, naked skin on top of their head, and their very large *tertial* (inner wing) feathers give the appearance of a bustle. Cranes forage by walking steadily, while herons stand very still and watch for the movements of nearby prey. Cranes fly with their neck fully extended, often in flocks, but herons fly singly, with their neck folded back. Cranes are very vocal, with sonorous, rolling gooselike calls, while herons are restricted to guttural croaks. Northern-hemisphere cranes are highly migratory, moving to distant wintering grounds. Most of Alaska's Sandhill Cranes winter in the central valleys of California. The only heron that occurs regularly in Alaska is the Great Blue Heron, and it is usually seen watching for prey on a mudflat or lake shore in the southern part of the state. Cranes, on the other hand, are usually seen in pairs or flocks on tundra, wet meadows, or fields.

Natural History
Ecology and Behavior

Cranes forage by walking slowly through their open habitat. They are omnivores, eating a wide variety of small vertebrates and large invertebrates, as well as seeds, tubers, grasses, and sedges – just about anything in their environment that they can swallow. In migration, cranes gather in flocks that move slowly northward or southward, reminiscent of geese and swans as they move overhead with loud, sonorous calls. Unlike waterfowl, they use the rising air of thermals just as migrating raptors do, circling higher and higher on set wings, then gliding off in the appropriate direction to find another thermal and repeat the maneuver. Their long wings with primary flight feathers separated at the end (into "fingers") look very much like the wings of eagles.

In spring as they migrate, or even on their wintering grounds, SANDHILL CRANES begin their impressive courtship behavior, often referred to as "dancing," that includes jumping in the air, giving elaborate bows and wingspreads, and pulling up and tossing of bits of plant material and soil. They continue this onto the breeding site, where pairs defend large territories.

Breeding
Cranes are monogamous and mate for life. The nest is a big pile of vegetation gathered by the adults, often in the middle of an extensive marsh or wet prairie but elevated sufficiently to keep the eggs dry. The 2 eggs laid are incubated by both sexes for 29 to 32 days. The young leave the nest soon after hatching and are fed by the adults at first; gradually they learn how to feed themselves. They first fly at about 9 to 10 weeks of age, then remain with their parents for their first year, accompanying them as they migrate south and then back north to their breeding grounds.

Lore and Notes
Cranes are a symbol of good luck, happiness, and long life in Japan, and they are everywhere in Japanese art and daily life. In part as a consequence of the atomic bombs dropped in Japan during World War II, school children all over the world now make *origami* cranes, cleverly folded pieces of paper, as a demonstration of their desire for world peace. The courtship "dances" of cranes have also influenced the dances of the Native people of North America, Australia, and Africa, and one wonders how many modern ballet choreographers have been similarly influenced.

Status
SANDHILL CRANES are abundant across most of western North America, although some of the eastern and southern USA populations have diminished greatly with the destruction of wetlands. The federal government and many state governments have programs to maintain and restore this striking species, but even more effort has been put into the recovery of the WHOOPING CRANE, the only other crane to occur in North America. One of America's most spectacular birds, the Whooper was very nearly lost to extinction. It nested widely in northern North America and wintered along the Gulf Coast, but it was subject both to hunting during migration and to disturbance on its nesting grounds; by 1941, it was thought that no more than two dozen of them remained. With complete protection, public education, and a substantial captive-breeding program, numbers gradually increased to the present total of several hundred birds. There is a large captive flock and also a good population that nests in Wood Buffalo National Park in Canada and winters on the Texas coast. Captive-bred birds are being used to start a second, non-migratory, flock in Florida, but mortality is very high in the released birds (powerline strikes, Bobcat predation), and the success of this endeavor remains to be seen. Not out of danger, the Whooping Crane is at least holding its own at present.

Profiles
Sandhill Crane, *Grus canadensis*, Plate 21d

8. Shorebirds

Shorebirds are among the birds that make Alaska a compelling destination for the serious birder. If you like diversity, the list of breeding species will satisfy you, because most species of North American shorebirds breed at Alaska latitudes.

They breed in both the open tundra that wraps itself around the state and the muskeg-dotted forest that fills its center. The arctic tundra resounds through the 24-hour daylight of summer with the songs that are given by sandpipers and plovers as they perform their spectacular display flights. If you like seeing large numbers of animals, go to one of the bays along the southern coast in spring, for example, the Copper River delta or Kachemak Bay. Tens to hundreds of thousands of migrant shorebirds use these estuaries as sites where they can feed and put on fat for the last stage of their long flight to their more northerly breeding grounds.

Shorebirds are traditionally placed along with the gulls in the avian order Charadriiformes. They are global in distribution and often occur in large numbers – the primary reason being that the sandy beaches and mudflats on which they forage usually teem with their food. There are several families, three of which require mention. The *sandpipers* (family Scolopacidae) are a worldwide group of 88 species. Thirty-nine of them occur regularly in Alaska, including 32 breeding species; another 18 species are irregular visitors, mostly from Siberia (shorebirds are well-known as long-distance wanderers). The *plovers* (family Charadriidae), with 66 species, likewise have a worldwide distribution but are more common in the tropics. Eight species occur regularly in Alaska, of which five are known to breed in the state, and another two species are rarer visitors. Finally, a single species of *oystercatcher* (family Haematopodidae) occurs in Alaska; although there are only 11 species, oystercatchers occur on all continents.

All shorebirds, regardless of size, are recognizable as shorebirds. They walk or run on sandy beaches, mudflats, or rocks or wade in shallow fresh or salt water; the waders typically have long, slender legs. The sexes look alike, or nearly so, in most shorebirds (but see under Breeding). They are usually drably colored during the nonbreeding season, darker above and lighter below – perfectly camouflaged on the sand, mud, or vegetation on which they forage. Many shorebirds molt into a bright breeding plumage in spring, and this plumage can be seen during much of their brief stay in Alaska. Alaska sandpipers range from 15 to 48 cm (6 to 19 in) in length. They are generally slender birds with straight or curved bills of various lengths, each adapted to feeding in a specific habitat and even at a specific depth below the surface of the sand or mud. Plovers, 15 to 30 cm (6 to 12 in) long, are small to mid-sized, thick-necked shorebirds with short tails and straight, relatively thick bills. They are mostly shades of gray and brown above and white below, but some have bold color patterns such as a broad white or dark band on the head or chest. A few Alaska species are boldly marked with large areas of black in the breeding season. The BLACK OYSTERCATCHER (Plate 32) is an unmistakable large black shorebird with a bright red chisel-shaped bill.

Some of the small shorebirds, such as SANDERLINGS (Plate 38), resemble amusing wind-up toys as they spend hours running up and down the beach, chasing, and then being chased by, the outgoing and incoming surf. Shorebirds are often conspicuous and let themselves be watched, as long as the watchers maintain some distance. When in large flying groups, sandpipers such as DUNLINS (Plate 38) and WESTERN SANDPIPERS (Plate 36) provide some of the most compelling sights in nature, as their flocks rise from sandbar or mudflat to fly low and fast over the surf, wheeling quickly and tightly in the air as if they were a single organism, or as if each individual's nervous system were joined to that of the others.

Natural History
Ecology and Behavior

Shorebirds are typically seen in the open, associated with coastlines and inland wetlands. They are all excellent flyers, but when chased they often seem to prefer running to flying away. Sandpipers characteristically forage by moving slowly and steadily forward, picking their food from the ground or using their bills to probe for it in mud or sand. In the breeding season, most of them eat insects and spiders, but in migration and on their marine wintering grounds, they take many kinds of small invertebrates, including worms, snails, and crustaceans. They will also snatch bugs from the air as they walk and from the water's surface as they wade or swim. The larger species, such as godwits and curlews, with longer bills, probe deep in the mud for large polychaete worms and small crabs. Plovers forage by alternately running and stopping to pick prey from the surface, and they can easily be distinguished from sandpipers at a great distance by this characteristic behavior. Alaska oystercatchers, alas, can find no oysters to catch, but their bill is surpassingly well adapted for prying limpets off rocks or stabbing partially open mussels so they relax their protective valves. *Phalaropes* are the most unusual shorebirds; although members of the sandpiper group, these tiny shorebirds spend much of their life on the ocean's surface, where they pick planktonic crustaceans from the top few centimeters of the water. They often *spin* (swim in small circles), creating a vortex that draws tiny invertebrates closer to the surface.

Some shorebirds, for example SPOTTED SANDPIPERS (Plate 34) and SANDERLINGS, establish winter feeding territories along stretches of beach; they use the area for feeding for a few hours or for the day, defending it aggressively from other members of their species. On the other hand, most sandpipers and plovers are gregarious birds, often seen in large groups, especially when they are travelling. Flocks of thousands of DUNLINS and WESTERN SANDPIPERS are commonly observed. Several species make long migrations over expanses of open ocean, a good example being the PACIFIC GOLDEN-PLOVER (Plate 33), which flies nonstop over the Pacific in spring and autumn between Alaska breeding grounds and Hawaiian or even Tahitian wintering locales.

Breeding

Shorebirds breed in a variety of ways. Most species breed in monogamous pairs that defend small breeding territories and share in parental care. Others are *polygynous*, the males in species such as RUFFS coming together in communal displays called *leks*. Females are attracted to these groups but typically mate with only certain of the males. Many of the males mate with more than one female. In this system, males provide no parental care. Other species practice *polyandry*, the least common type of mating system among vertebrate animals, in which some females have more than one mate in a single breeding season. This type of breeding is exemplified by the SPOTTED SANDPIPER. In this species, the normal sex roles of breeding birds are reversed: the female establishes a territory on a lakeshore that she defends against other females. More than one male settles within the territory, either at the same time or sequentially during a breeding season. After mating, the female lays a clutch of eggs for each male. The males incubate their clutches and care for the young. Females may help care for some of the broods of young provided that there are no more unmated males to try to attract to the territory. In phalaropes, also polyandrous, there has been a substantial switch in sex roles; females are distinctly larger and more brightly colored than males (quite unusual in the bird world), and actively court the smaller, duller males. After laying her eggs in a nest constructed by the male, a female contributes no additional parental care.

Most shorebird nests are simply shallow depressions in the ground in which the eggs are placed; some of these *scrapes* are lined with dead leaves or lichens, which apparently are excellent insulating material, holding in the heat generated by the incubating bird's body. Sandpipers and plovers typically lay 4 relatively large eggs, this exact clutch size probably determined by how many eggs can be successfully incubated. Incubation, depending on species, is by the male alone, the female alone, or both parents, for 20 to 28 days. Oystercatchers lay clutches of 3 eggs, which are incubated for 24 to 29 days by both male and female. Like waterfowl and grouse, shorebird young are precocial, that is, soon after they hatch they are mobile, able to run from predators, and can feed themselves (but oystercatchers and snipes feed their young). One or both parents usually stay with the young to lead them to feeding areas and guard them until they can fly, 2 to 5 weeks after hatching.

Shorebirds are famous for their *distraction displays*, in which one or both parents flop along the ground as if they have a broken wing or are otherwise incapacitated. A predator that might go for their eggs or young instead follows the apparently guaranteed meal that the adult represents, and is lured away from the nest or young until the adult, having accomplished its goal, flies away. A specialty of arctic shorebirds is called the *rodent run*. Performing this behavior, an adult shorebird scurries across the tundra like a lemming or vole, its dark rump with white on either side perhaps simulating a rodent's tail. To a predator, the presence of a bird may indicate a nest worth searching for, but the presence of a rodent doesn't necessarily indicate a rodent nest; so the predator follows the shorebird away from its nest, just as intended.

Ecological Interactions
Shorebirds often gather in very large flocks at what are known as *staging areas*, sites where the birds can find abundant food and put on the fat they need for long-distance migration. In some species, only a few such sites exist on the route between breeding and wintering ground, and the birds, at these sites, put enormous predator pressure on the invertebrates on which they feed. In fact, shorebirds are the main avian predators on intertidal invertebrates. When researchers construct exclosures on mudflats to keep sandpipers and plovers out of small areas, the invertebrates within those exclosures remain at much greater densities than in the areas where the birds can feed freely.

Lore and Notes
The manner in which flocks of thousands of birds, particularly shorebirds, fly in such closely regimented order, executing abrupt maneuvers with precise coordination, such as when all individuals seem to turn together in a split second in the same direction, has puzzled biologists and engendered some research. What is the stimulus for the flock to turn – is it one individual within the flock, a "leader," from which all the others take their "orders?" Or is it a stimulus from outside the flock that all members respond to in the same way? And how are the turns coordinated? Everything from "thought transference" to electromagnetic communication among flock members has been advanced as an explanation. After studying films of DUNLINS flying and turning in large flocks, one biologist suggested that the method birds within these flocks use to coordinate their turns

is similar to the way people in a chorus line know the precise moment to raise their legs in sequence or how "the wave" in a sports stadium is coordinated. That is, one bird, perhaps one that has detected some danger, such as a predatory falcon, starts a turn, and the other birds, seeing the start of the flock's turning, can then anticipate when it is their turn to do the same – the result being a dazzlingly quick wave of turning coursing through the flock. To acknowledge where he got it, the researcher called his idea the *chorus-line* hypothesis.

Birds are very hot animals, their body temperatures averaging around 40°C (104°F). Because of this, the temperature of the air around them, except in the world's hot deserts, will always be lower than their body temperature. Birds' feathers give them the insulation they need to maintain their high body temperature, but they lose heat from uninsulated parts of their bodies: their eyes, bill, and feet. The response of shorebirds to this heat-loss problem is easy to see. When they are not active, many of them will tuck their bill under their shoulder feathers, pull one leg up within the body feathers, and close their eyes. They are not necessarily sleeping (if you watch them you will see an eye open and close at intervals), but they are conserving heat. They also furnish much amusement to the human onlooker who sees one of them hopping rapidly down the beach on one leg, just to avoid putting that other leg out in the air. When you see a one-legged shorebird, it is very unlikely that it has lost the other leg; we have even seen them attempting to feed while hopping on one leg.

Status

Alaska's most vulnerable shorebird from the standpoint of its worldwide numbers is surely the BRISTLE-THIGHED CURLEW, the entire population of which totals perhaps 7000 individuals. This curlew's breeding range is confined to the Seward Peninsula and Yukon Delta, and, amazingly, this bird of such a restricted breeding range winters widely on tiny islands scattered across the Pacific (including small numbers in Hawaii). It epitomizes the long-distance migration characteristic of shorebirds. It also points out the need to manage vulnerable populations of migratory birds everywhere within their range, because losses can occur not only on breeding grounds and wintering grounds but even in migration. A strong North Pacific storm in spring 1998 deposited many of these curlews on the American West Coast, where they are not usually seen, and biologists wonder how many of them were lost at sea. Alaska has several other shorebirds with restricted nesting ranges, which makes them vulnerable.

Shorebirds were hunted for the pot at the end of the 19th and beginning of the 20th centuries, and many species had declined to obvious rarity before the Migratory Bird Treaty Act of 1918 was enacted into law. Signed by the United States and Great Britain (for Canada), the act gained real power when it was also signed by Mexico in 1936, thereby protecting all birds of North America. Sadly, it was perhaps too late for the ESKIMO CURLEW, a small curlew that bred on Arctic tundra and wintered on the pampas of southern South America. While the AMERICAN GOLDEN-PLOVER (Plate 33), BUFF-BREASTED SANDPIPER, and other species with similar distribution and migration routes recovered from the market hunting, the curlew did not, and it is either extinct or so rare that years go by with no definite sighting.

The fact that shorebirds are so picky about where they stop in migration makes it obvious that an environmental catastrophe at even one of a species' major stop-over sites would not bode well for that species. In other words, even a very abundant species can be at risk if its populations are highly concentrated at any time of the year.

Profiles

Black Oystercatcher, *Haematopus bachmani*, Plate 32a
Whimbrel, *Numenius phaeopus*, Plate 32b
Bar-tailed Godwit, *Limosa lapponica*, Plate 32c
Marbled Godwit, *Limosa fedoa*, Plate 32d
Black-bellied Plover, *Pluvialis squatarola*, Plate 33a
American Golden-Plover, *Pluvialis dominica*, Plate 33b
Pacific Golden-Plover, *Pluvialis fulva*, Plate 33c
Semipalmated Plover, *Charadrius semipalmatus*, Plate 33d

Greater Yellowlegs, *Tringa melanoleuca*, Plate 34a
Lesser Yellowlegs, *Tringa flavipes*, Plate 34b
Spotted Sandpiper, *Actitis macularia*, Plate 34c
Wandering Tattler, *Heteroscelus incanus*, Plate 34d
Ruddy Turnstone, *Arenaria interpres*, Plate 35a
Black Turnstone, *Arenaria melanocephala*, Plate 35b
Surfbird, *Aphriza virgata*, Plate 35c
Rock Sandpiper, *Calidris ptilocnemis*, Plate 35d
Semipalmated Sandpiper, *Calidris pusilla*, Plate 36a
Western Sandpiper, *Calidris mauri*, Plate 36b
Least Sandpiper, *Calidris minutilla*, Plate 36c
Baird's Sandpiper, *Calidris bairdii*, Plate 36d

Pectoral Sandpiper, *Calidris melanotos*, Plate 37a
Common Snipe, *Gallinago gallinago*, Plate 37b
Short-billed Dowitcher, *Limnodromus griseus*, Plate 37c
Long-billed Dowitcher, *Limnodromus scolopaceus*, Plate 37d
Dunlin, *Calidris alpina*, Plate 38a
Sanderling, *Calidris alba*, Plate 38b
Red-necked Phalarope, *Phalaropus lobatus*, Plate 38c
Red Phalarope, *Phalaropus fulicaria*, Plate 38d

9. Jaegers, Gulls, and Terns

The family Laridae contains 105 species, including eight *jaegers* and *skuas*, 50 *gulls*, 44 *terns*, and three *skimmers*. Alaska's waters are inhabited by four jaegers and skuas, 20 gulls, and six terns at different times of year, although eight of these 30 species are very rarely seen in the state. Members of this family (called *larids* as a group) are long-winged, long-distance fliers; the ARCTIC TERN (Plate 41) has the longest migration route of any bird. Jaegers and skuas are brown or brown and white. Most adult gulls and terns are gray and white, with bright colors restricted to their eyerings, bills, and legs (sometimes very bright). Gulls typically have either an all-white or an all-dark head in breeding plumage, while many terns have a black cap in that plumage. Terns are generally smaller and more slender-bodied than gulls, with more buoyant flight. Jaegers and skuas, because of their heavy, hooked bills, brown coloration, and predatory nature, seem allied to the hawks and eagles, but in fact they are very closely related to the gulls.

Natural History
Ecology and Behavior

The members of this bird family are mostly fish-eaters. Terns dive for their fish. They fly well above the water surface and watch for prey, often hovering in one place to get a better view, then plunge their entire body into the water, beak-first, to capture the fish. Then they take off, get rid of much of their water load with a vigorous shake, quickly flip the fish around to swallow it headfirst, or carry it crosswise in their bill to bring it to hungry young birds. Some of Alaska's terns, while on their freshwater breeding grounds, pick insects from the surface. Gulls also dive into the water for fish, but they don't usually go as deep as terns, and they often pick their prey from the surface. Gulls are much more variable in foraging behavior than the rather conservative terns; in addition to fish, they eat dead animals floating on the sea surface or on the beach, hunt for invertebrates by walking around in the intertidal, follow plows to pick up unearthed worms and grubs, and use all sorts of human activities as food sources (see below).

Jaegers, predators on lemmings and bird eggs and young on the breeding grounds, are the unsurpassed *kleptoparasites* of the bird world (only the tropical frigatebirds are their equals) on their migration routes and wintering grounds. Kleptoparasitism is the forceful taking of prey from other animals that have already captured it. The three Alaska jaegers are of different sizes, and each pursues fish-catching birds that are slightly smaller than itself. The POMARINE JAEGER (Plate 39) pursues medium-sized gulls and shearwaters out at sea, the PARASITIC JAEGER (Plate 39) especially prefers BONAPARTE'S GULLS (Plate 40) and COMMON TERNS feeding nearer shore, and the LONG-TAILED JAEGER (Plate 39) follows ARCTIC TERNS on their long migration up and down the world's oceans. A jaeger in migration is eternally vigilant, whether in flight or resting on the water, when around fishing birds. When the jaeger sees a bird make a capture, it approaches it, accelerating amazingly rapidly and often catching the bird unaware. The jaeger, being larger and apparently tougher, has an unquestioned advantage, and the original captor usually drops its prey quickly after a minimal chase. Small gulls and terns often attempt escape, but it seems futile: the jaeger can fly faster, it is as agile in flight as the smaller bird it is chasing, and as the tern turns, so does the jaeger, right on its tail. If the prey is not dropped quickly, the jaeger will merely grab the bird it is chasing by the wing or tail and spin it around in the air. The fish is dropped, and the jaeger almost always is able to catch it before it hits the water, no mean feat in itself. The black wings and white wing patches of menacing jaegers may make them quickly recognizable to other birds, causing victims to give up their prey more readily.

Kleptoparasitic behavior is not restricted to jaegers and, in fact, is common in their nearest relatives, the gulls and terns. A tern that has been unsuccessful in foraging may harass another tern carrying a fish until it drops it; and gulls perform this sort of behavior all the time, not only on smaller species but on their own. It is easy to observe this wherever gulls are fed by humans, either on purpose or as a consequence of our propensities for producing garbage. Around fish-processing plants, fishing boats, garbage dumps, and even drive-in restaurants, large gulls such as GLAUCOUS-WINGED GULLS (Plate 40) hang around and gather up waste, and they seem to spend as much time chasing one another for tidbits as they do finding their own. In fact, the energy spent by a bunch of gulls chasing one with food in its bill seems far out of proportion to the energy gained by stealing the item – especially when it makes the thief the object of another chase!

Breeding

All members of the larid family practice *courtship feeding*, in which the male presents a recently caught fish to the female with which he will breed. This ritual not only makes and strengthens the pair bond but also gives the female extra metabolic energy to put into her developing eggs. The eggs growing within the female's body may make her too heavy and slow to be a successful predator, so courtship feeding by the male may sometimes be very important in providing nutrition to breeding females. Courtship behavior in gulls and terns involves much calling. Courtship in terns is especially spectacular. Members of a pair, next to one another, fly higher and higher and then come swooping down in a long, spiral flight with depressed wings, a *pas de deux* with no music other than the sounds of the sea and the birds' own voices. Gull courtship occurs on the ground and involves movements of the head, with bows and head-ups and choking motions; the long, loud calls of courting males ring through the colony at the height of the mating season. Jaeger courtship is rather similar to that of gulls, with fewer vocalizations.

In most members of this group, the nest is an open cup on the ground, usually lined with whatever plant material is available. At lower latitudes, most gulls and terns breed in colonies on islands, where they are safe from ground predators. Arctic-nesting jaegers, SABINE'S GULLS (Plate 41), and ARCTIC TERNS breed as solitary pairs on the open tundra, where visibility is such that they can see predators approaching from far away and, if necessary, leave their nest in time to avoid the nest being located. BONAPARTE'S and MEW GULLS (Plate 40) breed in forested areas at the edge of small lakes. They build somewhat flimsy stick nests in trees, probably because, being white and very conspicuous, they would be subject to intense nest predation if they nested on the ground. Jaegers lay 2 eggs, gulls and terns typically 3. Incubation is for 23 to 28 days in jaegers, 23 to 30 days in gulls, and 20 to 24 days in Alaska terns. Larids protect their nests vigorously, diving on approaching predators and hitting them from behind with strong feet. They react the same way to human intruders, and the only ways you can protect yourself are to wear a floppy hat or keep your eyes on the approaching birds; they won't hit you from the front. After one aggressive experience with a jaeger or large gull, you'll never forget it. Even delicate Arctic Terns, when they hit you, typically elicit four-letter Anglo-Saxon words such as "ouch."

All of these birds have *semiprecocial* young. They are fluffy and alert soon after hatching, but unlike the precocial young of shorebirds and waterfowl, which leave the nest area quickly after hatching, larid young remain at or very near the nest and are fed by the adults for up to two or three months, until they are well able to fly. These birds often breed in large colonies, and the young, especially of terns, often associate in large groups away from the nests. How do adults recognize their own young and vice versa? It is all vocal; an adult coming in with fish begins to call, and its own chicks answer it from the group. They all sound about the same to us, but apparently not to each other. Gulls and especially terns follow their parents around for weeks after they fledge, often able to cajole a feeding out of them, and terns have even been seen feeding young on their wintering grounds, months after leaving the nesting area.

Ecological Interactions

Although jaegers, gulls, and terns are closely related, they don't usually have amicable relationships with one another. Kleptoparasitism has already been discussed, but predation also occurs, by jaegers and gulls on tern chicks and eggs. On the North Atlantic coast of North America, HERRING GULLS nearly wiped out colonies of small terns before gull-control programs reduced gull populations on and around the tern nesting islands. These programs have remained ongoing, to protect both terns and Atlantic Puffins from the double pressure of kleptoparasitism and predation.

Lore and Notes

Gulls are smart birds, no doubt about it; they have to be to compete with crows and ravens to take advantage of human largesse. This can best be seen in parking lots of grocery stores and restaurants, where an open dumpster attracts flocks of these birds, vying for edible bits of garbage. The ensuing squabbles give insights into bird behavior – the advantages of large size, the dominance of adults over immatures, types of aggressive displays, and the different behavior styles of various species. Some people, of course, would rather watch avian interactions in more pleasant surroundings. Both gulls and crows have learned to pick up clams from the shoreline, fly up with them to heights of 10 m (33 ft) or so, then drop them on rocks until they break open. Gulls must be delighted with all the jetties, bridges, roads, and parking lots that we have added to their environments, because they use all of these as clam-smashers. Immature gulls go through a learning period during which they become able to distinguish an asphalt road from a sandy beach.

Status

Gulls are among the most successful of birds, especially the larger species, as they have learned to coexist with and even take advantage of human populations. The rarest gulls and terns of the world (none of which breed in Alaska) have specialized breeding habitats that may be in short supply. Alaska's gulls, such as MEW GULLS, that breed in a great variety of habitats and winter widely on salt water will be successful as long as Alaska retains a good part of her habitats. Large gulls, such as GLAUCOUS-WINGED, have even begun to nest on human structures, especially the tops of flat buildings with no roof access to people and abandoned piers with no connection to land.

Profiles

Pomarine Jaeger, *Stercorarius pomarinus*, Plate 39a
Long-tailed Jaeger, *Stercorarius longicaudus*, Plate 39b
Parasitic Jaeger, *Stercorarius parasiticus*, Plate 39c
Bonaparte's Gull, *Larus philadelphia*, Plate 40a
Mew Gull, *Larus canus*, Plate 40b
Glaucous-winged Gull, *Larus glaucescens*, Plate 40c
Glaucous Gull, *Larus hyperboreus*, Plate 40d
Black-legged Kittiwake, *Rissa tridactyla*, Plate 41a
Sabine's Gull, *Xema sabini*, Plate 41b
Arctic Tern, *Sterna paradisaea*, Plate 41c
Aleutian Tern, *Sterna aleutica*, Plate 41d

10. Puffins and Their Relatives

Although birds of the family Alcidae occur widely in both the North Atlantic and North Pacific oceans, Alaska is the world's center of diversity for this group. These birds have been given a variety of names, so rather than calling them *auks, murres, puffins, guillemots*, etc., ornithologists usually opt for the collective term *alcids*. They are in the same order, Charadriiformes, that includes the gulls, terns, and shorebirds. Of 23 species of alcids, no fewer than 16 occur in Alaska. All of them are common breeding birds somewhere in the state, with the exception of the DOVEKIE, a North Atlantic species that wanders very rarely to the Bering Sea. On the water, alcids show short necks, compact bodies, and scarcely any tail, and these same characteristics make them look like flying footballs in the air. When they take off from the water, they immediately spread their tail wide and flatten their big, webbed feet beside it; this maximizes their lift as they attempt to become airborne. Once in the air, they always fly with rapidly whirring wings; gliding is not an option. Their feet are webbed for surface swimming, but there is no hind toe. This is a good clue, when examining dead birds cast up on the beach, that you have found a member of this family.

Alcids are smallish diving birds, ranging in size from tiny 15-cm (6-in) LEAST AUKLETS (Plate 44) to substantial 38-cm (15-in) TUFTED PUFFINS (Plate 42). The bright colors of alcids are restricted to their bills and feet, just as in gulls and terns. Some of them are quite garishly colored, with bright red-orange bills and feet. These colors are enhanced in the breeding season in puffins and a few of the auklets by the growth of an additional hard plate at the base of the bill, which adds more size and color to it. In the RHINOCEROS AUKLET (Plate 43), that plate includes a "horn" that dramatically alters the shape of the bill during the breeding season. Long black or white feathers that form conspicuous head plumes are also grown during the breeding season in some species. Of all the alcids profiled here, only the PIGEON GUILLEMOT (Plate 43) changes plumage color dramatically for breeding.

Natural History
Ecology and Behavior
Alcids are diving birds, feeding underwater like loons, grebes, and cormorants and preying mostly upon fish just as those birds do. However, they approach underwater locomotion in a different way, using their wings for propulsion instead of their feet. They are called *wing-propelled divers*, in the same category as the unrelated penguins. In fact, alcids are often thought of as the northern-hemisphere equivalents of penguins. Unlike penguins, however, alcids fly. Their wings, although small enough to enable the birds to swim rapidly underwater, are still large enough for them to fly. Alcids swim faster than you might think and easily quick enough to chase down the herrings, sand lances, and bottom fish on which they feed. Not only are alcids fast, but they dive to amazing depths: COMMON MURRES (Plate 42) are known to have reached depths of 180 m (590 ft), and even small species such as the CASSIN'S AUKLET dive below 30 m (100 ft). At great depths, the sea is cold and dark, and thinking of birds swimming down there stretches our idea of them as air-loving, flying animals.

Breeding
Alcids are monogamous and probably mate for life, because both parents return to the same nest site each year. Alcid nesting sites are varied. Murres nest on cliff

ledges, precarious places where you would think their eggs would be subject to rolling off. But their eggs are pointed at one end and therefore tend to roll in a circle! Many species nest in rock crevices, including all the small Bering Sea alcids. Puffins and guillemots nest in crevices on rocky islands or dig their own burrows where there are no crevices. ANCIENT MURRELETS (Plate 43) and RHINOCEROS AUKLETS always dig their own burrows. KITTLITZ'S MURRELETS lay their single egg on the ground, with no nest but often at the base of a large rock. MARBLED MURRELETS (Plate 43) do likewise when they nest in tundra areas, but in forested areas they depart drastically from their seabird relatives in nesting high in old-growth conifers, the nest a depression on a wide, mossy branch. Most alcids must work hard to find enough prey to feed their young, especially because the prey is patchy in distribution and the adults may have to fly far and wide to find it. Thus almost all of them lay only a single egg, but guillemots are exceptions to this. They are inshore feeders on bottom fishes and are thus able to find their prey closer to home; they often lay 2 eggs. Ancient Murrelets also lay 2 eggs, because they don't have to make long flights to feed their young (see below). The incubation and fledging periods of alcids are both lengthy and quite variable, depending on conditions at that time and place. The range of incubation periods is 23 to 52 days.

The way alcids care for their chicks varies greatly. Young puffins remain in their nests for 6 or 7 weeks before they flutter down to the sea, independent of their parents. Marbled Murrelets are similar, the young not leaving the nest until it can fly at 27 to 28 days – but this young bird, if fledging from high in a conifer, doesn't have much choice but to fly from its nest; the young may head for rivers, and float down them to the sea. Murres nest on cliffs, and their young take to the sea by jumping, rolling, and falling down to the water when only 2 to 4 weeks old, before they can fly. The female deserts the family at this time, and the male takes the young bird out to sea and feeds it for another several weeks. Finally, probably to avoid long, costly flights back and forth from feeding grounds to their nesting island, Ancient Murrelets take their young to sea when they are only a few days old, and there they are fed, perhaps one by each parent, for another month.

Lore and Notes

Murre eggs are the most variable of those of any birds. Their ground color varies from white to cream to buff to blue, and they can be unmarked, lightly marked, or heavily marked with any combination of streaks, scrawls, spots, or blotches. It would probably be impossible to find two eggs exactly alike. This variation apparently serves for individual recognition, so murres that leave their nesting ledge can come back and find their own egg among a long line of murre eggs. This conclusion was reached by biologists who switched eggs between two adjacent nesting birds and found the birds returning to their own eggs.

Status

No Alaska alcid is imperiled by human activities, but MARBLED MURRELET populations have declined so much to the south that the species was listed as Threatened in Canada in 1990 and in Washington, Oregon, and California in 1992. Logging is surely the cause for this decline, because the murrelets need old-growth forest for nesting. They will only place their nests on large branches high above the ground, and therefore large, old-growth trees are required. About 90% of the original forest cover of the Pacific Northwest is gone, and accelerated logging late in the 20th century changed the Marbled Murrelet from a common species to a rare one in just a few decades. Like the Spotted Owl, the Marbled Murrelet is now a *flagship species*, used as a symbol by wildlife and conservation organizations in the fight to save the remaining old growth. Extensive logging in the Tongass National Forest, Alaska's finest stand of old growth, will surely move the murrelet even closer to extirpation. Its presence in the forest adds an important issue to the debate among environmentalists, government agencies, and lumber companies about the fate of this forest.

Profiles

Common Murre, *Uria aalge*, Plate 42a
Thick-billed Murre, *Uria lomvia*, Plate 42b
Horned Puffin, *Fratercula corniculata*, Plate 42c
Tufted Puffin, *Fratercula cirrhata*, Plate 42d
Pigeon Guillemot, *Cepphus columba*, Plate 43a
Marbled Murrelet, *Brachyramphus marmoratus*, Plate 43b
Ancient Murrelet, *Synthliboramphus antiquus*, Plate 43c
Rhinoceros Auklet, *Cerorhinca monocerata*, Plate 43d
Parakeet Auklet, *Aethia psittacula*, Plate 44a
Least Auklet, *Aethia pusilla*, Plate 44b
Whiskered Auklet, *Aethia pygmaea*, Plate 44c
Crested Auklet, *Aethia cristatella*, Plate 44d

11. Owls

Although some *owls* are common Alaska birds, most of them are *nocturnal*, active at night, and so are rarely seen. Two species are *diurnal*, active in the daytime, but being large, predatory birds, they are not present in large numbers. Most owls are members of the family Strigidae, a worldwide group of 156 species; the only other owls are 17 species of the *barn owl* family, Tytonidae. Owls are particularly diverse in the tropics and subtropics, but Alaska has a good number of them, with 10 regularly occurring species and three rare visitors. Owls are readily recognized as such because of several distinctive features. All have large heads with forward-facing eyes; small, hooked bills; plumpish bodies; and sharp, hooked claws. Most have short legs and short tails. Owls are clad mostly in mixtures of gray, brown, black, and white, the result being that they are highly camouflaged against a variety of backgrounds. They have large, fluffy, very soft feathers. Most are medium-sized birds, the Alaska species ranging in length from 18 to 84 cm (7 to 33 in). Males and females look alike, although females are a bit larger.

Natural History
Ecology and Behavior

In general, owls occupy a variety of habitats: forests, clearings, fields, grasslands, mountains, and marshes. They are considered to be the nocturnal equivalents of the day-active birds of prey – the hawks, eagles, and falcons. Most owls hunt at night, taking prey such as small mammals, birds (including smaller owls), and reptiles; smaller owls specialize on insects, earthworms, and other small invertebrates. Owls in Alaska regularly hunt during the day, because at high latitudes in summer, it's always daylight. The NORTHERN HAWK OWL (Plate 46) hunts during the day. The SNOWY OWL (Plate 45) and SHORT-EARED OWL (Plate 45) prefer to hunt at dusk (*crepuscular* activity). Owls hunt by sight and by sound.

Their vision is very good in low light, the amount given off by moonlight, for instance; and their hearing is remarkable. They can hear sounds that are much lower in sound intensity (softer) than most other birds, and their ears are positioned on their heads asymmetrically, the better for localizing sounds in space. This means that owls in the darkness can, for example, actually hear small rodents moving about on the forest floor, quickly locate the source of the sound, then swoop and grab. Additionally, owing to their soft, loose feathers, the flight of owls is essentially silent, permitting prey little chance of hearing their approach. Owls kill their prey by biting, much in the fashion of falcons. They swallow small prey whole, then instead of digesting or passing the hard bits, they regurgitate bones, feathers, and fur in compact *owl pellets*. These are often found at the base of trees or on rocks where owls perch, and when pulled apart tell the story of an owl's favored cuisine. In winter, some northern owls store prey for later consumption (that is, they *cache* it). For instance, a dead mouse might be placed in a clump of spruce needles, where it quickly freezes. To thaw it later, the owl will tuck the frozen mouse under its belly, as if incubating an egg.

Owls maintain territories that they defend by their deep hooting and higher-pitched whistled calls (hoots and toots). As might be expected in night birds, vocalizations as much as appearance may serve to distinguish between species.

Breeding

Owls are monogamous breeders. They do not build nests themselves, but they take over nests abandoned by other birds or nest on broken-off stumps or in cavities such as tree holes; a few small species have taken to nesting boxes. Incubation of the 1 to 10 or more eggs (often 2 to 4) is usually conducted by the female alone for 4 to 5 weeks, but she is fed by her mate. At first, the female broods the young while the male hunts and brings meals, then both feed the young as they grow larger. Because incubation begins soon after the first egg is laid, the eggs hatch in sequence, and a nest may include everything from an unhatched egg up to a 2-week old young. If the parents can bring in enough food, all the young survive, but if food is scarce, the smaller young, which don't beg as energetically as the older ones, don't get fed, and eventually starve to death. Female SNOWY OWLS have been seen feeding one of these freshly dead young to a larger sibling – the economy of nature. Because owl broods are often fairly large, the young in tree-cavity nests may have to leave them before they attain full size. The young climb out and hop onto nearby branches until they settle down on a preferred branch; they are called *branchers* at this point by students of owl biology. The parents continue to feed them until they are 4 to 6 weeks old.

Ecological Interactions

Most birds breed every year, but some arctic-breeding species, owls among them, are unable to do so. The reason is that in some years, their food is very scarce. Lemming populations vary from abundant to virtually nonexistent in many areas of the arctic tundra (see p. 220), and the birds that depend on them for sustenance must adjust their breeding efforts accordingly. SNOWY OWLS and Pomarine Jaegers, in particular, may go several years without breeding if there are few lemmings in the area in which they breed. The jaegers are in an all-or-nothing situation, either breeding or not, but the owls appear to be able to adjust their clutches to lemming populations. When both the mated male and female owl have arrived on their breeding territory, the male begins to hunt for the female, and if lemming populations are high, he is able to present her with many lemmings during his courtship. She will then lay a large clutch, up to 10 or more eggs. If populations are lower, she may lay as few as 3 eggs, and if no lemmings are forthcoming, she may not breed at all. It is not known whether this is consciously determined or results from a feedback system from the female's energy balance.

Lore and Notes

Their big heads and forward-directed eyes give owls a peculiarly human look, and this, together with their habit of sitting still when we see them, rather than rushing about like sparrows and chickadees, has given them a reputation for wisdom. But they're not especially wise – in most cases when we spot them, they've just been awakened from a sound sleep. The forward-facing eyes of owls are a trait shared with few other animals: humans, most other primates, and, to a degree, cats. Eyes arranged in this way allow for almost complete binocular vision (one eye sees the same thing as the other), a prerequisite for good depth perception, which, in turn, is important for quickly judging distances when catching prey and especially important when you're doing it at night. The very large eyes of owls (those of a GREAT HORNED OWL, Plate 45, being about the size of human eyes) take up so much space that the eyes cannot move much; thus, owls must swivel their heads to look left or right. An owl can turn its head over a very wide angle (more than 180 degrees), but, contrary to what you may have heard, it can't turn it around completely.

Owls have a reputation for fierce, aggressive defense of their young; many a human who ventured too near an owl nest has been attacked and had damage done. A book by the famous British bird photographer, Eric Hosking, is entitled *An Eye for Birds*. Most readers don't realize that the title is a direct reference to losing an eye to a TAWNY OWL as Mr. Hosking was photographing a nesting pair.

Status

All Alaska owls are secure, as far as we know, but owls *are* harder to keep track of than most birds. SHORT-EARED OWLS have inexplicably declined in parts of their North American range, perhaps because of the disappearance of both marshy wetlands and natural grasslands, their preferred habitats. The most famous owl from the standpoint of conservation in North America is, of course, the SPOTTED OWL, which usually requires for breeding large sections of undisturbed, old-growth forest. But this species is not threatened in Alaska because it occurs no farther north than southern British Columbia. If any of Alaska's owls were similarly dependent on old-growth forests, this state might be embroiled in the disputes between environmentalists and loggers that occur regularly in Washington, Oregon, and northern California. Fortunately, the owls of Alaska occur in a variety of forest types, and many of them occur in the more northerly parts of the state, where the trees are too small to make logging profitable. The WESTERN SCREECH-OWL, NORTHERN PYGMY-OWL, BARRED OWL, and NORTHERN SAW-WHET OWL, relatively rare residents of the forests of southeast Alaska, might be vulnerable to forest destruction but can survive as long as there are extensive forests at various stages of succession.

Profiles

Short-eared Owl, *Asio flammeus*, Plate 45a
Snowy Owl, *Nyctea scandiaca*, Plate 45b

Great Horned Owl, *Bubo virginianus*, Plate 45c
Great Gray Owl, *Strix nebulosa*, Plate 45d
Northern Hawk Owl, *Surnia ulula*, Plate 46a
Boreal Owl, *Aegolius funereus*, Plate 46b

12. Hummingbirds

Hummingbirds are birds of extremes. They are among the most easily recognized kinds of birds, the smallest of birds, and undoubtedly among the most beautiful, albeit on a diminutive scale. Fittingly, much of their biology is nothing short of amazing. The hummingbirds comprise a large family, Trochilidae, with 322 species. Hummingbirds are restricted to the New World and primarily to the tropics; there are only two regularly occurring and two rare species in southern Alaska. The variety of forms encompassed by the family, not to mention the brilliant iridescence of most of its members, is indicated in the names attached to some of the groups: emeralds, sapphires, sunangels, comets, metaltails, fairies, woodstars, pufflegs, sabrewings, thorntails, and lancebills. Although Alaska species are primarily birds of forest edge and suburbs, hummingbirds elsewhere occupy a broad array of habitat types, from exposed high mountainsides at 4000 m (13,000 ft) to mid-elevation deserts to sea level tropical forests and mangrove swamps, as long as there are nectar-filled flowers to provide necessary nourishment.

Almost everyone can identify hummingbirds (often called *hummers* by those who study them): tiny birds, usually gorgeously clad in iridescent metallic greens, reds, and violets. Their name refers not to their musical activity (most merely say "chip") but to the sound their wings make as the birds whiz by at high speeds.

Most hummers are in the range of only 6 to 13 cm (2.5 to 5 in) long, although South America's GIANT HUMMINGBIRD (what an oxymoron!) reaches 20 cm (8 in). The smallest among them resemble nothing so much as large bees. Alaska species weigh about 3 g – as light as a penny. Bill length and shape varies extensively among species, each bill closely adapted to the precise type of flowers from which a species draws its liquid food. Males are usually more colorful than females, and many of them have *gorgets*, bright, glittering throat patches in red, blue, green, or violet. Hummers have tiny legs and feet; in fact, they are included with the swifts in the avian order Apodiformes, meaning *those without feet*.

Natural History
Ecology and Behavior

Owing to their many anatomical, behavioral, and ecological specializations, hummingbirds have long attracted the research attention of biologists; the result is that we know quite a bit about them. These highly active birds that are so entertaining to watch are most often studied for one of four aspects of their biology: flying ability, metabolism, feeding ecology, and defense of food resources.

(1) Hummers are capable of very rapid, finely controlled, acrobatic flight, more so than any other kind of bird. Their wings are modified to allow for perfect, stationary *hovering* flight and also for the unique ability to *fly backwards*. The secret to these maneuvers is the hummers' ability to rotate the wing on its own axis and thus get power on both the downstroke and upstroke. Their wings vibrate at a speed beyond our ability to see each stroke – up to 80 times per second. Because people usually see hummers only during the birds'

foraging trips, they often appear never to land, remaining airborne as they zip from flower to flower, hovering briefly to probe and feed at each. But they do perch between flights, providing opportunities to get good looks at them.

(2) Hummingbirds have very high metabolisms, a necessary condition for small, warm-blooded animals. To pump enough oxygen and nutrient-delivering blood around their little bodies, their hearts beat up to 10 times faster than human hearts – 600 to 1000 times per minute. To obtain sufficient energy to fuel their high metabolism, hummingbirds must eat many times each day. Quick starvation results from an inability to feed regularly. At night, when they are inactive, they burn much of their available energy reserves, and on cold nights, if not for special mechanisms, they would surely starve to death. The chief method to avoid energy depletion on cold nights is to enter into a sleep-like state of *torpor*, during which the body's temperature is lowered to just above that of the outside world, from 17 to 28°C (30 to 50°F) below their daytime operating temperatures, saving them enormous amounts of energy. In effect, they set the thermostat down and hibernate overnight.

(3) All hummingbirds are *nectarivores* – they get most of their nourishment from consuming nectar from flowers. They have long, thin bills and specialized tongues to suck nectar from long, thin flower tubes, which they do while hovering. Because nectar is mostly a sugar and water solution, hummingbirds need to obtain additional nutrients, such as proteins, from other sources. Toward this end they also eat small insects and spiders, which they catch in the air or pluck off spider webs.

(4) Hummers are typically highly aggressive birds, energetically defending individual flowers or feeding territories from all other hummingbirds, regardless of species. This is always size-mediated – large species are able to dominate small ones.

Predators on hummingbirds include small, agile hawks and also frogs and large insects, such as praying mantises, that ambush the small birds as they feed at flowers. Even large spider webs and sticky plant seeds sometimes catch hummingbirds. Another hazard, not so easy to document, is the long migration Alaska species make between their breeding and wintering habitats. The RUFOUS HUMMINGBIRD (Plate 46) migrates to the mountains of western Mexico and back.

Breeding
Hummingbirds are promiscuous breeders in which males attempt to mate with as many females as possible and females supply all the parental care. The following refers to the common Alaska species, the RUFOUS. A male on his territory advertises for females by performing a wonderful oval display flight. He ascends high in the air and then dives full-speed toward the ground, pulling up at the last moment with a loud burst of staccato, musical sounds (made by jerking his tail, which has specially modified outer feathers). A female enters the territory and, following an intense courtship display, mates. Afterwards, she leaves the territory to nest on her own. Nests are placed on small horizontal branches of trees, usually within 10 m (30 ft) of the ground. On the outside, nests have a coating of lichens, which is carefully applied by the female and probably provides both camouflage and waterproofing. The female lays 2 eggs, incubates them for 15 to 17 days, and feeds regurgitated nectar and insects to her young for about 21 days, until they fledge.

Ecological Interactions

The relationship between hummingbirds (nectar consumers) and the flowering plants from which they feed (nectar producers) is mutually beneficial. The birds obtain a high-energy food that is easy to locate and always available because various flowering plant species, as well as groups of flowers on the same plant, open and produce nectar at different times. The flowering plants, in turn, use the tiny birds as other plants use bees – as pollinators. The nectar is produced and released into the part of the flower that the hummer feeds from for the sole reason of attracting the birds so that they may accidentally rub up against the parts of the flower (*anthers*) that contain pollen grains. These grains are actually reproductive spores that the flower very much "wants" the bird to pick up on its body and transfer to other plants of the same species during its subsequent foraging, thereby achieving for the flower *cross-pollination* with another member of its species. Flowers that are specialized for hummingbird pollination place nectar in long, thin tubes that fit the shape of the birds' bills and also protect the nectar from foraging insects. Hummingbird-pollinated plants often have red, pink, or orange flowers, colors that render them easily detectable to the birds but indistinguishable from the background environment to insects, most of which lack red color vision. Furthermore, these flowers are often odorless because birds use color vision and not smell to find them, and this prevents visits from inappropriate pollinating insects that use odor to guide them.

Lore and Notes

Hummingbirds seem quite unafraid of people. Bright red anywhere on your person is almost a guaranteed hummingbird attractant, and some hikers add a red scarf to their apparel just for this pleasure. Think of yourself as a walking flower.

Status

Alaska's hummingbirds are doing fine, prospering in part because so many people put out feeders for them, but many species of limited range in tropical countries are rare if not endangered.

Profiles

Rufous Hummingbird, *Selasphorus rufus*, Plate 46d

13. Kingfishers

Kingfishers are bright-colored birds most often encountered along rivers and streams or along the seashore. Classified with the *motmots*, *bee-eaters*, and several other colorful tropical bird families in the order Coraciiformes, the 95 kingfisher species of the family Alcedinidae range throughout the tropics, with a few of them pushing deeply northward and southward into temperate areas. Only six kingfisher species reside in the New World, and only one of those makes it to Alaska. Kingfishers vary in size from 12 to 46 cm (5 to 16 in), but all are of a similar form: large heads with long, robust, straight bills, short necks, short legs, and, for some, large, bushy crests. The kingfisher color scheme in the New World is also fairly standardized: dark green or blue-gray above, white and/or chestnut-orange below. Old World kingfishers are much more varied in size and shape, and, belying their names, many are terrestrial predators, feeding on insects and lizards in tropical forests and savannahs.

Natural History
Ecology and Behavior

Many kingfishers, as the name suggests, are fish eaters (that is, they are *piscivores*). Usually seen hunting alone near water, they sit quietly, attentively on a low perch – a tree branch or a telephone wire – while scanning the water below. When they locate suitable prey, they swoop and dive, plunging head-first into the water (to depths up to 60 cm, or 24 in) to seize it. If successful, they quickly emerge from the water, return to the perch, beat the fish against the perch to stun it, then swallow it whole, head first. Thus, kingfishers are sit-and-wait predators of the waterways. They will also, when they see movement below the water, hover over a particular spot before diving in. BELTED KINGFISHERS (Plate 46) commonly fly out 500 m (a quarter mile) or more from a lake's shore to hover 3 to 10 m (10 to 33 ft) above the water, searching for fish. Kingfishers fly fast and purposefully, usually in straight and level flight, from one perch to another; often they are seen only as flashes of blue darting along waterways.

Kingfishers are highly territorial, aggressively defending their territories from other members of their species with noisy, chattering vocalizations, chasing, and fighting. They inhabit mostly lowland forests and waterways, but some range up to elevations of 2500 m (8000 ft).

Breeding

Kingfishers are monogamous breeders that nest in holes. In the BELTED KINGFISHER, both members of the pair defend the territory in which the nest is located, and both take turns digging the 1 to 2 m (3 to 6 ft) long nest burrow into the soft earth of a river or stream bank. In recent times, road excavations near water have become prime habitat for kingfisher nests. Both parents incubate the 6 or 7 eggs for a total of 22 to 24 days. The young are fed increasingly large fish by both parents until they fledge at 27 to 29 days old. Fledglings continue to be fed by the parents for another 3 weeks. At some point after they are independent, the parents expel the young from the territory. Many juvenile kingfishers apparently die during their first attempts at diving for food. Some have been seen "practicing" predation by capturing floating leaves and sticks.

Lore and Notes

Kingfishers are the subject of a particularly rich mythology, a sign of the bird's conspicuousness and its association with water throughout history. In some parts of the world, kingfishers are associated with the biblical Great Flood. It is said that survivors of the flood had no fire and so the kingfisher was chosen to steal fire from the gods. The bird was successful, but during the theft, burned its chest, resulting in the chestnut-orange coloring we see today. According to the ancient Greeks, Zeus was jealous of Alcyone's power over the wind and waves and so killed her husband by destroying his ship with thunder and lightning. "In her grief, Alcyone threw herself into the sea to join her husband, and they both turned immediately into kingfishers. The power that sailors attributed to Alcyone was passed on to the Halcyon Bird, the kingfisher, which was credited with protecting sailors and calming storms" (D. Boag 1982). Halcyon birds were thought to nest 7 days before and 7 days after the winter solstice and these days of peace and calm were referred to as *halcyon days.*

Status

The BELTED KINGFISHER remains abundant throughout much of North America. In fact, none of the New World species is rare. But some kingfisher species on islands in the South Pacific are threatened by habitat destruction with the clearing of already limited forest stands, and a few island populations have already become extinct.

Profiles

Belted Kingfisher, *Megaceryle alcyon*, Plate 46c

14. Woodpeckers

We are all familiar with *woodpeckers*, at least in name and in their cartoon incarnations. These are industrious, highly specialized birds of the forest; where there are trees in the world, there are woodpeckers (excepting only Australia and some island nations). The woodpecker family, Picidae, includes 216 species, from the 9-cm (3.5-in) *piculets* to large woodpeckers up to 50 cm (20 in) long. Six regularly occurring species and three rare species occur in Alaska, and they occupy diverse wooded habitats. Woodpeckers have strong, straight, chisel-like bills, very long tongues that are barbed and often sticky-coated, and toes that spread widely, firmly anchoring the birds to tree trunks and branches. They come in various shades of black and white, brown, and olive-green, usually with small but conspicuous head or neck patches of red or yellow, more prominent in males. Some have red or brown crests. A few woodpeckers are quite showy, mostly in striking patterns of red, black, and white. Because of the tapping sounds they produce as they hammer their bills against trees and wooden structures, and owing to their characteristic stance – braced upright on tree trunks – woodpeckers often attract our notice and so are frequently observed forest-dwellers.

Natural History

Ecology and Behavior

Woodpeckers are associated with trees and are adapted to cling to a tree's bark and to move lightly over its surface, searching for insects. They also drill holes in bark and wood into which they insert their long tongues, probing for hidden insects. They usually move up tree trunks in short hops, using their stiff tail as a prop. Woodpeckers find most of their insect prey on the surface or below the bark of twigs, branches, and trunks of many kinds of trees. They also are not above a bit of flycatching, taking insects on the wing, and many tropical species supplement their diets with fruits, nuts, and nectar. *Sapsuckers* are woodpeckers that use their bills to drill small holes in trees that fill with sap, which is then eaten. Some woodpeckers, including the NORTHERN FLICKER (Plate 47), also forage on the ground, especially for ants.

Woodpeckers are monogamous, but some non-Alaskan species live in large family groups. Woodpeckers sleep and nest in cavities that they excavate in trees. They hit trees with their bills for three very different reasons: for drilling bark to get at insect food; for excavating holes for roosting and nesting; and for *drumming*, sending signals to other woodpeckers. The characteristic drumming sound, equivalent to the spring song of songbirds, is much more rapid than those steady or irregular taps that indicate feeding or digging a new home. Woodpeckers typically fly with a characteristic up-and-down (*undulating*) flight.

Breeding

A mated male and female woodpecker carve a nesting hole in a tree. Sometimes they line the cavity with wood chips. In Alaska woodpeckers, both sexes incubate the 3 to 8 eggs for 12 to 16 days, males typically taking the entire night shift. Young are fed by both parents for 20 to 30 days until they fledge. Juveniles often remain with the parents for several months more, or longer in those species in which families of up to 20 individuals associate throughout the year.

Ecological Interactions

Woodpeckers are often used as examples of the evolutionary consequences of competitive interactions in nature. One way for ecologically similar species to avoid competition is to specialize on prey of different sizes. Woodpeckers, most of which forage for insects on bark, are very similar ecologically, and different-sized woodpeckers do indeed specialize on different-sized prey, thereby reducing the negative effects of competition. There are small (for instance, DOWNY WOODPECKER, Plate 47) and medium-sized (NORTHERN FLICKER) species in Alaska and much larger species to the south. When there are two or more woodpecker species of about the same size inhabiting the same place, for example the HAIRY WOODPECKER (Plate 47) and THREE-TOED WOODPECKER (Plate 47) in Alaska, these potential competitors usually forage in different ways, or for different items – again, eliminating competition that could drive one of the species to extinction in the region in which they overlap.

Woodpeckers use dead trees or dead branches on live trees for most of their foraging and nesting. Dead wood is softer than live, thus easier to chip away, and it is often infested with boring beetles. Live poplars and aspens, with their very soft wood, are also favored trees for nest holes. Woodpeckers are usually considered beneficial by people, because they consume great quantities of insects such as tree borers that can significantly damage forests. On the other hand, the persistent early-morning drumming of a Northern Flicker on the side or roof of a house can drive a home-owner to distraction.

Because other birds use tree holes for roosting and/or nesting, but do not or cannot dig holes themselves, sometimes the carpenter-like woodpeckers end up doing the work for them. Many species, ranging from swallows to small owls and small ducks, occupy deserted woodpecker holes. More problematically, some birds "parasitize" the woodpecker's work by stealing holes. For instance, European Starlings, although smaller than flickers, have been observed evicting them, as well as other woodpeckers, from their nest holes. Fortunately for woodpeckers and other hole nesters, starlings are still uncommon in Alaska.

Lore and Notes

In ancient Roman mythology, Saturn's son, Picus, was a god of the forests. The sorceress Circe, attracted to the handsome Picus, courted him but was rejected. In her wrath, she transformed Picus into a woodpecker, providing the basis for the woodpecker family's name, Picidae. The Mayans of ancient America thought that the woodpecker was a lucky bird, possessor of a lucky green stone that it kept under its wing. The legend was that the luck would be transferred to any person who could find a woodpecker hole and cover it. The bird would excavate a new hole, but that one, too, should be covered. After nine excavations, the woodpecker would drop the charm, allowing the person to claim it. During the Mayan civilization, presumably, there were quite a few highly frustrated woodpeckers.

Woodpeckers damage trees and buildings and also eat fruit from gardens and orchards (especially cherries, apples, pears, and raspberries), and so in some regions are considered significant pests and treated as such. Sapsuckers, which reach their northern limit in southern Alaska, drill holes in living trees to eat the sap that flows from them and the insects attracted to fermenting sap, and enough sapsucker holes can lead to diseased and damaged trees.

Status

No Alaska woodpeckers are at risk, but one North American member of the group is, sadly, on the list of extinct species. The large and spectacular IVORY-BILLED WOODPECKER was common in southeastern swamp forests when Europeans began to colonize the continent, but the woodpeckers were tame and easily shot. More important, they were probably dependent on the mature trees of old-growth forest for nesting and foraging. The eastern forests were logged surprisingly rapidly as the East was settled, and birds such as the Ivory-bill, that needed about 8 sq km (3 sq miles) of undisturbed forest for each pair, could not persist. Their numbers dropped markedly by the end of the 19th century, and only a few birds persisted to nearly the middle of the 20th century. They are gone now, and a similarly precarious population of the species in eastern Cuba has probably met the same fate.

Profiles

Downy Woodpecker, *Picoides pubescens*, Plate 47a
Hairy Woodpecker, *Picoides villosus*, Plate 47b
Three-toed Woodpecker, *Picoides tridactylus*, Plate 47c
Northern Flicker, *Colaptes auratus*, Plate 47d

All of the bird groups considered below are *passerine*, or *perching birds*, members of order Passeriformes (see p. 106).

---

15. Flycatchers

The *flycatchers* comprise a huge group of birds that is broadly distributed over most habitats from Alaska and northern Canada to the southern tip of South America. They are the first *passerine* birds discussed in this book. The flycatcher family, Tyrannidae, is considered among the most diverse of avian groups. With 394 species, flycatchers usually contribute a hefty percentage of the avian bio-diversity almost anywhere in the New World. For instance, it has been calculated that flycatchers make up fully one tenth of the land bird species in South America, and perhaps one-quarter of Argentinian species. Even at the northern end of their range in Alaska, there are eight regularly occurring and seven rarely seen species. Of course, they are present in Alaska only during the summer, when flies are available to catch.

Flycatchers range in length from 6.5 to 40 cm (2.5 to 16 in). At the smallest extreme are some of the world's tiniest birds, weighing only 7 g (1/4 oz). Their bills are usually broad and flat, the better to snatch flying bugs from the air. Tail length is variable, but some species have very long, forked tails, which probably aid the birds in their rapid, acrobatic, insect-catching maneuvers. Most flycatchers are dully turned out in shades of gray, brown, and olive-green, but many tropical species have bright yellow in their plumage, and a few are quite flashily attired in, for example, bright expanses of vermilion. A great many of the smaller, drabber flycatchers, clad in olives and browns, are extremely difficult to tell apart in the field, even for experienced birdwatchers, and most of Alaska's species look so similar that they are not illustrated here. Flycatcher sexes are usually similar in size and coloring.

Natural History

Ecology and Behavior

Flycatchers are common over a large array of different habitat types, from high mountainsides and lowland moist forests to treeless plains and grasslands, marshes, and mangrove swamps; they are especially prevalent in rainforests. In Alaska, most species inhabit forests, although SAY'S PHOEBE (Plate 48) is a bird of open country. As their name implies, most flycatchers are *insectivores*, obtaining most of their food by employing the classic flycatching technique. They perch motionless on tree or shrub branches or on fences or telephone wires, then dart out in short, swift flights to snatch from the air insects foolhardy enough to enter their field of vision; they then return to the same perch to repeat the process. After a period of scanning the sky in vain, they will move to another perch. Many flycatchers also fly up to and snatch insects from foliage, and many tropical species also supplement their diets with fruits. Some of the larger flycatchers will also take small frogs and lizards, and some, such as the GREAT KISKADEE, consider small fish and tadpoles delicacies to be plucked from shallow edges of lakes and rivers. Almost all of the relatively few flycatchers that have been studied inhabit exclusive territories that mated pairs defend for all or part of the year. In Alaska, this means the breeding season, May to July.

Breeding

Flycatchers are mainly monogamous. Many tropical flycatchers are known for spectacular courtship displays, males showing off to females by engaging in aerial acrobatics, including flips and somersaults. In some monogamous species, males help the females build nests. Alaska flycatchers are much more conservative than their varied tropical relatives. They all build cup nests (lined with mud in the case of the SAY'S PHOEBE), but tropical species may build roofed nests or globular hanging nests placed in trees or shrubs. Other tropical flycatchers build mud nests that they attach to vertical surfaces such as rock walls, and still others place their nest in holes in trees or rock crevices. Alaska flycatchers generally lay 3 to 4 eggs that are incubated by the female for 12 to 17 days; the nestlings fledge when 13 to 23 days old. Flycatchers, as do all passerines, have *altricial* nestlings, born naked, blind, and helpless, that slowly develop the ability to take care of themselves as they grow while in the nest.

Ecological Interactions

Some flycatchers show marked alterations in their lifestyles as seasons, locations, and feeding opportunities change. Such ongoing capacity for versatile behavior in response to changing environments is considered a chief underlying cause of the group's great ecological success. An excellent example is the EASTERN KINGBIRD'S drastic changes in behavior between summer and winter. Breeding during summer throughout much of North America (but only a rare visitor to Alaska), these flycatchers are extremely aggressive in defending their territories against other birds and defending their eggs and young against anything that moves; they feed exclusively at that time on insects. But a change comes over the birds during the winter, as they idle away the months in South America's Amazon

Basin. There, Eastern Kingbirds congregate in large, nonterritorial flocks with apparently nomadic existences, and, for food, they share tree fruit with a host of resident tropical fruit-eaters.

Lore and Notes

Of all the groups of birds, it is probably among the flycatchers that the most undiscovered species remain. This distinction is owing to the group's great diversity, its penetration into essentially all terrestrial habitats, and the inconspicuousness of many of its members. In fact, as people reach previously inaccessible locations – hidden valleys, cloud-draped mountain plateaus – in the remotest parts of South America, previously unknown flycatchers are indeed found. New species of flycatchers were described in 1981 from Peru, in 1987 and 1992 from Brazil, and in 1988 from Colombia. The last of Alaska's flycatcher species was described in 1895, however.

Status

Alaska's flycatchers are secure for now, but members of this family elsewhere in the world have suffered from habitat destruction. Several species known only from southeastern Brazil, for example KAEMPFER'S TODY-TYRANT, are considered at great risk, because they have been sighted only a few times in recent years. That part of the world has had the vast majority of its forested habitats cleared for agricultural use, negatively affecting many forest bird populations. The newly described RESTINGA TYRANNULET is found only along a stretch of coastal beach in Brazil that is rapidly being developed for recreation.

Profiles

Alder Flycatcher, *Empidonax alnorum*, Plate 48a
Say's Phoebe, *Sayornis saya*, Plate 48b

16. Larks and Pipits

There are 91 species of *larks*, family Alaudidae, distributed throughout Eurasia and Africa, but one species, the HORNED LARK (Plate 48), long ago crossed the Bering Strait and colonized much of North America, with isolated populations in the northern Andes of South America. There are 65 species of *pipits* and *wagtails*, family Motacillidae, and they are wider-ranging, with pipits on every continent and wagtails throughout Eurasia and Africa; two of the latter, the WHITE WAGTAIL and YELLOW WAGTAIL, have colonized Alaska from the west and can be seen on the Seward Peninsula. Larks and pipits are small birds, the Alaska species, at 15 to 20 cm (6 to 8 in), typical of their families. Members of these families are supremely adapted for ground living, with long toes and especially long hind claws (toenails) to furnish additional support as they walk. Most other ground-dwelling passerine birds have curved claws and hop rather than walk; they belong to bird families adapted for tree- and shrub-living but include some members that forage on the ground.

Wagtails are brightly marked birds – with mixtures of black and white and gray and yellow in the different species – that may be conspicuous because they are such active foragers and have nothing to gain by being cryptically colored. They wag their long, black and white tails frantically and, when flushed, fly in huge arcs through the air, calling loudly. Larks and pipits have shorter tails, also with white edges that are conspicuous when they fly, but they are brown above and very well camouflaged – for instance, when they are feeding among dried grasses. They call when flushed, but less noisily than the wagtails, and their flight does not show the extreme bounding undulations of wagtail flight.

Natural History
Ecology and Behavior
The HORNED LARK and AMERICAN PIPIT (Plate 48) are characteristic breeding birds of Alaska tundra. The lark is largely restricted as a breeding species to alpine tundra but also occurs sparsely in arctic tundra north of the Brooks Range. The pipit breeds much more widely in both mountain and lowland tundra across the state. Both species may be seen in migration in open areas, for example beaches, tide flats, and agricultural lands, anywhere farther south in the state. But the pipit is much more commonly seen in migration than the lark. American Pipits, in fact, are among the most familiar birds in Alaska because of their tameness and propensity for feeding in the open. Both larks and pipits walk or run through open areas, where the vegetation is usually quite short, and pluck their prey from the ground. The pipit has a very fine bill and is a confirmed insectivore, whereas the lark's bill is thicker, somewhere between that of a pipit and that of a sparrow. It is basically a seed-eater, feeding on seeds during the winter but taking many more insects when they are available during the summer. Interestingly, pipits will turn to a seed diet on their wintering grounds when weather conditions cause an insect scarcity. Both larks and pipits form flocks in the nonbreeding season. These birds are often invisible until flushed, at which point they ascend, circle, and either fly away or drop back to the ground. Pipits come down in jerks, as if descending an invisible stairway, and their loud, two-noted calls sound enough like "pi-pit" to be memorable.

Breeding
Many open-country birds have aerial displays, and pipits and larks are no exceptions. Males of both species profiled here ascend into the air and sing in flight, sometimes for minutes at a time. Then they drop suddenly or spiral conspicuously down to the ground, where they can be found by an interested female. Flight songs make it possible for open-country birds to advertise their territories and attract mates much more effectively than if the birds were confined to the ground. The Horned Lark is one of the earliest breeding birds in its tundra environment, nesting as early as late May and early June, but pipits are on their nests in late June and July. Both larks and pipits nest on the ground, constructing cup nests in depressions. Lark nests are placed in the open, but pipit nests are often sheltered by a rock or overhanging grass. Horned Larks lay 3 or 4 eggs, and the female incubates them for 10 to 12 days. The young leave the nest after another 10 to 12 days but cannot fly until they are another week older. American Pipits have similar breeding habits, although they lay a slightly larger clutch, 4 to 6 eggs; incubation lasts 13 to 16 days. The young pipits leave their nest at about 14 days of age and continue to be fed by their parents for another week or two. Larks seem to have an accelerated development in comparison to pipits, perhaps because they nest in slightly more exposed areas and are thus a bit more likely to be seen by sharp-eyed predators.

Lore and Notes
The SKYLARK, a species accidental on Bering Sea islands, is said to have one of the most beautiful songs of any bird, and it delivers it from high in the air, as do many larks. Percy Bysshe Shelley's 1820 poem *To a Skylark* makes it clear that this

species deserves its reputation: "Hail to thee, blithe Spirit! Bird thou never wert, That from Heaven, or near it, Pourest thy full heart In profuse strains of unpremeditated art."

Status

Much of the world is open space, and it would seem surprising that birds of open country, including larks and pipits, would be vulnerable to habitat destruction. But in fact, natural grasslands (*steppes*) are among the most threatened environments. Because our grain crops (wheat, corn, rye, sorghum, rice) are grasses, areas of grassland are the natural places to plant them, and in North America   in particular, scarcely any of the original grassland remains. Fortunately, HORNED LARKS seem very adaptable, and they have readily taken to farmland. But they are one of the few grassland birds to be so adaptable, and many other species, for example the SPRAGUE'S PIPIT and Greater Prairie-Chicken of the American Great Plains, have become scarce in most parts of their ranges.

Profiles

American Pipit, *Anthus rubescens*, Plate 48c
Horned Lark, *Eremophila alpestris*, Plate 48d

17. Swallows

Swallows are easily identified by their habit of catching insects on the wing during long periods of sustained flight. Members of the family Hirundinidae, they are a group of songbirds, 89 species strong, with a worldwide distribution. Six regularly occurring species and two rarities are found in Alaska, all present only as summer migrants from far southerly wintering areas. Swallows are small, streamlined birds, 11.5 to 21.5 cm (4.5 to 8.5 in) in length, with short necks, bills, and legs. Adapted for moving rapidly through the air with high maneuverability, they have long, pointed wings, and most of them have forked tails. Some are colored in shades of blue, green, or violet, but many are gray or brown. The sexes look alike in most species, although male and female VIOLET-GREEN SWALLOWS (Plate 49) are quite easily distinguished by the male's greater brightness and contrast.

Natural History
Ecology and Behavior

Among the birds, swallows and the unrelated *swifts* represent pinnacles of flying prowess and aerial insectivory. It seems as if they fly all day, circling low over water or land or flying in erratic patterns high overhead, all the while snatching insects from the air. The length of a swallow's tail and the depth of its fork are good indicators of where it forages. CLIFF SWALLOWS (Plate 49) have a very short, unforked tail, and they forage high in the air, mostly gliding around in circles as they search for insects. TREE SWALLOWS (Plate 49), with tail slightly forked, are more agile fliers, turning more readily to chase elusive prey, but they still fly well above the ground. BARN SWALLOWS (Plate 49), with a very long, deeply forked tail, forage near the ground, where they must be able to turn very suddenly to capture low-flying insects and avoid obstacles.

Some swallows, for example the TREE SWALLOW, are able to winter fairly far north because they can subsist on berries if insects are scarce. Not quite so aerially restricted as swifts, swallows land more often, often resting during the hottest parts of the day. At dawn and dusk, swallows seem always to be airborne, and their calls are sometimes heard from overhead during the night-time.

Breeding

Some species of swallows breed in dense colonies of dozens to a thousand or more nesting pairs. Although swallows are thought of as monogamous like so many other passerines, colonial breeding furnishes abundant opportunities for deviating from this mode. Male BANK SWALLOWS (Plate 49) are ready to attempt copulation with any female, and thus when the female of a pair leaves the nest early in the reproductive cycle, her mate will fly right behind her to keep other males away. Many female CLIFF SWALLOWS lay part of their clutch in a nearby nest, if given the opportunity, a literal example of the saying "don't put all your eggs in one basket," and with the same reasoning. If the swallow's own nest is unsuccessful, that of the neighbor may survive, and the swallow's reproductive efforts are not entirely in vain.

Nests are constructed of plant pieces placed in a tree cavity, burrow, or building, or, alternatively, consist of a mud cup or chamber attached to a vertical surface such as a cliff. The mud-nesting species must find their mud somewhere, so this need determines where they can nest, although in Alaska it's usually not too far to the nearest mud puddle. BARN SWALLOWS forage for mud for their nests singly, but Cliff Swallows do it in groups, and one of the more striking sights of summer is a mud puddle with dozens of Cliff Swallows landing and taking off and gathering mud in their bills, their wings fluttering in the air. Apparently the wing flutter – in both sexes – is to prevent another swallow from trying to mate with the preoccupied bird! Most swallows line their nests with an inner coat of feathers, obviously of value for insulation, and feathers are in great demand among these birds. A single white duck feather in a farmyard might be plucked from the ground by a TREE SWALLOW, which is then chased around and around by others of the same species, the feather dropped and caught in midair repeatedly until one bird finally gets it into its nest hole. In Alaska swallows, either the female alone or both sexes incubate the 3 to 7 eggs for 13 to 16 days. The nestlings fledge after 18 to 24 days, and the parents continue to feed them for several days after that, the young often "parked" in conspicuous groups on dead tree branches or fence wires.

Ecological Interactions

Swallows are small, vulnerable lightweights, and as such are often under competitive pressure for breeding space from other hole-nesting species. European Starlings and House Sparrows, for instance, sometimes try to take over nests built by swallows, especially TREE and VIOLET-GREEN. CLIFF SWALLOWS may locate their colonies near to or actually surrounding the cliff-situated nests of large hawks, basking in the protection afforded by having a nest close to a fearsome predator.

Because swallows depend each day on capturing enough insects, their daily habits are largely tied to the prevailing weather. Flying insects fill the air on warm, sunny days but are relatively scarce on cold, wet ones. Therefore, on good days, swallows can catch their fill of bugs in only a few hours of flying, virtually anywhere. But on cool, wet days, they may need to forage all day to find enough food, and they tend to fly low, where under such conditions insects are more available. They are especially attracted to water at that time, perhaps because it is easiest to capture low-flying insects when they are not flying among plants or because aquatic insects continue to emerge from ponds and lakes even during cool weather.

Lore and Notes

Swallows have a long history of beneficial association with people. In the New World, owing to their insect-eating habits, they have been popular with people going back to the time of the ancient Mayan civilization. Mayans, it is believed, respected and welcomed swallows because they reduced insect damage to crops. CAVE SWALLOWS nest in almost all the old Mayan ruins, and Cozumel (the word refers to swallows), off Mexico's Yucatan Peninsula, is the Island of Swallows. People's alterations of natural habitats, harmful to so many species, are often helpful to swallows, which adopt buildings, bridges, road culverts, road banks, and quarry walls as nesting areas. In fact, very few populations of BARN SWALLOWS continue to use cliffs and cave mouths, probably their original nesting sites. CLIFF SWALLOWS very often use human structures for nesting, although they are much more colonial than Barn Swallows, sometimes occurring in colonies of hundreds of pairs. BANK SWALLOWS originally nested in sandy river banks and still do, but a colony can form anywhere earth-moving machinery leaves a sand pile. TREE and VIOLET-GREEN SWALLOWS, both cavity nesters, are quite willing to accept bird houses as substitutes. All but the Bank Swallow are familiar sights in Alaska's cities and villages. The result of the close association between people and swallows is that, going back as far as ancient Rome, swallows have been considered good luck. Superstitions attached to the relationship abound; for example, it is said that the cows of a farmer who destroys a swallow's nest will give bloody milk. Arrival of the first migratory Barn Swallows in Europe is considered a welcoming sign of approaching spring, as is the arrival of Cliff Swallows at Capistrano, an old Spanish mission in California. The swallows don't actually return to Capistrano on the same day each year, but their arrival dates are close enough to be notable.

Status

Swallows are among the more successful birds of the world, in part because many of them have incorporated the products of our architects and construction workers as nesting sites. Nevertheless, two species of swallows, one in the Middle East and the other in Thailand, are known only from one or a few specimens taken on their wintering grounds; their breeding sites are unknown, and they are obviously very rare if not extinct.

Profiles

Violet-green Swallow, *Tachycineta thalassina*, Plate 49a
Tree Swallow, *Tachycineta bicolor*, Plate 49b
Bank Swallow, *Riparia riparia*, Plate 49c
Cliff Swallow, *Petrochelidon pyrrhonota*, Plate 49d
Barn Swallow, *Hirundo rustica*, Plate 49e

18. Crows and Jays

The *crows, ravens, magpies,* and *jays* are members of the Corvidae, a passerine family of 118 species of *cosmopolitan* (worldwide) distribution. In other words, corvids occur just about everywhere. Six species are locally common residents in Alaska, and a rare visitor adds a seventh to the list. *Corvids* are known for their versatility, adaptability, and undoubted intelligence; jays, in addition, are strikingly handsome. Members of this group are also usually quite noisy, and the *caw* of the AMERICAN CROW is one of the best-known of bird vocalizations.

Members of the family range in length from 20 to 71 cm (8 to 28 in), many near the higher end; they are large for passerine birds. Corvids have robust, fairly long bills and strong legs and feet; some species have quite long tails. Jays hop, but the usual locomotion on the ground of the larger crows and ravens is a jaunty walk that, at higher speeds, could easily be called a drunken swagger. Species on the crow side of the family are all or mostly black, but jays are attired in bright blues, purples, greens, yellows, and white. American jays tend to be blue, and many have conspicuous crests (for example, the STELLER'S JAY, Plate 50). Alaska's GRAY JAY (Plate 50) is an exception, being rather dull and crestless; but it makes up in personality what it lacks in flashiness. In corvids, the sexes generally look alike. The COMMON RAVEN (Plate 50) is the largest songbird and may be Alaska's most ubiquitous bird.

Natural History
Ecology and Behavior
Crows and jays eat a large variety of foods and so are considered *omnivores*. They feed on the ground, but also in trees, taking bird eggs and nestlings, carrion, insects (including some in flight), and fruits and nuts. Bright and versatile, they are quick to take advantage of new food sources and to find food in agricultural and other human-altered environments. All use their feet to hold food down while processing it with their bills. GRAY JAYS can actually carry food items in their feet, a very unusual accomplishment for a songbird but one that allows them to remove large bits of flesh from a carcass before larger scavengers take over. Hiding food for later consumption, *caching*, is practiced widely by the group. You can watch a crow or jay that has been fed a peanut, for example, hop over the ground for a while, find an acceptable spot, and push the peanut into the ground by a few blows with its powerful bill. It then stands back, surveys the situation, and then pulls a few leaves and bits of moss over the spot. Caching is what allows members of this family to be resident at high latitudes and altitudes, because they can use their stored food throughout the winter. Gray Jays can cache up to 1000 items in a 17-hour summer day in Alaska, more than one per minute, and their salivary glands produce a sticky saliva that allows them to stash their caches just about anywhere. The memory they have had to evolve to remember where they have hidden so many individual tidbits surely plays a part in the substantial intelligence of this group, which is at the peak of bird braininess.

Corvids are usually quite social, and Alaska's species are no exception. NORTHWESTERN CROWS (Plate 50) gather in large flocks at winter roosts, dozens of COMMON RAVENS in a group may visit a garbage dump, and Gray Jays wander through the forest in small groups of relatives, 5 to 10 strong, that forage together within a restricted area, or *home range*. Many jays are raucous and noisy, giving loud calls, some of them harsh and some of them musical, as the foraging flock straggles from tree to tree.

Breeding
Courtship feeding is common in corvids, the male feeding the female before and during incubation, which she performs alone. Bulky, open nests, constructed primarily of twigs (an impressive pile with a hole in the side in the BLACK-BILLED MAGPIE, Plate 50), are placed in trees (or on cliff ledges in the COMMON RAVEN). Three to 7 eggs are incubated for 16 to 22 days, and the young are then

fed in the nest by both parents for 22 to 29 days. Young GRAY JAYS remain with the parents for a month after leaving the nest. Corvid breeding in Alaska is accomplished from May through July, beginning before the majority of Alaskan passerines, which are migrants from the south. Alaska's jays are mainly monogamous, but quite a few jays of lower latitudes, for example the FLORIDA SCRUB-JAY, breed cooperatively. In these species, generally the oldest pair in the group breeds, and the other members serve only as *helpers*, assisting in nest construction and feeding the young. By doing this, helpers are guaranteed a breeding territory when the adult of the same sex of the breeding pair dies.

Ecological Interactions

Jays and other corvids are often scavengers. Specialist carrion-eating birds exist, such as vultures, but jays and crows and their relatives contribute a good deal to breaking down dead animals so that the nutrients bound up in them are recycled into food webs. And where there are roads, civic-minded corvids assist highway departments in keeping them clear of road kills.

The omnivory of corvids also drives them to be predators on bird nests – generally on species that are smaller than they are, of which there are many. Jays, crows, and magpies all tear up nests and eat eggs and nestlings. They are considered to be responsible for a significant percentage of the nest predation on many songbird species, particularly those with cup nests. Ravens are especially important predators on the nests of open-country birds, and Alaska, with its huge expanses of tundra, has more than its share of ravens.

Owing to their seed-caching behavior, corvids are important to trees as dispersal agents. In eastern North America, for example, the BLUE JAY'S acorn-burying habit must surely result in the maintenance and spread of oak forests, and the CLARK'S NUTCRACKER does the same for certain species of pines in the western mountains. This is because corvids never find all the seeds they've stashed. The best caching corvid from a plant's standpoint is a very active but somewhat forgetful one!

Lore and Notes

Corvid folklore is rife with tales of crows, ravens, and magpies as symbols of ill omen. This undoubtedly traces to the group's frequent all-black plumage and habit of eating carrion, both sinister traits. COMMON RAVENS, in particular, have long been associated in many Northern cultures with evil or death, although these large, powerful birds also figure more benignly in Nordic and Middle Eastern mythology. Several groups of indigenous peoples of Northwestern North America consider the raven sacred and sometimes, indeed, as a god. Haida legends have it that Raven, although a man, was raised by a bird; he was saved from death by wearing a bird's skin to fly when Raven's angry uncle called forth a flood to drown him.

Status

Unlike the highly endangered HAWAIIAN CROW, Alaska's corvids remain unthreatened. In fact, they are all probably increasing in numbers, because the intelligence of the species in this family seems to fit them well for coexisting with humans. Crows and ravens raid garbage dumps and garbage cans, eat pet food, and scrounge for French fries at Alaska's relatively few drive-in restaurants. They are among the short list of species that are often called *human commensals* (commensals are animals that feed in association with other animals), and the species on that list should remain on the planet long after many less adaptable species have disappeared.

Profiles

Gray Jay, *Perisoreus canadensis*, Plate 50a
Steller's Jay, *Cyanocitta stelleri*, Plate 50b
Northwestern Crow, *Corvus caurinus*, Plate 50c
Black-billed Magpie, *Pica pica*, Plate 50d
Common Raven, *Corvus corax*, Plate 50e

19. Chickadees, Nuthatches, and Creepers

There are 53 species of *chickadees* and *titmice*, family Paridae; 25 species of *nuthatches*, family Sittidae; and six species of *creepers*, family Certhiidae. The members of these families are characteristic forest birds of all north temperate regions, although nuthatches also occur in the lowland tropics in Asia, and titmice and creepers occur throughout forested parts of Africa. Alaska's forests hold four chickadees, a nuthatch, and a creeper, although the representatives of the latter two families are to be found mostly in the southern part of the state. Chickadees (called "tits" in the Old World) are small, active, gray or brown or reddish birds with dark caps and throats and contrasty white cheek patches. Their bills are short and pointed, thicker at the base than those of some other insect-eaters. The wings of chickadees are short and their tails long; they are not strong fliers, and all species are resident all year, even at high latitudes. Nuthatches have considerably longer bills and shorter tails than chickadees and are usually blue-gray above and paler below, with dark caps. Creepers are brown and black striped above and white below, with a very long, slender, pointed, and obviously down-curved bill; their tail is fairly long, and the feathers are pointed. Alaska nuthatches and creepers are migratory, and many of them leave the state during winter.

Natural History
Ecology and Behavior

Chickadees are very social and move about the countryside in small flocks during the nonbreeding season. These *feeding flocks* may be joined by a few nuthatches and, at times, a creeper or two, and provide characteristic sights and sounds of northern forests. The birds in these flocks probably stay in touch as they move through the forest by their regular vocalizations (usually some variation of *chick-a-dee dee dee* in the chickadees). The pointed bills of chickadees, small but strong, are used to catch insects and pound open seeds. Chickadees often feed by hanging upside down and sometimes hover beneath a branch to pluck a small insect from it. Owing to these feeding specializations, chickadees can spend the winter at high latitudes. This is because, although their insect food is in dormant stages in winter, the chickadees can extract insect eggs and pupae from beneath leaves and twigs. Nuthatches use their long, slender bills to probe into cracks in tree bark and pry up loose pieces of bark. They also move out onto small branches and probe moss clumps and leaf masses. Creepers, with their even more slender, curved bills, probe more deeply into crevices in bark; they usually forage on larger tree trunks, with thick bark. The creeper method of foraging is characteristic and unmistakable; a bird flies to the bottom of a tree trunk, spirals its way up it nearly to the top, then drops down to a nearby tree and spirals up again. This bird seems to have a very effective defense against its predators, perhaps birds such as accipiter hawks and pygmy-owls. It is extremely well camouflaged and, when stationary, is virtually invisible against a tree trunk. Even its foraging method may be designed to avoid detection, because the creeper dropping from one tree to the next often looks like nothing more than a falling leaf.

Like crows and jays, chickadees and nuthatches cache thousands of seeds in the fall and visit their caches throughout the winter, when times are hard. Their memories seem as good as those of their larger relatives.

Breeding

The species in these groups are the smallest hole-nesting birds. We think of woodpeckers as being able to dig nest holes in tree trunks, but it is a bit surprising to learn that a tiny chickadee or nuthatch can do the same. Both chickadees and nuthatches excavate their own nests in dead trunks or branches or enlarge small natural cavities. Creepers, on the other hand, place their nests behind loose pieces of bark. Hole-nesting birds tend to lay large clutches of eggs, because their young are relatively well protected from predators, and they can thus stay in their nests for a longer time than the young of cup-nesters. Accordingly, the industrious adults can capture enough prey items to feed a larger number of more slowly growing offspring. Alaska's chickadees lay 5 to 10 eggs, which are incubated for 11 to 18 days, and the young leave the nest after about 16 to 20 days. The RED-BREASTED NUTHATCH (Plate 51) lays 5 or 6 eggs, which are incubated for about 12 days, and the young fledge about 2 to 3 weeks after hatching. The BROWN CREEPER (Plate 51) also lays 5 or 6 eggs, but incubation takes 14 to 17 days, and the young fledge after 13 to 16 days. In all three families, only the female incubates. Why, in these similar-sized birds, the incubation period should be shorter and the fledging period longer in the nuthatch than in the creeper is a subject for ornithologists to ponder. Perhaps the nuthatch's enclosed nest keeps the eggs warmer, so the embryos develop more rapidly, and perhaps the young are more exposed in the creeper's nest, so they leave earlier to avoid attracting predators.

Ecological Interactions

Small insectivorous birds such as the ones discussed here eat billions of insects each year. However, they probably have relatively little effect on insect populations, because they are likely to eat the species that are more common and switch to other species when their preferred prey becomes rare. Then the original prey species, relieved of predator pressure, probably increases again. One of the interesting phenomena that occurs in foraging animals is the formation of a *search image*. When a particular prey type is common, the animals that feed on it apparently quickly develop a clear picture of that organism in their mind and can pick it out from the background more readily. When the prey decreases, either because of heavy predation pressure or some other reason, the search image can switch to another prey item. This attribute in birds has been thought to have contributed to the almost unbelievable diversity of forms of tropical insects. Presumably many of them evolved bizarre shapes so they were not part of a group of insects for which certain birds had developed a search image.

Lore and Notes

The BROWN-HEADED NUTHATCH of southeastern USA pine forests is one of the very few tool-using birds. Some individuals learn to break off small pieces of bark and use them to pry up other such pieces and dislodge insects that would otherwise be inaccessible.

CHESTNUT-BACKED CHICKADEES (Plate 51) and GOLDEN-CROWNED KINGLETS (Plate 52) occur together throughout the range of the chickadee and have rather similar calls. Some researchers speculate that the chickadee's calls, originally more like the typical *chick-a-dee* of the BLACK-CAPPED CHICKADEE (Plate 51), may have converged with those of the kinglet over evolutionary time to facilitate their flocking together.

Status

Alaska's rarest member of this group is the GRAY-HEADED CHICKADEE, restricted to willow and low spruce stands along streams, north of the continuous forests inhabited by the other species of chickadees. In Europe it is known as the SIBERIAN TIT, because it occurs all across Siberia. The Old World populations are moderately well studied, but almost nothing is known of the biology of this rare species in Alaska.

Profiles

Black-capped Chickadee, *Parus atricapillus*, Plate 51a
Chestnut-backed Chickadee, *Parus rufescens*, Plate 51b
Boreal Chickadee, *Parus hudsonicus*, Plate 51c
Red-breasted Nuthatch, *Sitta canadensis*, Plate 51d
Brown Creeper, *Certhia americana*, Plate 51e

20. Wrens and Dippers

Wrens are small, brownish passerines with an active manner and characteristically upraised tails. The 75 wren species comprise a group for the most part confined to the western hemisphere and much more diverse in the tropics than at high latitudes. Among other traits, wrens are renowned for their singing ability, vocal duets, and nesting behavior. Nests are often placed in crannies and crevices within buildings or other structures. In fact, many wrens nest in naturally occurring cavities, hence the family name, Troglodytidae; *troglodytes* are cave dwellers. Wrens are slender-billed insect-eaters, and some of them, for example the HOUSE WREN, root about near and in human settlements, looking for their prey. Only a single wren species occurs in the Old World, the WINTER WREN (Plate 52), and it must have colonized that hemisphere during some former interglacial period by moving from Alaska to Siberia. No other wren thrives at such high latitudes, and the Winter Wren remains the only wren in Alaska. Wrens range in length from 10 to 20 cm (4 to 8 in) and appear mainly in shades of brown or reddish brown, with white, gray, and black markings. Their wings and tails are usually embellished with finely barred patterns. Some of them are tiny, weighing in at 10 g, or a third of an ounce. Wrens have rather short, broad wings and because of this are poor flyers. The sexes look alike. Their tails may be the group's most distinguishing feature, much of the time being held stiffly erect, at military attention. Tails are waved back and forth during displays, both for courtship and aggression. Holding the tail up is characteristic of small songbirds of many families that inhabit dense thickets, as do many wrens; wrens of open habitats such as deserts and rock cliffs keep their tails down.

Dippers represent a much smaller family, Cinclidae, of only five species. They are scattered around the mountains of the northern hemisphere and extend in the Andes to southern South America. Only one, the AMERICAN DIPPER (Plate 52), occurs in North America, and it is common in Alaska. All dippers are easy to recognize – take a wren and make it into a water bird, and you've got a dipper. Dippers are compact, short-tailed, thick-plumaged inhabitants of rocky streams. They are so named because they dip, or bob their body up and down, every few seconds while foraging or just standing. This movement may facilitate communication between members of a pair or parents and young, because the bobbing birds stand out by their vertical movement against the horizontal movement of a rushing stream's water. All dipper species are about the same size, gray or brown above and either *unicolored* (entirely the same color) or with white or reddish brown areas below; the sexes look alike. The gun-metal gray of the American Dipper is relieved each time the bird closes its lower eyelid, which is pure white.

Natural History
Ecology and Behavior

Wrens are *cryptically colored* and fairly secretive in their habits. They hop and poke around through forest undergrowth, thickets, grasslands, and marshes, searching for insects. Some are restricted to rocks and canyon sides. They are *insectivorous*, except for a few desert species that frequently eat berries and seeds. Wrens forage in places foreign to most birds – under logs and into rock crevices and seemingly impenetrable tangles. In fact, it is easier to mistake a WINTER WREN for a mouse than another bird! Wrens at lower latitudes remain in pairs all year and defend winter territories in which they will nest during the breeding season. Some of the larger tropical wrens spend their days in small family flocks, and, perhaps safer because of larger size and social behavior, are a bit more conspicuous than is typical of wrens. Some of these social species are very noisy, with harsh calls that do not sound very birdlike. After the breeding season, wrens use their nests as roosting places – or "dormitories," as one researcher puts it. The vocalizations of wrens have been studied extensively. A pair will call back and forth as they lose sight of each other while foraging in thickets, keeping in contact. In some species, mated pairs sing some of the bird world's most complex duets, male and female rapidly alternating in giving parts of a continuous song, so rapidly and expertly that it actually sounds as if one individual utters the entire sequence. Such duets probably function as "keep-out" signals, warning *conspecific* (same species) in-dividuals away from the pair's territory, and in maintaining the pair bond between mated birds. The Winter Wren has amazingly complex songs, long trains of notes in varied sequences up to 10 seconds or more in duration; researchers place the song of this bird at the very pinnacle of bird-song complexity.

Dippers not only forage along the banks of their mountain streams but also enter the water at every chance. Although the two South American species avoid submergence, the other species of dippers have switched their foraging behavior substantially to invade the underwater realm, a foraging niche otherwise unknown to songbirds. Dippers are supremely adapted to their way of life: they float on the surface like a duck and paddle with their unwebbed toes; they swim under water like a puffin with their short, rounded wings; and they walk on the bottom with sharp toenails clinging to the slippery rocks. Their goal is to snatch aquatic insect larvae living on and under the rocks, and they do it very well indeed. They are sufficiently at home in the water even to capture small fish. The song of dippers is as complex and beautiful as the songs of many of the wrens, and both Winter Wren and AMERICAN DIPPER songs celebrate the coming of spring in Alaska long before migratory songbirds (and spring itself) appear.

Breeding

Wrens and dippers are mainly monogamous, but some tropical wrens breed *co-operatively*, with members of the small family group helping out at the single nest of the parents. Many wrens construct their untidy nest in tree cavities; others build elaborate nests in the open, roofed and with inconspicuous side entrances. Interestingly, the roofed nests of both WINTER WREN and AMERICAN DIPPER are constructed primarily of mosses, the former on earth banks in the forest, the latter on banks above streams. The best place to look for dipper nests used to be behind waterfalls; now, many pairs build their nests on crosspieces below bridges. In some wren species, the male builds many more nests on his territory than his mate (or mates, in *polygynous* species) can use, apparently as a courtship signal. These multiple nests may also confuse predators, which check a few nests, find them empty, and ignore the rest. The wren's 5 or 6 eggs are incubated for 14 to 16 days, and the dipper's 4 or 5 eggs are incubated for 13 to 17 days; only females incubate. Nestlings are fed by both parents for about 19 days in the wren, longer in the dipper, until fledging. Wren and dipper breeding in Alaska occurs rather early, from April to July, so their songs are waning just at the time many migrant songbirds arrive, in full song, to breed.

Lore and Notes

There are so many wonderful aspects of nature that books can scarcely contain them. Think, for example, of the geographic distribution of animals and plants. Why are some species widely distributed and others are not? The WINTER WREN occurs all around the northern hemisphere, including on small islands in the North Atlantic Ocean and Bering Sea. Its distribution is measured in millions of square kilometers. Similarly common in New England, southern Alaska, the Himalayas, and the English countryside, its distribution is especially impressive because it is a tiny bird that spends more of its day creeping about the forest floor or in and out of rock piles than flying over long distances. However, many populations are migratory, and individual wrens must have substantial wing power to be able to fly from Ontario, Canada to Georgia, USA, or from Finland to Israel. A not-distantly-related species, the COZUMEL WREN, occurs only on tiny Isla Cozumel off the Yucatan Peninsula, its entire range about 350 square kilometers. Given the powers of flight of the even smaller Winter Wren, why can't the Cozumel Wren reach the Mexican mainland, about 18 km (11 miles) away?

Status

No wren is known to have gone extinct, but Mexico has two wrens of such restricted distribution that they are certainly vulnerable to extinction because of introduced predators (eating the wrens) and herbivores (eating their habitat) on their home islands. The SOCORRO WREN and CLARION WREN are restricted to the Revillagigedo Archipelago off the west coast of Mexico, where they live on small, offshore islands. These islands are even smaller than Cozumel, mentioned above. A natural catastrophe such as a hurricane could eliminate either species just as readily as changes caused by human activities.

Profiles

Winter Wren, *Troglodytes troglodytes*, Plate 52d
American Dipper, *Cinclus mexicanus*, Plate 52e

21. Kinglets and Arctic Warbler

There are six species of *kinglets*, placed in their own small family, Regulidae, which occurs all across the northern hemisphere; the GOLDEN-CROWNED KINGLET (Plate 52) and RUBY-CROWNED KINGLET (Plate 52) are both common in Alaska. The ARCTIC WARBLER (Plate 52) is in the *Old World warbler* family, Sylviidae, with 383 species. This family includes many of the common small songbirds of Eurasia and Africa. The Arctic Warbler breeds from Scandinavia to Siberia and winters in southern Asia but has extended its breeding range into Alaska. Kinglets are the tiniest passerine birds in Alaska, about 10 cm (4 in) long, and the Arctic Warbler is only slightly larger, at 13 cm (5 in). Kinglets are olive-green above and whitish below, with conspicuous pale wing bars and either stripes or an eyering attracting attention to their head. Both kinglet species have bright colors on their crown, in the Ruby-crowned only the male. The males' fiery-red (Ruby-crowned) or orange (Golden-crowned) crown patches are hidden most of the year but can be exposed and erected during singing, courtship, and antagonistic interactions. (This patch is a good example of a *coverable badge*, a patch of color that can be hidden or exposed depending on the bird's motivation.) Arctic Warblers are duller than kinglets, mostly brownish, and not quite so active. All of these birds have slender, pointed bills for insect-catching.

Natural History
Ecology and Behavior
Kinglets are frenetically active as they move through the forest, seemingly never slowing down in their search for insects, hanging and fluttering under branches as much as they are on top of them. Their prey is sufficiently abundant that kinglets are among the most common small birds in forests all across Alaska. The RUBY-CROWNED is much more widespread, being an inhabitant of coniferous and mixed woodland, the habitats characteristic of central Alaska. That region becomes uninhabitable to most birds in winter, so Ruby-crowns are highly migratory. The GOLDEN-CROWNED is confined to the dense, taller conifer forests of southern Alaska, and in that region of somewhat less seasonal change, the eggs and other overwintering stages of insects are more available on the trees, and the Golden-crown is mostly a year-round resident species. It forms mixed flocks with Chestnut-backed Chickadees in the nonbreeding season.

Both kinglet species spend much of their time in the forest canopy, although during migration they can be seen all the way down to the low shrubbery. They sing thin, wiry songs, although the Ruby-crowned song starts at a high frequency like that of the Golden-crowned, then descends to a loud, musical warble, surprisingly forceful for such a tiny bird.

Breeding
The Alaska species of both of these families are monogamous, pairs defending territories in the breeding season. Kinglets build small nests of varied materials, usually including lichens and mosses, that hang between slender branches high in trees and are usually well camouflaged under a canopy of leaves. Both species lay surprisingly large clutches for open-nesting birds, the 7 to 9 (rarely to 12!) eggs incubated by the female for 13 to 15 days. The young fledge in about 14 to 19 days. Arctic Warblers are similar in breeding biology but build their well-hidden nest on the ground in the dwarf willow and alder thickets they inhabit. Ground nesting is hazardous, and smaller broods can be fledged more quickly, so their

clutch size is smaller than that of the kinglets, 6 to 7 eggs, and the incubation period is shorter, 11 to 13 days. Arctic Warbler young also fledge more quickly, at 12 to 14 days.

Lore and Notes

The ARCTIC WARBLER is only one of quite a number of species of Old World birds that have extended their ranges across the Bering Straits to nest in Alaska. All of them withdraw to their proper hemisphere in winter, some of them migrating all the way down to southern Africa at that time. Arctic Warblers spend the winter in Southeast Asia. An Arctic Warbler may breed next to a Ruby-crowned Kinglet in a patch of willows on the slopes of Mount Denali, yet as the summer draws to an end, the warbler will embark on its long flight to Thailand, and the kinglet will head for California. If they could communicate with each other, what stories they could tell!

Status

Fortunately, small songbirds of wide distribution in the temperate zone are usually not at risk of extinction, and thus kinglets should be among the last birds to qualify for endangered-species listing. However, some of the Old World warblers are restricted to specific river valleys, mountain ranges, or tropical islands. The ALDABRA WARBLER, restricted to the island of Aldabra in the Seychelles Islands in the Indian Ocean, is probably extinct, but the SEYCHELLES WARBLER, similarly restricted to the nearby island of Cousin, is stable at a population of several hundred birds, probably as a consequence of the island being taken over as a nature preserve and intensively managed. Even if thriving, populations on small islands are always at risk of being wiped out by a single environmental catastrophe such as a typhoon, a fire, or something as seemingly inconsequential as a lighthouse-keeper's cat.

Profiles

Golden-crowned Kinglet, *Regulus satrapa*, Plate 52a
Ruby-crowned Kinglet, *Regulus calendula*, Plate 52b
Arctic Warbler, *Phylloscopus borealis*, Plate 52c

22. Thrushes

The 179 species of *thrushes* inhabit most terrestrial regions of the world. Eleven species occur regularly in Alaska, although some of them are Siberian migrants seen only on Bering Sea islands, and another six are rare and irregular visitors. Although many people would recognize a bird as a thrush, the family Turdidae has few defining features that set all its members apart from other groups. One such characteristic, perhaps a bit esoteric, is a *booted tarsus*, which means the horny covering on the lower legs is not divided into scales as in most birds. As could be expected; so large an assemblage of species is sure to include a significant amount of variation in appearance, ecology, and behavior. Thrushes as a group are tremendously successful birds, especially when they have adapted to living near humans and benefiting from our environmental modifications. Some thrushes are among the most common and recognizable park and garden birds, including North America's AMERICAN ROBIN (Plate 53), Europe's BLACKBIRD, and Central America's CLAY-COLORED ROBIN. Thrushes are slender-billed birds, and the North American species range from 15 to 24 cm (6 to 9.5 in) in length. Most thrushes are not brightly colored; instead, they come in drab browns and reddish-browns, grays, olive, and black and white. The bluebirds are glorious exceptions, with bright blue or blue and orange males and duller blue females, and the VARIED THRUSH (Plate 53) is surely one of the most striking of Alaska's songbirds. Other than in these species, the sexes are similar in appearance. In the nest and for a short while after they leave it, the young of most thrushes are clad in distinctively spotted plumages.

Natural History
Ecology and Behavior
Among the thrushes are species that employ a variety of feeding methods and that take several different food types. Many eat fruits (*frugivorous*), some are primarily *insectivorous*, and most are at least moderately *omnivorous*, taking both plant and animal foods. Although arboreal birds, many thrushes also forage on the ground for insects, other arthropods, and, a particular favorite, delicious earthworms. Ground-foraging thrushes hop and run along the ground, stopping at intervals and cocking their heads to peer downwards. Thrushes are residents of many kinds of habitats – forest edge, clearings, and other open areas such as shrub areas and grasslands, gardens, parks, suburban lawns, and agricultural areas. Some of them are quite social, spending their time during the nonbreeding season in flocks of the same species, feeding and roosting together. All of Alaska's thrushes are migratory, disappearing from the state each winter to return the following spring, although a few AMERICAN ROBINS and VARIED THRUSHES spend the winter in the more moderate climate of the far South. The frozen soil surface of most of the state in winter offers little in the way of earthworms or arthropods to feed these ground-foragers.

Breeding
Thrushes breed monogamously, male and female together defending exclusive territories during the breeding season. Nests, usually built by the female and placed in the branches of trees and shrubs or in crevices, are cup-shaped, made of grass, moss, and similar materials, and often lined with mud. Three to 6 eggs (usually 3 or 4) are incubated by the female for 12 to 17 days. Young are fed by both parents for 10 to 14 days prior to their fledging and, in some species, for another several weeks after fledging. In the hole-nesting MOUNTAIN BLUEBIRD, the young may not fledge until 23 days old and are then fed by the parents for another 3 to 4 weeks.

Ecological Interactions
The AMERICAN ROBIN represents a rather unusual way of life. It does much of its foraging on the ground in the open, yet it needs trees for nesting, so it is distinctly a forest-edge bird. Because of this, it has thrived on a continent in which not only are forests opened up by logging and development of cities and towns, but also trees are planted everywhere on the prairies. Thus much of the Lower 48 and southern Canada has become optimal robin habitat, and the populations of this species have probably increased as much as those of any bird of North America in historic times. Alaska's robins thrive in suburban areas, but most of them still breed in original robin habitats, woodlands with many clearings.

Lore and Notes
English colonists in the New World gave the AMERICAN ROBIN its name because it resembled England's common ROBIN – both birds are thrushes, and both have reddish breasts. The New World bird, however, is more closely related to Europe's

BLACKBIRD, also a common garden bird. Not content with incorrectly labeling birds that were new to them with English names, British settlers around the world, homesick, it is thought, imported birds from the British Isles to their new domains so that familiar birds would surround them. Thus European thrushes such as the SONG THRUSH and Blackbird, among many other birds, are now naturalized inhabitants of New Zealand. In fact, a British visitor to these distant islands would feel right at home with the city birds.

In fall, GRAY-CHEEKED THRUSHES (Plate 54) that have bred on the Chukotka Peninsula of Siberia head east across the Bering Strait, on their way to wintering grounds in South America. They fly past other thrushes going in the opposite direction, NORTHERN WHEATEARS and BLUETHROATS that had nested in Alaska and are on their way to their wintering grounds in Africa.

Status

In the huge and relatively undisturbed land mass that is Alaska, all breeding thrushes are still common, but not so to the south, in the tiny, environmentally beleaguered islands of Hawaii, where the SMALL KAUAI THRUSH is barely holding on. A recently instituted breeding program may give some hope, because captive-reared young released in 1999 almost immediately mated, built nests, and laid eggs.

Profiles

American Robin, *Turdus migratorius*, Plate 53d
Varied Thrush, *Ixoreus naevius*, Plate 53e
Gray-cheeked Thrush, *Catharus minimus*, Plate 54a
Swainson's Thrush, *Catharus ustulatus*, Plate 54b
Hermit Thrush, *Catharus guttatus*, Plate 54c

23. Miscellaneous Perching Birds

The three birds discussed here are all passerines but are not particularly closely related; each represents the only member of its family that occurs commonly in Alaska. *Waxwings*, family Bombycillidae, are fairly small, soft-plumaged silky brown birds with yellow tail tips (red in a Japanese species), jaunty, pointed crests, and wing-feather tips modified to look like little red drops of wax. There are three species of waxwings distributed around the northern hemisphere, of which two occur in Alaska.

Shrikes are slightly larger black, gray, and white birds with long tails and heavy, hooked bills. The 30 species of shrikes, family Laniidae, are found widely in the Old World, with Africa the center of diversity of the group. Only two species occur regularly in North America, one of them in Alaska.

The *blackbird* family, Icteridae, is a New World family, very diverse in the tropics, that includes not only the *typical blackbirds* but also groups as different as *meadowlarks* and *orioles*. It includes 97 species quite varied in size and coloration, although many of them are all or partly black, as one would hope. Some are colored with bright patches of yellow, orange, or red, and some of the black species are highly iridescent. The smallest species are just larger than sparrows, and the largest species are crow-sized. Most species have long, pointed bills that are somewhat flattened from top to bottom; as is always the case with birds, this correlates with their way of feeding (see below). Eight species have been recorded in Alaska, but only three are known to breed in the state, and two of the three breeding species are quite local and uncommon.

Natural History
Ecology and Behavior

The three birds profiled here are very different from one another. Waxwings are primarily fruit-eaters, forming nomadic flocks during winter and roaming the countryside looking for trees and shrubs that have held their berries through the fall. They also eat fruit in summer on the breeding grounds but switch their diet to take more insects then, even catching some of them in the air, from a perch like a flycatcher or from the air like a swallow. Their bill is flattened somewhat like the bill of a flycatcher, and their wings are pointed somewhat like those of swallows, so they are well adapted to capture insects. Just about any shape bill is adequate for eating soft fruits.

Shrikes, on the other hand, are predators. The NORTHERN SHRIKE (Plate 53), although a songbird, specializes in vertebrate prey – small birds and mammals. Because these prey types are widespread and common, Northern Shrikes have a very wide range all across the northern hemisphere and winter farther north than the many songbirds that specialize in insects. Shrikes hunt from a perch in the open, alert to all signs of movement around them. In completely open country, they can hover over a spot and dive down on a prey animal just about as effectively as a hawk. They kill with a quick bite through the spinal nerve with their heavy, notched bill. Shrikes have an interesting way of *caching* prey that probably stemmed from the inability of the shrike's passerine feet, not at all like those of a hawk or owl, to hold prey firmly while tearing off bite-sized pieces. Thus the shrike had to wedge or snag its prey somehow to hold it in place – on a large thorn, for instance. A mouse or sparrow so secured was then available for the shrike to return to later to finish its meal. Shrikes have been known to return to such a cache – mummified but perhaps still edible – months after it was made. Sharp-eyed observers from time to time see one of these shrike caches on a stiff branch or thorn, or on a barbwire fence where this sign of civilization is prevalent.

Blackbirds are again quite different birds, and Alaska's most common species, the RUSTY BLACKBIRD (Plate 53), is typical of the family. It is an insect-eater during the summer but a seed-eater in winter. Like the waxwing and many other migratory birds, its diet changes between seasons, depending on what is available (insects aren't available during winter), what types of prey its bill is adapted to capture (the long, slender bill is good for capturing insects in summer although not optimal for seed-cracking), and what its young need to grow quickly (insects, not seeds). Blackbirds share with starlings a unique method of feeding by *gaping*. They push their pointed bill into the soil or the base of a leaf and spread it apart by opening the bill; the flattened shape facilitates this prying action. By doing this, they can uncover insects and seeds unavailable to other birds. Unlike waxwings and shrikes, blackbirds are comfortable on the ground and spend much time walking around in moist areas looking for their food.

Breeding

These birds are all typical passerines, with monogamous mating and cup nests built in trees and shrubs. Courtship feeding is charming to watch in the waxwing, with the male "capturing" berries and feeding them to the female. Both sexes construct the nest in waxwings and shrikes, but only the female performs that task in blackbirds. The female incubates the 4 to 6 eggs in all three species.

Incubation lasts about 2 weeks, and the young fledge in another 2 weeks after hatching (slightly longer in the shrike), with both sexes providing their food.

Ecological Interactions

Shrikes are noteworthy for the very large size of their territories. Eating higher up on the food chain, they need much more space to find an adequate number of small birds and rodents than an insect-eater like the blackbird or a fruit-eater like the waxwing needs to find sufficient prey.

Lore and Notes

BOHEMIAN WAXWINGS (Plate 53) received their first name because of their nomadic lifestyle; their propensity to wander about the countryside apparently recalled the similar behavior of Bohemians. "Shrike" comes from the same source as "shriek," originally a bird with a shrill cry. Shrikes are also called "butcher birds" because of their habits of hanging their prey on thorns and branches. The meaning of "blackbird" is obvious, and "rusty" comes from the reddish fall colors of the species.

Status

Waxwings must surely be more common and widespread than they were originally on this continent, because very large numbers of them seem dependent on planted fruit trees. Such trees are common, for instance, all across the Great Plains, where no trees, much less fruiting trees, grew a few centuries ago. Shrikes, on the other hand, are much less common, perhaps because of a decline in their prey populations. Populations of LOGGERHEAD SHRIKES, the other North American species, have declined to nearly zero in northeastern USA while maintaining healthy populations in the South and West. This decline was first thought to indicate some significant environmental problem, but researchers more recently have come to the conclusion that many open areas (optimal shrike habitat) in the Northeast have grown up into closed woodland (poor shrike habitat) since the early farming days. RUSTY BLACKBIRDS have not benefited greatly by human activities, but other blackbirds have. Mixed flocks of blackbirds, mainly RED-WINGED BLACKBIRDS and COMMON GRACKLES, have been estimated in the millions in winter roosts in eastern North America, and these vast flocks are supported by nearby agricultural fields with their heavy seed crops.

Profiles

Bohemian Waxwing, *Bombycilla garrulus*, Plate 53a
Northern Shrike, *Lanius excubitor*, Plate 53b
Rusty Blackbird, *Euphagus carolinus*, Plate 53c

24. Warblers

Warblers are small birds that occur in all wooded habitats, as well as brushy second-growth and even marshes. Although they are beautiful little birds, because of their quick movements and great diversity, even experienced birders sometimes despair of trying to differentiate the various species. This same diversity makes them important birds in the *boreal forests* of North America, making up more of the birdlife in many such forests than all other birds combined. Many warblers migrate long distances to tropical wintering grounds, where they are especially evident in areas of disturbed woodland where resident tropical species are less common. American warblers (family Parulidae), also known as *woodwarblers*, are a group of 115 species, with wide distribution over the New World. Alaska is home to 12 species that migrate north from tropical wintering grounds to breed somewhere in the state every summer, and to another eight species that visit rarely. Members of this family are brightly colored, predominantly yellow or greenish, often mixed with varying amounts of gray, black and white; a few have even more color, with patches of red and orange. A few are brown like thrushes or wrens, to match the forest floor where they live.

Natural History
Ecology and Behavior
Warblers are commonly found in forested and shrubby habitats; in migration and winter many of them move into gardens, parks, and plantations. They forage in lively fashion, mainly for insects and spiders; in the winter, some of them pierce berries to drink juice and partake of nectar from flowers. Most of them capture their prey by *gleaning*, a very common behavior in insectivorous birds in which the bird moves slowly along branches or hops from branch to branch, looking for insects on twigs and leaves. Some species specialize in creeping along larger branches and tree trunks to do this, even *probing* like a nuthatch or creeper. Some species also forage by *hover-gleaning*, in which they hover briefly next to or beneath a leaf and pluck an insect or spider from it. Others capture flying insects by *sallying* into the air after them, as true flycatchers do. This can be seen commonly in Alaska wherever there are hatches of small insects such as midges. In the breeding season, warblers are territorial birds, a male and a female defending a piece of real estate from other members of their species. Male warblers have two different types of songs, one to advertise their territory ownership and repel other males of their species, and another to attract females.

Breeding
Warblers are monogamous, but partners do not necessarily make equal contributions to breeding efforts. They build open cup or roofed nests in trees or shrubs or on the ground. Surprisingly, even some treetop foragers build ground nests, which may be safer from predators just because they are not so obvious when nestled into the ground. Usually the female alone builds the nest and incubates the 4 to 6 eggs for 11 to 13 days; the male may feed his incubating mate. Young fledge after 8 to 13 days in the nest. Breeding takes place from May to July, as in virtually all migratory songbirds in Alaska.

Ecological Interactions
For many years, North American scientists interested in warblers and other migratory songbirds concentrated their research on the birds' ecology and behavior during breeding, essentially ignoring the fact that the birds spent half of each year wintering in the tropics, many of them in Mexico and Central America. Now, with the realization that the birds' biology during the nonbreeding season is also important for understanding their lives, their ecology and behavior during the winter have become areas of intense interest. Researchers are now addressing a diverse set of questions. Are species that are territorial during breeding also territorial on their wintering grounds, and if so, in what way? Why do some birds remain territorial and solitary, but others move about in flocks, either with their own species or in multispecies mixed flocks? Do individual birds return to the same spot in the tropics each year in winter as they do for nesting during the

North American summer? Do species have similar diets on breeding and wintering grounds, or do some of them change drastically? Do migratory birds compete for food on their wintering grounds with those species that remain all year in the tropics? Why do some species retain their bright, species-specific breeding plumage on their winter habitat, whereas others molt into an entirely dull plumage?

Lore and Notes

Warblers are among the favorites of North American birders because they are brightly colored, active, very diverse, and highly migratory. "Warbler waves" in the eastern states may involve migratory movements of a dozen or more species, and with the right conditions in spring and fall, trees can be full of these beautiful little birds. Alaska is at the far northwestern end of the breeding range of North American warblers, and they arrive in the spring with some fanfare, immediately proclaiming territorial rights by singing from conspicuous perches; but after breeding is completed, they quietly disappear, as if they could barely wait to get to their warm, productive wintering grounds. The TOWNSEND'S WARBLER (Plate 55) of southern Alaska winters mostly in Mexico, but the BLACKPOLL WARBLER (Plate 55), which breeds all the way up to the Seward Peninsula, has a much lengthier migration. Birds leave Alaska in fall and fly all the way to the Atlantic coast, feeding voraciously in the Canadian Maritimes or New England. They then set out on a 3800 km (2400 mile) flight over the Atlantic Ocean to northern South America, where most of them arrive safely but much lighter, having burned up the extensive stores of fat they deposited under their skin during their premigratory feeding frenzy. Each fall, natural selection takes its toll on those birds not effective enough as foragers to put on the weight needed for the flight. Some of these birds are fortunate and land in Bermuda, but even then they may be out of luck, because on those small oceanic islands they may not find enough food to meet their needs for a further flight.

Status

No warbler is threatened in Alaska, but a few species elsewhere in North America have not fared well. The BACHMAN'S WARBLER of southeastern swamps is extinct, perhaps lost because of the destruction of thickets of giant canes, the tall grasses in which they nested. Habitat destruction on their wintering grounds in Cuba might have also played a part in their demise. KIRTLAND'S WARBLER of jack-pine forests near the Great Lakes and the GOLDEN-CHEEKED WARBLER of juniper woodlands in Texas are just holding their own, threatened as much as anything by intense pressure from Brown-headed Cowbirds. Cowbirds are *brood parasites*, laying their eggs in the nests of other birds. The young cowbirds are usually larger and grow faster than their nest mates, and thus are able to obtain more food from their "parents," causing the parents' real young to starve. It is thought that aggressive programs to control cowbird populations have eliminated that particular threat to these two warblers. However, *natural succession* (the continued growth and change in species composition of shrubs and trees) constantly changes the landscape and, in the preferred habitats of these warblers, is producing habitats that are less favorable for them. In addition to cowbird trapping, controlled burning is now being used to set back succession and keep habitats in their optimal states for these two rare species.

Migrant birds, including many warblers, are also vulnerable to habitat destruction in their winter range. So much tropical lowland and mid-elevation forest has been destroyed that this loss surely has had an effect on populations of wintering birds (so-called *Neotropical migrants*) there, as well as the resident tropical species. Fortunately, at least some of the migrants do well in disturbed habitats. A recent controversy involves growing conditions for coffee, plantations of which have replaced natural forest in many areas. Where the upper story of shade trees is left intact (above low-growing coffee plants), or fast-growing leguminous trees are planted, this "shade coffee" supports substantial populations of birds (enough so that these wintering grounds could rightly be called "coffee grounds"). Where the shade trees are removed ("sun coffee"), very few birds persist. Imagine the environmental effect if all coffee drinkers insisted on shade coffee!

Profiles

Wilson's Warbler, *Wilsonia pusilla*, Plate 54d
Northern Waterthrush, *Seiurus noveboracensis*, Plate 54e
Yellow Warbler, *Dendroica petechia*, Plate 55a
Orange-crowned Warbler, *Vermivora celata*, Plate 55b
Townsend's Warbler, *Dendroica townsendi*, Plate 55c
Yellow-rumped Warbler, *Dendroica coronata*, Plate 55d
Blackpoll Warbler, *Dendroica striata*, Plate 55e

25. Sparrows

Totaling 157 species, the New World *sparrows* and Old World *buntings* are a large, diverse, almost worldwide group that includes some of Alaska's most common and visible passerine birds. Their family, Emberizidae, is one of a number of closely related families including the cardinals, tanagers, warblers, and blackbirds. Members of these families occur just about everywhere in the New World, in all kinds of habitats and climates, from Alaska and northern Canada south to Tierra del Fuego. In fact, one species, the SNOW BUNTING (Plate 58), breeds farther north than any other land bird, in northern Alaska, Canada, and Greenland. Alaska is home to 15 species of the sparrow/bunting family, with another 12 as rare visitors; half of the latter are sparrows from farther south and east in North America, the other half buntings from Siberia that occasionally visit western parts of the state. Most of the species of regular occurrence leave Alaska during winter, but some of them remain throughout that season in the warmer southern parts of the state.

For our purposes here, we will speak of all birds in this group as sparrows. Sparrows are generally small birds, 10 to 17 cm (4 to 6.75 in) in length, with relatively short, thick, conical bills, that are specialized to crush and open seeds. In some species, the upper and lower halves of the bill can be moved from side to side, the better to manipulate small seeds. Sparrows have relatively large feet that they use in scratching the ground to find seeds. Coloring varies greatly within the group, but the plumage of most is the epitome of camouflage for a ground bird, various shades of brown and gray, with streaked backs. Distinctions among the species are typically seen in their head and breast patterns; the sexes generally look alike.

Natural History
Ecology and Behavior

Sparrows are mostly seed eaters, although they feed insects to their young, as do most passerine birds. They are birds of thickets, forest edge, and open country, foraging mostly on the ground or at low levels in shrubs or trees. Because many species spend large amounts of time in thickets and brushy areas, they can be quite inconspicuous. Their songs vary from buzzy and insectlike (species of open grassland) to loud and musical (especially species of dense thickets). The sweet, whistled songs of the WHITE-CROWNED SPARROW (Plate 56), GOLDEN-CROWNED SPARROW (Plate 56), and FOX SPARROW (Plate 57) are familiar spring sounds over large parts of Alaska. Some sparrows show local *song dialects*, with all the birds in one region singing more or less similarly and birds in another region sounding quite different.

Most species are strongly territorial, a mated pair aggressively excluding other members of the species from sharply defined areas. These territorial proclivities usually disappear in winter, although SONG SPARROWS (Plate 57), among a few other species, maintain winter territories as well. Some species within the group travel in small flocks during the winter; the DARK-EYED JUNCO (Plate 56) is a good example of this behavior.

Breeding

Most sparrows are monogamous breeders. The female of the pair usually builds a cup-shaped nest out of grasses and fine rootlets. Nests are concealed on the ground or low in a shrub or tree. SNOW BUNTINGS normally hide their nests in rock crevices but have been able to extend their breeding localities by nesting in human structures where rocks aren't available. Females of the Alaskan species in this family incubate 3 to 7 eggs for 10 to 16 days. Both males and females feed nestlings, which fledge after 7 to 17 days in the nest but are fed for another few weeks. LAPLAND LONGSPURS (Plate 58) leave the nest when surprisingly young, perhaps better able to avoid predators by not attracting them to one spot.

Ecological Interactions

Members of this group are the most common seed-eating birds in North America. Many of them form flocks in the nonbreeding season, and the flocking behavior of several species has been studied from the standpoint of predation. It appears clear that foraging in flocks confers some real advantages. Birds in larger flocks spend more time eating and less time looking around than birds in smaller flocks or single birds, presumably because the more birds there are, the less likely a predator will be able to surprise them. Of course, foraging in a flock isn't all to the good; birds in this situation are pushed into direct competition for resources with their flock mates. To alleviate the problem of constant bickering, birds develop *dominance hierarchies* (first called "peck order" in chickens). Subordinate birds give way before dominant ones, if they encounter a choice food morsel at the same time. This is most easily studied at artificial feeding stations, where birds are forced into competition; but the situation may be a bit more relaxed in nature, where birds are usually spread out more when searching for seeds.

Lore and Notes

In addition to their reputation for ecological success, the New World sparrows are known especially as a group that is the subject of frequent scientific research, and therefore as one that has contributed substantially to many areas of our knowledge about birds. For instance, studies of the North American SONG SPARROW and Neotropical RUFOUS-COLLARED SPARROW provided the basis for much of the information we have about avian territoriality and many other kinds of behavior. Also, the WHITE-CROWNED SPARROW has been the species of choice for many researchers for investigations of bird physiology and the relationships between ecology and physiology, especially with regard to the timing of breeding and migration. Song dialects also have been thoroughly studied in this species.

Status

Sparrows are among the most common birds in Alaska, and no species is known to be rare or threatened. The most restricted distribution is shown by MCKAY'S BUNTING, a close relative of the SNOW BUNTING that breeds on St. Matthew and Hall islands and, rarely, on the Pribilofs and St. Lawrence Island; most individuals move to the nearby mainland in winter. This is the whitest of all songbirds, the breeding males pure white except for a bit of black at the wingtips, and it is a thrill to see one in circling song flight drop from the sky onto the green and brown tundra. Restricted in range as it is, its populations should be monitored, but so far there seems to be no threat to it on these isolated and uninhabited islands.

Profiles

American Tree Sparrow, *Spizella arborea*, Plate 56a
Dark-eyed Junco, *Junco hyemalis*, Plate 56b
Golden-crowned Sparrow, *Zonotrichia atricapilla*, Plate 56c
White-crowned Sparrow, *Zonotrichia leucophrys*, Plate 56d
Savannah Sparrow, *Passerculus sandwichensis*, Plate 57a
Lincoln's Sparrow, *Melospiza lincolnii*, Plate 57b
Song Sparrow, *Melospiza melodia*, Plate 57c
Fox Sparrow, *Passerella iliaca*, Plate 57d
Snow Bunting, *Plectrophenax nivalis*, Plate 58a
Lapland Longspur, *Calcarius lapponicus*, Plate 58b
Smith's Longspur, *Calcarius pictus*, Plate 58d

26. Finches

There are 140 *finches* in the Fringillidae, a family found on all the forested continents but Australia. The greatest diversity of species is in the north temperate zone, and most of the tropical species occur on higher mountains, although a few of them have become specialized for desert life. Finches occur in all temperate forest types, but no species occurs in tropical rain forest, probably because most tropical forest trees have seeds too large even for the larger-billed finch species to crack open.

Finches are seed-eating birds with conical bills, the high base of the bill furnishing mechanical advantage for cracking seeds. Larger finches eat larger seeds and have considerably stronger bills, and the smallest finches – *redpolls* and *siskins* – have more slender bills adapted for opening tiny seeds; most species fit in-between these extremes. Many finches are colorful, with reds and yellows predominating in otherwise brown-streaked plumages. Males are brighter than females in most species. Alaska's finches range in size from the 13 cm (5 in) redpolls and PINE SISKIN (Plate 59) to the 23 cm (9 in) PINE GROSBEAK (Plate 58), and this range encompasses finch size variation worldwide.

Natural History
Ecology and Behavior

Finches are the most confirmed seed-eaters among the birds. One of the more recently evolved families, their evolutionary radiation probably occurred during the similar radiation of the flowering plants, especially woody plants of the north temperate zone. Many finches are specialists, eating seeds of a particular size range in their environment and thus often specializing on particular trees. For example, redpolls are especially fond of birch seeds and siskins are fond of alder seeds, so flocks of these tiny seed-eaters can often be found in the nonbreeding season by checking groves of their favorite trees. They are not specialists to the point of starving to death without their preferred seeds, however, and most species of the family come readily to bird feeders stocked with mixed bird seeds. Many birds of other families are also seed-eaters, but those birds feed insects to their young, the insects a good source of the protein that the young need for growth. True finches, on the other hand, can raise their young on a seed diet. GRAY-CROWNED ROSY-FINCHES (Plate 58), which breed in rocky areas, may have an easier time finding insects than seeds, and their young are fed a larger proportion of insects than is the case in other finches. Rosy-finches have learned to hunt for insects that land on snow banks and, becoming quickly chilled, are unable to take off again.

Finches are an unusual group in being more nomadic and less territorial than most other songbirds. Whether birds defend a territory depends usually on whether it is an economically viable option. If the amount of energy that can be gained from feeding on the territory exceeds the costs of defense (including forcefully evicting intruders), then owning and defending a territory is worthwhile. But finches feed on seeds and fruits that are *patchy* in time and space, abundant at a locality today but scarce or gone next week or next month, and such patches are not worth defending as territories, except perhaps temporarily. Also, the plant resources that finches use for food are more abundant than the insects that most other passerines need to feed their young, so even when territorial, finches can thrive on smaller territories.

Breeding

Finches breed in monogamous pairs like most other passerines. Courtship feeding is common in this family, the males offering tidbits to their mates at regular intervals. This may serve both to strengthen the pair bond and to add to the female's energy resources while eggs are developing in her body. Nests are made of twigs and a variety of finer plant material. They are placed in shrubs and trees in most species but often on the ground in redpolls and in a rock crevice in rosy-finches. Ground nests usually lack twigs, which are obviously important for support in nests built in trees. Finches lay clutches of 4 or 5 eggs, about the average for passerines nesting at high latitudes, and the female incubates them for about 2 weeks (less in redpolls). The young remain in the nest for 2 to 3 weeks (slightly less in redpolls).

Ecological Interactions

Crossbills are finches famous for their tight association with conifer trees. In fact, the tip of the crossbill bill is "crossed" (see Plate 59) so that it can lift each scale of a conifer cone while snipping off the seed beneath the scale. Temperate-zone conifers are known to practice *mast fruiting*, in which huge seed crops appear at intervals of a few years, with few or no seeds in-between. This may be an adaptation on the part of the trees to flood the region with seeds, many of which will hatch before insect seed predators collect in sufficient numbers to harvest them. Only some stands of trees in a given region have seeds in any one year. This phenomenon causes crossbills to be among the most nomadic of birds, moving about the countryside until they find one of these large stands of seed-bearing trees, and settling to breed there.

The WHITE-WINGED CROSSBILL (Plate 59) eats primarily spruce seeds and is common all across Alaska's spruce forests. The RED CROSSBILL (Plate 59), on the other hand, eats a wider variety of conifer seeds, and this has led to a surprisingly complex evolutionary situation. Apparently, different populations of Red Crossbills specialized, over time, on the seeds of different conifers. Little by little they evolved slight changes to make them more effective at harvesting their particular conifer type, and their body and bill sizes changed to adapt to larger and smaller seeds. Now Red Crossbills that specialized in large pine seeds are robust, big-billed birds, and those that specialized on tiny hemlock and spruce seeds are much smaller birds with petite bills. Interbreeding would have negated this evolutionary fine-tuning, so the birds mated with their own "types," and evolved distinctive calls to facilitate recognition. They are probably now distinct species, and there may be as many as eight *sibling species* (species so similar they are difficult for scientists to distinguish) of "Red Crossbills" in North America. As the diversity of conifers is relatively low in Alaska, only one or two of these crossbill types occur in the state.

Lore and Notes

Crossbills are not the only nomads among the finches; many species lack specific wintering areas but instead "invade" different parts of their wintering range in subsequent winters, presumably moving to regions where their food is more abundant in different years. People who feed birds expect to see redpolls or siskins at their feeders one winter, then perhaps none the following winter, and another invasion in the third or fourth year.

Status

No finch is in jeopardy in Alaska, but the *Hawaiian honeycreepers*, near relatives of finches, include numerous extinct and endangered species. This colorful and fascinating group of birds descended from a finchlike ancestor that reached the Hawaiian Islands millennia ago and radiated into most of the niches that could be occupied by a perching bird – seed-eaters, insect-eaters, nectar-feeders, even woodpeckerlike probers. Subsequent waves of humans, first Polynesians and then Europeans, destroyed lowland habitats and introduced mosquitos that carry bird malaria, and bird populations plummeted, many of them to extinction. A quantification of this makes clear the sad tale: of 43 species of this group known to have occurred on the islands, only 20 are still in existence.

Profiles

Gray-crowned Rosy-Finch, *Leucosticte tephrocotis*, Plate 58c
Pine Grosbeak, *Pinicola enucleator*, Plate 58e
Red Crossbill, *Loxia curvirostra*, Plate 59a
White-winged Crossbill, *Loxia leucoptera*, Plate 59b
Common Redpoll, *Carduelis flammea*, Plate 59c
Hoary Redpoll, *Carduelis hornemanni*, Plate 59d
Pine Siskin, *Carduelis pinus*, Plate 59e

Environmental Close-up 4:
How do Birds and Mammals Survive at High Latitudes?

How do so many birds manage to thrive at high latitudes? About 115 species of birds nest above the Arctic Circle in Alaska, ranging from puffins and owls to ravens and chickadees. They must face long, dark, cold winters, with frozen fresh water and often with heavy snow cover that makes their prey difficult to locate. The first important factor involved in their survival is their feather coat, which, like the hair of mammals, has an insulating function. These birds have a high body heat that is produced by their high metabolic rate and spread throughout their body by their efficient circulatory system. They would lose this heat very quickly to the cold air (and recall that almost all the air in the world is cooler than a bird's 40°C [104°F] body temperature) if it weren't for the layer of air trapped within their fluffy feathers. Just as your dog or cat puts on a heavier coat during the winter (and sheds it all over the house in spring), a bird grows a denser feather layer in fall. Black-capped Chickadees, quintessential Alaska winter birds, have a feather coat so efficient that the temperature difference between their skin and the air can be more than 45°C (113°F) on a cold winter day – and this gradient occurs over only a centimeter and a half (half-inch) distance! To reduce this temperature difference, which must take tremendous metabolic energy to maintain, chickadees become dormant at night, dropping their body temperature by 10°C (18°F) below their normal temperature.

Other birds partake of a different survival strategy. Redpolls, as small as chickadees, feed frantically all day long, depositing a substantial layer of fat by afternoon, and then burn up that fat to stay warm overnight. They also have an unusual three-stage feeding method that fits them for life in the Far North. In the first stage, they knock many birch seeds from their fruits onto the snow below, wasting as little time as possible up in a tree exposed to the wind. In the second stage, they drop to the snow and swallow the seeds. They can do this quickly, minimizing the time they are so exposed to potential predators, because they have a pair of pockets on either side of the esophagus to store the uncracked seeds. In the third stage, they fly to dense cover where they are safe from both wind and predators, and then regurgitate, crack, and swallow the seeds one by one. They do this into the night.

The Common Raven, another common winter bird of the high Arctic, eats just about anything. Ravens scrounge for garbage around human settlements when they can't find enough to eat in nature. Because of their larger size and therefore more favorable surface to volume ratio, they are not so stressed to maintain overnight body temperatures as are the small birds.

A few birds – redpolls, chickadees, ravens, Snowy Owls – can find enough to eat in central and northern Alaska to survive the winter, but how about the many birds that can't? Having an insulating layer does a bird no good when it can't acquire fuel to stoke its metabolic fires. Many of the birds that breed in Alaska are insect-eaters, and insects are quite unavailable in winter. Fish are equally inaccessible, covered by sheets of ice in both fresh and salt waters in many areas. So birds that cannot find food in winter migrate south for that adverse season. In fact, the great majority of Alaska birds are migratory, only a few dozen species wintering regularly as far north as Fairbanks in the interior. Even at the Copper River delta, with its unfrozen marine waters, no more than three dozen species are common in winter. Migrant species range from strong-flying shorebirds, some of which winter as far away as Chile or Tahiti, to small passerines with much weaker flight that move to Mexico; even some members of that group make it as far as northern South America.

Birds migrate in response to conditions at both ends of their migratory routes. An Arctic Tern stays in perennial summer, foraging at a time of large fish populations in the Arctic in the northern summer and in the southern oceans in the southern summer. It is able to find enough to eat during its rapid passage through relatively unproductive tropical waters to get it between its far-flung summer and winter homes. An Alaskan White-crowned Sparrow, on the other hand, may spend the winter in southern California, with abundant weed seeds to sustain it; it leaves there in spring, at a time when the seed crop may have been decimated by all the other winter seed-eating birds and rodents. There are both more competitors and more nest predators (snakes, for example) in southern California than there are in Alaska. Thus in order to breed it makes sense for the sparrow to go back to Alaska, where there are fewer competitors, fewer predators, and a flush of insects that appear as temperatures rise during the spring.

There are far fewer mammals than birds in the Arctic. Twenty-four species of land and freshwater mammals live in northern Alaska – two shrews, a hare, a marmot, a ground squirrel, five voles and lemmings, a porcupine, three canids, a bear, four mustelids, a cat, two deer, and two members of the antelope/sheep family. Note first the high proportion of carnivores (9 of 24); they can feed on any sort of animal smaller than themselves, so they have a good chance of surviving. Polar Bears are not included in this list, because they are basically marine mammals during the winter. Shrews, voles, and lemmings remain active under the snow; the lemmings can find plenty of vegetation in this protected environment, and the shrews take what they can, mostly insects and spiders they root out of their winter hiding places but even, when times are hard, plant matter. The Alaska Hare, Porcupine, and four species of hoofed animals are able either to graze in upland snow-free areas or browse on buds and branches of low shrubs that grow well north of the forest line, or both.

Finally, the Alaska Marmot and Arctic Ground Squirrel, which cannot find enough fresh greens to survive, go underground to *hibernate* through the winter. To do this, they must build up fat deposits of up to 80% of their lean weight in fall, and they do this by a bout of *hyperphagia* (intense eating). When they are snug in their winter retreat, their heart rate begins to fall, and their basal metabolic rate becomes about 1/50 of normal; their temperature lowers to 1/10 of normal, almost to the ambient temperature of their burrow, and they become completely dormant. They may arouse at intervals to urinate, apparently necessary to get rid of metabolic byproducts that would eventually poison them, and they may be able to check weather conditions at that time. But they remain dormant until spring, at which time their respiratory and heart rate rise quickly; they shiver, which raises their body temperature; and in three hours or so, they emerge from their burrow to face another summer.

Environmental Close-up 5:
Advantages of Colonial Nesting

Many of Alaska's birds nest in colonies, often on islands. These assemblages of breeding birds are often called "rookeries" (from the colonial nesting groups of Rooks, members of the crow family that are common in Eurasia). Many kinds of birds nest in colonies (about 12% of all bird species), so there must be some special advantage in doing so. In fact, there are probably several reasons for colonial nesting in birds.

One important reason is for *safety*. Birds that nest on the ground, as so many marine birds do, are subject to predation by snakes at low latitudes and mammals at all latitudes. One way to *avoid predation* is by nesting on islands, where snakes and mammals are scarce or absent. But islands are in short supply, relative to mainland territory, so many birds may be packed into a relatively small space. This in itself causes breeding densities to be high on many islands. But the birds realize real advantages from nesting in groups. Some predators are of a size that an individual bird or pair could not protect their eggs and young from them, but numerous individuals of the nesting species can sometimes gang up on such predators and *prevent predation*. When predators approach colonies of nesting gulls and terns, they are dive-bombed unmercifully and, even if not hit, are so distracted that they may turn around before they reach the first nest. Individual predators do learn to ignore the commotion, however, and some predators are even attracted to the noise and activity of a nesting colony. Both Great Horned Owls and Black-crowned Night-Herons have been known to visit colonies of terns every night and make off with both adult and young birds, the day-active terns having no defense against a nocturnal predator that can reach their offshore sanctuary from a nearby mainland.

Another factor provided by the high density of birds in colonies is *safety in numbers*. Research done in Alaska on River Otters preying on Fork-tailed Storm-Petrels showed that storm-petrels nesting at higher densities were less likely to be taken than those in outlying, smaller clusters at lower densities. Thus, not only does colonial nesting protect against predation, but larger colonies seem less at risk, and this makes colonies of tens of thousands and hundreds of thousands of birds more understandable. Furthermore, another safety factor provided by very large colonies is *predator saturation* (there are too many prey animals for predators to have much effect on their population). Most predators are territorial, and if the colony was in the territory of only one or a pair of predators, the birds could finish their breeding before that pair of predators could take many of their eggs or young. Of course, the overall success of the colony is not applicable to the relatively few birds that were actually eaten.

Besides predation, nesting in colonies also confers *benefits for feeding*. Seabirds are by definition marine animals, and nest sites should be situated as near as possible to rich oceanic feeding areas. But if prey species are patchily distributed, and especially if they move about, as fish schools do in the ocean, the best way birds could exploit their prey would be to breed in one spot in the midst of the area in which the prey might be encountered. An island represents a focal point where breeding can be accomplished, and yet the birds can still fly out in all directions to forage for fish and other marine life for themselves and their young. This is very different from the territoriality of terrestrial and freshwater birds, which defend a relatively restricted area in which they can find all or most of their food.

There is also the thought that breeding colonies may serve as *information centers* for birds to learn about good foraging areas. Imagine if you were a bird on a nest on an island, and your neighbors returning from the West all had beaks full of fish, whereas those coming from the East were empty-beaked. In which direction would you fly when your mate replaced you at the nest and it was your turn to go out and bring back breakfast for the kids? The idea of information centers is intuitively pleasing, and there is some evidence that birds do use each other as indicators or guides.

Another very good reason for nesting in colonies is the opportunity a large group provides for *mate-finding*. Most seabirds move over long distances and are spread out all over the ocean. By gathering at one place, they are just about assured of a mate. For the most part, if both members of a pair return to the nesting area, they come together again; this is considered monogamy, even though they go their own ways in the nonbreeding season. The importance of colonies to seabird mating is brought out very clearly by birds such as Kittlitz's and Marbled Murrelets, seabirds that nest as scattered pairs all along the coast and, accordingly, not only mate for life but actually remain together all year. We have no evidence for this other than the fact that they are typically seen in pairs throughout the winter, unlike other seabirds, which can occur in any size group. It's rather charming to watch a pair of Marbled Murrelets diving for fish. They dive together but then must go in their own directions, because they often come up well separated. Calling constantly, the two birds home in on one another and come together before they dive again.

Chapter 11

MAMMALS

- *General Characteristics and Natural History*
- *Seeing Mammals in Alaska*
- *Family Profiles*
  1. *Shrews and Bats*
  2. *Rabbits and Pikas*
     Rodents
  3. *Larger Rodents*
  4. *Smaller Rodents – Mice, Voles, and Lemmings*
     Carnivores
  5. *Wolves and Foxes*
  6. *Bears*
  7. *Seals and Sea Lions*
  8. *Weasels*
  9. *Cats*
  10. *Hoofed Mammals*
  11. *Whales and Dolphins*
- *Environmental Close-up 6: Mammal Population Cycles*

General Characteristics and Natural History

Looking at the color plates in this book, the reader will notice pictures of more birds than mammals. This may at first seem discriminatory, especially when it is recalled that we ourselves are mammals and, owing to that direct kinship, are probably keenly interested and motivated to see and learn about mammals. Why not include more mammals? There is a simple reason for this discrepancy. The total number of mammal species worldwide, and the number in any region, is less than the number of birds. In fact, there are only about 4600 mammal species, compared with 9700 birds, and the relative difference is reflected in Alaska's fauna. If species were illustrated in direct proportion to their likelihood of observation, the discrepancy would be much greater yet, because mammals are relatively rarely seen – especially by short-term visitors. Most mammals lack that basic protection from predators that birds possess, the power of flight. And because mammals are considered delicious fare by any number of predatory beasts (eaten in good numbers by reptiles, birds, and other mammals), most are active at night, or, if day-active, are highly secretive. Birds show themselves freely, mammals do not. Exceptions include those mammals that are beyond the pale of predation – huge mammals and fierce ones. There are no elephants or giraffes in Alaska, nor prides of lions, but there are sufficient mammals, both large and small, to keep the visitor on the lookout for them, and some members of the squirrel family are seen about as commonly as birds.

If birds are feathered vertebrates, mammals are hairy ones. The group first arose, so fossils tell us, approximately 245 million years ago, splitting off from primitive reptiles during the late Triassic Period of the Mesozoic Era, before the birds did the same from a more advanced reptile group. Four main traits distinguish mammals and confer upon them great advantage over other types of animals: *hair* on their bodies that insulates them from cold and otherwise protects them from environmental stresses; the bearing of *live young* instead of eggs, allowing breeding females to be mobile and hence, safer than if they had to sit on eggs for several weeks; *milk production* for the young, freeing mothers from having to search for specific foods for their offspring; and *advanced brains*, with obvious enhancing effects on many aspects of animal lives. Note that mammals are also unique in having intense female parental care, with males freed from it entirely in most groups. In the majority of birds, both sexes share parental care, and in most reptiles, amphibians, and fishes, parental care is little developed.

Mammals are quite variable in size and form, many being highly adapted – changed through evolution – to specialized habitats and lifestyles. The development of various modes of locomotion has been especially great in mammals, with species adapted to walking, running, jumping, climbing, burrowing, and swimming in many different ways. Swimmers vary from Water Shrews with stiff hairs on their feet, through River Otters, and Muskrats, which use their tails to furnish propulsion, to pinnipeds (seals and sea lions) and especially cetaceans (whales and dolphins), supremely adapted to the ocean environment. Some mammals even fly; in fact, bats have the distinction of being one of only four groups of animals that have ever evolved flight – insects, pterosaurs (extinct), and birds being the others. The smallest mammals are the *shrews*, tiny insect eaters that weigh as little as 2.5 g (a tenth of an ounce). The largest are the *whales*, weighing in at up to 160,000 kg (350,000 lb, half the weight of a loaded Boeing 747) – as far as anyone knows, the largest animals ever.

Mammals are divided into three major groups, primarily according to reproductive methods. The *monotremes* are an ancient group that actually lays eggs and still retains some other reptilelike characteristics. Only three species survive, the *platypus* and two *echidnas*; they are fairly common inhabitants of Australia and New Guinea. The *marsupials* give birth to live young that are relatively undeveloped. When born, the young crawl along their mother's fur into her *pouch*, where they find milk supplies and finish their development. There are about 240 marsupial species, including kangaroos, koalas, wombats, and possums; they are limited in distribution to the Australian region and to South and Central America (the roadkill-prone Virginia Opossum also inhabits much of Mexico and the USA). The majority of mammal species are *eutherians*, or *true mammals.* These animals are distinguished from the other groups by having a well-developed *placenta*, which connects a mother to her developing embryos, allowing for long internal development. This trait, which allows the young to develop to a fairly mature form in safety, and for the female to be mobile until birth, has allowed the true mammals to be rather successful, becoming one of the dominant groups of vertebrates on land for millions of years. The true mammals include those with which most people are familiar from childhood: rats, rabbits, cats, dogs, bats, monkeys, pigs, horses, and whales – everything from elephants to ecotravellers.

The 4600 species of living mammals are divided into 26 orders and 137 families. Of the 96 species that occur in Alaska, 28 are considered marine mammals (the pinnipeds and cetaceans), a very high proportion for a mainland region. The Sea Otter and Polar Bear belong to terrestrial groups and are not included in the 28. Two of the 96 species, the House Mouse and Norway Rat, are native to Eurasia but have travelled all over the world as unintended baggage on ships; and they thrive everywhere they travel. Both species are surprisingly widespread in settled areas in Alaska but are not likely to be found in the wilderness areas sought by naturalists.

The social and breeding behaviors of mammals are quite diverse. Some are predominantly solitary animals, males and females coming together only to mate, and this may be only once in a year. Others live in family groups. Some are rigorously territorial, others are not. Details on social and breeding behavior are provided within the individual family profiles that follow.

Seeing Mammals in Alaska

As we suggested above, mammal watching is more difficult than bird watching, but that doesn't mean it's impossible to see mammals. Although it is certainly not Africa, Alaska has quite a few mammals to be seen – several species of bears that are predators as fierce as lions; magnificent whales bigger than any elephant and just as social; and diurnal, perennially active, and often curious squirrels to take the place of monkeys.

Marine mammals are as diverse and conspicuous in Alaska as anywhere in the world. Sea Otters are guaranteed in many areas, it would be impossible to cruise anywhere along the coast without seeing pinnipeds, and there is always a very good chance of seeing cetaceans. The island breeding grounds of some of the pinnipeds are among the primary ecotourist attractions in the state, so you can see the same species both on land and at sea. Although cetaceans show only a tiny part of themselves at the water's surface, most are readily identifiable even with a brief look at their backs as they roll at the surface to breathe. Some of them, including both Gray and Humpback Whales, may jump sufficiently high to present a brief view of the whole animal. All of the Alaska ferries pass through prime wildlife-viewing areas, and there are cruises out of some of Alaska's coastal cities specifically for viewing whales and other wildlife.

Other than these denizens of the deep, many other mammals show themselves to even the casual viewer. Moose and Brown Bears are often seen from the road in many parts of the state, and ecotravellers on foot would do well to beware of both of these species, formidable opponents if encountered in an aggressive mood. Dall's Sheep and Mountain Goats are likely to be spotted by a visitor who patiently scans rocky hillsides in national parks. Among the smaller carnivores, Red Foxes are probably most often seen, but a fortunate viewer could see a member of the weasel family – perhaps a Short-tailed Weasel or River Otter. Among the small mammals, members of the squirrel family are especially viewable, and it will be hard to miss Red Squirrels in the forests and Arctic Ground Squirrels on the tundra. More than any other animal group, mammals are often detected by their "sign" – scratches on trees, droppings in prominent places, and, above all, their distinctive tracks. Carrying a small book on animal tracks is a good idea, if you are especially interested in knowing what mammals are in the vicinity. Look in sandy and muddy places near water for good impressions of tracks.

The first rule for viewing mammals is to be a typical mammal – inconspicuous. Loud noises and sudden movements scare mammals just as they do birds. The sound made by a nylon jacket as you raise your binoculars might be enough to startle the hypersensitive ears of a small mammal. Many an interesting wildlife sighting has presented itself to people who sat quietly on a rock or log in the midst of a natural habitat for a half hour or more. Also, driving slowly at night on country roads, you may see mammals that aren't out and about in the daytime. Another rule for watching any animal is to be aware of its "personal space." As you approach a bird or mammal for a better view, stop as soon as it looks up at you. When it returns to whatever it was doing, try to approach slightly closer. If it retreats, you're too close, and it's time to depend on your binoculars or telescope for further observations. Above all, spend much time in the national parks and nature reserves, where mammals, left unmolested long enough, have little by little become less likely to disappear as soon as they see you coming.

Family Profiles

1. Shrews and Bats

Shrews are the smallest mammals. They occur in most parts of the world but are absent from Australia, most of South America, and many island groups. The largest of them is smaller than most rats and mice, and the smallest weighs about 2 g (1/14 oz), about half the weight of a penny. What they lack in size, however, they make up in activity. Just to keep their tiny bodies going, they must forage almost constantly and eat and eat and eat. Along with hummingbirds and a few bat species, they are at the smallest size possible for an *endothermal* (warm-blooded) vertebrate. The production of metabolic heat by an endotherm is proportionate to its body volume, the loss of body heat is proportionate to its surface area, and the smaller an animal, the higher its ratio of surface area to volume. Animals smaller than shrews and hummingbirds would have this ratio apparently too high to survive; that is, they would lose heat through their skin faster than they could produce it. Even by being more frantically active than a shrew, such a tiny animal probably could not get enough to eat.

Shrews are *insectivores*, meaning "insect-eaters." The term "insectivore" also has a taxonomic meaning, indicating members of the order Insectivora, which includes *moles, hedgehogs,* and other many-toothed insect-eaters. The order contains 428 species, of which 312 are shrews; new species are still occasionally being discovered. Insectivores are considered at the base of the evolution of placental mammals. There are only 10 species of shrews in Alaska, and we profile three of the more common ones. Shrews are common but small and secretive enough that they are rarely seen by humans. Still, they do appear on occasion, usually a quick glimpse of a tiny, sharp-nosed mammal, perhaps running out from a tangle of branches or scurrying under a pile of leaves. A WATER SHREW (Plate 60) may be seen while it is swimming, the air captured in its fur giving it a silvery look. A better look at a shrew will show a medium-length tail and the different fur colors of the different species, but a close-up is necessary to see details of the face – a very pointed snout with long, sensitive "whiskers," a mouth full of tiny sharp teeth, and eyes and ears small enough to make one wonder about their functionality. Never fear, shrews can see and hear, but their sense of smell is best developed. They find their prey by tracking scents, just as a dog or badger does.

Of all the kinds of mammals, *bats* seem the strangest to us. There are several reasons for this. Bats, like birds, engage in sustained, powered flight – the only mammals to do so (they have quite erroneously been called "mice with wings"). Bats are active purely at night. They navigate the night sky not by sight or smell but chiefly by "sonar," or *echolocation*. They broadcast ultrasonic sounds – extremely high-pitched chirps and clicks – and then gain information about their environment by "reading" the echoes. The exotic behavior of bats, particularly their nocturnal habits, has engendered fear and superstition among most humans. But recently, both because their lives are so very different from our own and because many species are becoming less common, bats have been increasingly of interest to us.

Bats are mammals of the order Chiroptera (*chiro* = hand, *ptera* = wing), in some ways similar to and almost surely descendants of the insectivores. They are widely distributed, inhabiting most of the world's tropical and temperate regions, excepting some oceanic islands. With a total of about 975 species, the bats are second in diversity among mammals only to the rodents. Ecologically, they can be thought of as nighttime equivalents of birds, which dominate the daytime skies. In tropical regions, bats are especially important mammals. Their diversity and numbers tell the story: 39% of all Neotropical (South and Central America) mammal species are bats, and there are usually as many species of bats in a Neotropical forest as of all other mammal species combined. Researchers estimate that most of the mammalian biomass (the total amount of living tissue, by weight) in any given Neotropical region resides in bats. In temperate regions, bats are much less diverse but may still be very abundant. Alaska has its own small complement of bats, although they rapidly decrease with increased latitude within the state. Only six species are known from Alaska, and only the LITTLE BROWN MYOTIS (Plate 60) ranges widely.

Bats have true wings, consisting of thin, strong, highly elastic membranes of skin that extend from the sides of the body and legs to cover and be supported by the elongated fingers. Other distinctive anatomical features include bodies covered with silky, longish hair; toes with sharp, curved claws that allow them to hang upside down and are used by some to catch food; scent glands that produce strong, musky odors; and, in many, very odd-shaped folds of skin on their noses (nose leaves) and prominent ears that aid in echolocation. Like those of birds, the bodies of bats have been modified through evolution to conform to the needs of energy-demanding flight: they have relatively large hearts, low body weights, and high metabolisms.

Alaska bats are relatively uniform in size and appearance, weighing from 9 to 18 g (⅓ to ⅔ oz) and with 15 to 25 cm (6 to 10 in) wingspans, but elsewhere in the world there are bats less than a fourth the weight of Alaska's smallest and others weighing up to 1 kg (2.2 lb), with 2 m (6.5 ft) wingspans. These large bats with pleasant-looking faces are called *flying foxes*. They live in Southeast Asia, Australia, and the Pacific Islands, and they are the only bats often seen roosting in the open and flying around during daylight hours.

Natural History
Ecology and Behavior
The frenzied activity of shrews is legendary. Probably all species are active night and day, and they are on the move much of that time. They take short rests when their hunger is satiated but quickly become active to hunt again. "Shrewnap" would be a better name than "catnap" for the common human behavior of taking a short nap, because cats sleep much of the time! When a shrew comes upon a prey item – most likely an insect or earthworm – it just grabs and keeps biting until it meets no more resistance. Then, just as quickly, it chews and swallows it. This is rather more spectacular when the prey is a large insect, another shrew, or a small mouse. A few species of shrews secrete venom from their salivary glands, using it to subdue the struggles of larger prey, but no Alaska shrew is venomous. Prey animals that are not fully devoured are stored for later use. Shrews have such a hyperactive metabolism that they are apparently living right on the edge; they are so sensitive to environmental stress that observers have seen them die from being picked up or even from a sudden loud noise.

Like shrews, most bats specialize on insects. They use their sonar not just to navigate the night but to detect insects, which they catch on the wing, pick off leaves, or scoop off the ground. Bats use several methods to catch flying insects. Small insects may be captured directly in the mouth, but some bats use their wings as nets to trap insects and pull them to their mouth, while others scoop bugs into the fold of skin membrane that connects their tail and legs, then somersault in midair to move the catch to their mouth. Small insects are eaten immediately on the wing, but larger ones, such as large beetles, are taken to a perch and dismembered. Not all bats, however, are insectivores. Tropical bats have also expanded ecologically into a variety of other *feeding niches*. Some specialize in eating fruit, feeding on nectar and pollen at flowers, preying on vertebrates such as frogs or birds, eating fish, or even, in the case of vampire bats, sipping blood.

Bats spend the daylight hours in day roosts, usually tree cavities, shady sides of trees, caves, rock crevices, or, these days, in buildings or under bridges. For most species, the normal resting position in a roost is hanging by their feet, head downwards, which makes taking flight as easy as letting go and spreading their wings. Many bats leave roosts around dusk, then move to foraging sites at various distances from the roost. Night activity patterns vary, perhaps serving to reduce food competition among species. Some tend to fly and forage intensely in the early evening, become less active in the middle of the night, then resume active foraging near dawn; others are relatively inactive early in the evening, but more active later on.

There are very few insects in flight, either day or night, during the long Alaska winter, so bats cannot be active then. They have two strategies for coping with northern winters: migration and hibernation. One very rare Alaska bat, the SILVER-HAIRED BAT, is known to migrate, but all the other species, including the LITTLE BROWN MYOTIS, are hibernators. Their hibernation is not as deep as that of a ground squirrel, but instead they are *torpid*, still awake but with much lowered metabolism and thus using fat reserves they built up during the fall at a very slow rate to get them through the winter.

Breeding

Alaska shrews breed throughout the summer, often producing two or three litters each year of about 5 to 10 young each; the TUNDRA SHREW (Plate 60) has especially large litters, perhaps an adaptation to high winter mortality. The female cares for the young for about 3 weeks. One of the most endearing sights in the mammalian world is a female shrew moving her young. One young bites down (gently) on the mother's tail base, and the next young do the same on their siblings' tails, the whole assemblage moving like a short train with a big engine.

Bat mating systems are diverse, various species employing monogamy, poly-gyny, and/or promiscuity; the breeding behavior of many species has yet to be studied in detail. Most bats at high latitudes practice *delayed fertilization*. LITTLE BROWN MYOTIS and many other temperate-zone bats mate in fall at communal roosts, and females store the sperm, in contact with and nourished by the walls of the oviduct. The female is thus independent of male attention after that time. Ovulation and fertilization take place in late winter, and the females give birth to one or two young in June. Parental care is well developed, as in all female mammals. In some species of bats, the female is able to carry a single young between roosting and feeding sites. As it grows, she can "park" it in a tree or cave and return to nurse it. In the Alaska species, however, the females nurse their young for about a month, then abandon them.

Ecological Interactions

Shrews are not as abundant as mice, as they feed higher on the food chain, on other animals instead of plants. However, they are common, with populations reaching 12 to 25 per hectare (5 to 10 per acre) in some areas. They are very difficult to observe, so most research has been either on basic information acquired by putting out pit traps and harvesting the shrews that fall into them or by keeping small numbers of them in captivity. They are difficult to keep together, as they will fight and even eat each other. If shrews were as big as house cats and were ferocious in proportion to their size, Alaska forests might not be safe for people.

Oddly, although shrews figure in the diets of many predatory birds and mammals, it is not unusual to find their dead bodies, apparently where a predator has killed one but not eaten it. Some shrews are thought to be distasteful, and perhaps their strong musk overpowers the hunger urge. It is also possible that these shrews were victims of small carnivores such as cats or weasels that kill prey even in the absence of hunger.

With their sonar, bats would seem to have an easy time detecting and capturing flying insects; but their prey, of course, have developed tactics to avoid becoming bat dinners (or is it breakfasts?). Several groups of moths, for instance, can sense the ultrasonic chirps of some echolocating insectivorous bats; when they do, they react immediately by flying erratically or diving down into vegetation, making them quite uncatchable. Fortunately for bats, not all moths do this. Some moths even make their own clicking sounds, which apparently confuse the bats, causing them to break off their approach. The interaction of bats and their prey animals is an active field of animal behavior research, because the predators and the prey have both developed many tactics to try to outmaneuver or outwit the other.

Relatively little is known about which predators prey on bats. The list includes birds of prey (owls, hawks), snakes, cats, people (large tropical fruit bats are eaten on Pacific islands), and even other bats, such as the carnivorous FALSE VAMPIRE BAT of the New World Tropics.

Lore and Notes

When William Shakespeare wrote *The Taming of the Shrew*, had he ever seen a shrew? There are shrews in England, but in Shakespeare's time the Middle English word *schrewe*, a malicious person, had been applied to ill-tempered women well before it was applied to the small, seemingly irritable, mammal. One could easily imagine a sequel – *The Taming of the Shrew II* – by the insectivore keeper at a large zoo.

Bats, on the other hand, have frightened people for a very long time. The result, of course, is that there is a large body of folklore that portrays bats as evil, associated with or incarnations of death, devils, witches, or vampires. Undeniably, it was bats' alien lives – their activity in the darkness, flying ability, and strange form – and people's ignorance of bats that were the sources of these myriad superstitions. Many cultures, worldwide, have legends of evil bats, and even Australian Aborigines were not immune. One of their legends concerning the origin of death features a large bat that guarded the entrance to a cave. The first man and woman on Earth were warned to stay away from the bat. The woman, curious, approached the bat, which grew frightened and flew away. The cave housed Death, which, with its bat guard gone, escaped into the world, with predictable consequences.

Many ancient legends tell of how bats came to be creatures of the night. But the association of bats with vampires – blood-sucking monsters – may have originated in recent times with Bram Stoker, the English author who in 1897 published *Dracula* (the title character, a vampire, could metamorphose into a bat). Vampire bats are native only to the Neotropics. Stoker may have heard stories of their blood-lapping ways from travellers, and for his book, melded the behavior of these bats with legends of vampires from India and from Slavic Gypsy culture. Although not all New World cultures imparted evil reputations to bats, it is not surprising, given the presence of vampire bats, that some did. The Mayans, for instance, associated bats with darkness and death; there was a "bat world," a part of the underworld ruled by a bat god, through which dead people had to pass.

Status

Bats are already rare in Alaska, so it would take little effort to place them on state lists of Threatened or Endangered species. However, they are so poorly known – as is the case with shrews in many parts of the state – that it serves no purpose to set them apart as of special concern until attempts are made to learn more about their distribution and abundance. All of Alaska's bats are much more common to the south of the state, and most of Alaska's shrews range outside the state as well. However, a few species are restricted to the state, the ST. LAWRENCE ISLAND SHREW to St. Lawrence Island and the PRIBILOF SHREW to the Pribilofs. These animals should remain common as long as large parts of these islands remain pristine, as is the case now. Another shrew, the GLACIER BAY WATER SHREW, is restricted to Alaska mainland areas, but it too is presumably secure in a relatively undisturbed part of the world.

Profiles

Little Brown Myotis, *Myotis lucifugus*, Plate 60a
Masked Shrew, *Sorex cinereus*, Plate 60b
Tundra Shrew, *Sorex tundrensis*, Plate 60c
Water Shrew, *Sorex palustris*, Plate 60d

2. Rabbits and Pikas

The order Lagomorpha, the *lagomorphs*, includes two families of long-eared, long-legged, short-tailed, thin-skinned, soft-furred, leaf-eating mammals. There are 54 species of *rabbits* and *hares*, family Leporidae, and the family occurs on every continent but Australia (where the EUROPEAN RABBIT was introduced, with disastrous consequences for the fragile Australian environment). The long hind legs of rabbits suit them for both long- and high-jumping, although their locomotion when they are not fleeing a predator consists of walking or running. *Pikas*, family Ochotonidae, with 26 species, are distributed primarily in the mountains and high plateaus of Asia, with two species in western North America. They are smaller than hares and rabbits, with shorter ears, and hind legs not evolved for jumping. The three Alaska lagomorphs nicely divide the state among them – the SNOWSHOE HARE (Plate 61) in the forests, the ALASKA HARE (Plate 61) in the tundra, and the COLLARED PIKA (Plate 61) in rocky areas. A much smaller group than the rodents, the lagomorphs are similarly modified to be herbivores, as anyone who has seen a Bugs Bunny cartoon can attest. Like the rodents, which are probably their closest relatives, they have two big incisors at the front of both their upper and lower jaws. Unlike the rodents, they have another smaller pair of incisors right behind the prominent upper pair. Lagomorphs also differ from rodents in having their scrotum in front of their penis, a characteristic shared only with marsupials. Females are slightly larger than males, unusual among mammals. The Alaska species just about encompass the range of size in the order, and the only additional attributes to be learned by scrutinizing species from elsewhere in the world is that many hares of hot lower latitudes have extremely large ears.

Natural History
Ecology and Behavior

Rabbits are classically portrayed as lettuce-eaters, and indeed they eat the leaves from lettuce and other garden vegetables. Wild rabbits and hares, of course, feed not only on leaves but also on buds, flowers, twigs, and roots of many plants, both herbaceous and shrubby. Favorite foods in Alaska include most of the common plants, for example willows, grasses, and saxifrages. During winter, their diet shifts to twigs, bark, and buds and even the rather indigestible needles of spruces. Most rabbit activity, both feeding and mating, takes place at night.

Leaf-eating animals have a hard time getting sufficient nutrition from their diets, because the cellulose that coats plant cells is difficult to digest. Thus many leaf-eaters feed almost continually, and they have a gut full of specialized bacteria to aid in digestion. Rabbits take it one step further; in one of the more fascinating adaptations in the animal kingdom, they practice *coprophagy*, eating their own feces. Their "pellets" come out in two forms, the first green and rather soft; these are eaten. The second time around, the pellet is hard and brown and remains where it drops. This two-timing behavior may have evolved to allow rabbits – very vulnerable to predation – to eat very rapidly while out in the open, then retire to a safe place and digest, defecate, and reingest at leisure.

Rabbits show exceptional development of their senses, presumably another adaptation against predation. Their eyes are large and bulging and are placed on the sides of their head in such a way that the animal can see both in front and behind. Their nose is very sensitive and always twitching, testing the air for odors coming from all directions. Finally, their ears are just about the largest for their size among all mammals, only some bats exceeding them. ALASKA HARES sometimes stand up on their hind legs, probably to watch for predators, and may even walk upright briefly.

Breeding

Hares and rabbits have complex mating behavior, with males in some species fighting for the opportunity to mate with territorial females. In most species, there are wild chases, the females often jumping right over the males. Hares and rabbits are fabled rapid breeders, although those at high latitudes are more limited by season than their lower-latitude relatives. Like most mammals, males and females come together only for mating; the female furnishes all parental care. Their 36-day gestation period allows SNOWSHOE HARES to produce several litters of about four young each during the summer, and the young hares grow very rapidly, within 2 weeks being able to feed on their own. COLLARED PIKAS may have their two to six young any time during the summer; like rabbits, they are rapid breeders, with a gestation period of about 30 days. The young are weaned at a small size, something that is possible for herbivorous mammals, for which food is abundant and finding it doesn't take much brain power.

Ecological Interactions

One of the most interesting animal stories of Alaska and Canada involves the population cycles of the SNOWSHOE HARE and LYNX. Although Lynx eat a wide variety of prey, they are very closely tied to their main prey, the Snowshoe Hare. From the records kept by 19th-century fur trappers, it soon became obvious that hare numbers fluctuated in a fairly regular fashion, with highs about every 10 years and much lower populations in-between. Lynx trapping showed a similar pattern, and it didn't take much thought to understand that these patterns were related. When hare populations are high, Lynx do very well and raise lots of kittens, so their populations rise. In years of low hare populations, Lynx have a much harder time existing and raise few kittens. For more information on mammal population cycles, see Close-up, p. 220.

Lore and Notes

The idea that a rabbit's foot will bring good luck is a long-held tradition in most English-speaking countries. In the British Isles, rabbits and hares were long associated with either bad luck or good luck. For example, a rabbit that crossed one's path in front was a bad omen and one that crossed behind was a good omen. Because rabbits were considered prolific breeders, a rabbit's foot also became a symbol of fertility. Finally, the hind foot is considered a powerful charm against evil because the rabbit's hind legs touch the ground before its front legs when it is running, and people thought this was so remarkable that they ascribed magical powers to it. According to one legend, the absolute best luck is to carry a rabbit's left hind foot in the left pocket after removing it from a rabbit killed during a full moon by a cross-eyed person.

Status

Alaska's lagomorphs have healthy populations, but some of their relatives at lower latitudes in North America have not fared so well, mostly because of habitat destruction. The PYGMY RABBIT and WHITE-TAILED JACKRABBIT, species of Great Basin sagebrush and grassland habitats that are easily altered to pasture and farmland, are now rare in much of their ranges.

Profiles

Collared Pika, *Ochotona collaris*, Plate 61a
Snowshoe Hare, *Lepus americanus*, Plate 61b
Alaska Hare, *Lepus othus*, Plate 61c

Rodents

Rodents (order Rodentia) are the gnawing mammals (rodent is from the Latin *rodere*, to gnaw). With their strong, sharp, chisel-like front teeth, rodents make their living gnawing, cutting, and slicing vegetation, bark, roots, fruit, and nuts, digging burrows, and, in the case of beavers, imitating lumberjacks. Some of them (for example, the grasshopper mice of the American Southwest) even kill and eat other small animals, including smaller mice. Their ecological success is likely related to their efficient, specialized teeth and associated jaw muscles; to the fact that most of them eat plant matter, which is very abundant; and to the small size of most of them, allowing large numbers of individuals to exist in a relatively small area. Rodents, like the similarly herbivorous lagomorphs and most hoofed mammals, have an interesting dental arrangement. Their two pairs of incisors, the "buck teeth" at the front of the mouth, are separated by a decided gap (the *diastema*) from the cheek teeth (premolars and molars) in the back of the mouth. The incisors are for biting, and the cheek teeth are for chewing, and these are such different functions that, over evolutionary time, the two groups of teeth became separated completely. With our continuous row of teeth, it is hard for us to relate to such a dentition. Through the animals' constant gnawing, rodents' chisel-like incisors wear down rapidly. But unlike those of most mammals, the incisors of rodents continue to grow throughout their lives, and their structure, harder on the front edges and softer in back, makes them perfect self-sharpening tools.

Ecotravellers discover among rodents an ecological paradox: although by far the most diverse and successful of the mammals, rodents are, with a few obvious exceptions (notably the squirrel family), relatively inconspicuous and rarely encountered. There are over 2000 rodent species globally, 43% of the known mammalian species, and new species are discovered regularly. For example, a cat-sized rodent never before seen by scientists was found in the Peruvian Andes in 2000. In just about every region of the world, rodents – including mice, rats, squirrels, chipmunks, marmots, gophers, beavers, and porcupines – are the most abundant land mammals. More individual rodents are estimated to be alive at any one time than individuals of all other types of mammals combined. Rodents' near-invisibility to people derives from the facts that most rodents are very small, most are secretive or nocturnal, and many live out their lives in subterranean burrows. That most rodents are rarely encountered, of course, many people do not consider much of a hardship.

Most of the world's rodents are small mouselike or ratlike mammals that weigh less than a kilogram (2.2 lb); they range, however, from tiny pygmy mice that weigh only a few grams to South America's piglike CAPYBARA, behemoths at up to 50 kg (110 lb). The larger and mid-sized rodents are here separated from the much smaller mice and rats for ease of discussion.

3. Larger Rodents

Squirrels are members of the family Sciuridae, a worldwide group of more than 350 species that occurs on all continents except Australia. They are relatively large rodents, and the largest members of the family, *marmots*, weigh up to 9 kg (20 lb). Even some tree squirrels are surprisingly large, the GIANT SQUIRRELS (1.5 kg, 3.3 lb) and GIANT FLYING SQUIRRELS (2.5 kg, 5.5 lb) of southeast Asian rainforests measuring up to 90 cm (35 in) in length. The family includes marmots, *prairie dogs*, *chipmunks*, and *ground*, *tree*, and *flying squirrels*; six species occur in Alaska. Most squirrels have relatively long and bushy tails, appropriate as balancing organs for their tree-climbing and jumping activities, but there are also many shorter-tailed species that remain on the ground and live in burrows.

The MUSKRAT (Plate 62) is in the very diverse mouse family, Muridae, and it is the largest species of the subfamily (Microtinae) that contains the *voles* and *lemmings* (p. 194). It is highly modified for aquatic life, with shiny, dense fur and a long, scaly tail compressed from side to side to serve as a sculling organ. The beaver family, Castoridae, is a small family, with a single Old World species and a single New World species, the AMERICAN BEAVER (Plate 62). Beavers are by far the largest rodents in northern latitudes, normally weighing up to 27 kg (60 lb). They are even more highly modified for aquatic life than Muskrats, with a similarly large, scaly tail that is broad and flat. The incisors are bright orange on the front surface on beavers and some other rodents, but the function of this color remains unknown. Like Muskrats, beavers may cross dry land when moving between water bodies. Finally, the family Erethizontidae contains the 15 species of New World *porcupines*, which are distributed throughout the Americas save for the southern third of South America. A single species, the COMMON PORCUPINE (Plate 61), is native to Alaska. It is nearly as large as the beaver (18 kg, 40 lb) and unmistakable because of its very long hairs, which only partially conceal the 30,000 or so hairs that have been modified as defensive quills.

Natural History
Ecology and Behavior
The squirrel family stands in strong contrast with other rodents, because most of its species are day-active. In fact, these unusual rodents are similar to birds in many ways. Some of them are relatively brightly colored and patterned for mammals (think of chipmunks), and many of them are highly vocal; RED SQUIRREL (Plate 63) calls are among the characteristic sounds of conifer forests, and marmot whistles startle hikers high in the mountains. The long, bushy tail of most squirrels makes them not only excellent jumpers but also quite attractive. Some of them quickly become tame enough to be fed by hand in areas where ecotourists congregate. Tree squirrels typically eat a great variety of foods, although Red Squirrels especially prefer conifer seeds and mushrooms; insects make up a substantial part of the diet of that species in summer, and a nestful of bird eggs is a special treat. Ground squirrels and marmots, on the other hand, have a much more restricted diet of green vegetation.

An exception in a usually day-active family, the NORTHERN FLYING SQUIRREL (Plate 63) is nocturnal like most other rodents. Sleeping all day in a tree cavity, they rouse at dusk, pop out of their nest hole, climb a few feet, and launch themselves into the air to begin their nightly foraging route. With their spread-out skin flaps and wide, bushy tails, flying squirrels can glide up to 80 m

(262 ft) at a time, and by doing so, they can cover a lot of area in a night's activities. Obviously they cannot flourish where the trees are too far apart, so intact forest is necessary to sustain a population of flying squirrels. Oddly, they forage as much on the ground (where they dig for fungi) as they do in the trees (where they eat lichens, seeds, fruits, insects, and bird eggs like their day-active relative, the Red Squirrel). Both Red Squirrels and Northern Flying Squirrels inhabit leafy or twiggy nests in summer, but during the winter flying squirrels move into tree cavities, and Red Squirrels go underground in tunnels under stumps and tree trunks. Both of them store seeds and whole cones in their winter nests to keep them well-fed during that difficult season.

BEAVERS and MUSKRATS are active during the day but may be active at night as well, and beavers are always nocturnal where disturbed by humans. Both of these rodents are aquatic, living in "lodges" they build or in burrows in sandy banks. Beavers, of course, are the best-known animal architects, constructing not only their fabled dams but also large lodges out of the same woody materials. A beaver lodge looks like nothing more than a huge pile of branches out in the water, but it is carefully built to have two underwater entrances and a large, dry chamber lined with finer material. Although eating a wide variety of plant parts in the summer, from both terrestrial and aquatic plants, beavers eat primarily twigs and branches during the winter. They store large quantities of these food items under water, both inside and outside their lodge, and, once their water body freezes, no predators can disturb them. Dams are constructed at any narrow point in a stream or small river, the beavers carrying branch after branch to the site, until the pile reaches across the stream and begins to slow its motion. The current deposits more and more detritus in the increasingly filled-in dam. The interstices are then filled with mud, the current stops, and the stream spreads out into a pond, ideal beaver habitat. Beavers have an uncanny ability to find the smallest leaks in their dams, and they fill them immediately. Biologists have been able to study beaver families at work by creating a small breach in the main dam and watching from a distance.

Muskrats, much smaller than beavers, feed on herbaceous rather than woody vegetation. Their lodges are also made of soft aquatic plants, and their home ranges are much smaller than those of beavers, so several lodges may be seen in the same marsh. Young Muskrats travel long distances over land to find new water bodies, and they are very vulnerable to predation by Minks and other carnivores at that time.

PORCUPINES are usually nocturnal, although they are sufficiently large that they are quite visible when encountered sleeping in a small spruce tree during the day. In summer, when plant growth is profuse, they eat a wide variety of buds, leaves, and twigs, but in winter most of their diet is made up of the soft inner bark of trees. They are amazing long-distance travellers, and individuals are often found far out on the tundra among low willows, and even in treeless grasslands.

Breeding

The first question one might ask here is "how do porcupines mate?" The traditional answer is "very, very carefully," but in fact they mate like most other mammals, with the female's quills relaxed and her spiny tail held over her back. Most of the rodents profiled here breed in late winter or early spring, the marmots somewhat later, and have their young in the period from April to June. PORCUPINES diverge from this pattern by mating in fall and having their young in early spring. Most large Alaska rodents breed once each year, but MUSKRATS manage to get in two litters during the short Alaska summer. The gestation period varies from about a month for the smaller squirrels to 3 to 4 months in the larger rodents. In most species, the young leave the nest soon after being weaned, but BEAVERS are somewhat more social, with the offspring remaining in the small colony until they reach breeding age at 2 years, when they are forced out by the adults. Porcupines are unusual among rodents in having quite *precocial* young, born with eyes open and able to move around on their own almost immediately. Fortunately for the mother, their quills are soft at birth, but they harden quickly in the air.

Ecological Interactions

Rodents are important ecologically primarily because of their great abundance. They are so common that they make up a large proportion of the diets of many carnivores, for instance, 70% of the prey eaten by Martens in one study in interior Alaska. Most of Alaska's carnivores, from Brown Bears and Gray Wolves down to Least Weasels, feed at least in part on rodents. In turn, rodents, owing to their ubiquitousness and numbers, are themselves important predators on seeds. They digest or damage the seeds, rendering them useless to the plants that produced them for reproduction. Of course, not every seed is damaged (some fall to the ground as rodents eat), and so rodents, at least occasionally, also act as seed dispersers. Where rodents eat fruits, as in tropical rain forests, they often carry them away from where they have fallen from a fruiting tree and, thus, may take them to a more favorable spot for sprouting and growth.

Burrowing is another aspect of rodent behavior that has significant ecological implications because of the sheer numbers of individuals that participate. When so many animals (for example, ground squirrels, pocket gophers, rats, and mice) move soil around, the effect is that over several years the entire topsoil of an area is turned, keeping soil loose and aerated, and therefore more suitable for plant growth. Rodents and earthworms have similar ecological effects in this way.

The different species of marmots have been used to show the relationship between habitats and mammal social systems. WOODCHUCKS (a type of marmot; Plate 62) live in rich environments and protect their own food resources by being territorial; their young leave home at an early age because it is easy for them to find an unoccupied territory. OLYMPIC MARMOTS live high in the Olympic Mountains of Washington state, where the heavy snow pack makes the growing season very short and conditions more adverse. In that species, the young remain with the parents through their second year, until they are experienced enough to move to their own home range. Along with this, the females breed only every other year, facilitating the long maturation period of their young.

Lore and Notes

All three species of marmots profiled here and the ARCTIC GROUND SQUIRREL (Plate 63) are true hibernators, spending the winter in a state of suspended animation with their metabolic rate greatly reduced and their body temperature greatly lowered, nearing that of the environment. They can hibernate only because they are deep in burrows, protected from the most intense cold and from predators that remain active during winter. All of these species are plant-eaters, and they spend a very busy fall feeding almost continually on the leaves of low-growing plants and building up fat to carry them through the winter. "Roly-poly" describes them well at that time. There are no other true hibernators among Alaska's mammals, although several species, including bears, may "hole up" and remain asleep for long periods with somewhat lowered body temperature.

Contrary to folk wisdom, PORCUPINES cannot "throw" their quills, or spines, at people or predators. Rather, the spines detach quite easily when touched, such that a predator attempting to bite a porcupine will be impaled with spines and, hence, rendered very unhappy. The spines have barbed ends, like fishhooks, which anchor them securely into the offending predator. Nonetheless, mammals such as Wolverines, Fishers, and Cougars commonly dine on porcupines by harassing them until they are tired, then attacking their unquilled underside. They are much better at this than foxes and other canids, many of which have been seen with porcupine quills in their muzzles.

Status

All of Alaska's large rodents are still common. A close relative of the HOARY MARMOT (Plate 62), the VANCOUVER MARMOT, is restricted to higher elevations on Vancouver Island, British Columbia. It has been critically reduced in population size by habitat destruction and is listed by the Canadian government as endangered. BEAVERS, which decreased substantially in many areas during the long history of beaver trapping in North America, have rebounded, and they continue to recolonize areas from which they had disappeared. Where tree cover is not extensive, they can replace a wooded stream with a treeless pond and then, having eliminated their own sources of food, move on. They thrive in some suburban and even urban wetlands, where they often bring "beaver control" onto themselves by cutting down trees in parks and yards and, more seriously, destroying narrow bands of trees growing along streams (*riparian* vegetation) that provide very important habitat for other wildlife.

Profiles

Common Porcupine, *Erethizon dorsatum*, Plate 61d
Hoary Marmot, *Marmota caligata*, Plate 62a
Alaska Marmot, *Marmota broweri*, Plate 62b
Woodchuck, *Marmota monax*, Plate 62c
Muskrat, *Ondatra zibethicus*, Plate 62d
American Beaver, *Castor canadensis*, Plate 62e
Red Squirrel, *Tamiasciurus hudsonicus*, Plate 63a
Northern Flying Squirrel, *Glaucomys sabrinus*, Plate 63b
Arctic Ground Squirrel, *Spermophilus parryii*, Plate 63e

4. Smaller Rodents – Mice, Voles, and Lemmings

Mice and *voles* are the most abundant mammals. Being small and for the most part plant-eaters, they can exist at very high densities because the world is their cafeteria. Plants not only occur in dense populations, but they continue to grow during the summer and thus constantly replenish the food supplies of little leaf- and seed-eating rodents. Many seed-eating mice collect seeds throughout the summer and cache them in burrows to eat during the winter. Leaf-eating rodents can survive the winter by eating older, lower-quality leaves left over from the summer before or, in a few species, by hibernating.

There are numerous small rodents called "mice," but the main rat and mouse family is a huge one, Muridae, with more than 1300 species all over the world.

One mouse, eight voles, and three *lemmings* of this family occur in Alaska, and the Muskrat, discussed previously, is actually a large, aquatic relative of the voles and lemmings. The *jumping mouse* is a member of a much smaller family, the Dipodidae, with 51 species in North America, Eurasia, and Africa. Mice are easily recognized as little long-tailed rodents with big ears; almost all of them are active at night. They travel about on the ground or up in shrubs and trees, a few species climbing quite high; some semi-aquatic species live in marshy areas or streams. *Rats* are really nothing more than large mice, usually similar in shape and habits. Voles and lemmings have shorter tails and smaller ears than mice, and most of them are active throughout the 24-hour day. Jumping mice have especially large hind feet and long tails. Their feet provide spring for a long jump, and the tail provides balance in the air. As would be expected, small rodents are all camouflaged in various shades of brown, but many of the nocturnal ones are white beneath, perhaps to cast less of a shadow in the moonlight.

Natural History
Ecology and Behavior
Most mice and rats eat seeds, with much variation on this theme, whereas voles and lemmings are primarily leaf-eaters. Leaves are found everywhere, but they don't furnish much nutrition; and this is probably why voles and lemmings must remain active day and night, foraging. Their food plants are common, so they don't have to move around a lot, which would make them conspicuous; thus they can forage in broad daylight. Also, they travel in a well-used system of partially hidden runways at the ground surface. Seeds are more localized sources of high nutritional value, and mice must spend some time harvesting each batch, perhaps out in the open, so it makes sense for them to be nocturnal, to avoid visual predators. Jumping mice are seed eaters, but they are apparently unable to find enough to eat during the winter, so they hibernate.

Lemmings are the rodents of the Arctic. They remain active all winter, burrowing under the snow that protects them from both the cold and their predators. Their bodies are very compact, with smaller ears and shorter tails even than voles, providing less surface area from which to lose body heat. The COLLARED LEMMING (Plate 65) turns white in the winter, the only rodent to do so, further protecting it from predators when it has to move about on the snow. It is also adapted for the Arctic by an amazing change that takes place in its anatomy. The two central claws on either forefoot lengthen in the fall, and the horny pads beneath them grow into big, laterally flattened paddles that the lemming uses to dig burrows through densely packed snow. When growth of the claws stops in the spring, they get worn back to their normal size.

Breeding
Small rodents are the most prolific of mammals. They have large litters (typically 5 to 10 young in Alaska species) and often have more than one litter per year. The young grow very rapidly, reaching independence from the mother in 2 weeks, and in some species can breed when they are only a month old! Females undergo hormonal recycling very rapidly and can breed within a few weeks of having weaned a litter of young. A. W. Banfield, in *The Mammals of Canada* (1974), wrote "The rabbit is generally considered to have reached the acme of fecundity, but it is not even in the same league as the meadow vole. These creatures meet, mate, and multiply almost before rabbits can get started." Voles and lemmings live such a fast life, in fact, that most of them live only about a year. They are *annuals*, just

like many familiar wildflowers that grow up from seed, flower, fruit, and die in the same summer.

Ecological Interactions

Alaska's small rodents range in abundance from the rather uncommon jumping mice to the superabundant deer mice, voles, and lemmings. Voles and lemmings in particular are so common that they serve as the primary diet of numerous carnivorous birds and mammals. Lemmings, in fact, are *keystone species* in the Arctic tundra ecosystem, their abundance influencing both the plants they eat and the animals that in turn feed on them. See under owls (p. 141) for more about the relationships of their predators.

Although we usually think of mice as eating seeds and other plant parts, some of them are quite carnivorous, as is true of many rodents. On Triangle Island, British Columbia, NORTHWESTERN DEER MICE (Plate 63) include in their diets the eggs of breeding seabirds such as Rhinoceros Auklets. Up to a third of the auklets' eggs were eaten by deer mice in one study, quite a surprise when you learn that the mice weigh about 44 g (1.5 oz), the eggs about 79 g (2.8 oz). Those gnawing incisors are very effective.

Lore and Notes

One of the first thoughts to cross the minds of many people when they hear the word "lemmings" is to think of little brown rodents hurling themselves off cliffs and into the sea in an orgy of follow-the-leader. In fact, the mass migration that brings about these actions every three or four years is a feature of the life of the NORWAY LEMMING of far northern Europe and does not seem to occur in North American species. Lemmings on this continent sometimes become very common during the peaks of their population cycles, but the animals move about individually when they disperse, without the frenzied mass migration of their Scandinavian relatives and without drowning themselves even when moving across unfamiliar terrain. This is not to say that any such journeys aren't fraught with extreme danger, because a small mammal that leaves its own home range is exposed to all the predators it passes without the safety of known escape routes.

Status

It would be hard to conceive of any of the northern rodents becoming rare; they are abundant within their habitats, and their habitats are still present in vast tracts. The smaller the animal, the easier preserved its populations are, because a preserve with a few hundred hectares (1 hectare = 2.47 acres) can easily serve as habitat for a large population of voles. However, the same area might not be able to support a single individual of a medium-sized predator such as a Marten, which is why planners of reserves should always set aside the largest tracts of land possible.

Profiles

Meadow Jumping Mouse, *Zapus hudsonius*, Plate 63c
Northwestern Deer Mouse, *Peromyscus keeni*, Plate 63d
Singing Vole, *Microtus miurus*, Plate 64a
Meadow Vole, *Microtus pennsylvanicus*, Plate 64b
Yellow-cheeked Vole, *Microtus xanthognathus*, Plate 64c
Tundra Vole, *Microtus oeconomus*, Plate 64d
Northern Red-backed Vole, *Clethrionomys rutilus*, Plate 65a
Northern Bog Lemming, *Synaptomys borealis*, Plate 65b

Brown Lemming, *Lemmus sibiricus*, Plate 65c
Collared Lemming, *Dicrostonyx groenlandicus*, Plate 65d

Carnivores

Carnivores are the ferocious mammals that are specialized to kill and eat other vertebrate animals. They include, of course, the cat that sleeps on your pillow and the dog that takes table scraps from your hand. There are 237 species of carnivores (order Carnivora) found around the world, and, as they are relatively common at high latitudes, Alaska has a good range of species, including the largest (Brown and Polar Bears) and smallest (Least Weasel) carnivores in the world. The 26 species of carnivores found in Alaska include members of seven families: dogs (Canidae), bears (Ursidae), weasels (Mustelidae), and cats (Felidae) among the land carnivores, and sea lions (Otariidae), walruses (Odobenidae), and true seals (Phocidae) among the pinnipeds, or marine carnivores. They have in common teeth customized to grasp, rip, and tear flesh – witness their large, cone-shaped canines. The terrestrial species eat other vertebrate animals, but some of them, especially the bears, are *omnivorous*, taking also fruits and other plant materials. Aquatic carnivores – the River Otter and pinnipeds – eat primarily fish; the Sea Otter and Walrus are unique among Alaska's mammals in that they specialize in eating shellfish.

5. Wolves and Foxes

Alaska is rich in *canids*, the members of the family Canidae; the group includes *dogs*, *wolves*, and *foxes*. They are often called *canines*, and the most prominent teeth in the carnivore mouth are named after them. The dog family is not a large one, but it is a familiar one to us because of our long association with the domesticated version. The willingness of both COYOTES (Plate 66) and GRAY WOLVES (Plate 66) to mate with domestic dogs, and the viable hybrids produced by such matings, shows the close genetic relationships among dogs and their relatives. There are 34 species of canids, with worldwide distribution if one counts the long-ago introduction of the DINGO, another domesticated canine, into Australia. The four species that occur in Alaska comprise some of the state's most charismatic animals; and the traveller has a fair chance to see one or more of them, because the two fox species may become accustomed to human presence and thus may be quite visible in their preferred habitats, and their larger relatives are also common and widespread, if less trusting.

    Wild members of the dog family are unmistakable to us, with their perky ears, pointy snouts, and bushy tails. Ear size and shape varies with temperature; desert dogs have very large ears not only to hear their surroundings better but also to shed heat, and the ARCTIC FOX (Plate 66) has the shortest ears in the family, fully furred and adapted to conserving heat in its icy environment. Seventy per cent of this fox's coat consists of *underwool*, coiled hairs that provide a dense layer of insulation. The Arctic Fox is the only canine to change color during the year, brown in summer and white in winter, with its winter coat twice as thick as its summer one. Bering Sea island populations can be blue-gray all year long, matching the monotonous rocky landscape.

Natural History
Ecology and Behavior

Canids take their prey opportunistically, eating just about anything they can catch. Rodents – abundant as they are – feature prominently in the diets of solitary species such as RED FOX (Plate 66) and ARCTIC FOX, but both of them also capture many birds, especially during the breeding season. Arctic Foxes are especially fond of lemmings, and an average litter of 10 fox young may consume about 127 kg (280 lb) of prey (equivalent to 2400 lemmings) before they become independent. GRAY WOLVES feed on much larger animals, including a wide range of large mammals, both because the wolves are larger than other canids and because they hunt in packs, allowing them to pull down animals the size of Moose. Wolf packs average eight or fewer individuals, but a pack of 36 was once observed in southern Alaska. Packs consist of a breeding pair and their pups and, usually, a few other wolves, and they appear to be held together by genuine affection (friendship).

All canids hunt by moving rapidly through the landscape, eyes, ears, and nose open to the presence of their prey. Foxes and COYOTES attempt catlike stealth and are often successful in sneaking up on small birds and mammals. They often capture voles and lemmings by following their movements in low vegetation with their sensitive ears and then, with precise position plotted, jumping into the air and coming down on the spot with front paws together. A stunned rodent is often there for the taking. Small prey is gulped down whole, and larger prey is dissected by the very sharp-edged *carnassial* teeth, molars and premolars modified very differently from our own. Dog and cat owners miss the chance to see the impressive working of these teeth as their pets gulp down processed pet food.

Breeding

Mating in Alaska's canids occurs in late winter; gestation periods vary from 52 to 66 days, with the larger species having longer periods. Females give birth in spring in a den that the parents dig in a well-drained hillside, and the adults (of a pair or a pack) cooperate in raising the young. ARCTIC FOXES are probably the most prolific breeders of all carnivores, if not of all mammals. Their average litter size is around 10 pups, and in a good year, when lemmings are abundant, a single female may give birth to and raise the astonishing number of 25 pups. One wonders at the condition of the adult pair at the end of the summer! Actually, all canids have a fairly high reproductive rate, able to raise so many young because males contribute to their feeding and care, a situation quite unusual among mammals (try to think of other mammals in which males participate in parental care). GRAY WOLVES average seven pups in a litter, COYOTES six, and RED FOXES four, although any of them may have up to a dozen or more young, perhaps dependent on the age and condition of the female. Females have only eight nipples, which leads to quite a bit of jockeying for position when litters of over eight are born. The young of smaller canids hunt with their parents for several months, those of larger species up to a year or more. For a carnivore, learning to hunt effectively is a lengthy process, so the extended period of parental care is not surprising.

Ecological Interactions

The predator–prey relationship between GRAY WOLVES and Moose has long been cited as an example of the way predators actually have a "good" effect on their prey. Of course, if you were a Moose attacked by wolves, you wouldn't think so. But Moose that are ill, crippled, or otherwise less than vigorous are more likely to fall under the onslaught of a wolf pack than their healthier relatives. Some of these infirmities have a genetic basis, so this constant weeding process probably improves the overall genetic makeup of Moose populations.

Predation occurs even among related carnivores. RED FOXES not only compete with their smaller cousins the ARCTIC FOXES but also prey on them, as do the much larger GRAY WOLVES. Wolves do the same to COYOTES when they can catch them, and it is thought that one of the reasons for the substantial increase in Coyote populations in parts of North America was the extirpation of wolves from those regions. To eliminate Arctic Fox populations on some bird breeding islands, sterile (so they couldn't breed and cause the same problems) Red Foxes were introduced, and the Arctic Foxes quickly disappeared. Arctic Foxes also interact with much larger carnivores, the Polar Bears with which they share the arctic ice. They follow the bears around to snatch scraps of their usually substantial seal meals, but they must remain vigilant, because an unwary fox may in turn become a meal for a bear.

Lore and Notes

The relationship between humans and GRAY WOLVES has been a long one, marked by active aggression in some regions and an uneasy truce in others. Wolves have been known to attack and kill people in Eurasia, but this behavior has been absent from North America, except for a single documented case in Ontario in 1942 (in which a wolf attacked, but the wolf was killed, not the person). Nevertheless, settlers killed wolves wherever they found them, just as they did the other big predators, and the species disappeared little by little from much of its former range in North America. The Gray Wolf was either the sole ancestor or one of the ancestors of the domestic dog, and many wolves must have been taken into captivity and bred generation after generation to result in their quite nonthreatening descendants.

Status

All of the species profiled here are surprisingly successful in North America, with only one exception. COYOTES have greatly expanded their range in historic times, from a basically western animal to one that now occurs through large parts of the East. As stated above, perhaps the decrease of wolves, and surely the opening up of the forests, aided and abetted this range expansion. Coyotes also seem to be able to coexist very well with humans, feeding on everything from garbage to pet cats. RED FOXES seem to do just about as well, as long as they are not systematically hunted, and they have expanded their range in the Arctic and Subarctic in recent years, the cause of which is not understood. ARCTIC FOXES, because so much of their range coincides with very sparse human populations, are still abundant in many areas. The exception to this general canid success is the GRAY WOLF, which disappeared from large parts of its very extensive range in North America over the last two centuries. It is probably no coincidence that this is the largest of the species, its packs needing the largest home range. The Mexican subspecies of the Gray Wolf is virtually extinct, and wolves are common in the Lower 48 states only in northern Minnesota, although they occur in scattered populations elsewhere along the border with Canada. They are still common in Alaska.

Profiles

Gray Wolf, *Canis lupus*, Plate 66a
Coyote, *Canis latrans*, Plate 66b
Red Fox, *Vulpes vulpes*, Plate 66c
Arctic Fox, *Alopex lagopus*, Plate 66d

6. Bears

The *bears*, family Ursidae, are the largest carnivores, huge mammals with stocky bodies, heads much like large dogs but with heavier skulls, moderate-length legs with large, flat feet and long claws, and very short tails. The eight species are spread through all the continents but Africa and Australia, with usually no more than one or two species occurring in a region. Alaska is fortunate to have three bears, although they're not the type to sit down with Goldilocks for a quiet meal of porridge. They include two of the largest and fiercest carnivores in the world, the POLAR BEAR (Plate 67) and BROWN (GRIZZLY) BEAR (Plate 67), as well as the much smaller but nonetheless imposing BLACK BEAR (Plate 67). The Brown Bears on Kodiak Island ("Kodiak Bears") are the very largest of land carnivores. For their size, bears are surprisingly agile and very fast runners; Grizzlies would be contenders in a horse race, unless they became distracted by their edible competitors. Black Bears can climb trees readily, but Browns, other than cubs, cannot. Bears are also great swimmers, and the Polar Bear is a champion, swimming for hours at a time at about 10 kph (6.5 mph). Its swimming style is unique among mammals, paddling with only its front feet.

The best time to watch Brown Bears is when they are preoccupied with hunting salmon rather than with your presence in their habitat. Numerous ecotours take advantage of this meeting of fish and bears. You may also see Black Bears on your own in Alaska, but to see Polar Bears you'll have to be especially intrepid, because there are no Polar Bear tours in the state as there are at Churchill, Manitoba, where every fall the bears come ashore from Hudson Bay.

Natural History

Ecology and Behavior

Like most carnivores, bears are solitary animals; males and females roam about on their home ranges independent of one another but come together to breed at the appropriate time. Females with cubs stay well away from males, because male bears are known to kill unprotected cubs when they come across them. On the other hand, bears are not as territorial as many other carnivores; they freely wander through each others' home ranges and collect at superabundant resources such as salmon streams, carcasses of large mammals, and, sadly, garbage dumps. Being big, bears have very large home ranges, varying from 2.3 to 112 sq km (0.9 to 43 sq miles) in four studies of BLACK BEARS, with males using two or three times as much space as females; 57 to 2600 sq km (22 to 1000 sq miles) in ten marked BROWN BEARS (Grizzlies in the Yellowstone ecosystem), distinctly larger in males; and not readily calculated in POLAR BEARS, which stay on the move and may wander thousands of kilometers during their lifetime, both on foot and drifting with the ice pack. At one time it was thought that individual Polar Bears roamed all the way around the Northern oceans, but recent research has shown that there are actually separate populations of this species with their own genetic identities, indicating confinement to specific regions and little interbreeding with other populations.

Bear vision is rather poor, but their sense of smell is well-developed, and all three species use smell to locate their prey, Polar Bears even detecting seals at their breathing holes in the ice. The three bears show a gradient in plant *vs* animal food, with the Black Bear being largely *herbivorous*, eating roots, berries, and fungi, even leaves and bark, as well as the occasional insect, clutch of bird eggs, or rodent. The Brown Bear is truly *omnivorous*, with a mixed diet of just about everything in its environment, from berries and roots and beetle grubs up to large hoofed animals; great numbers of these bears aggregate every summer and fall at rivers full of spawning salmon. Polar Bears are basically *carnivorous*, their main diet of seals augmented by a great variety of smaller animals and even a bit of plant matter when they come ashore in fall. One of the senior author's most memorable, and goriest, wildlife experiences was watching a Polar Bear kill and begin to eat an adult female Walrus on an ice floe in the Chukchi Sea. The Walrus surely weighed more than the bear, but she made no attempt to defend herself with her impressive tusks, although accounts have been written of male Walruses fighting off Polar Bears in that way.

The two terrestrial bears eat prodigiously in fall, put on layers of fat, and then disappear into their dens for the winter. They are not true hibernators (see p. 177), but their temperature falls a few degrees, and they sleep through much of the winter. Black Bears tend to use existing cavities under trees and in the ground, whereas Brown Bears dig their own dens. Polar Bears dig their dens in drifted snow, usually on shore but in some cases on drifting pack ice, and the Hudson Bay population excavates ground nests like their close relatives the Brown Bears. It is thought that the Hudson Bay bears, by digging down to the permafrost layer, can remain as cool as ice-denning bears. Polar Bears are scarce as breeders in Alaska, and the known denning sites are scattered along the Beaufort Sea coast east of Barrow. Bears avoid having to excrete wastes in their dens by swallowing roughage – leaves and bark and even their own hair – that forms a plug at the end of the digestive system that is voided when they emerge in spring.

Breeding

Bears mate in spring, but the fertilized embryos do not implant in the wall of the uterus until fall. This *delayed implantation* is characteristic of a number of groups of mammals, allowing mating and giving birth each to occur at the optimal time of year. Female bears bear their young in mid or late winter in their winter dens. The one to three young are born at a very small size (about the size of rats), smaller relative to adult size than in any other mammals but marsupials. The young grow rapidly on the female's very rich milk, and by the time the mother and cubs emerge from their winter den, the still quite small but active young can scamper after their mother. Typical litters are of two cubs, but they vary from one to four. The young nurse for about a year and stay with their mother for their first two years, and because of this, females breed only every other year.

Ecological Interactions

Bears at a salmon stream sort themselves out by size, the largest individuals easily displacing the smaller ones. What seems peaceful to us is actually a predetermined placement of individuals according to their rank in the *dominance hierarchy*, with the dominant animals at the best fishing spots and the subordinate ones at the less desirable spots. As bears grow older and larger, they can move up in the hierarchy. Males are larger than and remain dominant to females.

Lore and Notes

The southernmost of Alaska's Native people, the Haida, have a wonderful myth about a berry picker who was taken by a clan of bears back to their den. She married a bear chief and bore him two sons. Her brother came looking for her, and her noble ursine husband offered himself as a sacrifice, but not before he pulled the bear garments from his children, transforming them into two handsome boys who went on to become the greatest hunters of their people and start the Bear clan among the Haida.

Modern-day relationships of people and bears are just as complicated. Bears are among the most exciting of the animals that draw ecotravellers to Alaska, but they are at the same time the most dangerous wildlife element in the state. Bears are sufficiently uncommon that most visitors will never encounter one, unless they go specifically to one of the salmon-spawning sites where bears gather. On the other hand, they are widespread, one or more of Alaska's species occurring everywhere in the state except the Aleutian and Bering Sea islands (BROWNS are on Unimak and POLARS may reach St. Lawrence Island) and above snow line in the mountains. "You're never very far from a bear" is a statement often heard in Alaska. BLACK BEARS are relatively harmless, and ecotravellers in Alaska are very unlikely to encounter a Polar Bear, but Brown Bears (and their inland representatives, the Grizzlies) are potential hazards. If you are in open country, keep your eyes open and you'll be able to avoid distant bears, and if you walk through wooded or brushy areas, make plenty of noise, and the bears should avoid you. Keep a substantial distance between yourself and any bear with cubs.

How do Polar Bears keep warm? Their prey, the seals, have a dense layer of blubber to hold in their body heat, but Polar Bears depend on their hair. Black pigment absorbs heat, so for years biologists questioned why Polar Bears and some other arctic animals were white instead of black. A few decades ago, examination of Polar Bear hairs seemed to offer the answer. They were found to be hollow, and it was thought that sunlight actually travelled down these hollow hairs to the bear's dark skin, warming it as expected. Not until 1998 did further research finally show that the hollow nature of the hair was in fact to hold a layer of air against the skin, and the trapped air actually furnishes much of the insulating power of the fur, as is the case generally in land mammals. The hollow hairs of Polar Bears also probably increase their buoyancy, an advantage for an animal that spends much time in the water.

Status

The land-based BLACK and BROWN BEARS are much less common at lower latitudes in North America than they were at the time of Caucasian settlement of the continent, but they are still common in northern wilderness areas, as is the POLAR BEAR in its mostly uninhabited range. Nevertheless, all three are hunted, and populations of all three are considered vulnerable to environmental threats. The Black Bear is classified as threatened in some southern USA states, and the Brown (Grizzly) is classified as threatened everywhere in the Lower 48, where its range has shrunk dramatically in the last century. Once widespread throughout the western USA, it now occurs in any numbers only in the Rocky Mountains of Idaho, Montana, and Wyoming. The Brown Bear also occurs in the Old World, generally as a much smaller animal, but its populations there have been reduced even more than in North America. The Polar Bear is the subject of international concern, because individual bears wander between countries just as other marine mammals do.

Profiles

Black Bear, *Ursus americanus*, Plate 67a
Brown (Grizzly) Bear, *Ursus arctos*, Plate 67b
Polar Bear, *Ursus maritimus*, Plate 67c

7. Seals and Sea Lions

Seals and *sea lions* are called *pinnipeds* (*pinni* = fin, *ped* = foot), members of the suborder Pinnipedia of the order Carnivora; they are sea-going carnivores. Pinnipeds were probably derived from a bearlike ancestor early in the evolution of the carnivores, and they have gone on to inhabit all of the seas of the world. There are even freshwater seals landlocked in the Caspian Sea and Lake Baikal in Asia. Pinnipeds are very large animals, the smallest species weighing in the neighborhood of 40 kg (88 lb), larger than all but the largest dogs, and male elephant seals tipping the scales at over 3600 kg (4 tons), approaching the size of the huge land animals for which they are named. In many pinnipeds, males are much larger than females. There are 34 species of pinnipeds, divided among three families: 19 *true* (or *earless*) *seals* of the Phocidae, one *walrus* of the Odobenidae, and 14 *eared seals* (*sea lions* and *fur seals*) of the Otariidae. Although all are easily recognizable as pinnipeds, these families have gone in rather different evolutionary directions. Sea lions are relatively agile on land, with large, mobile forelimbs and hindlimbs that can be turned forward, producing a gait on land that could best be called scrambling. The true seals, on the other hand, have rearward-pointing hindlimbs and shorter forelimbs, and they move on land only by wiggling their bodies forward as much like inchworms (caterpillars) as anything. When not moving, they look much like slugs, to continue the invertebrate similes. Underwater, their locomotion is just as different. Sea lions swim by "flying" underwater with their long front flippers, steering with the hind ones. Seals are very different, propelling themselves forward with vertically held hind flippers, much like a pair of fish tails. Interestingly, WALRUSES (Plate 73) move like sea lions on land but like seals in the water. Also, sea lions have external ears, but walruses and seals lack them. The long tusks of walruses render them unmistakable. A visit to three pinniped colonies – one each of sea lions, walruses, and elephant seals – would provide a lasting education in pinniped locomotion as well as biology.

Natural History
Ecology and Behavior

All pinnipeds feed on marine animals. Seals and sea lions are *piscivores* (fish-eaters), and, with two very different modes of locomotion, they still manage to swim fast enough to capture a great variety of bottom and midwater fish, including rockfishes, greenlings, and salmon. The fish they catch are often quite large, and the mammal has to bring them to the surface and thrash them around a bit to kill them. As they feed on them, scraps spread out from the predator and attract a variety of seabirds. The seabirds should remain cautious, however, because sea lions are known to vary their fish diet with an occasional bird (some of those in the southern hemisphere are especially fond of penguins). We see pinnipeds only at the surface and have been limited in understanding their underwater lives, although most of them have been photographed beneath the surface in recent years. Scientists have developed more and more sophisticated apparatus to measure the dives of all sorts of marine animals, and what they have found is nothing short of astonishing. STELLER'S SEA LIONS (Plate 72) are known to dive to 180 m (600 ft), NORTHERN FUR SEALS (Plate 72) to 230 m (755 ft), and HARBOR SEALS (Plate 72) to 446 m (1460 ft), but the deepest dive ever recorded for an air-breathing vertebrate was by a NORTHERN ELEPHANT SEAL that reached a depth of more than 1500 m (almost a mile)!

WALRUSES are invertebrate-eaters. Their mouth anatomy is specially modified so they can suck a large clam right out of its shell, and clams are their primary food. But they eat other mollusks and crustaceans as well, all of which they find on the bottom by skating along on their tusks with head down, detecting animals in the mud with the sensitive bristles on their snout. The tusks, which are not used for invertebrate predation, can be used to kill a full-grown seal, an occasional walrus meal. The tusks are also used in defense, in display against other males while contesting for dominance, in combat between territorial males, to keep breathing holes open in the ice, and to help the walrus haul out on ice. These "tools" rival a Swiss army knife in their versatility.

Breeding

Many pinnipeds are *polygynous* (males mate with more than one female), in particular the members of the eared seal family. Elephant seals of the true seal family are also polygynous. Many things about the lives of these animals work together to produce this special mating system. First, most pinnipeds feed offshore, spending much of their time in cool to cold water, which produces the need for good heat conservation. Second, because of their extreme adaptations for aquatic locomotion, they have limited mobility on land. Third, the females must go on land to give birth, usually on isolated beaches on islands. Fourth, because of their limited mobility and the small number of suitable beaches, pinnipeds are highly gregarious on these islands. Fifth, males in these dense aggregations tend to be aggressive and territorial, although females are not. Males compete among themselves for territories and females, with the result that the females are monopolized by some males, while others are excluded and hang around the margins of the gregarious group.

The need for heat conservation at sea resulted in the development of heavy subcutaneous fat deposits (blubber) in sea lions. Furthermore, they evolved large body size, because larger animals have a lower surface-to-volume ratio and therefore lose heat less rapidly than smaller animals. These two features mean that sea lions have a relatively low metabolic rate and improved capacity for storage of energy, which in turn permits them to go without food for a long time. As a result, they can stay on land for long periods, without the need to go to sea to feed. Thus, males can occupy a territory for up to two months, without leaving to feed, which improves their chances of fertilizing females. The mature males (*beachmasters*) each vigorously and sometimes bloodily defend a stretch of beach against all other males, and mate with the females that come ashore in that territory (their *harem*). Typically, the larger the male, the better the fighter; the better the fighter, the longer stretch of beach defended and the more females mated. Because the largest males not only can remain on land longer because of their energy reserves, but also are likely to be the superior fighters, the advantage of being large, over time, has led to a very great discrepancy in size between the sexes. Male STELLER'S SEA LIONS weigh as much as six times as much as the females!

Some pinniped behavior borrows from the avian world: male WALRUSES perform courtship behavior, including some quite musical sounds, and male BEARDED SEALS (Plate 73) have long, eerie courtship songs that they "exhale" as they sink in a cloud of bubbles. Some pinnipeds mate in the water, and to facilitate this, the male Walrus has the largest *baculum* (penis bone) of any mammal. Called an *oosik*, this very hard bone has been used as a club by northern natives and bartenders. All pinnipeds must come out on land to bear their single young, so they are tied either to beaches on islands (mainlands in some areas) or ice. Female NORTHERN FUR SEALS and Steller's Sea Lions haul out on islands in summer and quickly give birth to their single pup. After a week of intense care, they begin to make foraging trips out to sea, returning for a day or more at a time to nurse the pup with milk extremely rich in fat and nutrients, and this goes on throughout the summer until the pups are weaned in late fall. The young may stay with their mothers for as long as their first year of life. Interestingly, in many pinnipeds mating takes place within days after the pups are born, so females are pregnant much of their adult life.

True seals are rather varied in their reproduction. HARBOR SEALS have their young in summer on the beach, often in the intertidal zone at low tide, and within minutes after birth the pup can follow the female into the water or higher up on the beach. They stay together until the pup is weaned in about a month, considerably faster than is the case with eared seals. SPOTTED SEALS (Plate 72) are similar but have their young on the pack ice in spring, the male associating with the female before and during the birth of the pup and then mating with her a month later; this is as close to monogamy as pinnipeds get. Quite different from the Harbor Seal, the Spotted Seal pup remains on the ice until after it is weaned. Bearded Seals and RIBBON SEALS (Plate 73) also have their young on ice, the fast-growing young weaned in 2 to 4 weeks. Female RINGED SEALS (Plate 73) are quite different from the rest of the species in digging pupping dens in the snow, usually near a breathing hole. The females forage and then return to nurse their pups in these protected lairs (they are protected against the elements, but Polar Bears are very good at finding them). Pups of seals that breed in the Arctic are born with a white, woolly coat called a *lanugo*, perhaps to camouflage them on the ice, and this coat is shed in about a month and replaced with the typical adult coat.

Female Walruses give birth in summer, but the calf (even the authors don't know why Walrus young are "calves" and those of all other pinnipeds "pups") goes into the water quickly, and the female, hanging upright, nurses her young there. These slow-growing young remain with the female for about two years, until they are weaned. The females don't mate again until the young is one year old.

Ecological Interactions

Pinnipeds are large animals, but nevertheless they have predators. Other than humans, Killer Whales and Polar Bears are their only major predators in Alaska, and both of those large, fierce marine species are very effective at capturing them. A seal in the water is much too fast for a Polar Bear to capture, but the bears stalk seals that are resting on the ice, and they also wait by seal breathing holes. Killer Whales have no trouble capturing pinnipeds, and the appearance of a group of these predators sends seals and sea lions into a panic, with sea lions leaping out of the water like dolphins to try to escape. Killer Whales in the southern hemisphere have learned to charge at high speed up onto gently sloping beaches and capture young sea lions resting at the shore; the whale then thrashes its powerful flukes and pulls itself back into the sea. Great White Sharks are also important seal predators, and it is thought that at least some shark attacks on humans were the consequence of a person on a short surfboard looking too much like a seal at the surface. By the time the shark takes a bite and discovers its mistake, it may be too late for the hapless surfer.

Lore and Notes

The physiology of deep diving has been studied extensively in pinnipeds and diving birds. These groups have special adaptations for diving, including an unusually large blood volume for their size, so the hemoglobin in their blood carries much oxygen, vital for metabolism. Their muscles are also rich in myoglobin, another source of oxygen. They can tolerate the high levels of carbon dioxide produced in their blood during a long dive (up to one hour underwater in some species). Numerous physiological changes take place during a dive. First, rather than taking a deep breath, as we might consider doing before ducking underwater, these better-adapted animals expel their air before they dive, so their buoyancy is reduced. Their heart rate and basal metabolic rate drop, so they need less oxygen, and blood flow is shunted away from nonessential organs such as the skin, many internal organs, and some of the skeletal muscles. Finally, their muscle metabolism temporarily becomes *anaerobic* (not needing oxygen). When they surface, marine mammals typically take several deep breaths in a row.

Status

STELLER'S SEA LION has been listed as threatened throughout its range because of a dramatic drop in numbers in the last decades of the 20th century. This decline has occurred throughout its range, including in Alaska, where it was once abundant. The cause of the decline is not certain but may relate to the crash of certain fish populations in the Bering Sea, particularly Walleye Pollock. The fish decline may be a consequence of overfishing or repeated El Niño conditions (warmer water that drastically affects local marine life), or perhaps the combined effects of both of them. NORTHERN FUR SEALS have declined historically but may be holding their own, and Alaska's other pinnipeds appear to be secure, well protected by the USA's Marine Mammal Protection Act of 1972.

Profiles

Northern Fur Seal, *Callorhinus ursinus*, Plate 72a
Steller's Sea Lion, *Eumetopias jubatus*, Plate 72b
Harbor Seal, *Phoca vitulina*, Plate 72c
Spotted Seal, *Phoca largha*, Plate 72d
Walrus, *Odobenus rosmarus*, Plate 73a
Ringed Seal, *Pusa hispida*, Plate 73b
Ribbon Seal, *Histriophoca fasciata*, Plate 73c
Bearded Seal, *Erignathus barbatus*, Plate 73d

8. Weasels

The weasel family, Mustelidae, comprises 65 species of small and medium-sized carnivores that are distributed globally except for Australia. Usually called *mustelids*, included in the family are *weasels, martens, skunks, otters,* and *badgers,* animals that occupy diverse habitats, including, in the case of otters, the water. Seven species of mustelids occur in Alaska, and visitors with much time to spend may see one or more of them, particularly the two species of otters and the SHORT-TAILED WEASEL (Plate 68). Mustelids generally have long, thin bodies, short legs, long tails, and soft, dense fur, but they nevertheless vary somewhat in shape and greatly in size. The LEAST WEASEL (Plate 68) is truly tiny, at 50 g (about 2 oz) the smallest of the carnivores, while the WOLVERINE (Plate 69) is 400 times as large, weighing up to 20 kg (44 lb) and, because it is so well-furred, reminiscent of a small bear. Because most of the body of a SEA OTTER (Plate 69) is underwater when we see it, it is hard to believe that this species is in fact the largest mustelid, large males weighing as much as 45 kg (100 lb). Males are larger than females in most mustelids. Weasels and their relatives have a characteristic bounding locomotion on land, the body of the more slender species bending upward in an obvious arc, much like an inchworm caterpillar, as the hind feet are brought forward. Both otter species have webbed feet for aquatic locomotion; in addition, the RIVER OTTER (Plate 69) also uses its long, powerful tail for swimming rapidly by flexing the rear part of the body up and down.

Natural History
Ecology and Behavior
Most of the mustelids are strongly carnivorous. These are powerful animals, capable of killing prey as large as, or even larger than, themselves (WOLVERINES have been known to kill Moose slowed down by deep snow). Like the cats, mustelids kill with swift bites to the head or neck, the long canines piercing the prey's spinal cord. All are potentially active day and night, an adaptation that broadens the types of prey with which they come in contact. MARTENS (Plate 68) are forest-dwelling tree climbers, with squirrels and birds their most important prey. Weasels are terrestrial, their slender bodies allowing them access to the burrows of the rodents that make up their diet. The SHORT-TAILED WEASEL is the most common mustelid in Alaska, and it occurs in all open and wooded habitats. Weasels are ferocious little "killing machines," and nothing much escapes them. The almost frantically active LEAST WEASEL eats more than half its weight in rodents each day, and to see one attack a vole of equal size is nothing less than primal. Few of us will have this opportunity, however, because Least Weasels, though common, are rarely seen. Even though voracious carnivores, Least Weasels are very small and thus can find enough to eat in a relatively small home range, only about 0.8 hectares (2 acres). MINKS (Plate 68) are semiaquatic, and their diet is the broadest in the family, ranging from mice and birds to frogs and fish. Although they are often seen on land, they are very much at home in the water and can dive to depths of 5 m (16 ft) after their prey. The large, active WOLVERINES are sufficiently fierce to put a bear or Cougar to rout. They eat just about anything, including carrion. Appearing always on the move, male Wolverines travel over a huge home range of up to 2600 sq km (1000 sq miles) that usually supports two or three females. RIVER OTTERS forage alone or in pairs, hunting in streams, rivers, and ponds for fish and frogs. Although River Otters are usually seen in or near the water, they spend their inactive time in burrows on land. Adapted for moving swiftly and smoothly through water, they move on land awkwardly, with a ducklike waddle. Finally, SEA OTTERS differ from the other members of their family in being not only restricted to the marine

environment but also largely aquatic (they spend relatively little time on land) and feeding largely on crabs, sea urchins, clams, and the like.

Breeding

Most female mustelids give birth in dens in rock piles or tree crevices, or in burrows under trees; SEA OTTERS, however, give birth in the open on rocks adjacent to the sea. Most Alaska species mate in fall, and the embryo stops developing at a very early stage, the *blastocyst*. After 6 to 10 months, the blastocyst becomes implanted in the wall of the uterus (this is called *delayed implantation*), and development continues. In a month or two more, the young are born; by this time, it is early spring. Exceptions to this include the LEAST WEASEL, in which implantation is not delayed, and gestation takes 34 to 37 days; this species may have two or even more litters in a year, the young born any time from spring to fall. Most of Alaska's mustelids have litters of two to five young, but the SHORT-TAILED WEASEL and MINK may have up to nine or ten at a time. As is true for carnivores in general, most mustelid young are born blind and helpless. However, Sea Otters give birth to a single (rarely two) larger young, born well-furred and with eyes open; this degree of maturity at birth, with protection against low temperatures, is necessary for it to survive in its cold aquatic habitat. Cared for by the female only, young mustelids become independent as they reach full size. Weaning of the young takes 5 to 6 weeks in the MINK and MARTEN but, surprisingly, somewhat longer in the much smaller Least Weasel. A young Sea Otter stays with its mother for a year or more, in some cases even when she has a new offspring.

Ecological Interactions

Because it takes many hares to feed one lynx and many antelopes to feed one lion, carnivores are generally much rarer than their prey. This of course is one reason why few carnivores are seen by the ecotraveller. However, weasels, because of their small size, prey on mice, which are very abundant. Thus weasels are relatively abundant compared with other carnivores. One facet of their natural history that is often overlooked is that these predators eat a staggering number of rodents. For instance, it has been calculated that weasels each year in New York State eat some 60 million mice and millions of rats. Someone should attempt such a calculation for Alaska, which presumably has both more mice and more weasels than New York.

Like Beavers, SEA OTTERS have a substantial effect on their environment. But it's not from building dams and ponds; it is from their food habits. Sea Otters eat a lot of sea urchins, especially where the latter are common, and the otters are voracious enough and occur in sufficiently high populations that they keep urchin numbers down. Because Sea Otter populations have waxed and waned in parts of Alaska, biologists have learned of the significance of this diet. When otter populations decrease, urchins increase and begin to have a negative effect on large algae such as kelp. In fact, where they have no predators, the urchins quickly eat up the kelp forests in the area, removing an important habitat for many other animals. Because the otter controls urchin populations, which in turn has a great effect on its habitat, it has been called a *keystone species*. Recently, overfishing in the Bering Sea has caused a decline in populations of sea lions and seals, and Killer Whales have begun to eat more Sea Otters as their preferred prey grows scarcer, with predictable effects on urchin populations and kelp forests.

Lore and Notes

Mustelids have a strong, characteristic odor produced by *musk* secreted from scent glands under their tails. The secretions are used to communicate with other members of the species and to mark territory ownership, or at least their presence in the landscape. In fact, the presence of mustelids often can be detected by their characteristic skunky smell. Mustelid musk is also sprayed during encounters with predators, and it may present an effective defense in at least some cases. Skunks have taken this defense mechanism to its highest level, their glands producing particularly strong, foul-smelling fluids that with precise aim can be violently squirted in a jet at potential predators. The fluids are not toxic and cannot cause blindness as is sometimes commonly believed, but they can cause temporary, severe irritation of eyes and nose. Predators that approach a skunk once rarely repeat the exercise, and skunks have evolved their characteristic black and white coloration to be easily recognizable.

As might be expected, the entirely aquatic SEA OTTER has no use for the musky aspect of weasel life. It has its own special adaptations, however, among them the densest fur of any mammal – 100,000 hairs per square centimeter. No, they weren't actually counted, but careful study of small patches of skin led to this figure. For the metrically disadvantaged, that's about 650,000 hairs per square inch. More impressive yet, this totals about 800 million such hairs over the whole animal. Sea Otters are the only marine mammals that lack a layer of insulating blubber, and their dense hair keeps them warm in frigid Alaska waters. Watch a Sea Otter to see how much time it spends taking care of this valuable coat. Not surprising, floating oil quickly subverts the otter's insulation, and oil spills cause great mortality in this species.

Status

No weasel is endangered or threatened in Alaska, and, fortunately, SEA OTTERS have recovered from relative scarcity when they were hunted for their fur well into the 20th century. In the mid-19th century, a Sea Otter pelt brought as much as $2500 (that would be far more in today's dollar), and as many as 120,000 of them were taken from their rightful owners, the otters, in a year. This family is full of fur-bearers, from the tiny SHORT-TAILED WEASEL (known as "ermine" in its white winter coat) and the MINK, now mostly raised in captivity, to the SABLE, a large Russian marten extirpated in many areas because of the very high value of its beautiful coat.

Profiles

Marten, *Martes americana*, Plate 68a
Mink, *Mustela vison*, Plate 68b
Short-tailed Weasel, *Mustela erminea*, Plate 68c
Least Weasel, *Mustela nivalis*, Plate 68d
Wolverine, *Gulo gulo*, Plate 69a
River Otter, *Lutra canadensis*, Plate 69b
Sea Otter, *Enhydra lutris*, Plate 69c

9. Cats

In total there are 36 species of *cats*, family Felidae, with representatives inhabiting all continents but Australia. Because both of the cats that occur in Alaska are fairly rare and quite shy, seeing even a single wild cat is a very infrequent occurrence on a visit to Alaska. More than likely, all that will be observed of cats are traces: some tracks in the mud near a stream or scratch marks on a tree trunk or log.

Cats are easily recognized as such, all of them some modification on the pussycat theme. The biggest variation is in tail length, and the two species that occur in Alaska, the LYNX (Plate 69) and the COUGAR (also called Mountain Lion), encompass that variation. Cougars are big, plain-colored, long-tailed cats, and Lynx are medium-sized, spotted, short-tailed cats. Because of their method of predation – sneakiness – cats are usually colored to match their environment very well, from the plain-colored Cougar and LION to the spotted LEOPARD and JAGUAR and striped TIGER, altogether including some beautifully patterned animals. Female cats usually are smaller than males, up to a third smaller in the Jaguar. Cats are not as smell-oriented as members of the dog family, but they have good hearing, even though their ears are short, compared with those of dogs. Their eyesight is superb, however, and cats hunt largely by sight. Most cats are nocturnal hunters, and their eyes are large, with large pupils that show as a vertical slit in the sunlight but are wide-open at night. Cats, like many other nocturnal animals, have a layer in the back of the retina, called the *tapetum lucidum*, which reflects light back into the light receptors of the retina, thus enhancing night vision. This reflective layer is what makes cats' eyes shine in the light of a flashlight. Both of Alaska's cats hunt by day or night, a necessity in a region in which either darkness or light may last 24 hours at some time of the year.

Natural History
Ecology and Behavior

As large predators that take a great variety of prey, cats are not usually limited to specific habitats. However, most species need cover from which to hunt, so they are not tundra animals. LYNX occur widely in Alaska forests, preying on mammals of hare size and birds of grouse size but taking just about any animal they can catch. COUGARS occupy forested habitats, especially where there are rocky areas, and prey on deer and other large mammals. Cougars, with a distribution that extends south to the tip of South America, are increasing in far southern Alaska but are still quite rare, the total population of the state probably no more than a few individuals.

Cats are finely adapted to be predators on vertebrate animals. They are the most carnivorous of the carnivores; their diets are more centered on meat than any of the other families. Hunting methods are extremely similar among the various species. Cats do not run to chase prey for long distances. Rather, they slowly stalk their prey or wait in ambush, then capture the prey after pouncing on it or after a brief, fast chase. The CHEETAH of Africa is the fastest land mammal, with a top speed of 110 kph (66 mph), and it can quickly catch up to a swift gazelle on the open plains. Biologists are often impressed by the consistency in the manner by which cats kill their prey. Almost always it is with a sharp bite to the neck or head, breaking the neck or crushing the skull. When killing prey larger than themselves, for example, a LION taking down a zebra, the cat may bite down on the other animal's neck with its powerful jaws, squeezing the windpipe and effectively suffocating the animal. Cat adaptations to carnivory include long, stabbing canine teeth; a rough tongue with which they can peel hair and skin from their prey; and very sharp cheek teeth to dissect their meal.

Cats have retractile claws, which are pulled in to give them a silent walk and extended to grab and hold prey. Their claws also give cats good climbing abilities, and some of them are partially arboreal animals, foraging and even sleeping in trees. Lynx have especially large feet for a cat, and these big feet allow them to travel across snow very easily to hunt their favorite prey, the Snowshoe Hare, which also has large, furry feet.

Aside from the highly social African Lion, cats are solitary animals, foraging alone and with individuals coming together only to mate. Some species are territorial, but in others individuals overlap in the areas in which they hunt. Cat territories are marked by feces (often including a scraped area), urine, and secretions from anal glands, and by scratches left on tree trunks. Young Lynx cover their feces, presumably to avoid detection, whereas adults leave their feces exposed, presumably to indicate their territory. When inactive, cats shelter in rock crevices, treefalls, or burrows dug by other animals.

Breeding
In almost all species of cats, males and females come together only to mate; the female bears and raises her young alone. She gives birth in a den in a burrow, rock crevice, or tree cavity. Pregnancy is about 2 months in the LYNX, about 3 months in the COUGAR. Most cats have one or two young at a time, although Lynx and Cougars may have up to four. This large litter size is probably an adaptation to high latitudes, where prey is very abundant during the time the female is feeding the young. The young are sheltered in the den while the female forages; she returns periodically to nurse and bring the kittens prey to eat. Juvenile Lynx remain with their mother for about 3 months, Cougars for up to 18 months; they must learn to be efficient hunters before they go off on their own.

Ecological Interactions
All cats are quite alike in form and behavior. Therefore, according to ecological theory, they should compete strongly for the same resources, competition that if unchecked, should drive some of the species to extinction. But are all cats really so similar? One major difference is size; of the cats occurring in Alaska, COUGARS are about four times the weight of LYNX. The smallest cats take small rodents and birds, medium-sized cats take larger rodents and birds, and large cats take larger prey such as large mammals. Biologists believe that these kinds of ecological differences among similar species permit sufficient "separation" to allow somewhat peaceful coexistence. Interestingly, the Lynx's southern relative, the BOBCAT, cannot travel on deep snow because of its smaller feet, and this difference in winter habitat prevents competition between these similar species in areas where they both occur.

Lore and Notes
Recently there have been widely circulated reports of COUGARS attacking people in North America, but this seems more due to people moving to live in prime Cougar habitat, which is increasingly limited, than to a newly acquired desire on the cat's part for human prey. Although Alaskans don't have to worry about this, because Cougars are quite rare in the state, there is good general advice if you happen to stumble across a large cat. Do not run, because that often stimulates a cat to chase you. Face the cat, make yourself large by raising your arms, make as much loud noise as you can, and slowly back away.

Status
Although LYNX have become quite rare in most parts of the Lower 48 where they historically occurred, they are still reasonably common in Alaska because so

much of it is wilderness. They are very sensitive to disturbance and can be expected to decrease in areas with much human use. COUGARS, unlike some other large carnivores, have increased in western North America in recent years, probably because of reduced hunting pressures. The species once occurred all over the USA, but most eastern populations disappeared by the end of the 19th century. The only Cougars persisting in the eastern part of the continent at present are part of a small population in southern Florida, listed as Endangered.

Profiles
Lynx, *Lynx lynx*, Plate 69d

10. Hoofed Mammals

Animals with hooves are usually called *ungulates* (*ungula* = hoof). They fall into two quite distinct orders: the *odd-toed* (1 or 3 toes) ungulates of the order Perissodactyla, which includes horses, tapirs, and rhinoceroses and has no present-day Alaska species; and the *even-toed* (2 or 4 toes) ungulates of the order Artiodactyla, which includes pigs, camels, deer, antelope, sheep, and their relatives. There are 220 species of *artiodactyls*, of which six occur naturally in Alaska, and two more, BISON and ELK, have been introduced from elsewhere in North America. These eight species are evenly divided between the *deer* family, Cervidae, with 43 species worldwide, and the *antelope/sheep* family, Bovidae, with 137 species worldwide. Both of these families are widespread, although there are no deer in Africa and no *bovids* in Central and South America; Australia lacks them all.

Artiodactyls are large animals. Males of the largest deer in Alaska, the MOOSE (Plate 70), weigh up to 725 kg (1600 lb) and stand as high as 2.25 m (7.4 ft) at the shoulders; the largest antlers on record measured just over 2 m (6.75 ft) in spread. The BISON is the largest North American bovid; shorter but much stockier and, therefore, heavier than the Moose, males can weigh as much as 900 kg (2000 lb).

Members of the two Alaskan artiodactyl families differ substantially in their armament; deer have antlers, bovids horns. *Antlers* grow rapidly out of the skull each summer, their blood supply furnished by the skin over them. Because the antlers are covered with fur when they are first grown, the deer are considered *in velvet* at that time. After the antlers are fully grown, the skin dries up and is rubbed off. Antlers are used by males primarily to intimidate and, ultimately, to fight other males in battles for dominance and, through this, the opportunity to mate. As the animal gets older, its antlers not only get larger but branch increasingly, and both size and branching are good measures of dominance. After the battles of the fall breeding period, big, branched antlers become a liability in an animal moving through dense woodland, and they are shed. CARIBOU (Plate 70), living in the open, hold onto their antlers longer, and female Caribou have smaller versions of them. *Horns*, on the other hand, are permanent, with a bony core like the antler but a covering of horny material (*keratin*, the same substance that makes up hair and fingernails). They grow as the animal grows, but they never branch. They are also used in fights between males, especially in sheep, in which they become massive in old males.

The hooves of hoofed animals vary, depending on where they live. Caribou hooves are quite large, and the two toes separate to provide a large surface for both snowshoeing and swimming. MOUNTAIN GOAT (Plate 71) hooves have a very spongy center, providing them with virtual suction cups as they clamber about on steep, rocky slopes.

Natural History
Ecology and Behavior

Hoofed animals are among the largest and therefore most conspicuous of mammals, and most of the Alaska species are likely to be sighted by wide-ranging ecotravellers. The only regional species that can hide easily is the BLACK-TAILED DEER (Plate 70), which lives in wooded areas. Where hunted it is quite wary, but it becomes tame in protected parks and reserves. The other species live in open environments where they are readily spotted, albeit only from a distance on lands where they are hunted (which most of them are, somewhere in the state). Walking and running on the tips of their toes on the end of long, slender legs, these animals evolved to roam, and their daily wanderings and lifetime home ranges are impressively large. CARIBOU are the most mobile, their loose herds moving 500 to 1000 km (300 to 600 miles) around the arctic lowlands through the passage of a year. By their large numbers they can overgraze local areas and trample the surprisingly delicate arctic tundra if they remain long in one spot. Concentrations of biting flies that are attracted to their herds also keep them on the move. Most Caribou herds winter in areas with some tree or shrub cover and an abundance of lichens for winter food. Their wintering grounds vary from year to year, but females unerringly return to their traditional calving grounds, usually the place they themselves were born. MUSKOX (Plate 71), the other tundra species, also move long distances over the landscape, from low, lush meadows in summer to drier ridges in winter, where the wind blows much of the snow off the sparse vegetation. The two mountain species, DALL'S SHEEP (Plate 71) and MOUNTAIN GOATS, move to lower elevations, where conditions are not quite so harsh, during the winter. MOOSE and Black-tailed Deer have smaller home ranges of 5 to 10 sq km (2 to 4 sq miles), being able to find whatever they need in the same area winter or summer.

Hoofed animals are plant-eaters. Those in open country *graze* on *herbaceous* (non-woody) vegetation growing up from the ground, especially grasses but including many *forbs* (herbaceous plants other than grasses and sedges). Some of them also *browse* on woody shrubs. Forest-dwellers such as Black-tailed Deer are also browsers, eating leaves from shrubs and low branches of trees and, during winter, twigs and buds of the same plants. Each species of plant produces chemicals to deter leaf-eaters, so a herbivore's best feeding strategy would be to move from plant species to plant species, not accumulating sufficient doses of any one of these chemicals to poison it. Observers studying deer have seen that that is exactly what they do. Deer also move out onto meadows at night to graze on the new, succulent leaves of the fast-growing herbaceous plants there. Moose vary these diets with aquatic plants during summer, and they are often seen belly-deep in a pond, with a mass of water lilies or pondweeds hanging from their mouth. Caribou have a harder time than some of the other species, subsisting mostly on lichens during the winter and usually losing weight on that not very nutritious diet.

Breeding

Ungulates usually have either promiscuous or polygynous mating systems, in which the males contribute no parental care. In *promiscuous* species such as MOOSE, males search for females and attempt to mate with them. Often two or more males converge on a receptive female, and they threaten or even fight one another for the opportunity to mate with her. In *polygynous* species such as CARIBOU, males display to and fight one another in order to control small groups of females, with which they then mate. Most young males of polygynous species, even though reproductively capable, are prevented from mating by their older and larger rivals. Mating takes place in late fall, when males are in prime condition with fully grown antlers. Gestation occurs through the winter, and the young are born in May or June, just in time for the flush of plant growth after the long winter. Younger female ungulates usually have one young, but older females often have twins; Caribou, however, never have more than a single calf. Young BLACK-TAILED DEER are spotted to match the dappled light of the forest floor, but the young of the other ungulates are colored like their parents. Caribou and Moose calves are among the favored prey of wolves and bears, and only one in three Moose and one in five Caribou survive to the end of their first year.

Lore and Notes

Quite a cottage industry has developed from the rear ends of MOOSE. Their droppings, called *moose nuggets* in Alaska, are dried, shellacked, and sold to tourists in various forms, even as earrings. As entrepeneurs, Alaskans have learned to use the natural resources available to them. Amazingly, there are several species of mosses, called dung mosses, that grow only on moose nuggets. Apparently no one has thought to name them "moose mess mosses."

Status

Alaska's grazing and browsing mammals are fortunate not to have to compete with the herbivorous livestock that humans take with them almost everywhere on Earth; none of the common livestock species from other parts of the world is suited for Alaska's climate. Although some MUSKOX are being domesticated in an attempt to harvest their underfur, the species is native to the region, and Alaska's tundra plants should not suffer from small herds of this species. The only domesticated animal adapted to the Arctic is the *reindeer* (the domesticated form of CARIBOU), and Native people raise them in western Alaska for their meat, milk, and hides. Recent estimates of Caribou have indicated an Alaska population of close to a million animals, which seems an astonishing total for such large animals. However, these herds are vulnerable to human disturbance in the form of mining and oil exploration and development. Caribou have become habituated to human activities in some locales, but disturbance, a persistent threat, will only increase. As well as raising the domestic relatives of Caribou, Alaska native people are becoming involved in protecting the traditional calving grounds of the wild ones.

Profiles

Black-tailed Deer, *Odocoileus hemionus*, Plate 70a
Caribou, *Rangifer tarandus*, Plate 70b
Moose, *Alces alces*, Plate 70c
Muskox, *Ovibos moschatus*, Plate 71a
Mountain Goat, *Oreamnos americanus*, Plate 71b
Dall's Sheep, *Ovis dalli*, Plate 71c

11. Whales and Dolphins

The 78 species of *dolphins*, *porpoises*, and *whales* belong to the order Cetacea, a group of mammals closest to the artiodactyls (the even-toed hoofed mammals; see p. 212); recent genetic analysis indicates they are perhaps descended from some hippopotamus-like ancestor. They colonized the oceans long ago, and there most of them remain, but a few of the smaller dolphins inhabit larger rivers and estuaries in Asia, Africa, and South America. *Cetaceans* never leave the water and generally come to the surface only to breathe. Their hind legs have been lost through evolution and their front legs modified into paddlelike flippers. Their tails have become broad and flattened into paddles called *flukes*. A single or double nostril, called a *blowhole*, is on top of the head. Up to a third of an individual's weight consists of a thick layer of fat (*blubber*) lying under the smooth, hairless skin; the fat serves to insulate the animal against the water temperature, almost always lower than its own. Although cetacean eyes are relatively small, some species can see quite well both below and above the water surface. Cetacean hearing is especially well developed, and toothed whales use high frequency sound (mostly clicking and popping sounds) for *echolocation*, like bats, for underwater navigation and to locate prey. The sounds are produced when a dolphin pushes air back and forth between chambers located next to the breathing tube. The bulging *melon* on the front of the head is full of fat that serves to direct the sounds produced for echolocation. The returning echoes are received in the fat-filled lower jaw, which directs the sound into the inner ear.

Whether a given cetacean species is called a whale or a dolphin has to do with size: whales generally are at least 4.5 to 6 m (15 to 20 ft) long, and dolphins and porpoises are smaller. Cetaceans are divided into two broad categories. One group of large whale species, the *baleen whales* (suborder Mysticeti), includes species with huge heads with mouths that look like immense car radiator grills, filled with long, vertical, brown or gray strands of *baleen*, or *whalebone*, hanging from the upper jaw. Dorsal fins vary from absent to fairly prominent. The largest animal that ever lived, the BLUE WHALE, is a baleen whale. Blue Whales, widespread in Alaska offshore waters, grow to 30+ m (100 ft) in length and 160+ tons in weight.

Baleen whales profiled here range in length from the huge BOWHEAD WHALE (Plate 74) and HUMPBACK WHALE (Plate 74) to the relatively small MINKE WHALE (Plate 74). The Bowhead is in a family (Balaenidae) of three species with very large, broad heads (up to 40% of the total length), no dorsal fins, and one or no throat grooves. The Minke and Humpback are in the *rorqual* family (Balaenopteridae), including six much more slender species with sharply pointed heads, well-developed throat grooves, and dorsal fins. The GRAY WHALE (Plate 74) doesn't seem to belong with either of the other two families and so has been given its own family (Eschrichtiidae). In Alaska coastal waters, baleen whales are represented most frequently by the Humpback Whale and Minke Whale of deep channels along the southern coast, and the Gray Whale that migrates along the coast on its way to and from the Bering Sea. Of these species, the Humpback is especially high on most whale-watchers' viewing wish lists and can be easily seen in Glacier Bay. The front flippers of the Humpback are huge (as long as a third of the body length), white, and winglike. When a Humpback initiates a deep dive (*sounds*), its large scalloped flukes (which measure up to 4.5 m, 15 ft, across) come well up off the water's surface to expose their undersides, which are mottled white and black.

The other group, known as the *toothed whales* (suborder Odontoceti), includes a few whales and all the porpoises and dolphins; they have mouths with teeth rather than baleen. Dolphins have a beaklike snout projecting from a bulging head, a backwards-curving dorsal fin, and sharp, pointed teeth; porpoises are blunt-nosed with a triangular dorsal fin and blunt teeth. Both families include some species without dorsal fins. The most commonly seen toothed whales in

Alaska waters are the small DALL'S PORPOISE (Plate 75) and HARBOR PORPOISE (Plate 75), the BELUGA (Plate 75), and the much larger KILLER WHALE (ORCA) (Plate 74). The two porpoises are members of the porpoise family (Phocoenidae), which contains six species, all of which occur mostly in cold waters; these small cetaceans vary in length from 1.4 to 1.8 m (4.5 to 6 ft). The Killer Whale is a member of the dolphin family (Delphinidae), with 32 species distributed throughout the world's seas but mostly in the tropics. Dolphins range in length from about 2 m (6.5 ft) to almost 4 m (13 ft), with the Killer Whale an especially large member of the family; male Killer Whales grow to 9.5 m (31 ft) long and weigh as much as 8 tons. The Beluga and NARWHAL (Plate 75) are the only members of the family Monodontidae, a cetacean family restricted to high northern latitudes and characterized by a large melon, no beak, and no dorsal fin. Males of these two species reach 6 m (20 ft) in length, females 5 m (16 ft), with Narwhals averaging larger than Belugas. They are both unmistakable, not least because no other species of small cetacean occurs in arctic waters.

Natural History
Ecology and Behavior

The common small cetaceans in Alaska waters are porpoises. Porpoises usually travel in small groups of a few up to 15 or so animals, although rarely they may gather in *pods* of up to several hundred individuals; a huge group of DALL'S PORPOISE was once seen off Japan occupying an area of 8 by 2.5 km (5 by 1.5 miles). Large groups apparently consist of many smaller groups, which usually are quite stable in membership for several years. There are dominance hierarchies within groups, the largest male usually being dominant. Porpoises eat primarily fish (including common Alaska species such as herring, cod, and hake) and squid, and they feed largely at night, when some of their prey species move closer to the surface. The two Alaska species probably don't compete very much, because Dall's is primarily an offshore species, and HARBOR PORPOISES usually remain near the coast. Dall's Porpoises are especially fast swimmers, and they part the surface in a big spray (they are also called "Spray Porpoise") at high speed and create a hollow in the water, allowing them to take a quick breath. Dall's Porpoises mature at about 7 or 8 years of age and probably live to be 25 years old, but the Harbor Porpoise, a smaller species, matures in only 2 or 3 years and doesn't live as long.

KILLER WHALES roam the world's oceans, covering up to 100 km (62 miles) each day at speeds up to 30 knots when on the move. They travel in pods of about 5 to 20 individuals, with a fifth of them adult males, a fifth calves, and the remainder females and immature males. At times pods traveling in different directions meet, and there is often much socializing, as if old friends are meeting again. They hunt cooperatively, feeding on everything from small fish and squids, up through porpoises and seals, to the largest baleen whales. In northern waters, there are both resident pods that specialize on salmon and transient pods that eat marine mammals; it makes sense that the groups that feed on much larger prey cover greater distances while foraging. Only a few eyewitness accounts are at hand for Killers taking large whales, but they are awesome accounts, not unlike a pack of Gray Wolves chasing down and systematically killing a Moose. Unlike the Moose, the large whales seem to have no defenses. Orcas often "play" with porpoises and pinnipeds, throwing them out of the water and perhaps teaching the young to hunt, much as a cat brings a live mouse to her kittens. Killer Whales are surpassingly intelligent predators, tipping over ice floes to slide seals off into a waiting mouth and even charging up on shore to catch young sea lions, then sliding back into the water with the next wave.

Shore-based whale watchers can enjoy the sight of BELUGAS as they cruise along the coast in groups of up to 10 individuals. This high-latitude species is at home at the edge of and even under the ice pack; they can break a breathing hole in ice up to 10 cm (4 in) thick. They are common in estuaries and travel hundreds of kilometers up larger rivers such as the Yukon. In autumn, they sometimes come together in large herds of hundreds to thousands of individuals. Like other toothed whales, they feed on a variety of marine animals, including numerous kinds of fishes, shrimps, and crabs. Sand lance and cod are among the preferred fish species. NARWHALS are much rarer in Alaska; they are generally similar in habits to Belugas but tend to feed more on bottom fish. Males have been seen ripping trenches in the sea floor with their tusks, but the significance of this behavior is unknown. Narwhal pods usually consist of an adult male and several females and their young, and Beluga pods consist of either females and their young or all-male groups that join the female groups during mating.

HUMPBACK WHALES migrate to feed in polar waters and return to equatorial waters to breed. Calves have no blubber so must remain in warmer waters until they have fed sufficiently to put on a layer of fatty insulation for the cold polar waters. Humpbacks are usually found in family groups of three or four individuals. It is greatly paradoxical that the baleen whales, behemoths so large they can only be measured in tons and tens of meters, feed mainly on planktonic crustaceans (they are called *krill* collectively), small shrimplike animals barely 5 to 10 cm (2 to 4 in) long. They swim through food-rich layers of water, especially in polar regions, with their mouths wide open. Then they close their mouths and use their immense tongues (some weighing 4 tons) to push water out through their 300+ baleen plates. The plates strain out the krill, which are swallowed in one gulp. In tropical waters, Humpbacks feed commonly on fish and squid using a similar method. However, they also have developed a spectacular fishing behavior. Once a Humpback locates a fish school, it swims under and around the fish, all the while releasing a stream of air bubbles. The stream of bubbles serves as a *bubble net* that frightens and concentrates the fish and forces them to rise as the bubbles rise. The whale then dives and turns to swim vertically up through the bubble net, its wide-open mouth closing only as it reaches the surface, entrapping and then swallowing large numbers of fish. If you are in an area where Humpbacks are using this fishing method, watch for a ring of air bubbles to break the surface; the whale will soon rise in its center, mouth first and up to several meters out of the water. Seabirds quickly learn of this behavior, and some of them wait at the rising bubbles to catch escaping fish; this probably explains the birds that have been found in Humpback stomachs.

Humpbacks also produce some of the most complex and fascinating songs of any animal. Each geographic group has its own song, or *dialect*, that all the individuals there copy and use, but the songs change from year to year. By choosing the right layer of water – the appropriate depth and temperature – a whale can have its songs travel hundreds of kilometers. Because they apparently can communicate over very long distances, Humpback social interactions – including mate attraction, group behavior, and territorial behavior – may be quite complex and difficult for us to understand. Humpbacks also frequently jump completely out of the water (*breaching*), usually in an arching back flip. This behavior may be associated with mate attraction and courtship or it may be to knock off parasitic barnacles that grow on the whales' skin.

GRAY WHALES have a migratory strategy similar to that of the Humpback, but rather than cross the ocean depths, they migrate along shore between the Bering Sea, where they feed prodigiously, and Baja California, where they breed. Gray Whales are unusual baleen whales in being mostly bottom feeders; with one side of their head, they scoop up bottom mud containing huge numbers of amphipod crustaceans and swim up through the water column, trailing muddy water behind. They make such a disturbance that their scrapes in clear, shallow waters can be seen from the air, and many birds are attracted to where they are feeding to pick up the animals that escape their mouths. An adult female Gray Whale can consume 880 kg (1900 lb) of amphipods per day in her 4 months in Alaska, gaining up to 18,000 kg (20 tons) of fat on top of her lean weight of 50,000 kg (55 tons). This will allow her to migrate 9000 km (5600 miles) to Baja California and spend the winter there, while metabolizing her fat stores. By doing this, she assures the birth of her calf in warm water, where it will not need to expend energy to keep warm. She pumps gallons of rich milk into it each day, and by the time mother and calf are ready to head north to Alaska, it is large enough to travel with her and has developed its own coat of blubber.

BOWHEAD and MINKE WHALES are relatively sedentary, spending their lives cruising around Alaska waters by themselves or in groups of a few individuals. The Bowhead is an arctic species, wintering at the edge of the ice pack and following it north in spring as it recedes; the Minke is widespread in cold waters. The much smaller Minke has relatively coarse baleen and feeds on schooling fish such as cod and herring in Alaska waters. The baleen of Bowheads, however, is very fine. Although the plates in their very large heads grow up to 3.7 m (12 ft) in length, these whales feed on the smallest of prey eaten by baleen whales, copepod and euphausiid crustaceans that may be only one or two centimeters (0.8 in) in length. They swim slowly through plankton "slicks" on the surface for some distance until they accumulate enough solid material on their baleen plates to justify scraping it off with their tongue for a gargantuan swallow. Minke Whales, by contrast, feed like their larger relatives, Humpback and BLUE WHALES, by rushing through a concentration of prey and then quickly shutting their mouth.

Breeding

The mating systems of cetaceans in the wild are not well known, for the obvious reason that it is difficult to observe underwater courtship and mating behaviors; also complicating observation is that males and females look much alike. BOTTLE-NOSED DOLPHINS, perhaps the best-known of the cetaceans, mate near the surface, and their courtship involves elaborate stroking, nuzzling, and posturing. Pregnancy lasts 12 months; birth is often attended by several female "midwives," which help nudge the newborn to the surface for its first breath. Mating takes place all year in the two porpoise species common in Alaska, and the single young is born after 10 to 11 months of gestation. When born, porpoises are almost a meter (3 ft) long; HARBOR PORPOISE calves are nursed for about 9 months, DALL'S PORPOISES up to 2 years. Females lie on their side at the surface while the calf is nursing, so it can breathe readily.

BELUGAS and NARWHALS mate in spring; their gestation period is 14 or 15 months, so the calves are born in midsummer in shallow water when it is at its warmest and food is most abundant. Young BELUGAS are dark gray and gradually become paler, to their final snow-white color at maturity at about 6 years of age. If they make it that far, they may live to a ripe old age of 50 years.

HUMPBACK WHALES reach sexual maturity at 9 to 10 years. Courtship is in shallow waters near the equator and involves a lot of splashing, churning, and breaching. Pregnancy is about a year, and calves nurse for an additional year. BOWHEAD whales may court in groups, several males attracted to a single female. Mating takes place with the pair upright in the water, holding on as best they can with their flippers.

Lore and Notes

Dolphins' intelligence and friendliness toward people have inspired artists and authors for thousands of years. Images of dolphins appear frequently on artworks and coins from at least 3500 years ago, and from both ancient Greece and Rome. Aristotle, 2300 years ago, noted that dolphins were mammals, not fish, and remarked on their intelligence and gentle personalities. Many other ancient writings tell stories of close relationships between people and dolphins. Dolphins are the only animals, aside from humans, that regularly assist members of other species that are in distress. There have been many reports of dolphins supporting on the water's surface injured members of their own and other dolphin species, as well as helping people in the same way.

Because BOTTLE-NOSED DOLPHINS were the first to be kept in captivity for long periods (they are the species often seen in aquarium shows and achieved fame in the entertainment industry under their collective stage name, "Flipper"), and because they are often found close to shore and so are easily observed, more is known of their biology than of other dolphin species. The members of this family, including the very large KILLER WHALES, are displayed in oceanariums all over the world, where they seem to thrive. We have learned much about their intelligence, if not their life in the wild, from these captive animals, which are easily trained to perform an amazing variety of "tricks." Many people, however, consider it a crime to keep any cetaceans – intelligent, highly social, long-lived animals like ourselves – in captivity.

Bottle-nosed Dolphins, among other claims to fame, were among the first species, during the 1970s, to be studied using photographs of individuals that allowed biologists to track and study individual animals. In this case, close photos of dorsal fins permitted researchers to identify individuals and follow their activities for extended periods. The same method is being used to track KILLER WHALES (differences in dorsal fins) and HUMPBACK WHALES (differences in flukes, seen when the whale dives). This method of identifying individuals by photographs is now also widely used to study the long-term behavior and movements of such terrestrial animals as elephants and lions.

Many small cetaceans will approach moving sea vessels to "ride" the bow pressure wave (the wave produced at the front of the boat as it slices through the water). They sometimes persist in "hitchhiking" in this way for 20 minutes or more, jostling and competing with each other for the best spots – where, owing to the water's motion, they need exert little energy to swim; they are essentially taking a free ride. In Alaska the DALL'S PORPOISE is most often seen in this situation, much to the delight of the people on board.

Status

All marine dolphins are CITES Appendix II listed as species not currently threatened but vulnerable if protective measures are not taken. DALL'S

PORPOISES are among the species caught accidentally in the nets of fishermen, and thousands have been killed in that way. Dolphins in some regions of the world are also sometimes killed by fishermen who consider them to be competitors for valuable fish, or to be used as bait – for instance, for crab fishing.

Many whale species were hunted almost to extinction during a 200-year period that ended in the early 1960s (when international controls and sanctions were placed on commercial whaling). During the 1830s, the American whaling fleet alone numbered more than 700 ships. Whales were killed by the thousands for the thin, transparent oil that is stored in a reservoir in the forward part of their heads; the oil was used in lamps. SPERM WHALES also produce *ambergris*, a terrible-smelling black residue found in their intestines, which was used in making expensive perfumes. As late as 1963, more than 30,000 Sperm Whales were killed in a single year. GRAY WHALES were hunted to extinction in the North Atlantic and almost to extinction in Pacific waters, and by the end of the 19th century, it was feared the species was in imminent danger of disappearing from the Earth. However, after protection by the International Whaling Commission in 1947, it has recovered to its former abundance of around 20,000 animals in the eastern Pacific. Likewise, the HUMPBACK WHALE (CITES Appendix I and USA ESA listed), with a worldwide population now of perhaps 10,000, seems to be doing well. BOWHEAD WHALES (CITES Appendix I and USA ESA listed) are also slowly recovering. There are about 8,000 of them in Alaska waters, and regulations have been set so that about 50 per year can be taken by native Alaska people. There is a constant pressure from the few countries that continue to hunt whales to rescind international rules against whaling, but this seems unlikely to happen, with the current attitudes toward these magnificent animals.

Profiles

Killer Whale (Orca), *Orcinus orca*, Plate 74a
Minke Whale, *Balaenoptera acutorostrata*, Plate 74b
Gray Whale, *Eschrichtius glaucus*, Plate 74c
Bowhead Whale, *Eubalaena borealis*, Plate 74d
Humpback Whale, *Megaptera novaeangliae*, Plate 74e
Harbor Porpoise, *Phocoena phocoena*, Plate 75a
Dall's Porpoise, *Phocoenoides dalli*, Plate 75b
Narwhal, *Monodon monoceros*, Plate 75c
Beluga (White Whale), *Delphinapterus leucas*, Plate 75d

Environmental Close-up 6:
Mammal Population Cycles

The up-and-down population cycles exhibited by some mammals are among the most studied biological phenomena of the Arctic and Subarctic. Two different cycles have been noted, the approximately 4-year cycles of lemmings and the approximately 10-year cycles of Snowshoe Hares and Lynx. Both Brown and Collared Lemmings show similar dramatic population cycles, but the two species may not be in synchrony in any given area.

Lemmings (Plate 65) are small plant-eating rodents. Because they eat plants, there is usually a lot for them to eat; this is especially true because they are fond of the majority of the most common arctic plants, especially sedges and grasses but also including broad-leaved plants of many kinds. Lemmings also feed on willow twigs and buds during the winter. Because they are small, they can occur at high densities; at highest densities, one animal may have a home range (the area in which it lives and seeks food) of as little as 3 to 5 sq m (32 to 54 sq ft), so many lemmings can inhabit each hectare (2.5 acres) of tundra. Because they are rodents, they have a high reproductive rate; females can have several litters during the summer, and litters commonly comprise 5 to 10 young.

With their high reproductive rate, lemming populations in an area increase over a period of a few years, finally reaching such numbers that they may even continue breeding through the winter. As the snow melts the following spring, the animals are forced to move to limited areas of higher ground, where their population density thus becomes even higher. The highest densities of Collared Lemmings have been estimated as over 600 times that of densities at the lowest population levels. These very large populations begin to overgraze the tundra, where plant growth is not as rapid as at lower latitudes. Some lemmings then cannot find enough to eat and either starve or leave their normal home range, looking for food. But even when food is still available, when at high densities the lemmings produce abnormally high levels of stress hormones, which causes them to become very agitated, even to the point of death. The Norway Lemming of Scandinavia undergoes mass migrations at such times, but the movements of Brown Lemmings in North America, although significant, are unspectacular, because the animals involved are scattered.

These higher populations also attract predators, especially Snowy Owls, jaegers, Rough-legged Hawks, Short-tailed Weasels, and Arctic Foxes. At these times, some of these species eat nothing but lemmings, which are easy prey. Snowy Owls and Pomarine Jaegers normally breed only during lemming population highs, which vary in timing from place to place; the jaegers accordingly are nomadic, moving about the Arctic after they arrive in spring to seek out lemmings. Predator densities reach unusually high levels where lemmings are abundant. For example, one area of 2.5 sq km (1 sq mile) near Barrow, Alaska, supported one pair of Snowy Owls, three pairs of Short-eared Owls, 19 pairs of Pomarine Jaegers, and an additional 16 to 20 nonbreeding Pomarine Jaegers, a very high density of large, predatory birds. Over a year or two, predation, starvation, and emigration all reduce the lemming populations to low levels. The predators disperse, the vegetation begins to recover, and the cycle begins again.

Snowshoe Hares (Plate 61) are much larger than lemmings, so their densities are always lower. Their reproductive rate is lower than that of lemmings but still impressive, with females often having two litters of about four young each per summer. They are herbivores, and their dietary preferences are at least as broad as those of lemmings, so, for hares also, the plant community represents an always available cafeteria. We have more precise information on Snowshoe Hare cycles than we do on lemmings, because the hares are trapped for their fur. A careful record was kept at the Hudson Bay Company for many years of all the hare pelts turned in by fur trappers, so biologists were later able to plot these numbers over almost a complete century. The resulting figures showed a striking cycle: over wide areas of Canada, peaks in the numbers of trapped hares occurred every 9, 10, or 11 years, with much lower numbers in-between. The cause of the cycles, as in the case of the lemmings, is by no means completely understood, but at high densities, the hares interact more frequently with one another, and the stress caused by the interactions may bring on hormonal malfunctions that lead to reproductive failure. Hare numbers diminish rapidly when this happens.

The hare's primary predator is the Lynx (Plate 69), another hunted fur-bearer, and by plotting numbers of Lynx similarly, it was clear that the predator also showed abundance cycles of about 10 years. It is not surprising that Lynx cycles lag one or two years behind those of the hare: as hare populations increase, Lynx would experience enhanced survival for both adults and young because of their more abundant prey. Lynx populations would increase accordingly but would be a bit behind hare populations. As Snowshoe Hare populations plummet, Lynx would experience poor feeding conditions, and their populations would decrease.

REFERENCES AND ADDITIONAL READING

Alaska Geographic Guides. (1996) *Mammals of Alaska*. The Alaska Geographic Society, Anchorage, USA.

Armstrong R. H. (1995) *Guide to the Birds of Alaska*. Alaska Northwest Books, Anchorage, USA.

Armstrong R. H. (1996) *Alaska's Fish: A Guide to Selected Species*. Alaska Northwest Books, Anchorage, USA.

Banfield A. W. F. (1974) *The Mammals of Canada*. University of Toronto Press, Toronto, Canada.

Boag D. (1982) *The Kingfisher*. Blandford Press, Poole, UK.

Burt W. H. and R. P. Grossenheider. (1964) *A Field Guide to the Mammals*. Houghton Mifflin Co., Boston, USA.

Chapman J. A. and G. A. Feldhamer. (1982) *Wild Mammals of North America: Biology, Management, and Economics*. The Johns Hopkins University Press, Baltimore, USA.

Committee on Management of Wolf and Bear Populations in Alaska. (1997) *Wolves, Bears, and their Prey in Alaska*. National Academy Press, Washington, USA.

Eschmeyer W. N., E. S. Herald and H. Hammann. (1983) *A Field Guide to Pacific Coast Fishes of North America*. Houghton Mifflin Co., Boston, USA.

Ford E. B. (1957) *Butterflies*. The New Naturalist. Collins, London, UK.

Gabrielson I. N. and F. C. Lincoln. (1959) *The Birds of Alaska*. The Stackpole Co., Harrisburg, PA, USA.

Gotshall D. W. (1994) *Guide to Marine Invertebrates – Alaska to Baja California*. Sea Challengers, Monterey, CA, USA.

Hultén E. (1968) *Flora of Alaska and Neighboring Territories*. Stanford University Press, Stanford, CA, USA.

Kaufman K. (1996) *Lives of North American Birds*. Houghton Mifflin Co., Boston, USA.

Kozloff E. N. (1983) *Seashore Life of the Northern Pacific Coast*. University of Washington Press, Seattle, USA.

Lamb A. and P. Edgell. (1986) *Coastal Fishes of the Pacific Northwest*. Harbour Publishing, Madeira Park, BC, Canada.

Leonard W. P., H. A. Brown, L. L. C. Jones, K. R. McAllister and R. M. Storm. (1993) *Amphibians of Washington and Oregon*. Seattle Audubon Society, Seattle, USA.

Margulis L. and K. V. Schwartz. (1997) *Five Kingdoms: An Illustrated Guide to the Phyla of Life on Earth*. W. H. Freeman and Company, New York, USA.

National Geographic Society. (1999) *Field Guide to the Birds of North America*. National Geographic Society, Washington, USA.

O'Clair R. M., R. H. Armstrong and R. Carstensen. (1997) *The Nature of Southeast Alaska*. Alaska Northwest Books, Anchorage, USA.

O'Clair R. M. and C. E. O'Clair. (1998) *Southeast Alaska's Rocky Shores – Animals*. Plant Press, Auke Bay, AK, USA.

Oldroyd H. (1964) *The Natural History of Flies*. W. W. Norton & Co., Inc., New York, USA.

Opler P. A. (1999) *A Field Guide to Western Butterflies*. Houghton Mifflin Co., Boston, USA.

Page L. M. and B. M. Burr. (1991) *A Field Guide to Freshwater Fishes*. Houghton Mifflin Co., Boston, USA.

Paulson D. (1993) *Shorebirds of the Pacific Northwest*. University of Washington Press, Seattle, USA.

Pratt V. E. (1989) *Field Guide to Alaskan Wildflowers*. Alaskakrafts Publishing, Anchorage, USA.

Riedman M. (1990) *The Pinnipeds: Seals, Sea Lions, and Walruses*. University of California Press, Berkeley, USA.

Scott J. A. (1986) *The Butterflies of North America*. Stanford University Press, Stanford, CA, USA.

Simmerman N. L. (1983) *Alaska's Parklands: The Complete Guide*. The Mountaineers, Seattle, USA.

Stebbins R. C. (1966) *A Field Guide to Western Reptiles and Amphibians*. Houghton Mifflin Co., Boston, USA.

Sydeman M. and A. Lund. (1996) *Alaska Wildlife Viewing Guide*. Falcon Press Publishing Company, Helena and Billings, MT, USA.

Viereck L. A. and E. L. Little, Jr. (1972) *Alaska Trees and Shrubs*. Agriculture Handbook No. 410. U.S. Department of Agriculture, Forest Service, Washington, USA.

Whitaker J. O., Jr. (1996) *National Audubon Society Field Guide to North American Mammals*. Alfred A. Knopf, New York, USA.

HABITAT PHOTOS

I Tundra and gravelly lake shore at Cape Mountain, Wales. © D. Paulson

2 Alders and willows along river through moist arctic tundra, Teller Road, Nome.
© D. Paulson

3 Dry alpine tundra, Council Road, Nome. © D. Paulson

4 Sedge/grass tundra in Brooks Range, Galbraith area, Dalton Highway. © C. Spaw

5 Low white spruce forest south of Brooks Range, Dalton Highway. © C. Spaw

6 Wild sweet pea along braided river with Alaska range in distance, Richardson Highway.
© C. Spaw

7 Black spruce forest along Trans-Alaska Pipeline in Alaska Range, Richardson Highway. © R. Droker

8 Broad-leafed willow herb, crowberry, and reindeer lichens in Alaska Range. © R. Droker

9 Freshwater lake and muskeg at Tazlina, Glenn Highway. © D. Paulson

10 White spruce forest with Chugach Mountains in distance, Glenn Highway.
© D. Paulson

11 Spruce forest in Chugach State Park, above Anchorage. © D. Paulson

12 Balsam poplar grove, Homer. © D. Paulson

13 Western hemlock/Sitka spruce forest, Copper River delta. © D. Paulson

14 Copper River wetlands and Chugach Mountains. © D. Paulson

15 Wind-pruned coastal conifer forest, McArthur Pass, Ragged Islands. © D. Paulson

16 Freshwater lake and mixed conifer forest, Tongass National Forest, Wrangell Island. © R. Droker

17 Freshwater wetland, Tongass National Forest, Wrangell Island. © R. Droker

18 South coast of Attu Island, westernmost of the Aleutians. © D. Paulson

19 Bird cliffs on St. Paul Island, Pribilofs © D. Paulson

20 Thick-billed Murres swarming around Bogoslof Island, Aleutians. © D. Paulson

21 Shishaldin Volcano on Unimak Island from Unimak Pass. © D. Paulson

22 Rocky coast, Wrangell Island.
© R. Droker

23 Rocky intertidal zone, Wrangell Island. © R. Droker

24 Intertidal zonation, Nazan Bay, Atka Island. © D. Paulson

25 Alaska intertidal invertebrates. © D. Paulson

Habitat symbols

= Tundra.

= Coniferous and mixed forest.

= Deciduous forest.

= Forest edge/shrub thicket.

= Meadows and grassland other than tundra.

= Freshwater. For species typically found in or near lakes, streams, rivers, marshes, swamps.

= Saltwater/marine. For species usually found in or near the ocean.

Regions (see Map 6, p.51):

SE   Southeastern Alaska; the southern peninsular part of the state, south of Yakutat and Skagway.

SC   Southcentral Alaska; includes the coastal lowlands from Yakutat west to Homer, including Anchorage and the Seward Peninsula.

SW   Southwestern Alaska; includes the Alaska Peninsula, Kodiak Island, and the Aleutian Islands.

W   Western Alaska; includes the Yukon Delta, Seward Peninsula, and generally the western edge of the state, as well as the Bering Sea islands.

N   Northern Alaska; includes the coastal plain from the Brooks Range north.

C   Central Alaska; includes the remainder of the state, the huge area centering around Fairbanks and including the Alaska and Brooks ranges and everything between them.

IDENTIFICATION PLATES

Abbreviations on the Identification Plates are as follows:

M;   male
F;   female
IM;   immature
J;   juvenile
B;   breeding
N;   nonbreeding

The species pictured on any one plate are drawn to scale. In a few cases, a horizontal line on a plate separates animals at different scales.

Plate A1
Black Spruce
Picea mariana
Common coniferous tree in boggy areas of interior, much like White Spruce but smaller (typically to 9 m, 30 ft, rarely to 18 m, 60 ft) and with smaller cones (length less than 2.5 cm, 1 in) that remain on tree after they mature. Top of tree usually with dense cluster of branches.

REGIONS: SC, C

Plate A2
White Spruce
Picea glauca
Dominant conifer over much of interior, grows in extensive pure stands over vast areas. Large tree, typically growing to 21 m (70 ft) in height, largest may reach 35 m (115 ft). Cones (length more than 2.5 cm, 1 in) drop from tree when mature.

REGIONS: SC, C, W

Plate A3
Western Hemlock
Tsuga heterophylla
Dominant coniferous tree in southern Alaskan spruce-hemlock forests, distinguished by relatively small, delicate needles and droopy tip of tree. Cones small, to 2.5 cm (1 in). Quite large, attaining 46 m (150 ft) in height.

REGIONS: SE, SC

Plate A4
Alaska Yellow Cedar
Chamaecyparis nootkatensis
Coniferous tree with flattened clumps of yellow-green needles; yellow wood gives it its name. Scattered through spruce-hemlock forests in the Southeast, where it grows to 24 m (80 ft) in height.

REGIONS: SE, SC

1 Black Spruce, *Picea mariana*

2 White Spruce, *Picea glauca*

3 Western Hemlock, *Tsuga heterophylla*

4 Alaska Yellow Cedar, *Chamaecyparis nootkatensis*

Plate B1

Balsam Poplar
Populus balsamifera

Most widespread large deciduous tree in Alaska, recognized by broad, sharply pointed leaves and gray, furrowed bark of mature trees. Grows commonly to 15 m (50 ft). Cottony seeds fill the air at times during summer. Replaced by Black Cottonwood (*Populus trichocarpa*) in Southeastern Alaska, hybridizing with it where they meet.

REGIONS: SC, SW, C, W, N

Plate B2

Quaking Aspen
Populus tremuloides

Striking deciduous tree, with pale orange to white bark and broad, pointed leaves that turn brilliant yellow in fall. Leaves "quake" because stalk (petiole) that attaches them to stem is flattened and quite long; trembling may cool leaf on a hot summer day. Aspens often grow in dense stands formed from suckers growing up from root system of a single tree.

REGIONS: SC, C

Plate B3

willows
Salix spp.

Willows are among the most ubiquitous deciduous trees and shrubs in Alaska, with larger species in southern forests and smaller species to the north. Some tundra species grow flat on the ground, their fuzzy flower heads poking up from among lichens. Seeds are cottony and airborne. There are 35 species in Alaska.

REGIONS: SE, SC, SW, C, W, N

Plate B4

Paper Birch
Betula papyrifera

Like aspen, Paper Birch has a white trunk and broad, pointed, deciduous leaves, but its leaves have more prominently toothed margins, and they don't flutter in the breeze. The white to reddish bark has dark horizontal lines scattered over it and peels off in paper-thin strips.

REGIONS: SC, C

Plate B5

Sitka Alder
Alnus sinuata

Alders are characteristic small deciduous trees and shrubs along rivers and streams. They also colonize burns, landslides, and clear-cuts, where they form dense pure stands. The finely toothed leaves and conelike fruits are characteristic.

REGIONS: SE, SC, SW, C, W

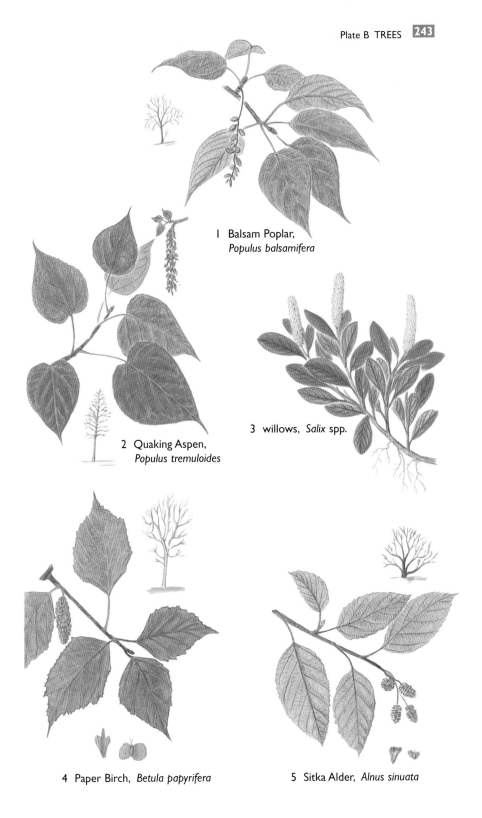

1 Balsam Poplar,
Populus balsamifera

2 Quaking Aspen,
Populus tremuloides

3 willows, *Salix* spp.

4 Paper Birch, *Betula papyrifera*

5 Sitka Alder, *Alnus sinuata*

Plate C1
Cloudberry
Rubus chamaemorus
Trailing, almost vinelike herb of peat bogs throughout the state. Leaves rounded, more or less five-lobed and finely toothed. Large white flowers with many long stamens; fruits orange, clustered like raspberries and just as tasty.

REGIONS: SE, SC, SW, C, W, N

Plate C2
Salmonberry
Rubus spectabilis
Deciduous shrub common in forest understory all along southern coast. Easily recognized by bright rose-pink flowers and red-orange (rarely yellow-orange) tasty fruits. Stems finely spiny, impeding progress in dense thickets.

REGIONS: SE, SC, SW

Plate C3
Prickly Rose
Rosa acicularis
Typical rose, with prickly stems, five-parted leaves with broad, toothed leaflets, and showy rose-pink five-petaled flowers. Locally common in shaded undergrowth of most forest types and in thickets in open areas. Fruits (rose hips) very rich in Vitamin C.

REGIONS: SC, C, W

Plate C4
Devil's Club
Echinopanax horridum
Common in forest undergrowth along southern coast, forming dense impenetrable thickets. Huge (to 35 cm, 14 in, in diameter) maple-shaped leaves and bright red berries characteristic, spiny branches unforgettable. Spiniest plant in Alaska; to be avoided.

REGIONS: SE, SC

Plate C SHRUBS **245**

1 Cloudberry, *Rubus chamaemorus*

2 Salmonberry, *Rubus spectabilis*

3 Prickly Rose, *Rosa acicularis*

4 Devil's Club, *Echinopanax horridum*

Plate D1

Kinnikinnick
Arctostaphylos uva-ursi

Ground-hugging evergreen shrub with small, prominently veined, rounded leaves wider toward tip. Flowers tiny, urn-shaped, white to pink; berries conspicuous, red. Often forms pure mats on dry ground in open forest.

REGIONS: SE, SC, SW, C

Plate D2

Mountain Avens
Dryas octopetala

Prostrate evergreen shrub, one of the more common plants of arctic and alpine tundra. Leaves wavy-edged and prominently veined, green above and white below, edges rolled under. Flowers with 8 to 10 white petals and yellow center; fruit begins as a twisted spike, turns into striking white furry-looking ball to 3.5 cm (1.5 in) in diameter.

REGIONS: SC, SW, C, W, N

Plate D3

Bunchberry
Cornus canadensis

Low shrub, forming ground cover in understory of many Alaskan forests. Oval leaves with nearly parallel veins characteristic, as are four large white bracts surrounding inconspicuous flower clusters. In late summer, each tiny plant topped by bright red berries.

REGIONS: SE, SC, SW, C, W

Plate D4

Twinflower
Linnaea borealis

Creeping evergreen shrub with long runners and erect stems at intervals, each stem with a few rounded, slightly toothed leaves, and pair of pinkish-white hanging flowers. Open forest, where it often carpets ground, and tundra.

REGIONS: SE, SC, SW, C, W

1 Kinnikinnick, *Arctostaphylos uva-ursi*

2 Mountain Avens, *Dryas octopetala*

3 Bunchberry, *Cornus canadensis*

4 Twinflower, *Linnaea borealis*

Plate E1
Crowberry
Empetrum nigrum
Low evergreen shrub forming dense mats with horizontal stems and profusion of small, thick, narrow leaves with rounded tips. Small maroon flowers inconspicuous, but fruit very obvious purple to black berry, persisting through winter beneath snow. Eaten by people and many animals. Abundant in tundra areas, locally common in forests and muskegs.

REGIONS: SE, SC, SW, C, W, N

Plate E2
Labrador Tea
Ledum groenlandicum
Small evergreen shrub with upright branches bearing narrow leaves with curled edges, upper sides dark green, lower sides coppery and fuzzy. White flowers with long stamens, fragrant and conspicuous. Characteristic of bogs and muskegs, also in drier, open White Spruce forests.

REGIONS: SE, C

Plate E3
Four-angled Cassiope
Cassiope tetragona
Creeping evergreen shrub forming almost mosslike mat, tiny grooved leaves pressed tightly against stems. Flowers white, bell-like, hanging from tips of long upright stalks. Alpine and arctic tundra; thrives where snow depth greatest.

REGIONS: C, W, N

Plate E4
Bog-rosemary
Andromeda polifolia
Low evergreen shrub with narrow, pointed leaves, green above and whitish below, the edges rolled in; flowers small, light pink, and urn-shaped. In bogs southward, wet sedge tundra north and west.

REGIONS: SE, SC, SW, C, W, N

Plate E5
Mountain-cranberry
Vaccinium vitis-idaea
Creeping evergreen shrub with dense, small, oval, shiny green leaves; small, pale pink, bell-shaped flowers; and prominent red berries clustered at branch tips. Common in bogs, in spruce and birch forests, on moist tundra, and on rocky slopes.

REGIONS: SE, SC, SW, C, W, N

1 Crowberry, *Empetrum nigrum*

2 Labrador Tea, *Ledum groenlandicum*

3 Four-angled Cassiope, *Cassiope tetragona*

4 Bog-rosemary, *Andromeda polifolia*

5 Mountain-cranberry, *Vaccinium vitis-idaea*

Plate F1
Bush Cinquefoil
Potentilla fruticosa
Low deciduous shrub with showy yellow roselike flowers and five-parted leaves; leaflets grayish beneath. Grows widely in dry and wet soils, usually in sun.

REGIONS: SC, C, W, N

Plate F2
Bog Blueberry
Vaccinium uliginosum
Low deciduous shrub (lying flat on northern tundra) with rounded dark green leaves; pink, urn-shaped flowers along branches; and tasty, blue to black berries. Common in bogs, open forests, and tundra habitats.

REGIONS: SE, SC, SW, C, W

Plate F3
Red-osier Dogwood
Cornus stolonifera
Smooth red twigs give this deciduous shrub of moist areas its name. Flat sprays of white flowers at top of plant turn into clumps of whitish or blue berries. Young twigs important winter food for deer and moose.

REGIONS: SE, C

Plate F4
Highbush Cranberry
Viburnum edule
Good-sized deciduous shrub of thickets and forest edge with large, thin, toothed and often three-lobed leaves; leaves turn red in fall. Small flowers in flat-topped clusters produce red or orange edible berries.

REGIONS: SE, SC, SW, C

1 Bush Cinquefoil, *Potentilla fruticosa*

2 Bog Blueberry, *Vaccinium uliginosum*

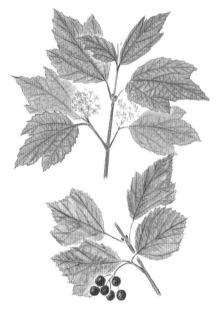

3 Red-osier Dogwood, *Cornus stolonifera*

4 Highbush Cranberry, *Viburnum edule*

Plate G1

Alaska Cotton
Eriophorum scheuchzeri

A sedge, with slender grasslike leaves. Grows in extensive beds, but each plant has a single slender stalk bearing a flower head with long, white, fluffy bristles, the effect being a field of marshmallows. Usually in wet, marshy areas and bogs.

REGIONS: C, W, N

Plate G2

Bistort
Polygonum bistorta

Herb with narrow, pointed leaves and tiny, light pink flowers clustered in spike at top of upright stalk. Common in alpine and arctic tundra. Leaves edible to humans, raw or cooked.

REGIONS: C, W, N

Plate G3

Northern Yarrow
Achillea borealis

Aromatic herb with very finely divided leaves and upright flower stalks with flat-topped heads of small white flowers. Dry, open areas; grows widely as a weed along roadsides. Dried leaves used for tea.

REGIONS: SE, SC, SW, C, W, N

Plate G4

Frigid Coltsfoot
Petasites frigidus

Flower stalk with pinkish to white flowers emerges from snow early in spring, then lengthens and produces dandelion-like seed heads. Leaves expand at that time, those along flower stalk narrow and pointed and those at base of plant large, rounded, and indented at base – something like a horse's hoof.

REGIONS: SW, C, W, N

1 Alaska Cotton, *Eriophorum scheuchzeri*

2 Bistort, *Polygonum bistorta*

3 Northern Yarrow, *Achillea borealis*

4 Frigid Coltsfoot, *Petasites frigidus*

Plate H1
Fringecup
Tellima grandiflora
Herb with cluster of heart-shaped, toothed, and slightly lobed leaves surmounted by long flower stalks with small, greenish, cup-shaped flowers all along their sides. Moist areas in and out of forest.

REGIONS: SE, SC, SW

Plate H2
Goatsbeard
Aruncus sylvester
Herb with large twice-divided compound leaves and tall (to 1.2 m, 4 ft), slender flower stalk bearing numerous spikes of tiny cream-colored flowers. Moist woods and meadows, common along roadsides.

REGIONS: SE, SC, SW

Plate H3
Partridge Foot
Leutkea pectinata
Prostrate shrub, forming mats over alpine meadows and rocks. Easily recognized by finely divided parsley-like leaves and elevated flower stalks with clusters of small white flowers.

REGIONS: SE, SC, SW, C

Plate H4
Cow Parsnip
Heracleum lanatum
Herb with large (30 cm, 12 in, wide), fan-shaped, deeply toothed leaves and tall (to 2.4 m, 8 ft) flower stalks with large, rounded heads consisting of 15 to 30 clusters of tiny flowers. Hairs on stems and leaves may be irritating to skin. Typically in moist woods and meadows.

REGIONS: SE, SC, SW, C, W

1 Fringecup, *Tellima grandiflora*

2 Goatsbeard, *Aruncus sylvester*

3 Partridge Foot, *Leutkea pectinata*

4 Cow Parsnip, *Heracleum lanatum*

Plate I1
Macoun's Poppy
Papaver macounii
Large yellow, shallowly cup-shaped flowers sway in wind at ends of long leafless stalks projecting above basal cluster of small, deeply divided leaves. Common in sandy and gravelly arctic and alpine tundra.

REGIONS: C, W, N

Plate I2
Roseroot
Sedum rosea
Herb with upright stalks completely ringed by broad, pointed, fleshy, gray-green leaves and topped by clusters of dark reddish flowers. Most common on rocky slopes. Name comes from cut roots smelling somewhat roselike.

REGIONS: SE, SC, SW, C, W, N

Plate I3
Purple Mountain Saxifrage
Saxifraga oppositifolia
Mat-forming plant of tundra regions, identified by rosettes of small, pointed leaves. One of first arctic wildflowers of spring, it becomes covered with bright pink flowers. "Saxifrage" means rock-breaker, in reference to the many kinds that grow on rocks.

REGIONS: SE, SC, SW, C, W, N

Plate I4
Woolly Lousewort
Pedicularis kanei
Flower stalk quite woolly while budding, then becomes longer as spike of bright pink flowers appears. Leaves very finely divided. Louseworts were so named because people thought they harbored lice that would infect their similarly woolly sheep.

REGIONS: SW, C, W, N

Plate I HERBS 257

2 Roseroot, *Sedum rosea*

I Macoun's Poppy, *Papaver macounii*

3 Purple Mountain Saxifrage, *Saxifraga oppositifolia*

4 Woolly Lousewort, *Pedicularis kanei*

Plate J1
Monkshood
Aconitum delphinifolium
Tall, slender herb with deeply divided, narrowly lobed leaves; blue-purple flowers distinctively shaped, with helmet-like "hood" above. Common in and out of forests, including moist tundra.

REGIONS: SE, SC, SW, C, W, N

Plate J2
Nootka Lupine
Lupinus nootkatensis
Robust herb with characteristic five-parted palmate leaves, blue-purple pea flowers, and hairy peapods. Drops of water that collect at base of leaflets add to photogenic quality of plant – beautiful but deadly, however, as most parts of plant are poisonous to eat. Moist areas, especially common along south coast.

REGIONS: SE, SC, SW

Plate J3
Wild Sweet Pea
Hedysarum mackenzii
Typical legume, with many leaflets in its compound leaves and bilaterally symmetrical rose-pink pea flowers. Named "sweet pea" from fragrance of bright pink flowers. Open areas, most common on disturbed land (river bars, rocky slopes).

REGIONS: C, N

Plate J4
Common Fireweed
Epilobium angustifolium
Aptly named beautiful tall herb with column of large, bright pink, four-petaled flowers flourishes on recently burned or cleared land; wind-borne fluffy seeds allow it quick access to such places. Pure stands of fireweed provide breathtaking displays of color in open and edge habitats all over state in late summer.

REGIONS: SE, SC, SW, C, W, N

1 Monkshood, *Aconitum delphinifolium*

2 Nootka lupine, *Lupinus nootkatensis*

3 Wild Sweet Pea, *Hedysarum Mackenzii*

4 Common Fireweed, *Epilobium angustifolium*

Plate 1a
Boreal Bluet
Enallagma boreale
ID: Mid-sized damselfly with wings closed over abdomen; males mostly bright blue, females with blue or brown thorax; conspicuous, often abundant; 3 cm (1.2 in).

HABITAT: Beds of vegetation in lakes and ponds, also over open water in flight; mated pairs lay eggs in vegetation.

REGIONS: SE, SC, C

Plate 1b
Common Spreadwing
Lestes disjunctus
ID: Large damselfly with wings usually held open; males with gray thorax and abdomen tip, females with striped thorax and black, thicker abdomen; 3.5 cm (1.4 in).

HABITAT: Marshy lake edges; males perch conspicuously on sedges, mating pairs lay eggs in sedge stems.

REGIONS: SE, SC, C

Plate 1c
Sedge Darner
Aeshna juncea
ID: Large, dark dragonfly with pale stripes on side of thorax and blue-spotted abdomen; 6 cm (2.4 in).

HABITAT: Open sedge marshes, marshy lake edges; males fly and hover over sedges or along lake shore; females much harder to see, lay eggs in plant stems at water level.

REGIONS: SE, SC, C, W

Plate 1d
Four-spotted Skimmer
Libellula quadrimaculata
ID: Mid-sized brown dragonfly with large dark marking at base of each hindwing and small spot at midwing; 4.5 cm (1.8 in).

HABITAT: Marshy and shrubby lake edges; males perch conspicuously on territory or guard females that drop eggs in open water.

REGIONS: SE, SC, C

Plate I 261

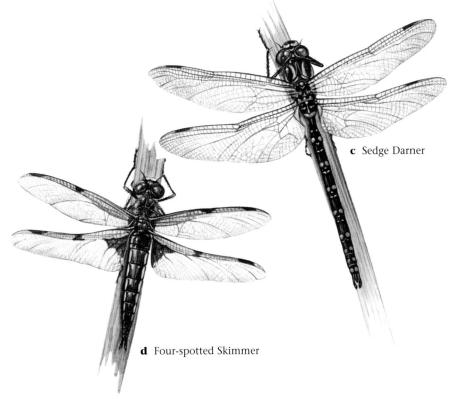

a Boreal Bluet

b Common Spreadwing

c Sedge Darner

d Four-spotted Skimmer

Plate 2a

horse fly
family Tabanidae

ID: Large flies with conspicuous, sometimes patterned, wings and large, often beautifully striped eyes; difficult to discourage as they circle persistently and land to bite fiercely; 1 to 2 cm (0.4 to 0.8 in).

HABITAT: Breed in wetlands of many kinds but females wander far from water to hunt blood meals; active during day.

REGIONS: SE, SC, SW, C

Plate 2b

black fly
family Simuliidae

ID: Tiny shiny black flies with prominent humped thorax, short wings and legs; very bothersome biters near breeding habitats; 0.2 to 0.5 cm (0.1 to 0.2 in).

HABITAT: Streams, rivers; active during day.

REGIONS: SE, SC, SW, C

Plate 2c

crane fly
family Tipulidae

ID: Largish, slender flies with very long legs that they lose if grabbed; 1 to 2.5 cm (0.4 to 1 in).

HABITAT: Marshes, wetlands of all kinds, also wet tundra; different species active day or night; often come to lights.

REGIONS: SE, SC, SW, C, W, N

Plate 2d

midge
family Chironomidae

ID: Tiny slender-legged insects in the fly order that *aren't* mosquitos (so don't immediately squash anything that lands on you); males, with feathery antennae like male mosquitos, often fly in dense sexual advertising swarms, localized over shrub or other prominent feature; 0.3 to 0.9 cm (0.1 to 0.35 in).

HABITAT: Wetlands of all kinds, lakes and ponds more than streams; more active during day.

REGIONS: SE, SC, SW, C, W, N

Plate 2e

mosquito
family Culicidae

ID: Small slender-legged insects in the fly order that irritate by buzz or bite; only females have long proboscis and bite; males with short mouthparts and feathery antennae; inimical to human comfort where abundant; 0.3 to 0.9 cm (0.1 to 0.35 in).

HABITAT: Wetlands of all kinds, primarily ponds and small water bodies without fish; active around the clock.

REGIONS: SE, SC, SW, C, W, N

Plate 2f

no-see-um (sand fly)
family Ceratopogonidae

ID: Very tiny insects of the fly order with short wings and legs, difficult to detect except by bite, which is way out of proportion to size; 0.1 to 0.2 cm (0.04 to 0.1 in).

HABITAT: Wetlands, especially ponds, lakes; often active at dusk.

REGIONS: SE, SC, SW, C

Plate 2   263

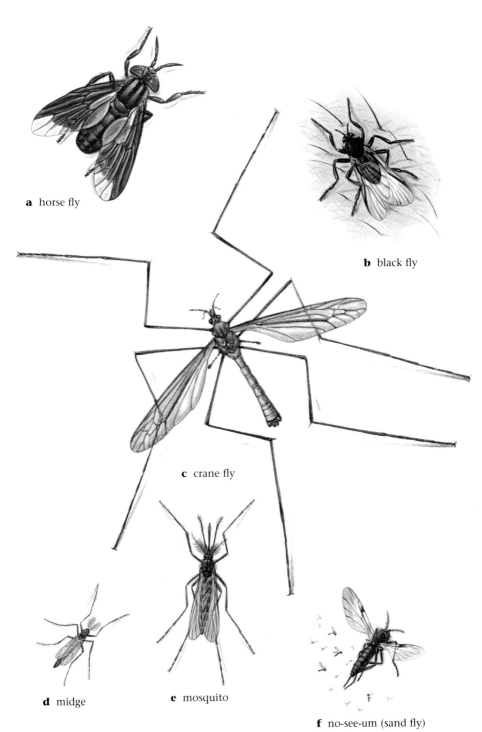

a horse fly

b black fly

c crane fly

d midge

e mosquito

f no-see-um (sand fly)

Plate 3a
Phoebus Parnassian
Parnassius phoebus
ID: Medium-large butterfly; wings snowy white with black markings, two large red spots on hindwings; female more heavily marked with black than male; flight straight and very fluttery; wingspan 5.5 cm (2.2 in).

HABITAT: Dry alpine and moist arctic tundra; larval food plant stonecrop.

REGIONS: SC, C, W

Plate 3b
Old World Swallowtail
Papilio machaon
ID: Large butterfly; wings yellow and black with gray-brown at base of forewings and orange spot at inner corner of hindwings; prominent tails on hindwings; rarely all dark; wingspan 7.5 cm (3 in).

HABITAT: Woodland, tundra, prairies, riparian, hillsides; larval food plants wild tarragon, arctic wormwood, cow parsnip.

REGIONS: SC, C, W, N

Plate 3c
Canadian Tiger Swallowtail
Papilio canadensis
ID: Large butterfly; like Old World Swallowtail but yellower (more restricted black markings), no brown at forewing base, tails longer; wingspan 7 cm (2.8 in).

HABITAT: Aspen parklands, mixed forest, forest edge; larval food plants birches, poplar, aspen.

REGIONS: SE, SC, C

Plate 3d
Arctic White
Pieris angelika
ID: Medium-small butterfly; wings white with gray to greenish lines along all wing veins, especially prominent in hindwings; wingspan 3.7 cm (1.5 in).

HABITAT: Moist woodlands and edges, alpine tundra; larval food plants various mustards.

REGIONS: SC, SW, C, W, N

Plate 3e
Hecla Sulfur
Colias hecla
ID: Medium-small butterfly; wings above orange with dusky margins; hindwings greenish below with small pink spot in middle; wingspan 4 cm (1.6 in).

HABITAT: Tundra; larval food plant alpine milk vetch.

REGIONS: C, W, N

Plate 3 **265**

a Phoebus Parnassian

b Old World
Swallowtail

c Canadian Tiger
Swallowtail

e Hecla Sulfur

d Arctic White

Plate 4a

Dorcas Copper
Lycaena dorcas

ID: Small butterfly; wings of male purplish above, of female brown with faint orange markings at outer edges; underside of hindwings orange, with red zigzag band near edge; wingspan 2.5 cm (1 in).

HABITAT: Meadows, bogs, streamsides; larval food plant cinquefoil.

REGIONS: SC, C

Plate 4b

Northern Blue
Lycaeides idas

ID: Small butterfly; wings of male blue above, of female brown with black lines and orange spots at outer edges; underside of wings gray; wingspan 2.5 cm (1 in).

HABITAT: Alpine tundra, subalpine meadows, edges of bogs; larval food plants legumes such as lupines and milk vetches.

REGIONS: SE, C, N

Plate 4c

Mourning Cloak
Nymphalis antiopa

ID: Large butterfly; wings dark brown above bordered outside by row of blue spots and vivid pale yellow edges; dead-leaf pattern below with pale edge; wingspan 7.5 cm (3 in).

HABITAT: Forest, woodland, riparian, wandering widely; larval food plants willows, birches, poplars.

REGIONS: SC, C, W, N

Plate 4d

White Admiral
Limenitis arthemis

ID: Large butterfly; wings above iridescent dark blue with conspicuous white band across each wing; orange spots on hindwings visible at close range; underwings with same white band but more prominent red-orange spots; wingspan 8 cm (3.1 in).

HABITAT: Deciduous and mixed forest, forest edge, clearings; larval food plants poplars, aspens, other deciduous trees.

REGIONS: C

Plate 4e

Painted Lady
Vanessa cardui

ID: Mid-sized butterfly; wings orange above, heavily marked with black, tips black with large white spots; below vividly patterned brown and white, exposed underside of forewing shows some red; wingspan 5.5 cm (2.2 in).

HABITAT: Open areas where thistles occur; also wandering widely and at times highly migratory; larval food plants very varied, especially thistles, but also mallows, legumes, other plant families.

REGIONS: SE

Plate 4 267

M

a Dorcas Copper

F

F

b Northern
Blue

M

c Mourning Cloak

e Painted Lady

d White Admiral

Plate 5a
Green Comma
Polygonia faunus

ID: Medium-small butterfly with very ragged wing edges; forewings orange above with black and yellow markings, hindwings with less orange, more brown; underwings vary from plain gray to very heavily patterned, some with small greenish spots along edges; wingspan 4.5 cm (1.8 in).

HABITAT: Openings and edges in forest, often along streams; larval food plants varied, including willows, aspens, birches, alders.

REGIONS: C

Plate 5b
Silver-bordered Fritillary
Boloria selene

ID: Medium-small butterfly; wings pale orange above with scattered black markings, outer edges white; hindwing below brown and orange with large silver spots; wingspan 4 cm (1.6 in).

HABITAT: Wet meadows, marshes, and bogs; larval food plants violets.

REGIONS: SC, C

Plate 5c
Common Alpine
Erebia epipsodea

ID: Medium-small butterfly; wings brown above with large orange patches containing rows of black eyespots near outer edges; wings similar below, exposed underside of forewing shows some orange; wingspan 4 cm (1.6 in).

HABITAT: Dry to moist grassy areas, from small forest clearings to extensive prairies; larval food plants grasses.

REGIONS: C

Plate 5d
Melissa Arctic
Oeneis melissa

ID: Medium-small butterfly; wings gray-brown above, very plain; underside of hindwing with fine complex pattern of black and white; wingspan 4 cm (1.6 in).

HABITAT: Open tundra, rocky hillsides and ridges; larval food plants sedges.

REGIONS: SC, C, N

Plate 5   269

a Green Comma

b Silver-bordered Fritillary

c Common Alpine

d Melissa Arctic

Plate 6a

Plumose Anemone
Metridium senile

ID: White, tan, or orange, slender-stalked, clustered intertidal and subtidal anemone with long, slender tentacles; best seen on pilings; height 10 cm (4 in).

HABITAT: Low intertidal and subtidal rocky shores in protected waters.

REGIONS: SE

Plate 6b

Giant Green Anemone
Anthopleura xanthogrammica

ID: Short, fat, green, solitary anemone with short tentacles; green color from symbiotic algae; best seen on rocks; height 30 cm (12 in).

HABITAT: Low intertidal and subtidal rocky shores, most common on exposed coasts.

REGIONS: SE

Plate 6c

Calcareous Tubeworm
Serpula vermicularis

ID: Twisted pencil-sized white calcium carbonate tube attached to rock, with worm inside; undisturbed animal extends crown of red to white, usually banded, gills out of tube for filter feeding; often in clumps; tube to 10 cm (4 in), crown width 2.5 cm (1 in).

HABITAT: Low intertidal and subtidal rocky shores in exposed and protected waters.

REGIONS: SE, SC

Plate 6d

Aggregating Anemone
Anthopleura elegantissima

ID: Small, flat, greenish clustered anemone with short tentacles tipped with pink or purple; best seen on rocks; height 5 cm (2 in).

HABITAT: Intertidal and subtidal rocky shores in exposed and protected waters.

REGIONS: SE, SC

Plate 6 **271**

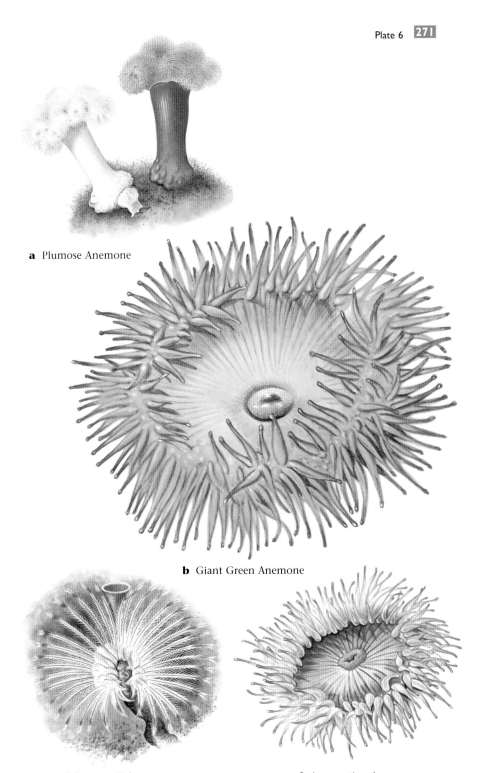

a Plumose Anemone

b Giant Green Anemone

c Calcareous Tubeworm

d Aggregating Anemone

Plate 7a

Giant Pacific Octopus
Octopus dofleini

ID: Unmistakable, largest octopus in world; arms three to five times length of body; variously colored depending on mood; armspread to 3 m (10 ft), largest on record 9.6 m (31 ft).

HABITAT: Low intertidal and subtidal areas of all bottom types, as long as crevice large enough for shelter is present.

REGIONS: SE, SC, SW

Plate 7b

Lion's Mane
Cyanea capillata

ID: Huge brownish to reddish jellyfish with very long tentacles; brown translucent blob when washed up on beach; diameter commonly to 50 cm (20 in), rarely much larger, tentacles to 2.0 m (6.6 ft) long. **Caution:** potent stinging cells on tentacles.

HABITAT: Open ocean and protected bays all along coast.

REGIONS: SE, SC, SW, W

Plate 7c

Red King Crab
Paralithodes camtschaticus

ID: Very large, light brown spiny crab with three pairs of walking legs and pair of feeding legs; body round at rear, pointed at front; carapace width to 28 cm (11 in).

HABITAT: Low intertidal (young only) to deep subtidal waters on variety of bottom types.

REGIONS: SE, SC, SW, W

Plate 7 **273**

b Lion's Mane

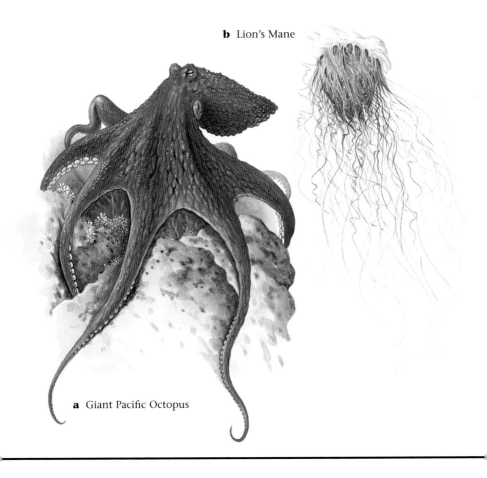

a Giant Pacific Octopus

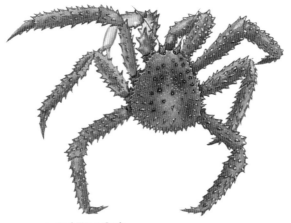

c Red King Crab

Plate 8a

Emarginate Dogwinkle
Nucella emarginata

ID: Thick-shelled, rather pointed snail with narrow aperture; low to prominent white ridges follow shell whorls, fine darker lines between ridges; to 4 cm (1.6 in).

HABITAT: Mid intertidal of exposed and protected rocky shores.

REGIONS: SE, SC

Plate 8b

Sitka Periwinkle
Littorina sitkana

ID: Thick-shelled, rather globular snail with wide aperture; low to prominent ridges follow shell whorls but pattern often does not; uniformly black or purple to brown or gray, plain or banded with orange, yellow, or white; to 2 cm (0.8 in).

HABITAT: High and mid intertidal of exposed and protected rocky shores.

REGIONS: SE, SC, SW, W

Plate 8c

Lined Chiton
Tonicella lineata

ID: Oval, flattened, eight-plated, reddish or purple mollusk with conspicuous lines on plates; girdle extending beyond shell also brightly patterned; large foot holds tightly to rock; to 5 cm (2 in).

HABITAT: Low intertidal to subtidal, usually on rocks, where it feeds on encrusting coralline algae.

REGIONS: SE, SC, SW

Plate 8d

Shield Limpet
Lottia pelta

ID: Cap-shaped (not spiral) snail, with high point just before center of shell; varies from smooth to radiating pattern of elevated ribs; large foot holds tightly to rock; differently colored on rock, mussel bed, and brown alga substrates; to 4 cm (1.6 in).

HABITAT: Mid intertidal of exposed and protected rocky shores.

REGIONS: SE, SC, SW

Plate 8e

Acorn Barnacle
Balanus glandula

ID: Crustacean in a shell, anchored to rock or piling and waving feathery legs in water through calcareous shell valves that open and close; diameter to 2 cm (0.8 in).

HABITAT: High and mid intertidal of rocky exposed and protected shores; attaches to rocks, pilings, and even boats.

REGIONS: SE, SC, SW

Plate 8f

Pacific Blue Mussel
Mytilus trossulus

ID: Blue-black bivalve, attached at narrow end to substrate and widening to bluntly rounded tip; to 13 cm (5 in).

HABITAT: Mid intertidal to subtidal of protected shores, attached to rocks or pilings.

REGIONS: SE, SC, SW, W, N

Plate 8 **275**

a Emarginate Dogwinkle

b Sitka Periwinkle

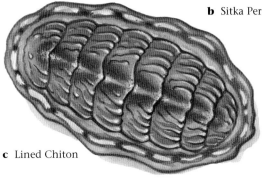

c Lined Chiton

d Shield Limpet   **e** Acorn Barnacle

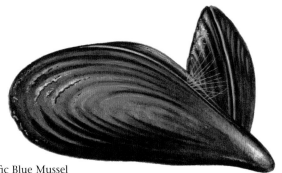

f Pacific Blue Mussel

Plate 9a
Ochre Star
Pisaster ochraceus
ID: Large, thick-armed starfish, usually purple in Alaska but rarely bright ochre (orange), with pattern of raised white bumps all over; diameter to 34 cm (13 in).

HABITAT: Mid intertidal to subtidal of rocky shores, more common on exposed coasts.

REGIONS: SE, SC

Plate 9b
Green Sea Urchin
Strongylocentrotus droebachiensis
ID: Somewhat flattened sphere, with moderate-length greenish spines; diameter to 8 cm (3 in).

HABITAT: Low intertidal to subtidal of all bottom types, more common in protected waters.

REGIONS: SE, SC, SW, W, N

Plate 9c
Red Sea Urchin
Strongylocentrotus franciscanus
ID: Large, somewhat flattened sphere, with long, densely packed, pointed, red to maroon spines; diameter to 17 cm (7 in).

HABITAT: Low intertidal to subtidal of exposed and protected rocky coasts.

REGIONS: SE, SC

Plate 9d
Sunflower Star
Pycnopodia helianthoides
ID: Very large, many-armed (up to 24) starfish, largest of its group in world; usually orange or purplish; fast-moving for starfish; diameter to 90 cm (35 in).

HABITAT: Low intertidal to subtidal of all bottom types, exposed and protected waters.

REGIONS: SE, SC, SW

Plate 9 277

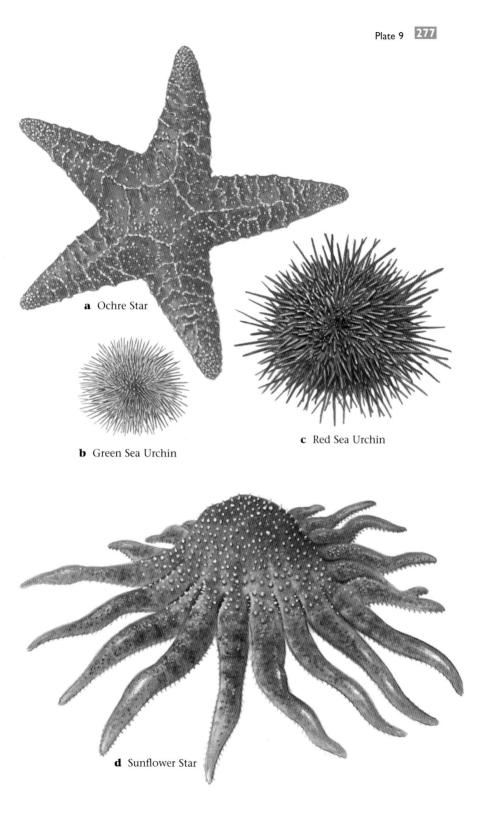

a Ochre Star

b Green Sea Urchin

c Red Sea Urchin

d Sunflower Star

Plate 10a

Alaska Blackfish
Dallia pectoralis

ID: Mottled brown bottom fish with large mouth, large, paddlelike pectoral fins, prominent rounded dorsal and anal fins toward rear, rounded tail; to 33 cm (13 in).

HABITAT: Freshwater; heavily vegetated ponds and marshes, also lakes and rivers with sufficient density of aquatic plants.

REGIONS: SW, C, W, N

Plate 10b

Pacific Lamprey
Entosphenus tridentatus

ID: Slender, eel-like "fish" with round sucking mouth instead of jaws, seven tiny gill openings, and no paired fins; two large dorsal fins toward rear; to 76 cm (30 in).

HABITAT: Anadromous: open ocean, adults ascending lakes and streams to spawn; larvae in gravel on stream bottoms for several years before returning to ocean.

REGIONS: SE, SC, SW, W

Plate 10c

Eulachon
Thaleichthys pacificus

ID: Slender, silvery, schooling fish with adipose fin and long anal fin, deeply forked tail; to 25 cm (10 in).

HABITAT: Anadromous; near shore, ascending coastal rivers to spawn; young move out into open ocean before returning toward shore.

REGIONS: SE, SC, SW, W

Plate 10d

Burbot
Lota lota

ID: Slender, large-mouthed mottled brown fish with very long dorsal and anal fins, rounded tail; long barbel ("whisker") on chin shows relatedness to marine codfish; to 84 cm (33 in).

HABITAT: Freshwater; deep, cold lakes and rivers.

REGIONS: SE, SC, SW, C, W, N

Plate 10e

Ninespine Stickleback
Pungitius pungitius

ID: Tiny, elongate, mottled or barred fish with about nine separated spines down back and three on belly (pelvic fins and first spine of anal fin); body very slender at rear, tail notched; breeding male may develop black belly; to 9 cm (3.5 in).

HABITAT: Anadromous and freshwater; shallow estuaries, rivers, streams, ponds, and lakes, usually in dense vegetation; marine populations move into fresh water to spawn.

REGIONS: SC, SW, C, W, N

Plate 10f

Threespine Stickleback
Gasterosteus aculeatus

ID: Tiny, big-eyed, elongate silvery or mottled or barred fish with three prominent spines down back and three large spines on belly representing pelvic and anal fins; marine populations may have series of bony plates down sides; breeding male develops bright red belly and blue eyes; to 10 cm (4 in).

HABITAT: Marine and freshwater; shallow estuaries, channels, streams, ponds, and lakes, usually over mud or sand bottom where vegetation present.

REGIONS: SE, SC, SW

Plate 10 279

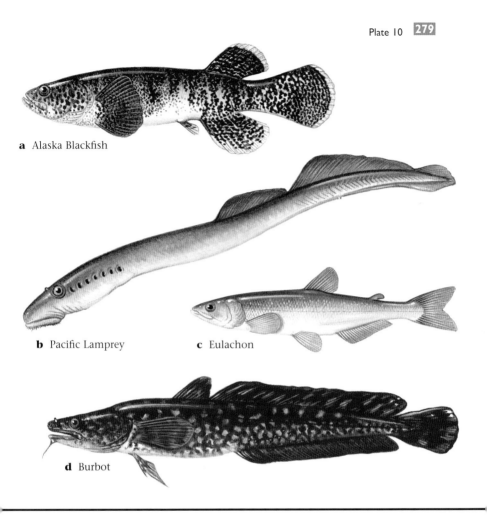

a Alaska Blackfish

b Pacific Lamprey   **c** Eulachon

d Burbot

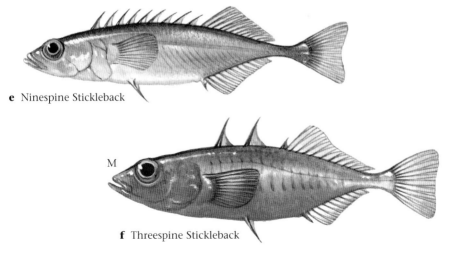

e Ninespine Stickleback

M

f Threespine Stickleback

Plate 11a

Inconnu
Stenodus leucichthys

ID: Silvery-white fish with large mouth, prominent adipose fin, forked tail; largest whitefish, to 125 cm (49 in).

HABITAT: Anadromous and freshwater; shallow estuaries and rivers, also large lakes; marine populations move into rivers to spawn.

REGIONS: C, W, N

Plate 11b

Arctic Grayling
Thymallus signifer

ID: Small-mouthed salmonid with sail-like dorsal fin; blue-gray above, bluish to pinkish on sides, with scattered black dots; to 76 cm (30 in).

HABITAT: Freshwater; clear, cold rivers and lakes, moving into smaller streams to spawn.

REGIONS: SC, SW, C, W, N

Plate 11c

Arctic Char
Salvelinus alpinus

ID: Chars are salmonids (long, streamlined body with relatively small fins and forked tail; share distinctive adipose fin with smelts) with pale instead of dark spots on sides, prominent white line on front of pectoral, pelvic, and anal fins; this species with pink to red spots on back and sides larger than eye; to 96 cm (38 in).

HABITAT: Anadromous and freshwater; coastal waters, rivers, and lakes, marine populations spawning in coastal rivers.

REGIONS: SW, C, W, N

Plate 11d

Dolly Varden
Salvelinus malma

ID: Much like Arctic Char, but red spots, when present, smaller than eye, fewer gill rakers on first arch (14 to 21 *vs* 23 to 32, seen by lifting gill cover); to 91 cm (36 in).

HABITAT: Anadromous and freshwater; coastal waters, ascending clear streams and rivers to spawn; some populations landlocked in lakes.

REGIONS: SE, SC, SW, C, W, N

Plate 11e

Rainbow Trout
Oncorhynchus mykiss

ID: Salmonid with back, sides, and all fins heavily spotted with black; freshwater populations with reddish stripe on sides; anal fin shorter (9 to 12 rays) than those of Pacific salmons (14 or more rays); to 114 cm (45 in).

HABITAT: Anadromous and freshwater; "steelheads" live in coastal waters, ascend coastal streams and rivers to spawn; "rainbows" widely distributed in streams and rivers of all sizes well into interior.

REGIONS: SE, SC, SW

Plate 11 281

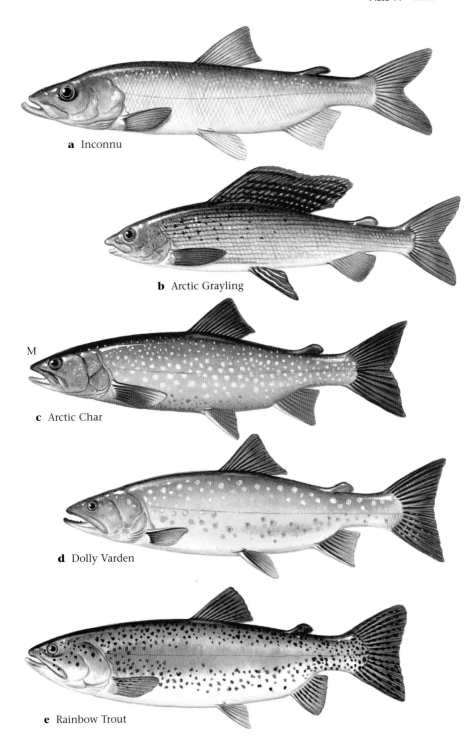

a Inconnu

b Arctic Grayling

M

c Arctic Char

d Dolly Varden

e Rainbow Trout

Plate 12a
Sockeye Salmon
Oncorhynchus nerka
ID: Salmonid lacking black spots; red with green head and white lower jaw when spawning, male with extremely hooked jaws; to 84 cm (33 in).

HABITAT: Anadromous; open ocean, ascending rivers and streams to spawn; also landlocked populations in lakes that spawn in small streams.

REGIONS: SE, SC, SW, W

Plate 12b
Chum Salmon
Oncorhynchus keta
ID: Lacks spots like Sockeye, but pelvic and anal fins white-tipped; reddish blotches or bars on sides when spawning; to 102 cm (40 in).

HABITAT: Anadromous; open ocean, ascending rivers and streams to spawn.

REGIONS: SE, SC, SW, W, N

Plate 12c
Chinook Salmon
Oncorhynchus tshawytscha
ID: Salmonid with irregular black spots on back and entire tail; darker when spawning, often with red suffusion on sides; to 147 cm (58 in).

HABITAT: Anadromous; open ocean, ascending rivers and streams to spawn.

REGIONS: SE, SC, SW, W

Plate 12d
Coho Salmon
Oncorhynchus kisutch
ID: Like Chinook but spots only on upper half of tail; back spotted, sides red when spawning; to 98 cm (39 in).

HABITAT: Anadromous; open ocean, ascending rivers and streams to spawn.

REGIONS: SE, SC, SW, W

Plate 12e
Pink Salmon
Oncorhynchus gorbuscha
ID: Like Chinook with spots on back and entire tail, but much smaller when adult, spots oval; brown above with reddish sides when spawning, male with greatly hooked jaws and huge hump on back; to 76 cm (30 in).

HABITAT: Anadromous; open ocean, ascending lower reaches of rivers to spawn.

REGIONS: SE, SC, SW, W, N

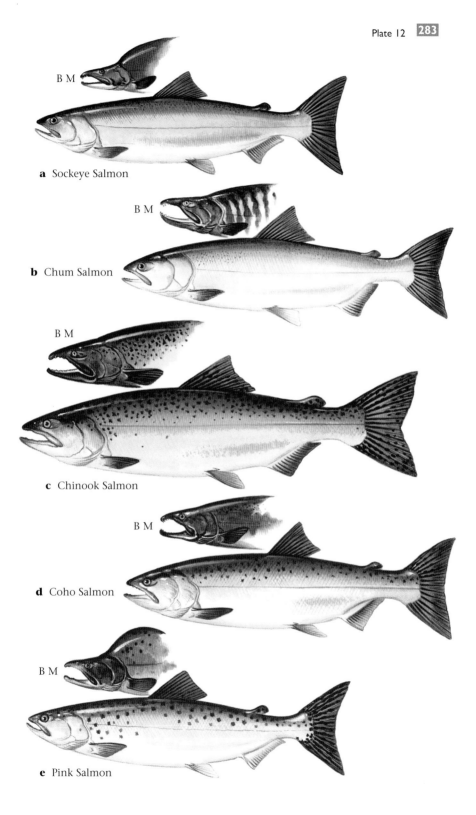

Plate 12 283

B M

a Sockeye Salmon

B M

b Chum Salmon

B M

c Chinook Salmon

B M

d Coho Salmon

B M

e Pink Salmon

Plate 13a
Pacific Staghorn Sculpin
Leptocottus armatus

ID: Stocky, somewhat flattened, large-mouthed, tan to greenish bottom fish with no scales and large fins (pectoral especially large); antlerlike spine projecting from gill cover, black blotch on front dorsal fin; to 46 cm (18 in).

HABITAT: Marine; shallow to moderately deep sand-bottomed bays and estuaries, occasionally moving into fresh water.

REGIONS: SE, SC, SW

Plate 13b
Pacific Ocean Perch
Sebastes alutus

ID: Chunky fish with large fins, first dorsal heavily spined; reddish above, white below, with dusky saddles on back; protruding knob on chin; to 51 cm (20 in).

HABITAT: Marine; deep open waters; best seen in fish markets

REGIONS: SE, SC, SW, W

Plate 13c
Yelloweye Rockfish
Sebastes ruberrimus

ID: As Pacific Ocean Perch but even stockier; bright red, with one or two narrow pale stripes down body; dark edges to posterior dorsal and anal fins and tail; to 91 cm (36 in).

HABITAT: Marine; rocky reefs in deep water; best seen in fish markets.

REGIONS: SE, SC

Plate 13d
Great Sculpin
Myoxocephalus polyacanthocephalus

ID: Chunky, mottled brown bottom fish with very large mouth and large, banded fins; long spine projecting from gill cover; to 76 cm (30 in).

HABITAT: Marine; intertidal to fairly deep waters with sand and mud bottoms.

REGIONS: SE, SC, SW, W

Plate 13e
Wolf-eel
Anarrhichthys ocellatus

ID: Long, sinuous, nightmare-looking bottom fish with large head and fierce-looking teeth, and wrap-around dorsal, caudal, and anal fins; gray to light brown or greenish with dark, pale-ringed spots all over body, more heavily spotted in young; to 203 cm (6.7 ft).

HABITAT: Marine; shallow to deep rocky bottoms.

REGIONS: SE, SC, SW

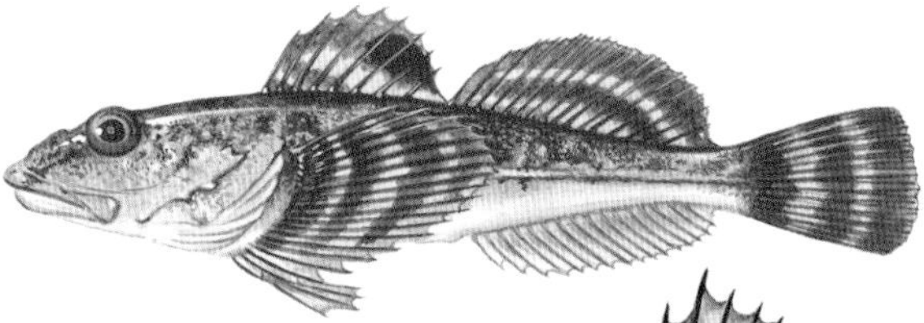

Plate 13   285

a Pacific Staghorn Sculpin

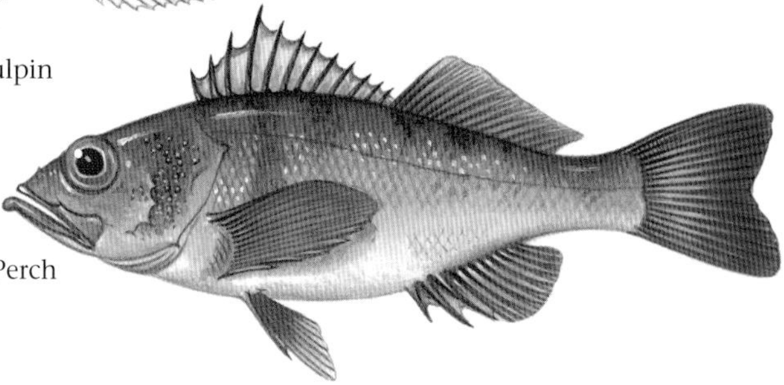

b Pacific Ocean Perch

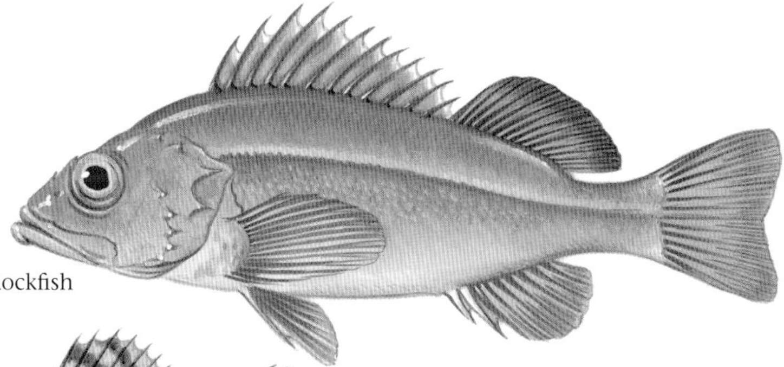

c Yelloweye Rockfish

d Great Sculpin

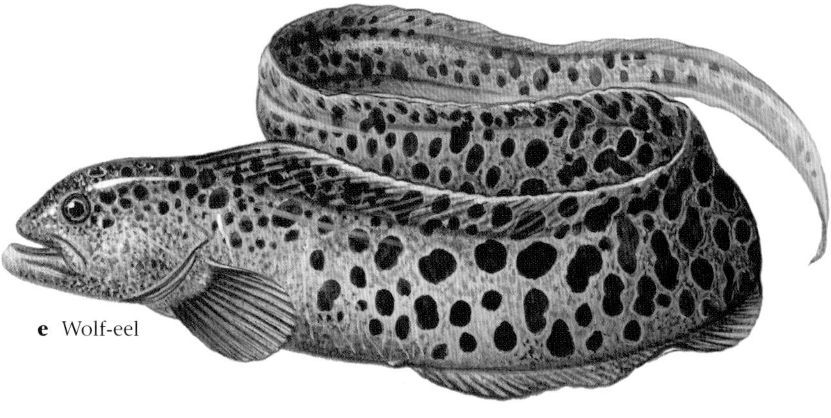

e Wolf-eel

Plate 14a
Petrale Sole
Eopsetta jordani
ID: Flatfish with eyes and color on right side, rounded tail, larger mouth than many other soles; light brown with faint darker blotches on dorsal and anal fins; to 70 cm (28 in).

HABITAT: Marine; moderate to deep sand bottoms; best seen on dinner plates.

REGIONS: SE, SC, SW, W

Plate 14b
Kelp Greenling
Hexagrammos decagrammus
ID: Narrow-bodied bottom fish with split dorsal fin extending over much of back; male olive-brown with scattered irregular blue spots at front, female covered with dark reddish brown spots arranged in wavy lines; to 53 cm (21 in).

HABITAT: Marine; shallow rock and sand bottoms, often among kelp.

REGIONS: SE, SC, SW

Plate 14c
Starry Flounder
Platichthys stellatus
ID: Flatfishes have eyes and color on one side, colorless with no eyes on other side (which rests on bottom); color and eyes may be on either side in this species; brown with distinctive alternating black and yellowish pattern on dorsal and anal fins and tail; to 91 cm (36 in).

HABITAT: Marine; shallow to deep sand bottoms, sometimes ascending lower reaches of rivers.

REGIONS: SE, SC, SW, W, N

Plate 14d
Lingcod
Ophiodon elongatus
ID: Long, slender predatory-looking bottom fish with large head and very large mouth, long dorsal fin typical of greenlings; light brown or gray, with black spots along back and sides; to 152 cm (60 in).

HABITAT: Marine; shallow to deep rock bottoms, young relatively shallow on sand and mud.

REGIONS: SE, SC

Plate 14e
Pacific Halibut
Hippoglossus stenolepis
ID: Very large flatfish with eyes and color on right side, indented tail; brown to blackish, with irregular dark blotches and light mottling; to 2.67 m (8.8 ft).

HABITAT: Marine; relatively deep waters of all bottom types, young shallower; best seen at fishing piers.

REGIONS: SE, SC, SW, W

Plate 14   287

a Petrale Sole

b Kelp Greenling

M

F

c Starry Flounder

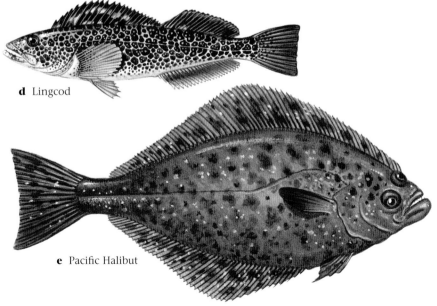

d Lingcod

e Pacific Halibut

Plate 15a
Pacific Herring
Clupea pallasii
ID: Narrow-bodied, large-mouthed, silvery schooling fish with single dorsal fin (no adipose), deeply forked tail; to 46 cm (18 in).

HABITAT: Marine; deep to shallow bays and inlets in large schools, spawning at shore.

REGIONS: SE, SC, SW, W, N

Plate 15b
Pacific Sand Lance
Ammodytes hexapterus
ID: Very long-bodied silvery schooling fish with very long dorsal fin, long anal fin, and forked tail; to 27 cm (11 in).

HABITAT: Marine; near shore in sand bottom or offshore in schools near surface; spawns in intertidal.

REGIONS: SE, SC, SW, W, N

Plate 15c
Pacific Cod
Gadus macrocephalus
ID: Long-bodied fish with three dorsal and two anal fins, large barbel ("whisker") on chin; brown to gray, with faint mottling; to 114 cm (45 in).

HABITAT: Marine; near bottom from shallow to deep water.

REGIONS: SE, SC, SW, W

Plate 15d
Walleye Pollock
Theragra chalcogramma
ID: As Pacific Cod, but more slender, lacking chin barbel, and lower jaw projects in front of upper; mottled brown above, silvery below; to 91 cm (36 in).

HABITAT: Marine; near bottom from shallow to deep water; best seen as *surimi* (simulated shellfish) on dinner table.

REGIONS: SE, SC, SW, W

Plate 15e
Pacific Hake
Merluccius productus
ID: Codlike, but long, notched posterior dorsal and anal fins rather than two separate fins, no chin barbel; mostly silvery, without mottling; to 91 cm (36 in).

HABITAT: Marine; near bottom to midwater, shallow to deep; in schools.

REGIONS: SE, SC, SW, W

Plate 15f
Sablefish
Anoplopoma timbria
ID: Codlike, but with only two well-separated dorsal fins and one anal fin; more slender, with more deeply forked tail; dark above and light below, with faint pale markings on upperside; to 102 cm (40 in).

HABITAT: Marine; adults near bottom in deep water, young considerably shallower but not near shore; best seen in Asian fish markets.

REGIONS: SE, SC, SW, W

Plate 15 **289**

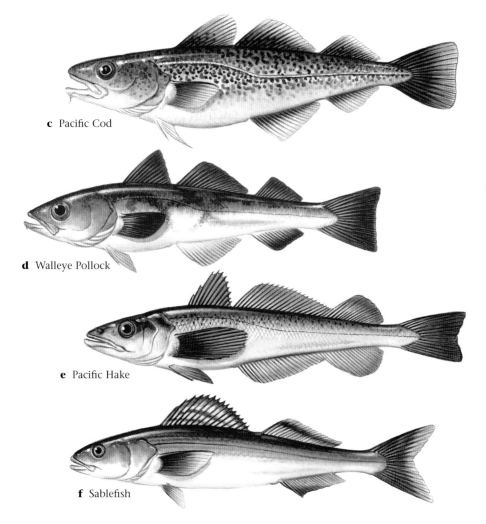

a Pacific Herring

b Pacific Sand Lance

c Pacific Cod

d Walleye Pollock

e Pacific Hake

f Sablefish

Plate 16a
Rough-skinned Newt
Taricha granulosa
ID: Brown, rough-skinned salamander with bright orange belly; to 9 cm (3.5 in) plus 9 cm (3.5 in) tail.

HABITAT: Moist woodland and other habitats near breeding lakes and ponds; usually seen in water but sometimes found travelling overland.

REGIONS: SE

Plate 16b
Long-toed Salamander
Ambystoma macrodactylum
ID: Blackish salamander with yellowish or greenish stripe down back; to 8 cm (3 in) plus 9 cm (3.5 in) tail.

HABITAT: Forest, woodland, or forest edge but must be near breeding pond or lake; most often found by turning over logs and debris.

REGIONS: SE

Plate 16c
Western Toad
Bufo boreas
ID: Squatty, short-legged frog with tubercles ("warts") all over upperparts; dark spots all over, light stripe down middle of back; black tadpoles and tiny dark toadlets often seen in great aggregations; to 10 cm (4 in).

HABITAT: Moist woodland, shrubby, and grassy areas, usually near breeding lakes and ponds but may travel well away from them.

REGIONS: SE

Plate 16d
Columbia Spotted Frog
Rana luteiventris
ID: Long-legged brown frog with prominent black spots above, red-orange on rear of belly and rear of legs; to 7 cm (3 in).

HABITAT: Pond and lake shores, usually seen in water.

REGIONS: SE

Plate 16e
Wood Frog
Rana sylvatica
ID: Long-legged rich or light brown frog with dark face mask; to 7 cm (3 in).

HABITAT: Wetlands and wet meadows; breeds in ponds and lakes but usually seen on land.

REGIONS: SC, C

Plate 16   **291**

a Rough-skinned Newt

b Long-toed Salamander

c Western Toad

d Columbia Spotted Frog

e Wood Frog

Plate 17a
Red-throated Loon
Gavia stellata
ID: Small loon with slender bill held uptilted; neck gray with rufous throat in breeding, gray above and white below in nonbreeding, dusky in juvenile; 58 cm (23 in).

HABITAT: Breeds on ponds and lakes in tundra and forest; winters along south coast, typically in shallow bays.

REGIONS: SE, SC, SW, C, W, N (winter SE, SC, SW)

Plate 17b
Pacific Loon
Gavia pacifica
ID: Small loon with slender bill held horizontal; neck gray above and black below in breeding, white back spots in patches; black above and white below in nonbreeding (hindneck gray in immatures); neck stripe straight; 58 cm (23 in).

HABITAT: Breeds on ponds and lakes in tundra and forest; winters along south coast, typically in deep marine passages.

REGIONS: SC, SW, C, W, N (winter SE, SC, SW)

Plate 17c
Yellow-billed Loon
Gavia adamsii
ID: Large loon like Common but with pale yellow or ivory-white bill held up at angle; in nonbreeding, paler than Common, with dark cheek spot; 76 cm (30 in).

HABITAT: Breeds on lakes in tundra; winters along south coast in all marine habitats.

REGIONS: W, N (winter SE, SC)

Plate 17d
Common Loon
Gavia immer
ID: Large loon with black upperparts uniformly spotted with white, white neck ring ("loon's necklace") in breeding; brown to black above and white below in nonbreeding, with jagged neck stripe; large loons fly higher than small ones; 76 cm (30 in).

HABITAT: Breeds on lakes in forest zone; winters along south coast in all marine habitats.

REGIONS: SE, SC, SW, C, W, N (winter SE, SC, SW)

Plate 17 293

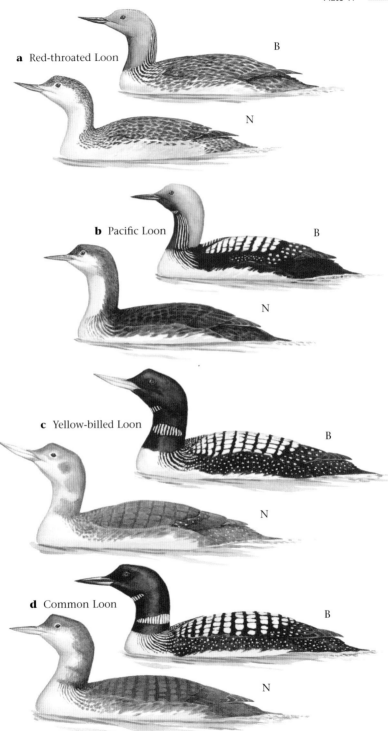

a Red-throated Loon

B

N

b Pacific Loon

B

N

c Yellow-billed Loon

B

N

d Common Loon

B

N

Plate 18a

Red-necked Grebe
Podiceps grisegena

ID: Large grebe with rufous neck and white cheeks in summer, all dull brown in winter; relatively longer neck than loons; 46 cm (18 in).

HABITAT: Breeds on open or marshy lakes and ponds in forest zone; winters along south coast in all marine habitats, often diving in kelp beds.

REGIONS: SC, C, W (winter SE, SC, SW)

Plate 18b

Horned Grebe
Podiceps auritus

ID: Small grebe with rufous neck and golden "horns" in summer, conspicuous white cheeks and foreneck in winter; 32 cm (12.5 in).

HABITAT: Breeds on marshy ponds and lakes in forest zone; winters along south coast in all marine habitats; often associates with diving ducks.

REGIONS: SC, SW, C, W, N (winter SE, SC, SW)

Plate 18c

Leach's Storm-Petrel
Oceanodroma leucorhoa

ID: Small, dark brown, long-winged seabird with conspicuous white rump, fluttering flight; 20 cm (8 in), wingspan 43 cm (17 in).

HABITAT: Breeding colonies in burrows on mostly small islands, where present at night; foraging on open ocean, may be blown near shore in storms.

REGIONS: SE, SW

Plate 18d

Fork-tailed Storm-Petrel
Oceanodroma furcata

ID: Small, light to medium gray, long-winged seabird with fluttering flight; 22 cm (8.5 in), wingspan 43 cm (17 in).

HABITAT: Breeding colonies in burrows or rock crevices on offshore islands, where present at night; foraging and winters on open ocean, may be blown near shore in storms.

REGIONS: SE, SC, SW

Plate 18 **295**

a Red-necked Grebe

B

N

b Horned Grebe

B

N

c Leach's Storm-Petrel

d Fork-tailed Storm-Petrel

Plate 19a
Black-footed Albatross
Phoebastria nigripes
ID: Large dark seabird with heavy, hooked bill, very long wings, gliding flight; older birds are paler on head and around tail; 81 cm (32 in), wingspan 1.9 m (6.2 ft).

HABITAT: Offshore ocean waters; nonbreeding summer visitor from Hawaiian Islands.

REGIONS: SE, SC, SW

Plate 19b
Northern Fulmar
Fulmarus glacialis
ID: Mid-sized seabird with variable color, from almost all white to all dark, not as dark as shearwaters; flies with stiff wingbeat, stubby bill angled down; 41 cm (16 in), wingspan 91 cm (36 in).

HABITAT: Breeding colonies on Bering Sea and Aleutian Island cliffs; foraging and wintering in offshore ocean waters.

REGIONS: SE, SC, SW, W (winter SE, SC, SW)

Plate 19c
Sooty Shearwater
Puffinus griseus
ID: Mid-sized dark, long-winged seabird with stiff wingbeat, whitish underwings, bill more slender, less angled down than fulmar; 43 cm (17 in), wingspan 96.5 cm (38 in).

HABITAT: Offshore ocean waters, mostly south of Aleutians; may be seen from shore; nonbreeding summer visitor from New Zealand.

REGIONS: SE, SC, SW

Plate 19d
Short-tailed Shearwater
Puffinus tenuirostris
ID: Mid-sized dark, long-winged seabird with stiff wingbeat, gray underwings; smaller than Sooty Shearwater, with shorter bill; 35.5 cm (14 in), wingspan 89 cm (35 in).

HABITAT: Offshore ocean waters, North Pacific and Bering Sea; nonbreeding summer visitor from Australia.

REGIONS: SC, SW, W, N

Plate 19   297

a Black-footed Albatross

light
form

b Northern
Fulmar

dark
form

c Sooty Shearwater

d Short-tailed
Shearwater

Plate 20a
Double-crested Cormorant
Phalacrocorax auritus

ID: Large black diving bird with long, hooked bill, yellow-orange bill base and throat; immature with light brown neck and breast; 71 cm (28 in), wingspan 1.07 m (3.5 ft).

HABITAT: Resident in all marine waters and fresh waters near coast, breeding colonies on coastal islands or in trees; cormorants roost on rocks, pilings.

REGIONS: SE, SC, SW (same in winter)

Plate 20b
Pelagic Cormorant
Phalacrocorax pelagicus

ID: Mid-sized glossy black long-tailed diving bird with slender, dark, hooked bill; white patch on flanks during spring; immature dull brownish black; 61 cm (24 in), wingspan 86 cm (34 in).

HABITAT: Resident in coastal marine waters, mostly along rocky coasts; breeding colonies on offshore islands and mainland cliffs.

REGIONS: SE, SC, SW, W (winter SE, SC, SW)

Plate 20c
Red-faced Cormorant
Phalacrocorax urile

ID: Like Pelagic Cormorant but slightly larger, browner wings in flight, bill pale at a distance; compare bill and face colors; immature like Pelagic; 63.5 cm (25 in), wingspan 91 cm (36 in).

HABITAT: Resident in coastal waters of Aleutians and Bering Sea; breeding colonies on islands.

REGIONS: SC, SW (same in winter)

Plate 20 299

a Double-crested Cormorant

IM

b Pelagic
Cormorant

c Red-faced
Cormorant

Plate 21a
Tundra Swan
Cygnus columbianus
ID: Smaller than Trumpeter Swan, usually with yellow at bill base; immature becomes whiter during winter; call higher-pitched, melodious, and varied, like honk of goose; 1.17 m (3.8 ft), wingspan 1.9 m (6.25 ft).

HABITAT: Breeds on tundra, often near lakes; migrates through large lakes, rivers, and marine estuaries.

REGIONS: SW, C, W, N

Plate 21b
Trumpeter Swan
Cygnus buccinator
ID: Very large white bird with very long neck; immature gray through first winter; call low-pitched and monotonous, like trumpet notes; 1.42 m (4.7 ft), wingspan 2.1 m (7 ft).

HABITAT: Breeds on lakes in forest zone; winters sparsely on lakes in south.

REGIONS: SC, C (winter SC)

Plate 21c
Snow Goose
Chen caerulescens
ID: White goose with black wingtips, pink bill and feet; immatures with much gray; aggregate in large flocks; 61 cm (24 in).

HABITAT: Breeds in small colonies on tundra; migrates along coast and locally through interior.

REGIONS: N (migration SE, SC, SW, C, W, N)

Plate 21d
Sandhill Crane
Grus canadensis
ID: Large, long-necked, long-legged, gray wading bird with loud, sonorous calls; immatures without red cap; 81 cm (32 in), wingspan 1.6 m (5.3 ft).

HABITAT: Breeds in marshes on tundra, rarely in forest zone; migrates through marshy wetlands and coastal salt marshes; flocks high in air in migration.

REGIONS: SW, C, W, N (migration SE, SC, SW, C, W, N)

Plate 21   301

a Tundra Swan

c Snow Goose

b Trumpeter Swan

d Sandhill Crane

Plate 22a

Greater White-fronted Goose
Anser albifrons

ID: Large brown goose with yellow-orange bill and feet; adult with white face and variable black belly markings; 66 cm (26 in).

HABITAT: Breeds on tundra; migrates through coastal salt marshes and inland meadows.

REGIONS: SW, C, W, N

Plate 22b

Emperor Goose
Chen canagicus

ID: Large gray goose with white head, black throat, pink bill, and orange feet; immature all gray; white tail conspicuous in flight; 66 cm (26 in).

HABITAT: Breeds on wet tundra near coast; migrates and winters in shallow saltwater bays and along beaches.

REGIONS: SW, W (winter SC, SW)

Plate 22c

Canada Goose
Branta canadensis

ID: Brown goose with black head and neck, white cheeks and throat, black bill and feet; different populations (subspecies) with birds of very different sizes and relative neck lengths; smaller birds have higher-pitched calls; 51 to 81 cm (20 to 32 in).

HABITAT: Breeds at lakes and ponds in forest and tundra, also coastal tundra; migrates through all aquatic habitats, winters on fresh and salt water along south coast.

REGIONS: SE, SC, C, W, N (migration SE, SC, SW, C, W, N)

Plate 22d

Brant
Branta bernicla

ID: Small dark goose with black head and neck, black bill and feet; white rump and undertail coverts conspicuous in flight; 56 cm (22 in).

HABITAT: Breeds on coastal tundra; migrates through coastal bays.

REGIONS: W, N (migration SE, SC, SW, W, N)

Plate 22 **303**

a Greater White-fronted Goose

b Emperor Goose

c Canada Goose

d Brant

Plate 23a
Green-winged Teal
Anas crecca

ID: Small, dark dabbling duck; male with brightly colored head, white vertical slash on side (white line along back in Aleutians), cream patches under tail; fast, twisting flight with green speculum visible; 36 cm (14 in).

HABITAT: Breeds at marshy and open ponds and lakes in forest and tundra; migrates through all freshwater and coastal wetlands; winters on south coastal estuaries.

REGIONS: SE, SC, SW, C, W, N (winter SE, SW)

Plate 23b
Mallard
Anas platyrhynchos

ID: Mid-sized dabbling duck reminiscent of barnyard; male light-colored with green head, white neck ring, rufous breast; blue speculum and white underwings in flight; 56 cm (22 in).

HABITAT: Breeds at marshy and open ponds and lakes in forest and tundra; migrates mostly through freshwater wetlands; winters on south coastal marshes and estuaries.

REGIONS: SE, SC, SW, C, W (winter SE, SC, SW)

Plate 23c
Northern Pintail
Anas acuta

ID: Long-necked, slender-looking, mid-sized dabbling duck; male very slender, with gray body, brown head and long white neck, and long pin tail; slender, with green-brown speculum in flight; M 61 cm (24 in), F 51 cm (20 in).

HABITAT: Breeds at shallow marshes, ponds, and lakes in forest and tundra; migrates through all freshwater and coastal wetlands; winters on south coastal estuaries.

REGIONS: SE, SC, SW, C, W, N (winter SE, SC, SW)

Plate 23d
Northern Shoveler
Anas clypeata

ID: Short-necked, mid-sized dabbling duck with huge bill; male with alternating dark-white-dark-white-dark along waterline; compact in flight, with powder blue wing patch and green speculum; 46 cm (18 in).

HABITAT: Breeds at shallow marshes, ponds, and lakes in forest and tundra; migrates through all freshwater and coastal wetlands; winters on freshwater marshes and coastal estuaries in south.

REGIONS: SC, C, W (migration SE, SC, C, W)

Plate 23 **305**

a Green-winged Teal

M

F

b Mallard

M

F

c Northern Pintail

M

F

d Northern Shoveler

M

F

Plate 24 (*See also*: Waterfowl, p. 117)

Plate 24a
American Wigeon
Anas americana

ID: Mid-sized, reddish brown dabbling duck with small bluish bill; male with white crown, green cheeks; large white wing patch in flight; 46 cm (18 in).

HABITAT: Breeds at shallow marshes, ponds, and lakes in forest and tundra; migrates through all freshwater and coastal wetlands; winters on south coastal estuaries and meadows.

REGIONS: SE, SC, SW, C, W, N (winter SE, SC)

Plate 24b
Greater Scaup
Aythya marila

ID: Mid-sized, large-billed diving duck; male with black head, breast, and rear end, white in middle; female brown with white patch around bill; long white wing stripe in flight; 48 cm (19 in).

HABITAT: Breeds at ponds and lakes in forest and tundra; migrates through freshwater lakes and coastal wetlands; winters on south coastal bays.

REGIONS: SC, SW, C, W, N (winter SE, SC, SW)

Plate 24c
Bufflehead
Bucephala albeola

ID: Small diving duck with puffy head, bluish bill; male black and white with large white head patch, female brown with white cheek patch; male with large, female with small white wing patches in flight; 34 cm (13.5 in).

HABITAT: Breeds in tree holes on lakes and ponds in forest; migrates through freshwater wetlands and all marine waters; winters on south coast and open fresh waters.

REGIONS: SW, C (winter SE, SC, SW)

Plate 24d
Harlequin Duck
Histrionicus histrionicus

ID: Small, small-billed, dark diving duck with pointy tail; male with bright rufous and white markings ("harlequin" is a clown), female very dark with two white cheek patches; all dark in low flight with shallow wingbeats; 41 cm (16 in).

HABITAT: Breeds in rock crevices on rivers and streams, usually in forest; winters on rocky coast south, often resting on rocks.

REGIONS: SE, SC, SW, C, W (winter SE, SC, SW)

Plate 24 **307**

a American Wigeon

F

M

b Greater Scaup

F

M

c Bufflehead

F

M

d Harlequin Duck

F

M

Plate 25a
Common Eider
Somateria mollissima
ID: Large diving duck with heavy head and bill; male mostly white above, black below, female barred brown; 63.5 cm (25 in).

HABITAT: Breeds on rocky coast and islands, also tundra lakes; winters on south coastal waters.

REGIONS: SC, SW, W, N (winter SC, SW)

Plate 25b
King Eider
Somateria spectabilis
ID: Large diving duck with puffy head and bill; male mostly white in front, black behind, with showy, colorful head; female like Common Eider but different bill proportions; 56 cm (22 in).

HABITAT: Breeds on tundra lakes and ponds; winters on south coastal waters.

REGIONS: W, N (winter SC, SW)

Plate 25c
Spectacled Eider
Somateria fischeri
ID: Large diving duck with large head and bill; male mostly white above, black below, with conspicuous white spectacles; female barred brown, shows trace of spectacles; 53 cm (21 in).

HABITAT: Breeds on tundra lakes and ponds; winters in openings in Bering Sea ice.

REGIONS: W, N

Plate 25d
Steller's Eider
Polysticta stelleri
ID: Mid-sized diving duck with smaller bill than other eiders; male garishly black, brown, and white; female darker than other eiders, with feather configuration around bill like other ducks; blue speculum like Mallard in flight; 43 cm (17 in).

HABITAT: Breeds on near-coastal tundra lakes and ponds; winters on south coastal waters.

REGIONS: SW, W, N (winter SC, SW)

Plate 25 **309**

a Common Eider

M

F

b King Eider

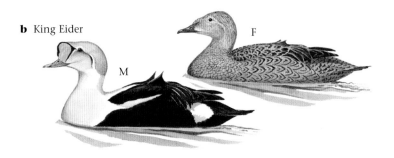

M

F

c Spectacled Eider

M

F

d Steller's Eider

M

F

Plate 26a
Long-tailed Duck
Clangula hyemalis
ID: Mid-sized diving duck with small bill, very long tail in mail; male mostly white in winter, brown in summer with white cheeks; female brown with paler head summer and winter; dark wings contrast with white body in flight; M 53 cm (21 in), F 41 cm (16 in).

HABITAT: Breeds on tundra lakes and ponds; winters on coastal waters, often deeper than other waterfowl.

REGIONS: SC, SW, C, W, N (winter SE, SC, SW, W)

Plate 26b
Black Scoter
Melanitta nigra
ID: Mid-sized, dark diving duck with smaller bill than other scoters; male black with orange bill base; female brown with conspicuous light cheeks; all dark in flight with paler primary feathers; 48 cm (19 in).

HABITAT: Breeds on lakes and ponds in tundra and forest; winters on south coastal waters, often rocky shores.

REGIONS: SC, SW, W (winter SE, SC, SW)

Plate 26c
Surf Scoter
Melanitta perspicillata
ID: Large, dark diving duck with heavy bill; male with brightly marked bill, white patches on head; female brown with pale nape patch; immatures with white cheek spots; all dark in flight; 52 cm (20.5 in).

HABITAT: Breeds on lakes and ponds in tundra and forest; winters on south coastal waters, often rocky shores.

REGIONS: SE, SC, SW, C, W, N (winter SE, SC, SW)

Plate 26d
White-winged Scoter
Melanitta fusca
ID: Large, dark diving duck with heavy bill; male with bill less brightly marked than Surf Scoter, small white patch around eye; adult female all dark brown, immatures with white cheek spots; white wing patch in flight; 56 cm (22 in).

HABITAT: Breeds on lakes and ponds, mostly in forest zone; winters on south coastal waters, especially large bays.

REGIONS: SE, SC, SW, C, W, N (winter SE, SC, SW)

Plate 26 **311**

a Long-tailed Duck

F winter

M winter

M summer

b Black Scoter

M

F

c Surf Scoter

M

F

d White-winged Scoter

M

F

Plate 27a
Common Goldeneye
Bucephala clangula

ID: Mid-sized diving duck with puffy head, short neck; male white with black back and head, white spot before eye; female with dark brown head, gray body; male with large, female with small white wing patches in flight; 48 cm (19 in).

HABITAT: Breeds in tree holes and crevices on lakes and ponds in forest zone; winters on south coastal waters and unfrozen lakes and rivers.

REGIONS: SW, C (winter SE, SC, SW)

Plate 27b
Barrow's Goldeneye
Bucephala islandica

ID: Much like Common Goldeneye but male with more black on back, including dark "finger" on breast, white crescent before eye; female with puffier head, orange bill in spring; 48 cm (19 in).

HABITAT: Breeds in tree holes and crevices on lakes and ponds in forest zone; winters on south coastal waters and unfrozen lakes and rivers.

REGIONS: SE, SC, SW, C (winter SE, SC, SW)

Plate 27c
Common Merganser
Mergus merganser

ID: Large, long-bodied diving duck with slender red bill; male with white (may look peach-colored) body, black back and head; female with gray body, contrasty brown head; male with large, female with small white wing patches in flight; 60 cm (23.5 in).

HABITAT: Breeds in tree holes and crevices on lakes and rivers in forest zone; winters on unfrozen lakes and rivers, also coastal waters.

REGIONS: SE, SC, SW (same in winter)

Plate 27d
Red-breasted Merganser
Mergus serrator

ID: Mid-sized, long-bodied diving duck with very slender orange bill; male contrastingly colored with black head, wispy crests; female with gray-brown body, not contrasty reddish brown head; male with large, female with small white wing patches in flight; 56 cm (22 in).

HABITAT: Breeds on lakes and rivers in tundra zone; winters on south coastal waters.

REGIONS: SE, SC, SW, W (winter SE, SC, SW)

Plate 27 313

a Common Goldeneye

F

M

b Barrow's Goldeneye

F

M

c Common Merganser

F

M

d Red-breasted Merganser

F

M

Plate 28a

Bald Eagle
Haliaeetus leucocephalus

ID: Huge raptor, adult with white head and tail conspicuous at great distance; immatures all dark brown at first with white under wings, increasing amounts of white on belly, then head and tail, as they mature; soars with wings flat, head and tail projecting about equally, hunting fish and birds; 79 to 86 cm (31 to 34 in), wingspan 1.9 m (6.25 ft).

HABITAT: Forests with large nest trees, also coastal areas and islands, where nests can be on ground; widespread but most common at water, with huge concentrations at southeast rivers in winter.

REGIONS: SE, SC, SW, C (winter SE, SC, SW)

Note: Until recently, considered threatened in parts of the USA (Lower 48 states); USA ESA and CITES Appendix I listed.

Plate 28b

Golden Eagle
Aquila chrysaetos

ID: Huge raptor, immatures dark brown with white tail base and white wing patch, both of which they lose with maturity; golden head from second year; soars with wings slightly above horizontal, tail projecting more than head, hunting mammals; 79 to 86 cm (31 to 34 in), wingspan 2 m (6.5 ft).

HABITAT: Resident in open arctic and alpine tundra with nesting cliffs, away from coast; never in large aggregations.

REGIONS: SW, C, W, N

Plate 28c

Osprey
Pandion haliaetus

ID: Large raptor, dark brown above and white below, with dark eyestripe; male with entirely white breast, female with band of short streaks there; soars with wings crooked up, bent in middle; hunting fish; 53 cm (21 in), wingspan 1.5 m (5 ft).

HABITAT: Breeds widely but sparsely at and near fresh and salt water; conspicuous nests on tops of tree trunks, poles.

REGIONS: SE, SC, SW, C

Plate 28d

Northern Harrier
Circus cyaneus

ID: Mid-sized hawk with long, narrow wings and tail, prominent white rump patch; male gray above, white below, superficially like gull in flight but head and tail gray; female brown above, white streaked with brown below; immature reddish brown below; flight low over ground, with uptilted wings, hunting mammals and birds; M 41 cm (17 in), F 48 cm (19 in), wingspan M 91 cm (36 in), F 102 cm (40 in).

HABITAT: Breeds in fresh and salt marshes, meadows, and tundra; migrates widely through open country; winters in coastal marshes and prairies.

REGIONS: SC, SW, C, W

Plate 28 315

a Bald Eagle

IM

c Osprey

b Golden Eagle

F

F

M

d Northern Harrier

Plate 29a

Northern Goshawk
Accipiter gentilis

ID: Large hawk with rounded wings, long tail, prominent white eyestripe; adult gray, heavily barred below; immature brown above, white streaked with brown below; flap and glide flight, pursues grouse and rabbits; M 51 cm (20 in), F 58 cm (23 in), wingspan M 91 cm (36 in), F 99 cm (39 in).

HABITAT: Resident in mature coniferous forest; wanders to other wooded habitats in winter.

REGIONS: SE, SC, SW, C (same in winter)

Plate 29b

Sharp-shinned Hawk
Accipiter striatus

ID: Small hawk with short, rounded wings, long tail; adult gray above, barred reddish below; immature brown above, white striped with brown below; flap and glide flight, agile chaser of small birds; M 27 cm (10.5 in), F 33 cm (13 in), wingspan M 51 cm (20 in), F 58 cm (23 in).

HABITAT: Breeds in coniferous and mixed forest; migrates widely; winters locally in wooded habitats along south coast.

REGIONS: SE, SC, C (winter SE, SC)

Plate 29c

Red-tailed Hawk
Buteo jamaicensis

ID: Large hawk with broad, rounded wings, short tail; adult with reddish tail, immature with brown barred tail; varies from white to black below; "Harlan's" Red-tailed of interior black all over or brown and white, with black and white barred tail; light birds have dark heads; soars with flat wings, looking for rodents; 53 cm (21 in), wingspan 116 cm (46 in).

HABITAT: Breeds in all forest and edge types with trees or cliffs for nesting; migrates widely.

REGIONS: SE, C

Plate 29d

Rough-legged Hawk
Buteo lagopus

ID: Large hawk with broad, rounded wings, fairly short tail; varies from mostly whitish below (adult male) through black-bellied (adult female and immature) to all dark brown (dark form); tail white, with narrow bars in adult female, crisp black tip in adult male, blended dark tip in immature; light birds have light heads; soars with flat wings and hovers in one place, looking for rodents; 53 cm (21 in), wingspan 122 cm (48 in).

HABITAT: Breeds on open tundra, usually nesting on rock outcrops and cliffs; migrates widely through open country.

REGIONS: SW, C, W, N

Plate 29 **317**

a Northern Goshawk

b Sharp-shinned Hawk

c Red-tailed Hawk

light form

light form

dark form

d Rough-legged Hawk

Plate 30a
American Kestrel
Falco sparverius
ID: Small falcon with long, pointed wings and long tail, dark head markings, bright reddish above; male with blue-gray wings, black tail tip; female with reddish wings, evenly barred tail; languid flight after insects, mammals, sometimes birds; often hovers, perches on wires; 25 cm (10 in), wingspan 56 cm (22 in).

HABITAT: Breeds in tree holes or rock crevices in forest zone, foraging in open areas.

REGIONS: C

Plate 30b
Gyrfalcon
Falco rusticolus
ID: Large falcon with long, pointed wings and long tail, head markings more obscure than in Peregrine; varies from blackish through gray-brown (common) to mostly white (rare); tail on perched bird extends farther beyond wingtips than in Peregrine; flight more leisurely than Peregrine, with broader-based wings; M 51 cm (20 in), F 58 cm (23 in), wingspan M 102 cm (40 in), F 112 cm (44 in).

HABITAT: Breeds on tundra where cliffs available for nesting; more widespread in open country, including along coast, in winter.

REGIONS: SW, C, W, N (winter SW, W)

Plate 30c
Merlin
Falco columbarius
ID: Small falcon with long, pointed wings and fairly long tail, striped below with barred flanks; males blue-gray to blackish above, females and immatures brown; head markings more obscure than in kestrel; rapid, powerful flight after birds, never hovers; 28 cm (11 in), wingspan 57 cm (22.5 in).

HABITAT: Breeds in coniferous and mixed forest, often near water; winters sparingly in same habitat, especially near coast.

REGIONS: SW, C

Plate 30d
Peregrine Falcon
Falco peregrinus
ID: Medium-large falcon with long, pointed wings and fairly long tail, strong head markings with thick or thin "mustache;" adult blue-gray above, barred below; immature brown above, streaked below; rapid, powerful flight after birds; M 38 cm (15 in), F 41 cm (17 in), wingspan M 91 cm (36 in), F 102 cm (40 in).

HABITAT: Breeds in forest, tundra, and coastal habitats where cliff ledges available for nesting; migrates widely; winters in coastal forests and islands.

REGIONS: SE, SW (winter SW)

Note: Listed as endangered (USA ESA and CITES Appendix I) but recovering and not globally threatened.

Plate 30 319

a American Kestrel

M

F

b Gyrfalcon

c Merlin

d Peregrine Falcon

Plate 31a
Ruffed Grouse
Bonasa umbellus
ID: Plump gray-brown chickenlike bird with small, pointed crest; gray-brown tail barred with black and with prominent black tip; black neck ruff in both sexes; 41 cm (16 in).

HABITAT: Resident in deciduous woodland, including aspen, poplar, birch, and willow groves and thickets.

REGIONS: C (same in winter)

Plate 31b
Spruce Grouse
Falcipennis canadensis
ID: Plump chickenlike bird with rufous-tipped tail; male gray-brown with black throat and breast, black and white barred belly, red comb over eye; female barred brown and black all over; very tame; 38 cm (15 in).

HABITAT: Resident in conifer forests, including those mixed with birches and poplars; more common in interior.

REGIONS: SC, C (same in winter)

Plate 31c
Rock Ptarmigan
Lagopus mutus
ID: White like Willow Ptarmigan in winter but with narrow black line between eye and bill; bill more slender than that of Willow; male barred brown, black and white, female barred brown in summer, browns more clay-colored, less reddish than in Willow; very tame; 33 cm (13 in).

HABITAT: Resident in arctic and alpine tundra, especially in rocky areas; two ptarmigan species may be found in same areas.

REGIONS: SE, SC, SW, C, W, N (same in winter)

Plate 31d
Willow Ptarmigan
Lagopus lagopus
ID: Plump chickenlike bird with black tail, otherwise entirely white in winter; male rich reddish brown in summer, white with reddish brown head/neck in spring; female barred brown in spring/summer; very tame; 33 cm (13 in).

HABITAT: Resident in arctic and alpine tundra, especially in low willow, alder, and birch thickets.

REGIONS: SE, SC, SW, C, W, N (same in winter)

Plate 31 **321**

a Ruffed Grouse

b Spruce Grouse

M   F

c Rock Ptarmigan

N

B

d Willow Ptarmigan

N

B

Plate 32a

Black Oystercatcher
Haematopus bachmani

ID: Unmistakable large shorebird, all blackish brown with bright red chisel-like bill and pale pinkish feet; flies with wings curved down, often in pairs; 41 cm (16 in).

HABITAT: Resident on rocky and gravelly marine shores and islands.

REGIONS: SE, SC, SW (same in winter)

Plate 32b

Whimbrel
Numenius phaeopus

ID: Large shorebird with long, down-curved bill; all brown with prominent black stripes on head; juvenile with white-spangled upperparts; all brown in flight; 41 cm (16 in).

HABITAT: Breeds in mostly dry tundra; migrates through coastal mudflats.

REGIONS: SC, SW, C, W, N

Plate 32c

Bar-tailed Godwit
Limosa lapponica

ID: Large shorebird with long, slightly upcurved bill; breeding male brown above and dark reddish below, female paler and more heavily barred; juvenile prominently striped above, buffy below; whitish lower back and tail visible in flight; feeds by probing; 41 cm (16 in).

HABITAT: Breeds in wet and dry tundra, mostly near coast; migrates through coastal mudflats.

REGIONS: SW, W, N

Plate 32d

Marbled Godwit
Limosa fedoa

ID: Large shorebird with long, slightly upcurved, pink-based bill; spangled brown and buff above, light reddish brown below; all brown in flight, with rich reddish wings; feeds by probing; 43 cm (17 in).

HABITAT: Breeds in coastal tundra, foraging on nearby mudflats.

REGIONS: SW (rare)

Plate 32 323

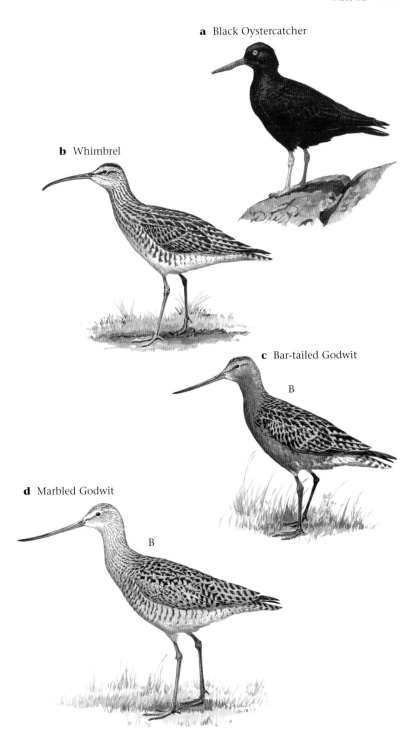

a Black Oystercatcher

b Whimbrel

c Bar-tailed Godwit

B

d Marbled Godwit

B

Plate 33a
Black-bellied Plover
Pluvialis squatarola
ID: Mid-sized shorebird with large head, short bill; breeding male mostly black below with white undertail, spangled black and white above; female duller, brown above and black mixed with white below; juvenile spangled brown and white above, white below with streaks and bars; white wing stripe and white tail in flight; 28 cm (11 in).

HABITAT: Breeds on dry tundra; migrates through mudflats and beaches.

REGIONS: SC, W, N (migration SE, SC, SW, W, N)

Plate 33b
American Golden-Plover
Pluvialis dominica
ID: Medium-small shorebird with large head, short bill; breeding male black and gold above, all black below, white side stripe on head and neck; female duller, black and white below; juvenile spangled brown and gold above, gray with dark streaks and bars below; all brown in flight; 25 cm (10 in).

HABITAT: Breeds on dry tundra; migrates through mudflats, beaches, and fields.

REGIONS: C, W, N (migration SE, SC, SW, C, W, N)

Plate 33c
Pacific Golden-Plover
Pluvialis fulva
ID: Like American Golden-Plover but slightly shorter wings don't project as far beyond tail tip; male with more white on sides and under tail; female and juveniles very similar; 25 cm (10 in).

HABITAT: Breeds on dry lowland and alpine tundra, more often near coast than American Golden-Plover; migrates through mudflats, sandy beaches, and fields.

REGIONS: W (migration SC, W)

Plate 33d
Semipalmated Plover
Charadrius semipalmatus
ID: Small shorebird with short bill and yellow-orange legs; brown above, white below, with conspicuous breast band black in breeding adults, brown in juveniles; conspicuous white wing stripe and tail edges in flight; 18 cm (7 in).

HABITAT: Breeds on tundra, rivers, and lakes; migrates through mudflats and sandy beaches.

REGIONS: SE, SC, SW, C, W, N

Plate 33 **325**

a Black-bellied Plover

B

N

b American
Golden-Plover

B

J

c Pacific Golden-Plover

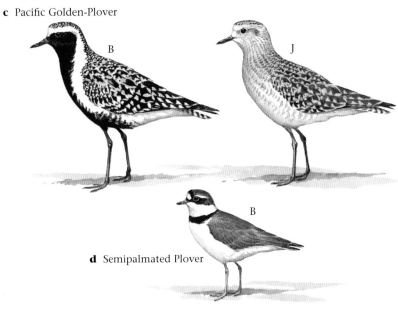

B

J

B

d Semipalmated Plover

Plate 34a
Greater Yellowlegs
Tringa melanoleuca
ID: Mid-sized shorebird with moderate length straight or slightly upcurved bill and long yellow legs, gray-brown above and white below; breeding adults heavily marked with black above and on sides; juveniles with white spangles above but no black on back or sides; wades and runs in shallow water with head-bobbing; dark wings, white rump and tail, three-noted call in flight; 30.5 cm (12 in).

HABITAT: Breeds in marshy meadows in forest zone; migrates through freshwater wetlands, estuaries, and mudflats.

REGIONS: SE, SC, SW

Plate 34b
Lesser Yellowlegs
Tringa flavipes
ID: Much like Greater Yellowlegs but smaller, with shorter (no longer than head), straight bill; two-noted flight call; 27 cm (10.5 in).

HABITAT: Breeds in marshy meadows in forest; migrates through freshwater wetlands, estuaries, and mudflats.

REGIONS: SC, C, W (migration SE, SC, C, W)

Plate 34c
Spotted Sandpiper
Actitis macularia
ID: Small shorebird with straight, yellow-based bill and short yellow legs; breeding adults flecked with black above and heavily spotted below, females more so than males; juveniles unspotted and with white barring on wing coverts; bobs rear end of body up and down, sometimes constantly; white wing stripes in flight don't reach wing base or tip; 17 cm (6.75 in).

HABITAT: Breeds on lakes, ponds, and rivers, and coastal beaches; migrates through freshwater wetlands and sandy, muddy, and rocky marine shores; nonflocking.

REGIONS: SF, SC, SW, C, W, N

Plate 34d
Wandering Tattler
Heteroscelus incanus
ID: Medium-small gray shorebird with straight bill, short yellow legs; breeding adults barred below, juveniles unbarred; all gray in flight; 28 cm (11 in).

HABITAT: Breeds on gravelly streams in alpine tundra; migrates through rocky marine shores; nonflocking.

REGIONS: SC, C, W (migration SE, SC, SW, C, W)

Plate 34　327

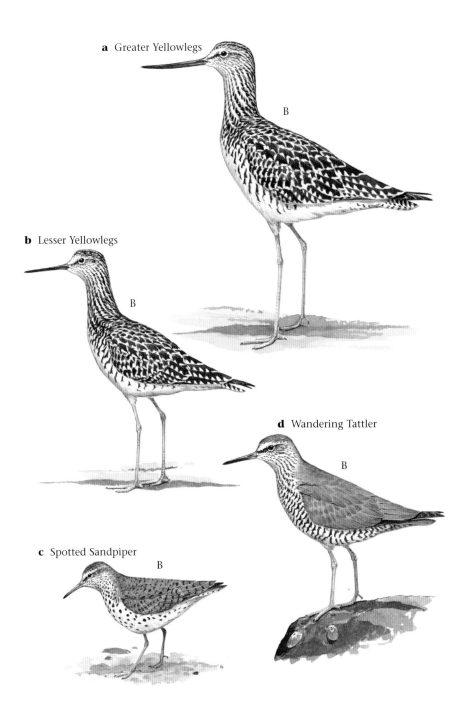

a Greater Yellowlegs

B

b Lesser Yellowlegs

B

d Wandering Tattler

B

c Spotted Sandpiper

B

Plate 35a

Ruddy Turnstone
Arenaria interpres

ID: Small shorebird with short, wedge-shaped bill and short orange legs; breeding adult vividly marked with black and orange; juvenile more subdued browns; brown, black and white harlequin back and wing pattern in flight; 23 cm (9 in).

HABITAT: Breeds on dry tundra; migrates through sandy, muddy, and rocky marine shores.

REGIONS: SW, W, N (migration SE, SC, SW, W, N)

Plate 35b

Black Turnstone
Arenaria melanocephala

ID: Small shorebird with short, wedge-shaped bill and short brownish orange legs; breeding adult with white markings on head and breast; juvenile duller, without those white markings; black and white harlequin back and wing pattern in flight; 23 cm (9 in).

HABITAT: Breeds on wet tundra; migrates through and winters locally on rocky and sandy marine shores.

REGIONS: SC, SW, W (migration SE, SC, SW, W)

Plate 35c

Surfbird
Aphriza virgata

ID: Medium-small shorebird with short bill and short yellow legs; breeding adult with orange to cream spots on back, conspicuous black chevrons below; winter adult gray, with white belly; juvenile similar with white feather edgings on back; conspicuous white wing stripe and white tail base in flight; 25 cm (10 in).

HABITAT: Breeds on dry alpine tundra; migrates through and winters locally on rocky shores.

REGIONS: SC, C (migration SE, SC, C)

Plate 35d

Rock Sandpiper
Calidris ptilocnemis

ID: Small shorebird with moderate-length, slightly drooped bill and short legs; breeding adult with much reddish above, dark cheek patch and breast smudge, and dark legs; winter adult gray with white belly, spotted sides, and yellow legs; juvenile browner; conspicuous white wing stripe, white sides of rump in flight; 21 cm (8.25 in).

HABITAT: Breeds on tundra; migrates through and winters on rocky marine shores (mudflats in Pribilofs).

REGIONS: SW, W (migration SE, SC, SW, W)

Plate 35 **329**

a Ruddy Turnstone

J

B

b Black Turnstone

B

c Surfbird

B

N

d Rock Sandpiper

B

N

Plate 36 (*See also*: Shorebirds, p. 129)

Plate 36a

Semipalmated Sandpiper
Calidris pusilla

ID: Very small shorebird with short, thick bill, black legs; breeding adult marked with brown and black on back, heavily streaked breast; juvenile with buffy to white breast; narrow white wing stripe, white sides of rump in flight; 15 cm (6 in).

HABITAT: Breeds on tundra; migrates through mudflats and freshwater wetlands.

REGIONS: W, N (migration SC, C, W, N)

Plate 36b

Western Sandpiper
Calidris mauri

ID: Very small shorebird with moderate-length, slender bill, black legs; breeding adult marked with reddish and black on head and back, dark markings on side; juvenile with buffy to white breast, no markings on side; as Semipalmated in flight; 16.5 cm (6.5 in).

HABITAT: Breeds on tundra; migrates through mudflats, sandy beaches, and freshwater wetlands.

REGIONS: SC, W, N (migration SE, SC, SW, W, N)

Plate 36c

Least Sandpiper
Calidris minutilla

ID: Very small shorebird with short, slender bill, yellow legs; breeding adult with rich brown markings on back, heavily streaked breast; juvenile with white lines on back, unstreaked buffy breast; as Semipalmated in flight; 14 cm (5.5 in).

HABITAT: Breeds on wet tundra and muskeg; migrates through freshwater wetlands and mudflats.

REGIONS: SE, SC, SW, C, W, N

Plate 36d

Baird's Sandpiper
Calidris bairdii

ID: Small, long-winged shorebird with short, straight bill, black legs; breeding adult with rich brown markings on back, heavily streaked breast; juvenile with buff scallops on back; as Semipalmated in flight; 18 cm (7 in).

HABITAT: Breeds on dry tundra; migrates through freshwater wetlands, including alpine lakes, and mudflats.

REGIONS: C, W, N (migration SE, SC, SW, C, W, N)

Plate 36 **331**

a Semipalmated Sandpiper

B

b Western Sandpiper

B

c Least Sandpiper

B

d Baird's Sandpiper

B

Plate 37a
Pectoral Sandpiper
Calidris melanotos
ID: Small shorebird with short, straight bill, yellow legs, heavily streaked breast sharply demarcated from white belly; breeding adult with brown back, juvenile with reddish and white markings above; narrow white wing stripe, white sides of rump in flight; M 22 cm (8.5 in), F 20 cm (8 in).

HABITAT: Breeds on wet tundra; migrates through freshwater wetlands and mudflats.

REGIONS: C, W, N (migration SE, SC, SW, C, W, N)

Plate 37b
Common Snipe
Gallinago gallinago
ID: Medium-small shorebird with very long bill, vivid stripes on head and back, white belly; all dark above in rapid, high escape flight, *scaip* call; 27 cm (10.5 in).

HABITAT: Breeds in and migrates through freshwater marshes, occasionally in salt marshes; nonflocking.

REGIONS: SE, SC, SW, C, W, N (winter SE)

Plate 37c
Short-billed Dowitcher
Limnodromus griseus
ID: Medium-small shorebird with very long bill, greenish legs; breeding adult all reddish and spotted below; juvenile with buff breast and unspotted white belly; plain wings, conspicuous white wedge up back, multinoted *tu-tu-tu* call in flight; 27 cm (10.5 in).

HABITAT: Breeds on marshy meadows in forest zone; migrates through freshwater wetlands and mudflats.

REGIONS: SC, SW (migration SE, SC, SW)

Plate 37d
Long-billed Dowitcher
Limnodromus scolopaceus
ID: Much like Short-billed Dowitcher but bars on sides of breast in breeding plumage; much plainer above in juvenile plumage; similar in flight but single *peep* call; 28 cm (11 in).

HABITAT: Breeds on low tundra; migrates through freshwater wetlands and mudflats.

REGIONS: C, W, N (migration SE, SC, SW, C, W, N)

Plate 37 **333**

a Pectoral Sandpiper

B

b Common Snipe

J

c Short-billed Dowitcher →

B

B

d Long-billed Dowitcher

Plate 38a

Dunlin
Calidris alpina

ID: Small shorebird with moderate-length droopy bill, black legs; breeding adult with rich reddish back, pale breast and large black belly patch; juvenile similar but duller, more streaky; winter adult gray-brown with white belly; conspicuous white wing stripe, white sides of rump in flight; 21 cm (8.25 in).

HABITAT: Breeds on wet tundra; migrates through and rarely winters on mudflats and sandy beaches.

REGIONS: SW, W, N (winter SE, SC, SW)

Plate 38b

Sanderling
Calidris alba

ID: Small shorebird with short, straight bill, black legs; only sandpiper to lack hind toe; breeding adults orangey-brown with white belly; winter adults very pale gray-brown above, white below; juveniles with black and white spangles on back, white below; as Dunlin in flight; 19 cm (7.5 in).

HABITAT: Breeds rarely on northern tundra; migrates through sandy and rocky beaches, less often mudflats.

REGIONS: SC (migration SE, SC, SW, W, N)

Plate 38c

Red-necked Phalarope
Phalaropus lobatus

ID: Small swimming shorebird occasionally seen on shore; slender, black bill and very short legs with lobed toes; breeding adult with dark head, white throat, and reddish neck patch (all brighter in female), dark back; nonbreeding adult gray above, white below, with vivid black ear patch; juvenile light-striped above; conspicuous white wing stripe, white sides of rump in flight; 18 cm (7.25 in).

HABITAT: Breeds on ponds in tundra and forest; migrates through lakes, estuaries, and open ocean.

REGIONS: SE, SC, SW, C, W, N

Plate 38d

Red Phalarope
Phalaropus fulicaria

ID: Small swimming shorebird rarely seen on shore; short, fairly thick bill and very short legs with lobed toes; breeding adult with dark cap, white face, dark, buff-striped, back, and reddish underparts (duller and washed-out in male); nonbreeding adult pale gray above, white below, with vivid black ear patch; juvenile light-striped above; as Red-necked in flight; 22 cm (8.5 in).

HABITAT: Breeds on tundra ponds; migrates over open ocean.

REGIONS: SW, W, N (migration SC, SW, W, N)

Plate 38 **335**

a Dunlin

B

N

b Sanderling

B

N

c Red-necked Phalarope

J

B F

d Red Phalarope

J

B F

Plate 39a

Pomarine Jaeger
Stercorarius pomarinus

ID: Gull-like seabird with dark cap, back, and wings, white flash near wingtip, long, blunt central tail feathers; either white below or entirely dark; juvenile with barred wings and body, lacks long central tail feathers; flight heavy, like big gull; 56 cm (22 in), wingspan 1.07 m (3.5 ft).

HABITAT: Breeds on wet tundra; migrates along shore and over open ocean.

REGIONS: SW, N (migration SE, SC, SW, W, N)

Plate 39b

Long-tailed Jaeger
Stercorarius longicaudus

ID: Smaller than Parasitic Jaeger, with longer central tail feathers, paler gray back and darker gray belly, no dark form; less white in wings; juvenile like Parasitic but more gray-brown, with central tail feathers rounded; flight light, ternlike; 51 cm (20 in), wingspan 96.5 cm (38 in).

HABITAT: Breeds on wet lowland and dry alpine tundra; migrates over open ocean.

REGIONS: SW, C, W, N

Plate 39c

Parasitic Jaeger
Stercorarius parasiticus

ID: Much like Pomarine Jaeger, but smaller, with long central tail feathers pointed; juvenile like Pomarine but slightly elongate central tail feathers pointed; all jaegers chase other seabirds to rob them; 51 cm (20 in), wingspan 1.02 m (3.3 ft).

HABITAT: Breeds on wet tundra; migrates along shore and over open ocean.

REGIONS: SE, SC, SW, W, N

Plate 39 **337**

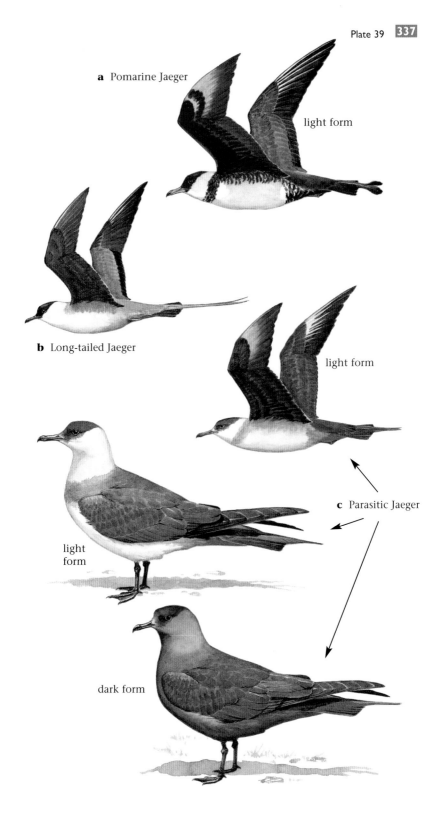

a Pomarine Jaeger

light form

b Long-tailed Jaeger

light form

c Parasitic Jaeger

light form

dark form

Plate 40a

Bonaparte's Gull
Larus philadelphia

ID: Small gull with tiny, black bill; adult with extensive white wingtips bordered behind by black, red-orange legs, black head in summer, black ear spot in winter; immature with striped wing pattern, black tail tip, yellow legs; light ternlike flight; 34 cm (13.5 in), wingspan 74 cm (29 in).

HABITAT: Breeds on lakes and ponds in forest zone, nest in trees; migrates through all marine habitats.

REGIONS: SE, SC, SW, C, W

Plate 40b

Mew Gull
Larus canus

ID: Medium-small gull with small bill; adult medium-gray above with black wingtips, yellow bill and legs; head white in summer, heavily mottled with gray in winter; immature light brown with darker wingtips and tail, pink-based bill and pinkish legs; gray back, white underparts, narrow black tail tip in second year; large white spots in black wingtips of adult distinctive in flight; 42 cm (16.5 in), wingspan 1.02 m (3.3 ft).

HABITAT: Breeds on lakes, ponds, rivers, and islands in forest zone; migrates through and winters in all marine habitats.

REGIONS: SE, SC, SW, C, W (winter SE, SC, SW)

Plate 40c

Glaucous-winged Gull
Larus glaucescens

ID: Large gull with large bill; adult light gray above with gray wingtips, yellow bill with red spot, pink legs; head white in summer, mottled with gray in winter; juvenile light brown all over with black bill, pink legs; changes gradually until maturity at 4 years; gray wingtips of adult distinctive in flight; 53 cm (21 in), wingspan 1.37 m (4.5 ft).

HABITAT: Breeds on low sandy and high rocky coastal islands; migrates through and winters in all marine habitats, also well up lowland rivers and in cities and towns.

REGIONS: SE, SC, SW, W (winter SE, SC, SW)

Plate 40d

Glaucous Gull
Larus hyperboreus

ID: Large gull with large bill; adult light gray above with white wingtips, yellow bill with red spot, and pink legs; juvenile light cream or white with brown flecks all over, bill bright pink with conspicuous black tip; 58 cm (23 in), wingspan 1.47 m (4.8 ft).

HABITAT: Breeds on coastal cliffs, islands, and lakes in tundra; migrates through and locally winters in all marine habitats.

REGIONS: SW, W, N (winter SW)

Plate 40 **339**

a Bonaparte's Gull

B

N

B

b Mew Gull

J

c Glaucous-winged Gull

J

B

d Glaucous Gull

B

Plate 41a

Black-legged Kittiwake
Rissa tridactyla

ID: Medium-small gull with black legs; adult with yellow bill, white head in summer, black half-collar in winter, sharply defined black wingtips; immature with black stripes extending length of wings, black tail tip, black bill; choppy wingbeat compared with other gulls; 41 cm (17 in), wingspan 96.5 cm (38 in).

HABITAT: Breeds on coastal cliffs and islands, foraging widely over ocean; winters in all marine habitats.

REGIONS: SE, SC, SW, W, N (winter SE, SC, SW)

Plate 41b

Sabine's Gull
Xema sabini

ID: Small gull with contrastingly patterned wings; breeding adult gray above with dark gray head, black bill with yellow tip; juvenile brown above with black tail tip, black bill; light ternlike flight; 33 cm (13 in), wingspan 74 cm (29 in).

HABITAT: Breeds on tundra ponds and lakes; migrates over open ocean and through inshore waters.

REGIONS: SW, W, N (migration SC, SW, W, N)

Plate 41c

Arctic Tern
Sterna paradisaea

ID: Mid-sized tern, pale gray with white rear and underwings, black cap, red-orange bill, very long outer tail feathers; juvenile brown-barred above with shorter tail, black bill and black on rear of head; very dainty flight; 37 cm (14.5 in), wingspan 71 cm (28 in).

HABITAT: Breeds on ponds, lakes, and coastal beaches; migrates through inshore waters and over open ocean.

REGIONS: SE, SC, SW, C, W, N

Plate 41d

Aleutian Tern
Sterna aleutica

ID: Much like Arctic Tern but black bill, white forehead, darker gray back and underparts contrast with white rump and tail; juvenile similar to Arctic but darker overall, no black on rear of head; 36 cm (14 in), wingspan 71 cm (28 in).

HABITAT: Breeds on coastal islands, lakes, and rivers; migrates over open ocean.

REGIONS: SC, SW, W

Plate 41 **341**

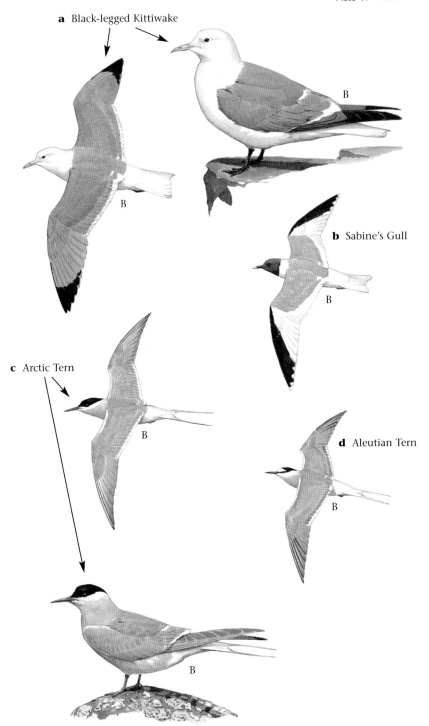

a Black-legged Kittiwake

B

B

b Sabine's Gull

B

c Arctic Tern

B

d Aleutian Tern

B

B

Plate 42a

Common Murre
Uria aalge

ID: Large alcid, looks black above and white below; breeding adult with black head and breast; winter adult and juvenile with white throat and breast, dark stripe behind eye; fine dark streaks on sides; football-shaped in flight, all alcids with very rapid wingbeat; 41 cm (17 in).

HABITAT: Breeds on coastal and island cliffs, foraging at sea; winters on all marine waters.

REGIONS: SE, SC, SW, W (same in winter)

Plate 42b

Thick-billed Murre
Uria lomvia

ID: Much like Common Murre but with blacker back, lacks fine streaks on sides; white line on bill in adult visible at close range, also white V of breast farther up on neck than in Common in summer; entirely dark cap down to eye in winter adult and juvenile; blacker back evident in flight; 41 cm (16 in).

HABITAT: Breeds on coastal and island cliffs, foraging at sea; winters on marine waters, especially offshore.

REGIONS: SW, W (same in winter)

Plate 42c

Horned Puffin
Fratercula corniculata

ID: Large alcid, black above and white below; breeding adult has white face, especially large red and yellow bill; winter adult loses red bill base, has pale gray patch on head; juvenile similar but with smaller bill; like murre in flight, but pale face and blocky-looking head; 37 cm (14.5 in).

HABITAT: Breeds in rock crevices and burrows on coastal cliffs and islands, foraging offshore; winters offshore.

REGIONS: SC, SW, W (winter SW)

Plate 42d

Tufted Puffin
Fratercula cirrhata

ID: Large black alcid with large, colorful bill; breeding adult has white head with yellow tufts, huge yellow and orange bill; winter adult with dark head, loses yellow at bill base; juvenile all dark, much smaller dull yellow bill; often flies around boats; 38 cm (15 in).

HABITAT: Breeds in burrows and rock crevices on coastal cliffs and islands, foraging offshore; winters offshore.

REGIONS: SE, SC, SW, W (winter SW)

Plate 42   343

b Thick-billed Murre

a Common Murre

c Horned Puffin

d Tufted Puffin

Plate 43a
Pigeon Guillemot
Cepphus columba

ID: Mid-sized alcid with dark, slender bill, large white patch on wing, and bright red-orange mouth lining and feet; breeding adult all black except for wing patch; winter adult mostly whitish; juvenile dark brown above, white below, somewhat murrelike but with small wing patch; white wing patches distinctive in flight; 33 cm (13 in).

HABITAT: Breeds in rock crevices and burrows on coastal cliffs and islands and on beams under docks and bridges, foraging near shore; winters in all inshore marine waters.

REGIONS: SE, SC, SW, W (winter SE, SC, SW)

Plate 43b
Marbled Murrelet
Brachyramphus marmoratus

ID: Small alcid with dark, slender bill; breeding adult all dark brown with white barring on underparts; winter adult black above, white below, with white stripe on either side of back; juveniles similar but more mottled; singles or pairs fly very fast and low with almost beelike flight, rocking from side to side; characteristic high-pitched calls heard over coastal forests at night; 23.5 cm (9.25 in).

HABITAT: Breeds in trees in old-growth forest near coast and on ground on treeless islands; forages and winters in all inshore marine waters; occasionally on freshwater lakes near coast during breeding.

REGIONS: SE, SC, SW (same in winter)

Note: Considered threatened in parts of USA (Washington, Oregon, and California); USA ESA listed.

Plate 43c
Ancient Murrelet
Synthliboramphus antiquus

ID: Small gray and white alcid with dark head and short, yellowish bill; breeding adult with white streaks on black head; winter adult and juvenile without streaks, juvenile often with white throat; flies without rocking motion of Marbled, small flocks may dive directly into sea; 24 cm (9.5 in).

HABITAT: Breeds in burrows on forested and open islands, foraging near shore; winters in offshore and inshore marine waters.

REGIONS: SE, SC, SW (same in winter)

Plate 43d
Rhinoceros Auklet
Cerorhinca monocerata

ID: Mid-sized dark brown alcid with white eye, restricted white belly (not visible at waterline), and thick, pale bill; summer adult with "rhinoceros" horn at base of orange bill, white facial stripes; winter adult lacks these ornaments; juvenile smaller, with smaller bill; 33 cm (13 in).

HABITAT: Breeds in burrows on south coastal islands, foraging on nearby waters.

REGIONS: SE

Plate 43   345

a Pigeon Guillemot

B

N

b Marbled Murrelet

B

N

c Ancient Murrelet

B

d Rhinoceros Auklet

B

Plate 44a

Parakeet Auklet
Aethia psittacula

ID: Small black and white alcid with white eye and round, red bill; winter adult and juvenile have white foreneck and breast; wings look relatively broad in flight; 25 cm (10 in).

HABITAT: Breeds in rock crevices on coastal islands; winters offshore.

REGIONS: SC, SW, W (winter SW)

Plate 44b

Least Auklet
Aethia pusilla

ID: Tiny black and white alcid with white eye and short, thick bill; breeding adult with white plume behind eye, belly varies from pure white to mottled; winter adult and juvenile without plume; 15 cm (6 in).

HABITAT: Breeds in rock crevices on coastal islands; winters offshore; incredibly abundant at breeding colonies

REGIONS: SW, W (winter SW)

Plate 44c

Whiskered Auklet
Aethia pygmaea

ID: Tiny gray-brown alcid with white eye, tall plume on crown, white facial stripes, and short, thick, reddish bill; winter adult with less-developed plumes and crest, juvenile with none; 18 cm (7 in).

HABITAT: Breeds in rock crevices on coastal islands; winters offshore; very local breeder.

REGIONS: SW

Plate 44d

Crested Auklet
Aethia cristatella

ID: Small gray-brown alcid with white eye, prominent head plume, white facial stripes, and short, thick, reddish bill; winter adult with smaller bill, no face stripes; juvenile with no plume or stripes and even smaller, dark bill; 25 cm (10 in).

HABITAT: Breeds in rock crevices on coastal islands; winters offshore; fantastically abundant at breeding colonies, sometimes flying around and around above colony in swarms.

REGIONS: SW, W (winter SW)

Plate 44 **347**

a Parakeet Auklet

B

b Least Auklet

B

c Whiskered Auklet

B

d Crested Auklet

B

Plate 45a

Short-eared Owl
Asio flammeus

ID: Mid-sized buffy-brown owl with short head tufts; pale, heavily streaked underparts; in flight shows buffy wing patches from above and black markings on wings from below; 34 cm (13.5 in).

HABITAT: Breeds on low tundra and all grassland and meadow types; migrates through all open country, including beaches and tide flats; active during day, especially at dusk and dawn, in mothlike flight over open areas, hunting rodents.

REGIONS: SC, SW, C, W, N

Plate 45b

Snowy Owl
Nyctea scandiaca

ID: Large, mostly white owl without head tufts; adult male almost pure white, female with much fine barring, juvenile heavily barred with brown, contrasting white face; 58 cm (23 in), wingspan 1.32 m (4.3 ft).

HABITAT: Breeds on tundra; migrates through and winters in any open habitats, including meadows and beaches; perches on ground, fences, poles, buildings; active day and night, hunting rodents and birds.

REGIONS: W, N (winter SC, SW, W)

Plate 45c

Great Horned Owl
Bubo virginianus

ID: Large owl with prominent head tufts (sometimes folded down); looks dark and mottled brown all over, with finely barred underparts, reddish face, and white throat visible at close range; about five (male) or eight (female) loud hoots with syncopated rhythm; 56 cm (22 in), wingspan 1.22 m (4 ft).

HABITAT: Resident in all forest types with larger trees or cliffs for nesting; wanders elsewhere during winter; active at night, hunting varied prey.

REGIONS: SE, SC, SW, C, W (same in winter)

Plate 45d

Great Gray Owl
Strix nebulosa

ID: Large gray owl with huge facial disk with concentric rings, no head tufts; moderately long tail; voice very deep single hoots; 61 cm (24 in).

HABITAT: Breeds in forests, especially where interspersed with meadows; active day and night, hunting small rodents.

REGIONS: C (same in winter)

Plate 45 **349**

a Short-eared Owl

b Snowy Owl

c Great Horned Owl

d Great Gray Owl

Plate 46a

Northern Hawk Owl
Surnia ulula

ID: Mid-sized gray-brown, heavily barred, long-tailed owl, black markings around facial disk; 36 cm (14 in).

HABITAT: Resident in open conifer and deciduous forest, moving to river bottoms in winter; active during day, hunting birds and mammals.

REGIONS: SC, C, W (winter SC, SW, C, W)

Plate 46b

Boreal Owl
Aegolius funereus

ID: Small brown owl with broadly striped underparts, black around large, square facial disk; juvenile dark brown with white on face; voice a series of loud, mellow whistled notes, also a startling *skyew*; 25 cm (10 in).

HABITAT: Resident in conifer and mixed forest; active at night, hunting rodents.

REGIONS: SC, SW, C (same in winter)

Plate 46c

Belted Kingfisher
Megaceryle alcyon

ID: Shaggy-headed, large-billed waterside bird, blue-gray above and white below; male with blue-gray band on breast, female with reddish band behind it; juvenile of both sexes with some reddish in gray breast band; loud, rattling calls; 32 cm (12.5 in).

HABITAT: Breeds at freshwater and saltwater wetlands, wherever sand or clay banks available for nest burrows; winters more widely along coastal beaches and lowland rivers.

REGIONS: SE, SC, SW, C, W (winter SE, SC, SW)

Plate 46d

Rufous Hummingbird
Selasphorus rufus

ID: Tiny bird with long, slender bill that hovers at flowers or perches on wires, twigs, conifer tips; male bright reddish with white breast; iridescent red-orange throat conspicuous in sun (looks black in shade); female and juvenile metallic green above, white below, with reddish sides and tail base; male has flight display with loud, staccato, electronic sound at end; 7.5 cm (3 in).

HABITAT: Breeds in wet forest edge and shrubby areas, typically where "hummingbird flowers" such as salmonberry and paintbrush are common.

REGIONS: SE, SC

Plate 46   351

a Northern Hawk Owl

b Boreal Owl

c Belted Kingfisher

F

M

d Rufous Hummingbird

M

F

Plate 47a

Downy Woodpecker
Picoides pubescens

ID: Small woodpecker with conspicuous black and white pattern, including striped head, white stripe down back, and spotted wings; small black spots on outermost tail feathers; male with red spot on back of head, lacking in female; juveniles of both sexes with red spot on top of head; 16 cm (6.25 in).

HABITAT: Resident in all forest types as well as shrubby thickets where dead trees of sufficient size available for nest holes.

REGIONS: SE, SC, C (same in winter)

Plate 47b

Hairy Woodpecker
Picoides villosus

ID: Colored exactly as Downy but considerably larger and longer-billed; no black spots on outermost tail feathers; woodpeckers fly with undulating flight; 22 cm (8.5 in).

HABITAT: Resident in all forest types where dead trees available for nest holes.

REGIONS: SE, SC, C (same in winter)

Plate 47c

Three-toed Woodpecker
Picoides tridactylus

ID: Mid-sized woodpecker, somewhat like Hairy but with black bars on white back, sides, and tail; male with yellow crown; 22 cm (8.5 in).

HABITAT: Resident in conifer and mixed forests where dead trees available for nest holes.

REGIONS: SE, SW, C, W (same in winter)

Plate 47d

Northern Flicker
Colaptes auratus

ID: Medium-large woodpecker differing from all others in being mostly brown, with black bars above and black spots below; southeastern Alaska ("Red-shafted Flicker") birds have reddish wing and tail feathers, male with red "mustache" on side of face; interior birds ("Yellow-shafted Flicker") have yellow wing and tail feathers, male with black "mustache;" 30.5 cm (12 in).

HABITAT: Breeds in all forest types where dead trees available for nest holes; forages on ground as well as in trees.

REGIONS: SE, SC, C

Plate 47 353

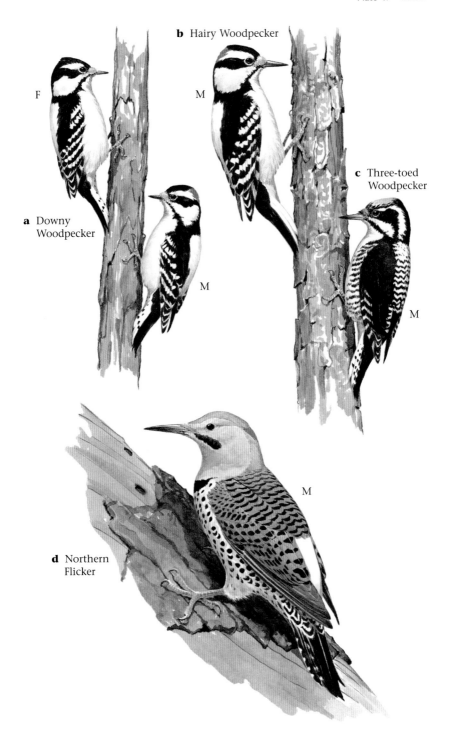

b Hairy Woodpecker

F

M

a Downy
Woodpecker

M

c Three-toed
Woodpecker

M

M

d Northern
Flicker

Plate 48a

Alder Flycatcher
Empidonax alnorum
ID: Small upright-perching olive-brown bird with pale underparts and white wingbars; bill broad at base, yellowish beneath; flycatchers fly out after flying insects and return to perch; loud *wee-bee-o* song, *peep* call; 13 cm (5.25 in).

HABITAT: Breeds in alder and willow thickets and forest edge, usually near water.

REGIONS: SE, SC, SW, C, W

Plate 48b

Say's Phoebe
Sayornis saya
ID: Small brown flycatcher with black tail, brighter buffy-brown belly; perches alertly upright in open areas and flies out after flying insects, also feeds on ground; wags tail down-up; plaintive *pee-ur* call; 18 cm (7 in).

HABITAT: Breeds in open country, where it nests on cliffs, in buildings or under bridges.

REGIONS: C, W, N

Plate 48c

American Pipit
Anthus rubescens
ID: Small ground-feeding bird, brown above and buffy below, with finely streaked breast, white outer tail feathers; thin bill and walking gait distinguish it from sparrows; wags tail as it forages; flight call *tsi-tsip, tsi-tsip* ("pipit"), song a series of short, high notes, also given in flight; 15 cm (6 in).

HABITAT: Breeds on tundra; migrates through grasslands, meadows, beaches, and mudflats.

REGIONS: SE, SC, SW, C, W, N

Plate 48d

Horned Lark
Eremophila alpestris
ID: Small ground-feeding bird, reddish brown above and white below, with black feathers forming tiny "horns" and black facial stripes and breast band; female has duller head markings, less obvious "horns" than male; juvenile with light-spotted back and dark-spotted breast, no black markings; black tail with white outer feathers contrasts with white belly in flight; tinkling song given from high in air, also *tsee-titi* flight calls; 18 cm (7 in).

HABITAT: Breeds on dry alpine tundra; migrates through grasslands, meadows, and beaches.

REGIONS: C, W, N (migration SE, C, W, N)

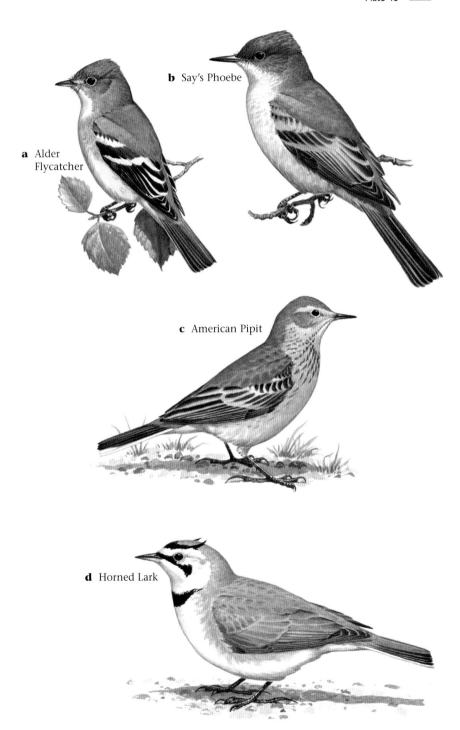

Plate 48 **355**

b Say's Phoebe

a Alder
Flycatcher

c American Pipit

d Horned Lark

Plate 49a
Violet-green Swallow
Tachycineta thalassina
ID: Swallows are aerial feeders with tiny bill, long, pointed wings; Violet-green has relatively short, forked tail; black and white at a distance, at close range green back and violet rump obvious; female duller than male, with brownish crown and obscure head pattern; distinctive fluttery wingbeat, with white rump patches prominent in flight; 13 cm (5 in).

HABITAT: Breeds in all forested habitats and human settlements, where tree holes, crevices, or humanmade structures available for nesting; migrates throughout.

REGIONS: SE, SC, SW, C

Plate 49b
Tree Swallow
Tachycineta bicolor
ID: Like Violet-green but all dark blue-green above, with no rump patches; dark of head extends below eye; first-year female and juvenile duller, brown-backed; flight less fluttery than Violet-green; 14 cm (5.5 in).

HABITAT: Breeds in forested habitats at or near water, where tree holes available for nesting; also in crevices or bird boxes at human settlements in tundra; migrates throughout.

REGIONS: SE, SC, SW, C, W

Plate 49c
Bank Swallow
Riparia riparia
ID: Smallest swallow, brown above and white below with brown breast band obvious at rest and in flight; 12 cm (4.75 in).

HABITAT: Breeds along rivers, where sand banks available for nest holes; migrates throughout.

REGIONS: SE, SC, SW, C, W

Plate 49d
Cliff Swallow
Petrochelidon pyrrhonota
ID: Short-tailed swallow with dark throat and white forehead patch; juvenile with darker forehead, paler throat; buffy rump and squarish tail obvious in flight; typically flies higher than other swallows, with much gliding; gathers around puddles for nest mud; 14 cm (5.5 in).

HABITAT: Breeds along rivers or at human settlements, where cliffs, bridges, and buildings available as substrate for gourd-shaped mud nests; migrates throughout.

REGIONS: SE, SC, SW, C, W, N

Plate 49e
Barn Swallow
Hirundo rustica
ID: Swallow with blue-black back, orange underparts, and long, deeply forked tail; juvenile with paler underparts, shorter tail; typically flies smoothly, low over ground; 17 cm (6.75 in).

HABITAT: Breeds in any habitat, typically near water, especially where human structures such as buildings and bridges available as substrate for cup-shaped mud nests; migrates throughout.

REGIONS: SE, SC

Plate 49   357

a Violet-green Swallow

M

M

b Tree Swallow

c Bank Swallow

d Cliff Swallow

e Barn Swallow

Plate 50a

Gray Jay
Perisoreus canadensis

ID: Mid-sized, long-tailed forest bird, mostly gray above and white to gray below with dark wings and tail, white forehead; juvenile almost all blackish; steady flap-and-glide flight; loud, whistled calls, *whee-oh* typical, also mimic owls; attracted to campgrounds and hikers (also called "camp robber"); 25 cm (10 in).

HABITAT: Resident in conifer and mixed forests of all heights.

REGIONS: SW, C, W (same in winter)

Plate 50b

Steller's Jay
Cyanocitta stelleri

ID: Mid-sized, robust black and blue forest bird with expressive crest; often around campgrounds, overlooks; steady flight with flaps and glides; loud, harsh *shook-shook-shook* calls, others more musical; 28 cm (11 in).

HABITAT: Resident in taller conifer and mixed forests; local movements after breeding.

REGIONS: SE, SC (same in winter)

Plate 50c

Northwestern Crow
Corvus caurinus

ID: Crow-sized black bird, half size of raven with shorter, more rounded tail; voice a flat *kaaa, kaaa, kaaa*; in pairs or flocks; flies with wings flat (Black Oystercatcher flies with wings curved downward); 41 cm (16 in).

HABITAT: Resident in southern coastal forests, needing trees for nesting but foraging in all habitats, including beaches and mudflats.

REGIONS: SE, SC (same in winter)

Plate 50d

Black-billed Magpie
Pica pica

ID: Mid-sized but very long-tailed black-and-white bird of open country; strikingly iridescent at close range; flight like rowing, with conspicuous white wing patches; 48 cm (18 in).

HABITAT: Resident in forest edges, open woodland, and tall shrub thickets; some movement during winter.

REGIONS: SC, SW, C (winter SE, SC, SW, C)

Plate 50e

Common Raven
Corvus corax

ID: Huge, large-billed, crowlike black songbird the size of Red-tailed Hawk, often seen in pairs; wedge-shaped tail obvious in flight, which includes soaring with flat wings and aerial acrobatics; voice a loud, musical croak, often doubled; attracted to dumps; 69 cm (27 in).

HABITAT: Resident in all habitats at all elevations, near or away from human settlements; needs large trees or cliffs for nesting.

REGIONS: SE, SC, SW, C, W, N (same in winter)

Plate 50   **359**

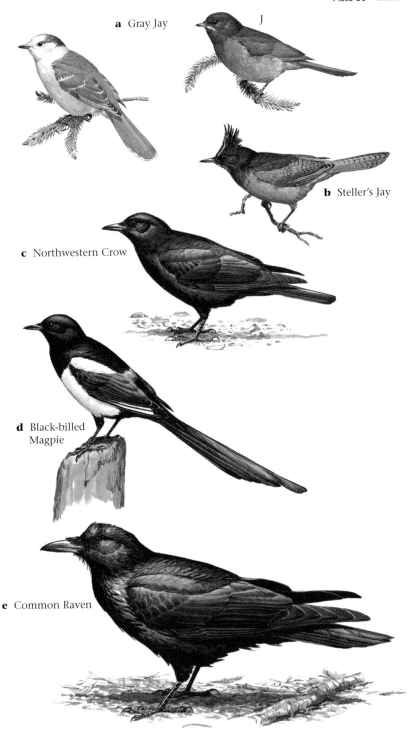

a Gray Jay

J

b Steller's Jay

c Northwestern Crow

d Black-billed Magpie

e Common Raven

Plate 51a

Black-capped Chickadee
Parus atricapillus

ID: Tiny forest songbird, gray above and whitish below, with black cap and throat, white cheeks; flocks in winter; song a high-pitched two-noted whistle, flock call *chick-a-dee-dee-dee* and musical notes; 13 cm (5 in).

HABITAT: Resident in mixed and deciduous forests of all heights and edges, typically along rivers.

REGIONS: SE, SC, SW, C, W (same in winter)

Plate 51b

Chestnut-backed Chickadee
Parus rufescens

ID: Like Black-capped but smaller, dark chestnut on back and sides (dark sides good distinguishing mark), cap dark brown; flock call sibilant *zitta-zitta-zee* somewhat like Golden-crowned Kinglet; 11 cm (4.5 in).

HABITAT: Resident in dense conifer forests, moving into other forest types during winter.

REGIONS: SE, SC (same in winter)

Plate 51c

Boreal Chickadee
Parus hudsonicus

ID: Like Black-capped but browner all over, cap brown and white cheek patch less extensive; *chick-a-dee* call more nasal, slower, no whistled song; 13 cm (5 in).

HABITAT: Resident in conifer and mixed forests of all heights.

REGIONS: SW, C, W (same in winter)

Plate 51d

Red-breasted Nuthatch
Sitta canadensis

ID: Tiny trunk-foraging songbird with long, slender bill, short tail; gray above and reddish below with prominent white eyestripe; male with black cap and cheeks, female gray; call nasal *nya-nya-nya-nya*, very excitable; 11 cm (4.25 in).

HABITAT: Breeds in all taller forest types, reduced numbers and some wandering in winter.

REGIONS: SE, SC

Plate 51e

Brown Creeper
Certhia americana

ID: Tiny trunk-foraging songbird with brown streaked back, white underparts; bill slender and curved, tail long and pointed as prop; ascends trees into crown, then drops down to base of nearby tree; song and call very high-pitched; 13 cm (5 in).

HABITAT: Resident in all taller forest types, moving into more open forests in winter.

REGIONS: SE, SC, SW (same in winter)

Plate 51   **361**

b Chestnut-backed Chickadee

a Black-capped Chickadee

c Boreal Chickadee

d Red-breasted Nuthatch

e Brown Creeper

Plate 52a
Golden-crowned Kinglet
Regulus satrapa
ID: Tiny olive-green songbird with white and yellow wing markings, prominent black head stripes; male with orange crown, female with yellow; flicks wings constantly while foraging; song and call very high-pitched, reminiscent of Brown Creeper and Chestnut-backed Chickadee that share its habitat; 9.5 cm (3.75 in).

HABITAT: Resident in dense, high conifer forests; also migrates through all wooded and shrubby habitats.

REGIONS: SE, SC, SW (same in winter)

Plate 52b
Ruby-crowned Kinglet
Regulus calendula
ID: Much like Golden-crowned Kinglet but no stripes on head, instead a white eyering; male with bright red crown patch that may be hidden but is prominently displayed during singing and interactions with other birds; song starts high and sibilant, descends to very musical; call a series of harsh, repeated *di-dit* phrases; 10 cm (4 in).

HABITAT: Breeds in all forest types of all heights, typically more open than Golden-crowned; migrates through all wooded and shrubby habitats.

REGIONS: SE, SC, C, W

Plate 52c
Arctic Warbler
Phylloscopus borealis
ID: Small thin-billed songbird with brown upperparts, whitish underparts, prominent white eyeline; duller than species of wood warbler family; song a buzzy trill; 11 cm (4.5 in).

HABITAT: Breeds in willow and alder thickets near streams in tundra zone.

REGIONS: SW, C, W, N

Plate 52d
Winter Wren
Troglodytes troglodytes
ID: Tiny dark brown forest songbird with slender bill, cocked short tail; barred wings and tail distinguish it from other brown birds; forages on ground and in understory; song long, musical, and complex; call *tsick tsick* like pair of kisses; 9.5 cm (3.75 in).

HABITAT: Resident in dense tall forest in south, beach detritus and rocky areas in Aleutians.

REGIONS: SE, SC, SW (same in winter)

Plate 52e
American Dipper
Cinclus mexicanus
ID: Small, plump, short-tailed gray songbird on streamside rocks and logs; constantly bobs body up and down, closes white upper eyelid; swims and dives beneath running water; song loud and musical, even in winter; call loud *bzeet*, heard over rushing water; 18 cm (7.25 in).

HABITAT: Resident on rocky rivers and streams at all elevations, moving into lowlands, even to lakes and beaches, as streams freeze over.

REGIONS: SE, SC, SW, C, W (same in winter)

Plate 52 **363**

a Golden-crowned Kinglet

M

F

M

b Ruby-crowned Kinglet

c Arctic Warbler

d Winter Wren

e American Dipper

Plate 53a

Bohemian Waxwing
Bombycilla garrulus

ID: Small, smooth, upright-perching brown songbird with prominent crest, chestnut undertail coverts, white and yellow wing markings, yellow tail tip; juvenile with striped breast, duller markings; red "wax" on tips of flight feathers and white wing markings become larger after first year; flocks in fruiting trees in winter; high-pitched sibilant flight calls; 19 cm (7.5 in).

HABITAT: Breeds in open conifer forests; migrates through all wooded habitats; winters south where berry-bearing shrubs and trees available.

REGIONS: SC, C (winter SE)

Plate 53b

Northern Shrike
Lanius excubitor

ID: Mid-sized, long-tailed predatory songbird of open areas; black mask, wings, and tail contrast with gray/white body; immature duller, brownish above and with fine bars all over underparts, song of musical whistles and squeaky notes, call harsh *shack shack*; watch for prey – voles and small birds – impaled on branches and fences; 24 cm (9.5 in).

HABITAT: Resident at edge of all forest types and in open tree- and shrub-studded flats, migrates into completely open areas, if scattered elevated perches or utility wires present.

REGIONS: SC, SW, C, W, N (winter SE, SC, SW, W)

Plate 53c

Rusty Blackbird
Euphagus carolinus

ID: Mid-sized, slender, long-billed wetland songbird with white eyes; male shiny black, female dull gray-brown; both sexes heavily marked with rusty bars in fall, also prominent pale eyestripe; 22 cm (8.5 in).

HABITAT: Breeds in thickets and scattered shrubs and trees near water; migrates through other forested and open habitats, including around human settlements.

REGIONS: SW, C, W

Plate 53d

American Robin
Turdus migratorius

ID: Mid-sized songbird with robust yellow bill and fairly long legs and tail; gray-brown upperparts and reddish breast; female with brown instead of black head, paler breast than male; juvenile with heavily spotted breast; runs and stops on ground for earthworms; song loud, musical whistles with rolling phrases *cheerily cheerily*; call loud *pip pip*; 24 cm (9.5 in).

HABITAT: Breeds in all forested habitats, even those with scattered trees, and in human settlements where nests sometimes on buildings; winters rarely in south, mostly in settled areas where fruiting trees and shrubs available.

REGIONS: SE, SC, SW, C, W

Plate 53e

Varied Thrush
Ixoreus naevius

ID: Smaller than robin, with shorter tail and black bill; bright markings on head, breast, and wings distinctive; female duller than male; overturns leaf litter to forage; song a series of burry, ethereal single notes on different pitches; call low *took*; 23 cm (9 in).

HABITAT: Breeds in all dense forest types, foraging both in and out of forest; winters rarely in southern forests, mostly near coast.

REGIONS: SE, SC, SW, C, W

Plate 53 **365**

a Bohemian Waxwing

b Northern Shrike

c Rusty Blackbird

M

F

d American Robin

M

e Varied Thrush

M

F

Plate 54a

Gray-cheeked Thrush
Catharus minimus

ID: Brown-backed, spotted-breasted songbird of low forest; quite plain gray-brown, with no distinct head markings; song series of fluty phrases that go up and down, last note descending; call high *wheea*; 17 cm (6.75 in).

HABITAT: Breeds in willow and alder thickets and mixed forests.

REGIONS: SE, SC, SW, C, W, N

Plate 54b

Swainson's Thrush
Catharus ustulatus

ID: Like Gray-cheeked but richer brown above, with conspicuous buffy eyering; song series of rising fluty phrases; call high *whit*; 17 cm (6.75 in).

HABITAT: Breeds in conifer and mixed forests and dense deciduous thickets.

REGIONS: SE, SC, SW, C

Plate 54c

Hermit Thrush
Catharus guttatus

ID: Smaller than other spotted thrushes, with blacker breast spots and contrasty reddish tail; droops wings and cocks tail up; song series of fluty phrases beginning with long, clear note; call low *took*; 15 cm (6 in).

HABITAT: Breeds in conifer and mixed forests and deciduous thickets in forest zone.

REGIONS: SE, SC, SW, C

Plate 54d

Wilson's Warbler
Wilsonia pusilla

ID: Warblers are small, active, and thin-billed, this species olive-green above and bright yellow below; male with black cap, female and juvenile without it; relatively long tail cocked up like wren; song an even series of notes *chip chip chip chip chip*; 11 cm (4.5 in).

HABITAT: Breeds in dense forests and shrubby thickets.

REGIONS: SE, SC, SW, C, W

Plate 54e

Northern Waterthrush
Seiurus noveboracensis

ID: Thrushlike warbler, dark brown above and white, heavily striped with brown, below, conspicuous white eyeline; forages on ground at waterside, bobbing rear end up and down; song jumble of musical whistles, louder and slower at beginning; 14 cm (5.5 in).

HABITAT: Breeds in forest and dense shrub thickets at lakes and ponds and along streams.

REGIONS: SE, SC, SW, C, W

Plate 54 **367**

a Gray-cheeked Thrush

b Swainson's Thrush

c Hermit Thrush

d Wilson's Warbler

M

e Northern Waterthrush

Plate 55a

Yellow Warbler
Dendroica petechia

ID: Mostly bright yellow warbler with yellow tail patches; male brighter, with orange breast streaks; female dull yellow, without streaks; populations in Southeast duller, more greenish; song a series of pure whistles varying in length; one version *sweet sweet sweet I'm so sweet*, 11 cm (4.5 in).

HABITAT: Breeds in deciduous forest and shrubby thickets, typically near water.

REGIONS: SE, SC, SW, C, W

Plate 55b

Orange-crowned Warbler
Vermivora celata

ID: Entirely greenish warbler (brighter yellow below in Southeast); orange crown patch of male seen during display; song a weak, descending trill; 11 cm (4.5 in).

HABITAT: Breeds in low deciduous and mixed forests and shrubby thickets.

REGIONS: SE, SC, SW, C, W

Plate 55c

Townsend's Warbler
Dendroica townsendi

ID: Warbler with greenish back and bright yellow underparts striped with black; contrasty dark crown, cheek patch, and throat (black in male, greenish in female); song a series of high-pitched buzzy notes; 12 cm (4.75 in).

HABITAT: Breeds in dense conifer and mixed forests.

REGIONS: SE, SC, C

Plate 55d

Yellow-rumped Warbler
Dendroica coronata

ID: Warbler with bright yellow spot on crown, either side of breast, and rump; white throat in interior ("Myrtle" Warbler), yellow throat in Southeast ("Audubon's" Warbler); female similar but less brightly marked; immature brownish and streaked, yellow rump best field mark; often catches insects in midair; song a rather weak series of whistled notes, rising or falling at end; 13 cm (5.25 in).

HABITAT: Breeds in conifer and mixed forests in forest zone, deciduous shrub thickets in tundra zone; migrates throughout.

REGIONS: SE, SC, SW, C, W

Plate 55e

Blackpoll Warbler
Dendroica striata

ID: Warbler with both sexes greenish above, whitish below, heavily streaked and with white wingbars; male with black cap and white cheeks (lacks black throat of chickadees), female dull overall, may be yellowish or white below; only streaked warbler with yellow feet; song a series of weak high-pitched notes; 13 cm (5 in).

HABITAT: Breeds in conifer and mixed forests in forest zone, deciduous shrub thickets in tundra zone.

REGIONS: SW, C, W

Plate 55 **369**

a Yellow Warbler

F

M

b Orange-crowned Warbler

c Townsend's Warbler

M

d Yellow-rumped Warbler

F

M

e Blackpoll Warbler

F

M

Plate 56a

American Tree Sparrow
Spizella arborea

ID: Sparrows are brown songbirds, streaky above, with conical seed-cracking bills; this species mid-sized and long-tailed, with reddish cap, black breast spot, white wingbars; juvenile with streaked breast; song a sweet warble preceded by clear notes; 15 cm (5.75 in).

HABITAT: Breeds in willow and alder thickets in tundra zone and low forest near treeline; migrates throughout in open country.

REGIONS: SW, C, W, N (migration SE, SC, SW, C, W, N)

Plate 56b

Dark-eyed Junco
Junco hyemalis

ID: Plain-colored sparrow with white outer tail feathers; all gray with white belly in interior ("Slate-colored Junco") but black head, brown back, and buffy sides in Southeast ("Oregon Junco"); female duller in both populations, which mix in migration and winter; juvenile streaked all over, same white in tail; song a musical trill; 15 cm (5.75 in).

HABITAT: Breeds in conifer and mixed forest and forest edge; migrates throughout and winters rarely south in all habitats.

REGIONS: SE, SC, SW, C, W (winter SE, SC)

Plate 56c

Golden-crowned Sparrow
Zonotrichia atricapilla

ID: Large, long-tailed sparrow with unspotted breast, white wingbars; breeding adult with yellow crown, black head stripes; winter adult and immature with finely streaked crown and often yellow forehead; juvenile with streaked breast; song a few slow, sweet whistles; 17 cm (6.75 in).

HABITAT: Breeds in willow and alder thickets in tundra zone and low forest near treeline; migrates throughout in open areas.

REGIONS: SE, SC, SW, C, W

Plate 56d

White-crowned Sparrow
Zonotrichia leucophrys

ID: Like Golden-crowned but slightly smaller; adult with black and white head stripes; immature with same stripes brown and gray; juvenile with streaked breast; song a few sweet whistles, followed by trill; 15 cm (6 in).

HABITAT: Breeds in shrubby thickets and woodland edge in forest zone, willow and alder thickets in tundra zone; migrates throughout in open areas.

REGIONS: SW, C, W, N (migration SE, SC, SW, C, W, N)

Plate 56 **371**

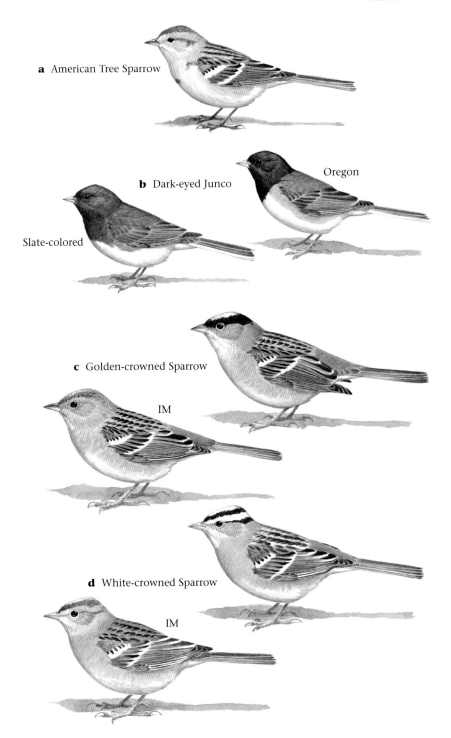

a American Tree Sparrow

b Dark-eyed Junco

Oregon

Slate-colored

c Golden-crowned Sparrow

IM

d White-crowned Sparrow

IM

Plate 57a

Savannah Sparrow
Passerculus sandwichensis

ID: Small, short-tailed, open-country sparrow, heavily streaked above and below; head with dark stripes and yellow around eye and bill; song high-pitched and buzzy, unlike other Alaska sparrows; 13 cm (5.25 in).

HABITAT: Breeds in wet meadows and wet and dry tundra; migrates through all open habitats, including beaches.

REGIONS: SE, SC, SW, C, W, N

Plate 57b

Lincoln's Sparrow
Melospiza lincolnii

ID: Small light brown sparrow with cleanly gray and black striped head, fine underpart streaks restricted to buffy breast and sides; song a rapid, bubbling trill; 13 cm (5.25 in).

HABITAT: Breeds in shrub thickets in wet areas; migrates throughout.

REGIONS: SE, SC, SW, C, W

Plate 57c

Song Sparrow
Melospiza melodia

ID: Mid-sized to large thicket- and beach-inhabiting sparrow with heavily striped head, back, and breast; cocks tail up; birds of Aleutians much larger and grayer than mainland birds; song staccato and musical and ending in a trill, for example *tsink tsunk tsi tsi tsi tsi tseeee*; 15 to 19 cm (6 to 7.5 in).

HABITAT: Resident in shrub thickets in or out of forest, mostly near coast, also on Aleutian Island beaches; some migrants away from breeding habitats.

REGIONS: SE, SC, SW (same in winter)

Plate 57d

Fox Sparrow
Passerella iliaca

ID: Large sparrow with spotted breast; heavily marked with rusty in interior, including head and back stripes, and white wingbars; plain brown head and back with rusty tail in South; yellow lower mandible distinctive; forages on ground with loud scratching; song a series of sprightly whistles; 16.5 cm (6.5 in).

HABITAT: Breeds in shrubby thickets in or out of forest; migrates through forest and shrub habitats.

REGIONS: SE, SC, SW, C, W, N

Plate 57   373

a Savannah Sparrow

b Lincoln's Sparrow

c Song Sparrow

d Fox Sparrow

Plate 58a
Snow Bunting
Plectrophenax nivalis
ID: Open-country sparrow with much white in wings and tail; breeding male spectacularly black and white; female streaked brown above; winter adult with much buffy brown; juvenile mostly dark gray; song a rapid warble, often given in flight; flight call a musical twitter and *tew*; 16.5 cm (6.5 in).

HABITAT: Breeds on tundra, especially rocky areas and associated with human settlements; migrates through all open habitats, including beaches.

REGIONS: SW, C, W, N (winter SE, SW, W)

Plate 58b
Lapland Longspur
Calcarius lapponicus
ID: Open-country sparrow with white outer tail feathers; male with black, white, and chestnut pattern on head and breast; female with subdued hint of same pattern; immature and winter adult sparrowlike, but brown cheek patch bordered all around by black; more likely than sparrows to fly high when flushed; song a rapid warble, often given in flight; flight call a dry rattle and *tew* notes; 15 cm (6 in).

HABITAT: Breeds on tundra; migrates through all open habitats, including beaches.

REGIONS: SW, C, W, N (migration SE, SC, SW, C, W, N)

Plate 58c
Gray-crowned Rosy-Finch
Leucosticte tephrocotis
ID: Dark brown and pinkish finch with much gray on head; female duller, less pink; juvenile dark brown; birds of Aleutians and Pribilofs much larger than mainland birds; call a loud *chew*; 16.5 to 20 cm (6.5 to 8 in).

HABITAT: Breeds in alpine tundra in rocky areas, also rocky beaches in Bering Sea islands, where resident; winters in coastal lowlands, often near human settlements.

REGIONS: SE, SC, SW, C, W (winter SW)

Plate 58d
Smith's Longspur
Calcarius pictus
ID: Open-country sparrow with bright black and white head markings, entirely buffy underparts, white outer tail feathers; female and winter adults more sparrowlike but largely buff, faintly streaked underparts distinctive; song a rapid warble, ending in *wee-chew*; flight call a dry rattle; 15 cm (6 in).

HABITAT: Breeds on wet or dry alpine tundra.

REGIONS: N

Plate 58e
Pine Grosbeak
Pinicola enucleator
ID: Large, heavy-billed, long-tailed finch with white wingbars; male mostly rose-colored, female gray with yellow to orange on head, rump, and underparts; call a loud double whistle, second note lower; 23 cm (9 in).

HABITAT: Resident in conifer forests of all heights; much movement in winter to deciduous forests with buds and fruits.

REGIONS: SE, SC, SW, C, W (same in winter)

Plate 58   375

a Snow Bunting

F

M

b Lapland Longspur

F

M

d Smith's Longspur

c Gray-crowned Rosy-Finch

M

F

M

F

e Pine Grosbeak

Plate 59a

Red Crossbill
Loxia curvirostra
ID: Short-tailed stocky finch, longish bill with crossed mandibles; adult males brick red, immature males orange and yellow, females yellowish green; juveniles streaked; hangs parrotlike when feeding; call a loud, repeated, musical *kip kip kip*; 15 cm (5.75 in).

HABITAT: Resident in conifer forests, but much movement throughout year; abundance varies from year to year.

REGIONS: SE (same in winter)

Plate 59b

White-winged Crossbill
Loxia leucoptera
ID: Like Red Crossbill but with conspicuous white wingbars contrasting with black wings; males pinkish red; call a drier *chiff chiff chiff*; 15 cm (6 in).

HABITAT: Resident in spruce forests, but much movement throughout year; abundance varies from year to year.

REGIONS: SE, SC, SW, C, W (same in winter)

Plate 59c

Common Redpoll
Carduelis flammea
ID: Tiny, heavily striped finch with red cap; male with reddish breast, female streaked below; rump pale, usually streaked; flight call rattling *jijijit*; 11 cm (4.5 in).

HABITAT: Resident in mixed woodlands in forest zone, shrubby thickets in tundra zone; movement into other habitats, including human settlements, in winter; abundance varies from year to year.

REGIONS: SE, SC, SW, C, W, N (winter SE, SC, SW, C, W)

Plate 59d

Hoary Redpoll
Carduelis hornemanni
ID: Like Common Redpoll but paler, rump usually unmarked white; bill slightly smaller, makes face look pushed in; both redpolls flock together; 11 cm (4.5 in).

HABITAT: Resident in mixed woodlands in forest zone, shrubby thickets in tundra zone; movement into other habitats, including human settlements, in winter; abundance varies from year to year.

REGIONS: W, N (winter SW, C, W)

Plate 59e

Pine Siskin
Carduelis pinus
ID: Tiny, heavily striped finch with no red; yellow in wings and tail varies from conspicuous to absent; flight call a long, ascending, buzzy *zhreeeee* and a redpoll-like rattle; 11 cm (4.5 in).

HABITAT: Resident in conifer forests; much movement into other forests and human settlements in winter.

REGIONS: SE, SC (same in winter)

Plate 59 **377**

a Red Crossbill

F

M

b White-winged Crossbill

F

M

c Common Redpoll

F

M

d Hoary Redpoll

M

e Pine Siskin

Plate 60a
Little Brown Myotis
Myotis lucifugus

ID: Little brown flying mammal, probably most likely to be seen of Alaska's bats; 5 cm (2 in), plus 3 cm (1.2 in) tail.

HABITAT: Any forested habitat, roosting in tree and rock crevices and caves; also urban and suburban areas, where it may roost in buildings; hibernates in caves and mine shafts, to which it may migrate from summer range; active at night.

REGIONS: SE, SC, C

Plate 60b
Masked Shrew
Sorex cinereus

ID: Shrews are tiny, hyperactive, pointy-nosed mammals with moderate-length tail; this species is brown above, slightly paler on sides; 5.5 cm (2 in), plus 3.5 cm (1.4 in) tail.

HABITAT: Moist situations in forests, shrublands, meadows, and tundra; active around the clock.

REGIONS: SE, SC, SW, C

Plate 60c
Tundra Shrew
Sorex tundrensis

ID: Like Masked Shrew but slightly larger and distinctly tricolored, with dark back, buffy sides, white belly; 7 cm (2.8 in), plus 3.5 cm (1.4 in) tail.

HABITAT: Wet tundra, edges of sphagnum bogs and marshes, and willow and alder thickets; active around the clock.

REGIONS: SC, SW, C, W, N

Plate 60d
Water Shrew
Sorex palustris

ID: Largest Alaskan shrew, as large as smallest mice; blackish brown, with pale belly; 8 cm (3 in), plus 7 cm (2.8 in) tail.

HABITAT: Wetlands of all kinds – ponds, marshes, bogs, and especially streams in conifer forest; active around the clock.

REGIONS: SE, SC

Plate 60 **379**

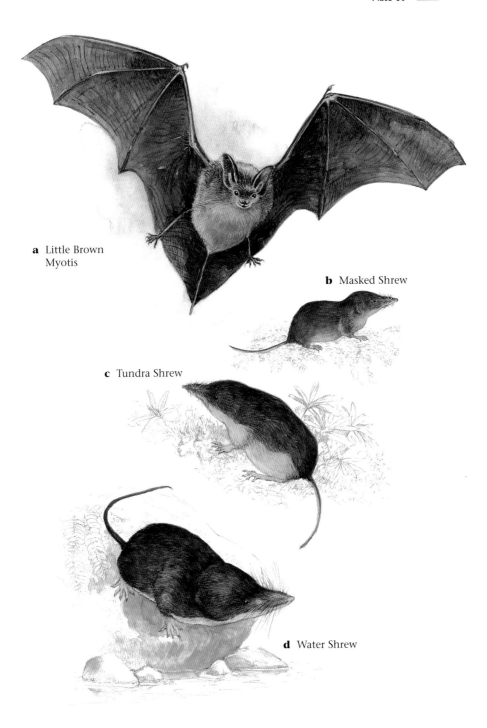

a Little Brown
Myotis

b Masked Shrew

c Tundra Shrew

d Water Shrew

Plate 61a
Collared Pika
Ochotona collaris
ID: Compact, short-eared, tailless, light brown rock-dwelling rabbit relative; high-pitched calls good sign of presence; 19 cm (7.5 in).

HABITAT: Rocky slopes with nearby herbaceous and shrubby vegetation; active during day.

REGIONS: C

Plate 61b
Snowshoe Hare
Lepus americanus
ID: Long-eared brown rabbit with brown tail and white feet; turns white with black ear tips in winter; 46 cm (18 in) plus 4 cm (1.6 in) tail.

HABITAT: Forest and woodland of all types, moving into clearings to feed; active at night but often seen during day.

REGIONS: SE, SC, C, W

Plate 61c
Alaska Hare
Lepus othus
ID: Large rabbit, gray-brown with white feet and tail in summer, white with black ear tips in winter; 56 cm (22 in) plus 8 cm (3 in) tail.

HABITAT: Open tundra, during winter moving into dry and rocky areas where snow shallow; active at night but must forage during day in arctic summer.

REGIONS: SW, W, N

Plate 61d
Common Porcupine
Erethizon dorsatum
ID: Large, rotund rodent with long dark and light hairs and yellow spines visible below them, especially toward rear; moderate-length tail also heavily spined; 51 cm (20 in) plus 20 cm (8 in) tail.

HABITAT: Forest and woodland of all types, including willow and alder shrublands, even moving cross-country over tundra and prairie; most active at night.

REGIONS: SE, SC, SW, C, W, N

Plate 61   381

a Collared Pika

b Snowshoe Hare

c Alaska Hare

d Common Porcupine

Plate 62a
Hoary Marmot
Marmota caligata
ID: Large pale brown to whitish rodent with moderate-length tail; black markings on head and black legs and feet; 50 cm (20 in) plus 15 cm (6 in) tail.

HABITAT: Talus slopes and other rocky areas from sea level to high in mountains; must have abundant herbaceous vegetation nearby; active during day; hibernates in winter.

REGIONS: SE, SC, C

Plate 62b
Alaska Marmot
Marmota broweri
ID: Like Hoary Marmot but with much of head, including snout, black, rump blackish, and feet pale; confined to Brooks Range; 46 cm (18 in) plus 13 cm (5 in) tail.

HABITAT: Talus slopes and other rocky areas with much herbaceous vegetation nearby, in Brooks Range; active during day; hibernates in winter.

REGIONS: N

Plate 62c
Woodchuck (also called Groundhog)
Marmota monax
ID: Large reddish brown rodent with moderate-length tail; 46 cm (18 in) plus 13 cm (5 in) tail.

HABITAT: Woodland edge with associated clearings and meadows; active during day; hibernates in winter.

REGIONS: C

Plate 62d
Muskrat
Ondatra zibethicus
ID: Mid-sized brown aquatic rodent with long, narrowly compressed, scaly tail; 28 cm (11 in) plus 23 cm (9 in) tail.

HABITAT: Lakes, ponds, and marshes with abundant herbaceous vegetation; active around the clock; active under ice in winter.

REGIONS: SE, SC, SW, C, W

Plate 62e
American Beaver
Castor canadensis
ID: Very large, brown aquatic rodent with wide, flat, scaly tail; 71 cm (28 in) plus 25 cm (10 in) tail.

HABITAT: Small, shallow streams, which they dam to make beaver ponds, but also existing lakes, ponds, and marshes; must be woody vegetation nearby for food; active around the clock, but mostly at night where disturbed by humans; active under ice in winter.

REGIONS: SE, SC, C

Plate 62 **383**

a Hoary Marmot

b Alaska Marmot

c Woodchuck

d Muskrat

e American Beaver

Plate 63a

Red Squirrel

Tamiasciurus hudsonicus

ID: Arboreal squirrel with long, bushy tail; reddish above and white below with black line down side and conspicuous white eyering; 19 cm (7.5 in) plus 13 cm (5 in) tail.

HABITAT: Conifer and mixed forest, especially where spruces are common; active during day.

REGIONS: SE, SC, SW, C, W

Plate 63b

Northern Flying Squirrel

Glaucomys sabrinus

ID: Arboreal squirrel with long, flattened, bushy tail and loose side skin for gliding; light brown above, white below; 15 cm (6 in) plus 13 cm (5 in) tail.

HABITAT: Conifer forests where trees are sufficiently close to glide between; somewhat social; active at night.

REGIONS: SE, SC, C

Plate 63c

Meadow Jumping Mouse

Zapus hudsonius

ID: Small mouse with tail longer than body, long hind legs for jumping, prominent ears; bicolored in side view, with brown back, rich buffy sides; 8 cm (3 in) plus 12 cm (5 in) tail.

HABITAT: A mixture of forest and shrub growth and moist meadows and clearings; active at night but sometimes flushed during day; hibernates in winter.

REGIONS: SE, SC, SW, C

Plate 63d

Northwestern Deer Mouse

Peromyscus keeni

ID: Small mouse with tail about same length as body, prominent ears; brown above (young gray), white below; 9 cm (3.5 in) plus 9 cm (3.5 in) tail.

HABITAT: Forests, woodlands, and shrubby areas of all types; active at night.

REGIONS: SE

Plate 63e

Arctic Ground Squirrel

Spermophilus parryii

ID: Squirrels are bushy-tailed, mostly day-active rodents; this species reddish brown to tan terrestrial squirrel with relatively short, skimpy tail; 30 cm (12 in) plus 13 cm (5 in) tail.

HABITAT: Open, well-drained tundra and rocky areas from sea level to high in mountains; active during day; hibernates in winter.

REGIONS: SC, SW, C, W, N

Plate 63 **385**

a Red Squirrel

b Northern Flying Squirrel

c Meadow Jumping Mouse

d Northwestern Deer Mouse

e Arctic Ground Squirrel

Plate 64a
Singing Vole
Microtus miurus
ID: Voles have small ears, relatively short tails; this species very small, with shortest tail of true voles; entirely brown with buff wash on sides; 11 cm (4.5 in) plus 3 cm (1.2 in) tail.

HABITAT: Alpine and arctic tundra and willow thickets, typically drier areas than Tundra Vole habitat but often near water; in colonies, active around the clock.

REGIONS: SC, C, W, N

Plate 64b
Meadow Vole
Microtus pennsylvanicus
ID: Like Singing Vole but slightly larger, distinctly longer tail, plainer dark brown; watch for voles in their runways; 12 cm (5 in) plus 5 cm (2 in) tail.

HABITAT: Any open area, from extensive moist meadows or drier grassland to small forest openings and agricultural lands; in colonies, active around the clock.

REGIONS: SE, SC, C

Plate 64c
Yellow-cheeked Vole
Microtus xanthognathus
ID: Slightly larger vole, with distinctive orangey patch on sides of snout; 15 cm (6 in) plus 5 cm (2 in) tail.

HABITAT: Wet forest and edge, shrub thickets, sphagnum bogs; in colonies, active around the clock.

REGIONS: C

Plate 64d
Tundra Vole
Microtus oeconomus
ID: Entirely brown like Meadow Vole but slightly larger, relatively shorter tail; 15 cm (6 in) plus 4.5 cm (1.8 in) tail.

HABITAT: Moist tundra and meadows with tall, rank grass and sedges, near water or in shallow marshy areas as long as runways not flooded; in colonies, active around the clock.

REGIONS: SE, SC, SW, C, W, N

Plate 64 **387**

a Singing Vole

b Meadow Vole

c Yellow-cheeked Vole

d Tundra Vole

Plate 65a
Northern Red-backed Vole
Clethrionomys rutilus

ID: Small vole with distinctly reddish back, paler sides than most others; 10 cm (4 in) plus 3.5 cm (1.4 in) tail.

HABITAT: Open forest or shrublands, sometimes in rocky areas; shuns open tundra; mostly active at night but seen during day in arctic summer.

REGIONS: SC, SW, C, W, N

Plate 65b
Northern Bog Lemming
Synaptomys borealis

ID: Small dark brown vole with very short tail; 11 cm (4.3 in) plus 2 cm (0.8 in) tail.

HABITAT: Bogs with sphagnum, black spruce, and Labrador tea, less often in moist spruce forest, wet meadows, alpine tundra; active around the clock.

REGIONS: SE, SC, C, W

Plate 65c
Brown Lemming
Lemmus sibiricus

ID: Largish brown vole with very short tail; lemmings travel in runways like voles; 15 cm (6 in) plus 2 cm (0.8 in) tail.

HABITAT: Moist low tundra, with dense grasses and sedges; in colonies, active around the clock.

REGIONS: SW, C, W, N

Plate 65d
Collared Lemming
Dicrostonyx groenlandicus

ID: Largish orange-brown vole with very short tail; brightly marked with black line down back and pale collar; turns entirely white in winter; perches on rocks like tiny pika; 15 cm (6 in) plus 1.5 cm (0.6 in) tail.

HABITAT: Dry, rocky tundra, often in rock piles; may move into wetter tundra with Brown Lemming; active around the clock.

REGIONS: SW, W, N

Plate 65 **389**

a Northern
Red-backed
Vole

b Northern Bog
Lemming

c Brown
Lemming

d Collared
Lemming

Plate 66a
Gray Wolf
Canis lupus
ID: Large doglike canine with bushy tail held straight back when running; varies from brown to gray to almost entirely white or black; some domestic dogs look very wolflike; 1.17 m (3.8 ft) plus 41 cm (16 in) tail.

HABITAT: All habitats, just as common in tundra and forested areas; active around the clock, although deep-voiced howling usually at night.

REGIONS: SE, SC, SW, C, W, N

Note: Considered endangered in parts of USA (Lower 48 states except Minnesota); USA ESA and CITES Appendix II listed.

Plate 66b
Coyote
Canis latrans
ID: Slender gray and reddish tan canine; about one third size of Gray Wolf, bushy tail held down when running; 86 cm (34 in) plus 33 cm (13 in) tail.

HABITAT: All habitats, a common situation with generalized predators such as this one, although absent from many areas of open tundra (perhaps susceptible to wolf predation in such exposed areas); active around the clock, but high-pitched barks and howls usually at night.

REGIONS: SE, SC, C, N

Plate 66c
Red Fox
Vulpes vulpes
ID: Slender canine with relatively large ears, long snout and legs, and very bushy tail; typically bright reddish with black legs and feet, varying to light brown with black stripe across shoulders and down back ("cross fox"), entirely black, or black with long white hairs ("silver fox"); 61 cm (24 in) plus 35 cm (14 in) tail.

HABITAT: All forest edge and shrubby habitats, also open prairie and tundra, where denning possible; rarely in dense forest; active mostly at night but often travel during day.

REGIONS: SC, SW, C, W, N

Plate 66d
Arctic Fox
Alopex lagopus
ID: Slender canine with relatively short ears, snout, and legs and very bushy tail; brown and white in summer, pure white and much fluffier in winter; Pribilof and Aleutian foxes dark blue-gray in summer, lighter in winter; 51 cm (20 in) plus 28 cm (11 in) tail.

HABITAT: Arctic and alpine tundra of all sorts and rocky cliffs on islands of Bering Sea, also open sea ice where they trail Polar Bears; active around the clock but hunting more at night.

REGIONS: SW, W, N

Plate 66 **391**

a Gray Wolf

b Coyote

c Red Fox

d Arctic Fox

Plate 67a

Black Bear
Ursus americanus

ID: Small bear without prominent hump on shoulders, black or cinnamon brown (often blue-gray along Gulf of Alaska coast) with tan snout; 1.7 m (5.5 ft), shoulder height 91 cm (3 ft). **Caution:** Can be dangerous to people.

HABITAT: Forest and woodland of all types, moving out into shrubby and open areas to forage for berries and other preferred food items; active around the clock, more so at night; dormant in den through much of winter.

REGIONS: SE, SC, C, W

Note: Considered threatened in parts of southern USA; USA ESA and CITES Appendix II listed.

Plate 67b

Brown (Grizzly) Bear
Ursus arctos

ID: Large bear with prominent hump on shoulders, varying from light brown to yellowish above and darker below in interior (Grizzly Bear) to entirely dark brown on coast (Brown Bear); coastal bears conspicuously larger; on Kodiak Island, known as "Kodiak Bears;" 2 to 2.4 m (7 to 8 ft), shoulder height 1.1 to 1.4 m (3.5 to 4.5 ft). **Caution:** Potentially very dangerous.

HABITAT: Open areas, including alpine and arctic tundra, prairies, and large clearings; also open forest and, on coast, beaches and intertidal zone; active around the clock; dormant in den through much of winter.

REGIONS: SE, SC, SW, C, W, N

Note: Considered threatened in parts of USA (Lower 48 states); USA ESA and CITES Appendix II listed.

Plate 67c

Polar Bear
Ursus maritimus

ID: Large yellowish white bear with relatively small head and long neck; 2.6 m (8.5 ft), shoulder height 1.2 to 1.4 m (4 to 4.5 ft). **Caution:** Potentially very dangerous.

HABITAT: Edge of arctic ice pack during winter, even swimming long distances between floes; comes ashore to beaches and coastal tundra in late summer; active around the clock.

REGIONS: W, N

Note: Regulated for conservation purposes; CITES Appendix II listed.

Plate 67 **393**

a Black Bear

b Brown Bear

c Polar Bear

Plate 68a

Marten
Martes americana

ID: Mustelids are very intense carnivores, some of them slender, all of them active and renowned for their ferociousness; this species mid-sized, brown arboreal mustelid with orange patch on chest, prominent ears, and long, bushy tail; 41 cm (16 in) plus 20 cm (8 in) tail.

HABITAT: Mature conifer and mixed forests; primarily active at night but may be seen during day.

REGIONS: SE, SC, C, W

Plate 68b

Mink
Mustela vison

ID: Mid-sized semiaquatic mustelid with long, bushy tail; all dark brown, with white on chin; 38 cm (15 in) plus 20 cm (8 in) tail.

HABITAT: Wetlands of all kinds, from slow streams to marshes, ponds, and lakes, even tide flats; travels cross-country through open and wooded terrestrial habitats; active mostly at night but often seen during day.

REGIONS: SE, SC, SW, C, W, N

Plate 68c

Short-tailed Weasel (Ermine)
Mustela erminea

ID: Small mustelid with small, rounded ears and moderate-length, thin tail; brown with black tail tip and white belly in summer, all white with black tail tip in winter (when it is called "ermine"); 18 cm (7 in) plus 8 cm (3 in) tail.

HABITAT: All habitats, from dry to moist, forest to tundra; especially common in talus and rocky areas; mostly active at night but seen during day in arctic summer.

REGIONS: SE, SC, SW, C, W, N

Plate 68d

Least Weasel
Mustela nivalis

ID: Like Short-tailed Weasel but even smaller and shorter-tailed; same color variation but tail without black tip; 15 cm (6 in) plus 3 cm (1.2 in) tail.

HABITAT: All habitats from tundra and meadows to forests; active at night but occasionally seen during day.

REGIONS: SE, SC, SW, C, W, N

Plate 68   **395**

a Marten

b Mink

c Short-tailed Weasel (Ermine)

d Least Weasel

Plate 69a

Wolverine
Gulo gulo

ID: Large mustelid with doglike face but short, rounded ears, very bushy tail – like a small, bushy-tailed bear; dark brown, with paler head and broad yellowish stripe on either side; 79 cm (31 in) plus 20 cm (8 in) tail.

HABITAT: Conifer forests, where now sparsely distributed, and tundra; active around the clock.

REGIONS: SE, SC, SW, C, W, N

Plate 69b

River Otter
Lutra canadensis

ID: Large semiaquatic mustelid with broad face, short ears, webbed feet, and thick-based, short-haired tail; entirely dark brown with paler chin and throat; 71 cm (28 in) plus 36 cm (14 in) tail.

HABITAT: Lakes, rivers, and marshes in all zones; often on beaches and foraging widely in all near-shore marine habitats; active around the clock, perhaps more so at night.

REGIONS: SE, SC, SW, C, W

Plate 69c

Sea Otter
Enhydra lutris

ID: Very large dark brown marine mustelid with pale head, big webbed feet, and short tail; fur very dense, guard hairs sometimes tipped with white; typically seen floating on back with head and feet above water; 84 cm (33 in) plus 30 cm (12 in) tail.

HABITAT: Kelp beds over rock and gravel bottoms, less often in open water; often social; active during day.

REGIONS: SE, SC, SW

Note: Considered threatened in parts of USA (Washington, Oregon, California); USA ESA and CITES Appendix I listed.

Plate 69d

Lynx
Lynx lynx

ID: Long-legged, big-footed cat with black-tufted ears, very short tail; pale silvery brown with scarcely any markings; 86 cm (34 in) plus 10 cm (4 in) tail.

HABITAT: Conifer forest, wandering into tundra and shrubby areas when forest hunting is poor; usually active at night but hunts by day by necessity during arctic summer.

REGIONS: SE, SC, SW, C, W, N

Plate 69 **397**

a Wolverine

b River Otter

c Sea Otter

d Lynx

Plate 70a

Black-tailed Deer
Odocoileus hemionus

ID: Long-legged ungulate, male with cylindrical, evenly branched antlers grown in late summer, shed in early winter; mostly reddish brown in summer, grayer in winter, tail black above; 1.5 m (5 ft), shoulder height 91 cm (3 ft).

HABITAT: Open woodland and brush to fairly dense conifer forest, also on beaches at coast; active at night where disturbed, around the clock where protected.

REGIONS: SE, SC

Plate 70b

Caribou
Rangifer tarandus

ID: Large, long-legged ungulate, both sexes with somewhat flattened antlers (fall and winter); color varies from brown with light neck and rump to light tan, almost whitish; 1.8 m (6 ft), shoulder height 1.1 m (3.8 ft).

HABITAT: Open moist and dry tundra, where most abundant, but also scattered populations in conifer forest and mixed woodland; very social; active during day.

REGIONS: SC, SW, C, W, N

Plate 70c

Moose
Alces alces

ID: Huge, very long-legged, dark brown ungulate with ungainly looking head, hairy "bell" hanging from throat; male antlers (in fall) flattened, palmate; 3.2 m (10.5 ft), shoulder height 1.9 m (6.2 ft). **Caution:** Can be dangerous to people.

HABITAT: Shrublands and open forest, especially poplar and aspen parkland, wandering into edge of prairie and tundra; much time near and in water during summer; most active at dawn and dusk.

REGIONS: SE, SC, SW, C, W, N

Plate 70 **399**

a Black-tailed Deer

b Caribou

c Moose

Plate 71a
Muskox
Ovibos moschatus
ID: Stocky, short-legged ungulate with broad face, shoulder hump, and slender, down- then upsweeping horns in both sexes (smaller in females); very long fur sheds in ragged clumps in spring; all brown except lighter legs and patch on back; M 2.2 m (7 ft), F 2 m (6.6 ft), shoulder height 1.2 m (4 ft).

HABITAT: Arctic tundra, moving into shrubby valleys in summer and onto windswept hillsides and ridges with less snow pack in winter; social; active during day.

REGIONS: W, N

Plate 71b
Mountain Goat
Oreamnos americanus
ID: Stocky, shaggy, white ungulate with slender, almost straight, black horns in both sexes (thicker in males); 1.6 m (5.2 ft), shoulder height 1 m (3.5 ft).

HABITAT: Cliffs and exposed rocky slopes, from sea level to high in mountains, moving to lower elevation in winter; social; active during day.

REGIONS: SE, SC

Plate 71c
Dall's Sheep
Ovis dalli
ID: Stocky, white ungulate with pale horns, thin and straight in females and young males, heavier and spiraled outward in mature males; less shaggy than Mountain Goat; M 1.5 m (5 ft), F 1.3 m (4.3 ft), shoulder height 97.5 cm (3.2 ft).

HABITAT: Alpine tundra, with or without rocks, moving to lower, more sheltered areas in winter; social; active during day.

REGIONS: SC, C, W, N

Plate 71 **401**

a Muskox

b Mountain Goat

c Dall's Sheep

Plate 72a

Northern Fur Seal
Callorhinus ursinus

ID: Dark gray-brown to blackish pinniped with short ears, thick coat, long whiskers, and very long black flippers; males much larger than females; agile on land, often holds flippers out of water; M 1.8 m (6 ft), F 1.4 m (4.5 ft).

HABITAT: Open ocean during nonbreeding season, breeding in summer in huge colonies on few islands in Pribilofs.

REGIONS: SE, SW, W

Plate 72b

Steller's Sea Lion
Eumetopias jubatus

ID: Light brown (commonly) to dark brown pinniped with short ears; much larger than Northern Fur Seal and with shorter hair and whiskers; males much larger than females; agile on land, active at water surface, with head pointed up; M 3.2 m (10.5 ft), F 2.1 m (7 ft).

HABITAT: Nearshore marine habitats, mostly in rocky areas, breeding in summer in island colonies.

REGIONS: SE, SC, SW

Note: Considered threatened; USA ESA listed.

Plate 72c

Harbor Seal
Phoca vitulina

ID: True seal, with no ears visible, awkward on land, quiet at water surface, with head held flat; varies from white, lightly to heavily spotted with black, through gray to almost solid black; 1.5 m (5 ft).

HABITAT: Nearshore marine habitats, hauling out socially on rocks or sand on islands and spits at low tide and breeding there in spring; ascends rivers; a population in Iliamna Lake.

REGIONS: SE, SC, SW, W

Plate 72d

Spotted Seal
Phoca largha

ID: Much like Harbor Seal, always light-colored and heavily spotted with black, but associated with ice; the two species barely overlap in summer at Kuskokwim Bay; 1.5 m (5 ft).

HABITAT: Pack ice, breeding solitarily on ice in spring and hauling out on sandy shores when ice recedes during summer.

REGIONS: SW, W, N

Plate 72 **403**

a Northern Fur Seal

b Steller's Sea Lion

c Harbor Seal

d Spotted Seal

Plate 73a

Walrus
Odobenus rosmarus
ID: Huge pinniped with characteristics of true seals; long white tusks (thicker in males); hair sparse, skin light brown in water, flushes to pink when hauled out; M 3.7 m (12 ft), F 2.7 m (9 ft).

HABITAT: Pack ice all year, but large numbers haul out at few islands in Bering Sea in summer.

REGIONS: W

Plate 73b

Ringed Seal
Pusa hispida
ID: Small true seal of pack ice; dark gray, with white rings all over body; 1.4 m (4.5 ft).

HABITAT: Pack ice and fast ice near shore, breeding on ice in spring.

REGIONS: W, N

Plate 73c

Ribbon Seal
Histriophoca fasciata
ID: Small true seal of pack ice and open water; medium to dark brown, with broad white rings around neck and body; pattern on female less contrasty; 1.5 m (5 ft).

HABITAT: Pack ice in winter, some following as it retreats, others remaining in open ocean; breeds on ice in spring.

REGIONS: W

Plate 73d

Bearded Seal
Erignathus barbatus
ID: Large true seal of pack ice, about twice size of other seals there; light gray to brown all over, without pattern; conspicuous white "whiskers" give it its name; M 3 m (10 ft), F 2.4 m (8 ft).

HABITAT: Pack ice in winter, most following as it retreats, few remaining in open ocean; breeds on ice in spring.

REGIONS: W

Plate 73 **405**

a Walrus

b Ringed Seal

c Ribbon Seal

d Bearded Seal

Plate 74a

Killer Whale (Orca)

Orcinus orca

ID: Very large toothed whale, shiny black with white markings on sides and underside head and body; tall and curved (female) or very tall and straight (male) dorsal fin at midlength with gray saddle behind it; 9 m (30 ft).

HABITAT: Inshore and offshore waters; social.

REGIONS: SE, SC, SW, W

Plate 74b

Minke Whale

Balaenoptera acutorostrata

ID: Smallish shiny black baleen whale with sickle-shaped dorsal fin well behind midlength and pale band across long flippers; 10 m (33 ft).

HABITAT: Inshore and offshore waters, north to pack ice.

REGIONS: SE, SC, SW, W

Note: Endangered; USA ESA and CITES Appendix I listed.

Plate 74c

Gray Whale

Eschrichtius glaucus

ID: Large, mottled gray baleen whale with bumps on back but no dorsal fin, usually seen near coastlines; conspicuous growth of barnacles on head; 14 m (46 ft).

HABITAT: Inshore waters of northern oceans in summer, migrates south in winter; social.

REGIONS: SE, SC, SW, W, N

Plate 74d

Bowhead Whale

Eubalaena borealis

ID: Huge tadpole-shaped black and white baleen whale of arctic waters; very large head and no dorsal fin; in still air, double V-shaped spout can be seen; 17 m (56 ft).

HABITAT: Open ocean near pack ice; social.

REGIONS: W, N

Note: Endangered; USA ESA and CITES Appendix I listed.

Plate 74e

Humpback Whale

Megaptera novaeangliae

ID: Large blackish baleen whale with prominent hump but no dorsal fin; very long flippers white below, as are flukes; 16.5 m (54 ft).

HABITAT: Inshore and offshore waters in summer, migrates south in winter.

REGIONS: SE, SC, SW

Note: Endangered; USA ESA and CITES Appendix I listed.

Plate 74 407

a Killer Whale (Orca)

b Minke Whale

c Gray Whale

d Bowhead Whale

e Humpback Whale

Plate 75a
Harbor Porpoise
Phocoena phocoena
ID: Small black porpoise, shows triangular dorsal fin in slow roll at surface; 1.8 m (6 ft).

HABITAT: Inshore and offshore waters; social.

REGIONS: SE, SC, SW, W, N

Plate 75b
Dall's Porpoise
Phocoenoides dalli
ID: Small black and white porpoise; typically fast-moving and with forward spray when surfacing to breathe, also rolls like other porpoises when feeding; often attracted to boats; 2 m (6.6 ft).

HABITAT: Inshore and offshore waters, farther at sea than Harbor Porpoise; social.

REGIONS: SE, SC, SW, W

Plate 75c
Narwhal
Monodon monoceros
ID: High-latitude mottled gray toothed whale with no dorsal fin; in male, one canine tooth extends forward as long, straight, spirally twisted "unicorn;" 3.7 m (12 ft).

HABITAT: Inshore northern waters, forced south in winter by pack ice; social.

REGIONS: N

Note: Regulated for conservation purposes; CITES Appendix II listed.

Plate 75d
Beluga (White Whale)
Delphinapterus leucas
ID: White, blubbery-looking toothed whale with no dorsal fin, prominent bulging forehead; born brown or gray, gradually turns white; 4.3 m (14 ft).

HABITAT: Inshore waters, often ascending rivers; social.

REGIONS: SC, W, N

Plate 75 **409**

a Harbor Porpoise

b Dall's Porpoise

c Narwhal

d Beluga (White Whale)

SPECIES INDEX

GENERAL INDEX

NOTES

Habitat symbols

= Tundra.

= Coniferous and mixed forest.

= Deciduous forest.

= Forest edge/shrub thicket.

= Meadows and grassland other than tundra.

= Freshwater. For species typically found in or near lakes, streams, rivers, marshes, swamps.

= Saltwater/marine. For species usually found in or near the ocean.

Regions (see Map 6, p.51):

SE   Southeastern Alaska; the southern peninsular part of the state, south of Yakutat and Skagway.

SC   Southcentral Alaska; includes the coastal lowlands from Yakutat west to Homer, including Anchorage and the Seward Peninsula.

SW   Southwestern Alaska; includes the Alaska Peninsula, Kodiak Island, and the Aleutian Islands.

W   Western Alaska; includes the Yukon Delta, Seward Peninsula, and generally the western edge of the state, as well as the Bering Sea islands.

N   Northern Alaska; includes the coastal plain from the Brooks Range north.

C   Central Alaska; includes the remainder of the state, the huge area centering around Fairbanks and including the Alaska and Brooks ranges and everything between them.